Damascus Life 1480–1500

Islamic History and Civilization

STUDIES AND TEXTS

VOLUME 168

The titles published in this series are listed at *brill.com/ihc*

Damascus Life 1480–1500

A Report of a Local Notary

By

Boaz Shoshan

BRILL

LEIDEN | BOSTON

Cover illustration: Umayyad Mosque Archway, Damascus. By American Rugbier, 2009 (CC BY-SA 2.0).

Library of Congress Cataloging-in-Publication Data

Names: Shoshan, Boaz, author.
Title: Damascus life 1480-1500 : a report of a local notary / by Boaz Shoshan.
Description: Leiden ; Boston : Brill, [2020] | Series: Islamic history and civilization : studies and texts, 0929-2403 ; volume 168 | Includes bibliographical references and index.
Identifiers: LCCN 2019037169 (print) | LCCN 2019037170 (ebook) | ISBN 9789004413252 (hardback) | ISBN 9789004413269 (ebook)
Subjects: LCSH: Ibn Ṭawq, Aḥmad ibn Muḥammad, 1430 or 1431-1509 or 1510 Taʿlīq. | Ibn Ṭawq, Aḥmad ibn Muḥammad, 1430 or 1431-1509 or 1510–Diaries. | Arabs–Syria–Damascus–Diaries. | Notaries–Syria–Damascus–Diaries. | Damascus (Syria)–History–15th century. | Damascus (Syria)–Social conditions–15th century. | Damascus (Syria)–Social life and customs.
Classification: LCC DS99.D3 S67 2020 (print) | LCC DS99.D3 (ebook) | DDC 956.91/4402–dc23
LC record available at https://lccn.loc.gov/2019037169
LC ebook record available at https://lccn.loc.gov/2019037170

Typeface for the Latin, Greek, and Cyrillic scripts: "Brill". See and download: brill.com/brill-typeface.

ISSN 0929-2403
ISBN 978-90-04-41325-2 (hardback)
ISBN 978-90-04-41326-9 (e-book)

This book is printed on acid-free paper and produced in a sustainable manner.

Printed by Printforce, the Netherlands

In memory of Andrew Rippin

Contents

Preface

This book has been many years in the making. My acquaintance with the *Taʿlīq*, the main source for it, which is a diary written in the last decades of the fifteenth century by the Damascus notary known as Ibn Ṭawq, goes back some 15 years now. At that time, when asked to contribute to a conference on Mamluk history, I was searching for a topic and hit accidentally upon the *Taʿlīq*, only the first volume of which edition was then published. The text struck me then as not entirely straightforward, and not always easy to understand, but at the same time a mine for all sorts of exciting information that I had not seen before and a window into a fascinating past reality. As sometimes happens, the conference proceedings were never published, and the paper I had written waited to see the light of day.

Although in subsequent years I became engaged with entirely different projects, Ibn Ṭawq's precious diary, in the meantime almost completely published, remained at the back of my mind all along. Occasionally, I was able to get to the approximately 1,900 printed pages and write a few short articles on select topics. But it was only after receiving a generous invitation from Professor Stephan Conermann to spend a few months at the Annemarie Schimmel Kolleg at Bonn University in the spring of 2014, there reading and struggling repeatedly with the four volumes of the edition of the *Taʿlīq*, that the idea occurred to me that not just a few articles but a whole book was possible—in fact, desirable—on the basis of the fascinating and demanding text. Also, Dr. Torsten Wollina's doctoral dissertation based on the *Taʿlīq* had appeared in German by that time. Its focus on a few topics was yet another reassurance about the richness of that unique source. A few more years have elapsed with some other obligations and, finally, after numerous days of close encounters with the old diary, interpreting and reinterpreting difficult passages—to this point, I am uncertain about quite a few—a book on late Mamluk Damascus is now complete.

As already mentioned, I owe special thanks to Professor Conermann for providing excellent conditions of work and habitation and a stimulating ambiance created by both senior and junior colleagues at the Kolleg. Of these I should mention in particular Professor Stuart Borsch for the numerous discussions we had and for a few bibliographical tips. A short-term stay at the Oriental Institute of Oxford University in the spring of 2016 was also beneficial for completing my research. Thanks go to Dr. Wollina for allowing me to see his work prior to its publication, and for a few discussions we had and questions he raised, which helped to fine-tune my thinking. Professor Yehoshua Frenkel, a long-time colleague, made some suggestions for further reading and sent to me some of his unpublished work. I thank Mr. Sali Turjeman for meticulously preparing the maps. An anonymous reader for Brill made me rethink parts of the manuscript and sharpen my arguments, even at the expense of vivid anecdotes recorded by Ibn Ṭawq, to which, as an excited reader of his diary, I was much attached and had a hard time leaving out. Finally, many thanks to Mr. Daniel Sentance for his meticulous copy-editing and his invaluable investment in order to improve the quality of my manuscript.

This book is dedicated to the memory of Professor Andrew Rippin, with whom I first corresponded in the 1990s, resumed contact on a few occasions, and finally met and spent some stimulating hours with when I was a visiting scholar at the Center for Studies in Religion and Society at the University of Victoria in 2011. It was an opportunity to get to know Andrew not only as an innovative and critical scholar but also as a fine human being. Subsequently, Andrew was kind enough to publish one of my previous books in the "Classical Islam" series he edited for Routledge. Although he was formally a student of *tafsīr*, and certainly one of the best in that field, he had a wide interest in many subjects, and I think the present book could fall into it. I grieve his premature death.

Abbreviations

AHR	*American Historical Review*
AI	*Annales Islamologiques*
BEO	*Bulletin d'Études Orientales*
BSOAS	*Bulletin of the School of Oriental and African Studies*
EI[2]	*Encyclopaedia of Islam*, 2nd edition, Leiden 1954–2004
EI[3]	*Encyclopaedia of Islam*, 3rd edition, Leiden 2007–
IJMES	*International Journal of Middle East Studies*
JAOS	*Journal of the American Oriental Society*
JESHO	*Journal of the Economic and Social History of the Orient*
JRAS	*Journal of the Royal Asiatic Society*
JSAI	*Jerusalem Studies in Arabic and Islam*
MSR	*Mamluk Studies Review*
REI	*Revue des Études Islamiques*

Maps

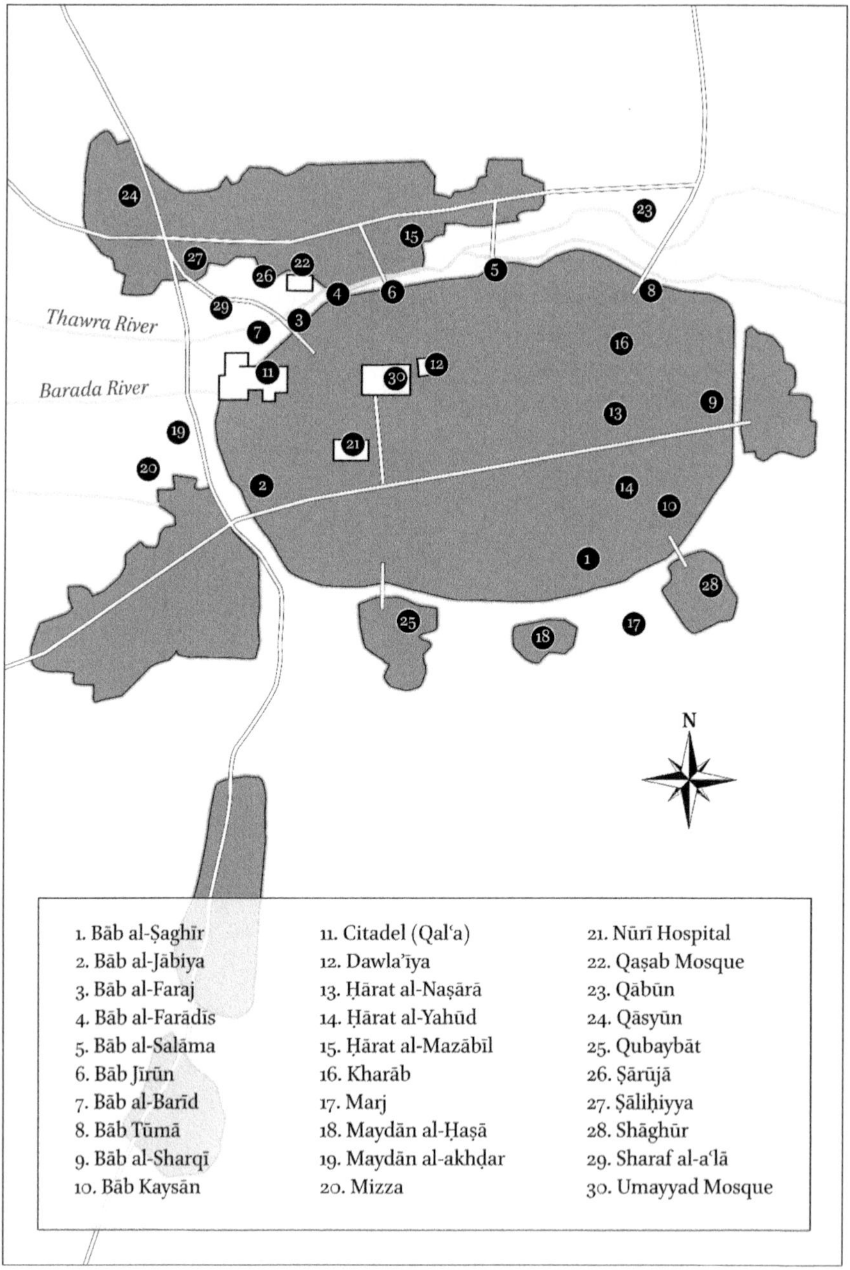

MAP 1 15th-century Damascus

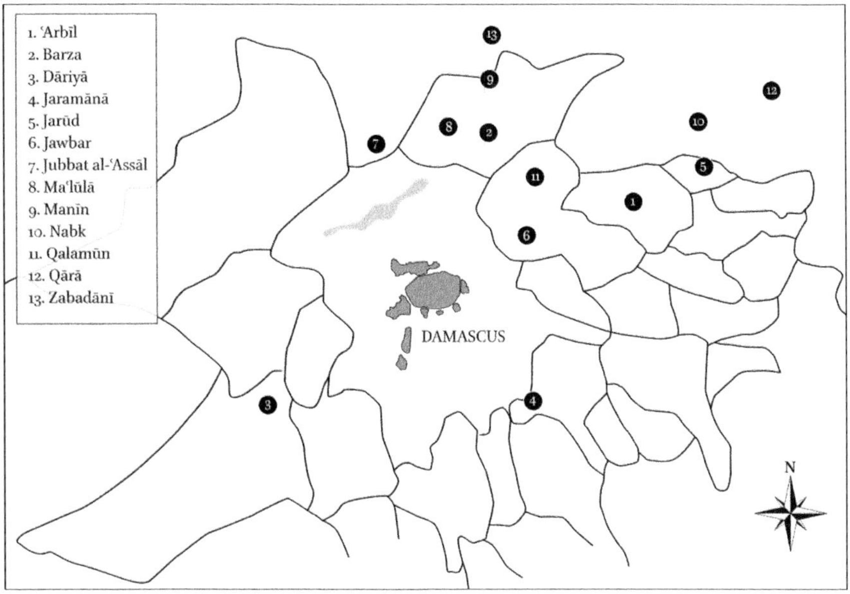

MAP 2 The Damascus region

Introduction

If it hadn't been for the attribution in the 1970s of a previously anonymous manuscript to Shihāb al-Dīn Aḥmad b. Muḥammad, known as Ibn Ṭawq (834–915/1430–1509), its author might have been destined to almost total oblivion.[1] At the most, he might have been considered fortunate enough—this, of course, said with a touch of irony—to have received a short reference, more than 100 years after his death, in a so-called biographical dictionary. There, Ibn Ṭūlūn, the leading historian of late Mamluk and early Ottoman Damascus, in an entry devoted to the Damascus *shaykh al-Islām* Taqī al-Dīn, of the prominent Shāfiʿī family Ibn Qāḍī ʿAjlūn, is cited as crediting Ibn Ṭawq for collecting Taqī al-Dīn's fatwas.[2] Elsewhere, Ibn Ṭawq is mentioned as a pupil of Burhān al-Dīn Ibrāhīm b. ʿAbd al-Raḥmān (d. 872/1467), also of the Ibn Qāḍī ʿAjlūn family, a deputy qadi and in charge of funds for orphans, as well as a teacher at the Umayyad Mosque.[3] However, these brief references fail to mention—not necessarily because their writers were unaware thereof, at least in the case of Ibn Ṭūlūn, as we shall see, he rather was aware—that Ibn Ṭawq recorded an immense number of notes on the Damascus of his day. Actually, he left a diary with the one-word title *Taʿlīq*, a title that, though vague, was not uncommon of contemporary works on different subjects.[4] Here, it may freely be translated as "a summary report."[5]

1 Unless otherwise indicated, dates are provided in the Hijrī/Common format. For the erroneous attribution of the work to al-Nuʿaymī in the 1947-published catalogue of the Damascus National Library (an attribution that, apparently, has yet to be corrected), see Wollina, *Zwanzig* 34.

2 al-Ghazzī, *al-Kawākib* i, 115. For a discussion of the office of *shaykh al-Islām* and of the role of the mufti, see Chapter 3.

3 al-Ḥaṣkafī, *Mutʿat al-adhhān* i, 186–187. For Burhān al-Dīn, see al-Buṣrawī, *Tārīkh* 28; Ibn al-Ḥimṣī, *Ḥawādith* i, 179.

4 For example, Ibn Ṭūlūn, the Damascene chronicler (on whom see further below), considered his *Iʿlām*, on the history of the Mamluk governors of Damascus, his scholarly autobiography, his *Naqd al-ṭālib li zaghl al-manāṣib*, as well as his short booklet on al-Mizza, all as a *taʿlīq*. See *Fulk* 21, 23, 44. Also, he refers to a book by one of his predecessors, Taqī al-Dīn al-Asadī (see on him Chapter 2), who wrote a history book (Ibn Ṭūlūn notes that he did not see it) at the beginning of the fifteenth century, as a *taʿlīq*. See *Iʿlām* 29–30. Ibn al-Ḥimṣī, another contemporary (see below), introduced his history book as a "rewarding" (*mufīd*) *taʿlīq*. Similarly, Taqī al-Dīn Ibn Qāḍī ʿAjlūn, the leading Shāfiʿī scholar in Damascus in Ibn Ṭawq's time, characterized his *fiqh* book, the *Iʿlām al-nabīh*, a *taʿlīq*.

5 I combine the rendering "report" in Makdisi, Diary 178, and "summary" in Hirschler, From archive 10.

 | DOI:10.1163/9789004413269_002

The importance of Ibn Ṭawq's diary—of which, at this stage, we are lucky to have, although with some lacunae, the part covering the time span between the later months of 885/1480 and the end of 906/1501—lies in the notes taken by the author on an almost daily basis.[6] Excepting days on which, for some reason, occasionally explained, he reports nothing, or days on which he notes that he had not entered the old city "between the walls,"[7] Ibn Ṭawq records all sorts of information about Damascus. No less important, the *Taʿlīq* contains also a great deal of what appears as its author's personal archive. This is what turns an otherwise little-known Muslim into an important source for students of premodern Islam. One could safely argue that we have no comparable source for the pre-Ottoman era in terms of the density and especially the sorts of information it provides for a short historical spell, about 20 years in this case. Being a notary who resided in Damascus during most of the years for which he kept his diary, Ibn Ṭawq provides modern readers with an unprecedented opportunity to glimpse a premodern society in a major Islamic city. Not simply providing a general view based on occasional references that enable the examination of Damascus in the larger context of other cities and for a long period,[8] the *Taʿlīq* gives us a rare opportunity to observe the trees for the forest, so to speak.

This has been recognized in some recent studies, notably in Torsten Wollina's pioneering research on the *Taʿlīq*.[9] In addition to the nature of the diary and some information on its author, Wollina discusses a select number of subjects that Ibn Ṭawq copiously reported about—his household, his daily itinerary, the food he and people of his milieu ate, and the clothes they wore. However, there is much more that remains unexplored. It is to some major aspects of Damascus life at the end of the fifteenth century, hitherto untouched, that the present book is devoted.

What is the *Taʿlīq* about? Nowhere is its purpose explicated, and the subheading "Diary" (*yawmiyyāt*) is the editor's addition. Surely, "diary" was a concept unknown to Ibn Ṭawq. Significantly, where he does reflect *en passant* on his "blessed *Taʿlīq*," as he occasionally refers to it, it is less about its concept,

6 Ibn Ṭawq, *Taʿlīq* 232–233, 662–663. The reports on 907 H and the early months of 908 H are yet to be published together with an index. For short lacunae that make the understanding of some passages quite impossible, see e.g. 1105, 1106, 1115, 1116, 1118.

7 For bad weather, see e.g. Ibn Ṭawq, *Taʿlīq* 205; for catching a cold, 353.

8 This has been done in Lapidus, *Muslim cities*, which is the pioneering study on Mamluk cities. Of course, at that time Ibn Ṭawq's diary had not yet been published.

9 Wollina, *Zwanzig* is a slightly revised Ph.D. thesis submitted to the Freie Universitat of Berlin in 2012. Studies of a limited scope are Shoshan, Mini-dramas; Shoshan, On divorce; and Shoshan, On the marital regime. The latter two are expanded on in Chapter 6. For the importance of the *Taʿlīq*, see also the brief remark in Martel-Thoumian, *Délinquance* 23–24.

as if not fully grasping what his project is about, but, more practically, about the content. Thus, in the preamble to his account of the year 886/1481–1482 he notes that it includes information on events, obituaries (mostly of men) known to him, "and whatever deserves attention." This does not lead us very far, because this is what Muslim historians before (and after) him had been doing all along. Similarly, at the beginning of 888/1483–1484 Ibn Ṭawq adds that he recorded whatever involved him personally, in particular in his capacity as a *shāhid* (a professional witness or, more broadly interpreted, a notary).[10] Even this brief statement does not reveal the richness of his records, their uniqueness, and their importance for modern students of Islamic history, intrigued as they ought to be by bits and pieces of history that are otherwise rare to come by. In the course of this book we shall see a great deal that is more than the modest scheme that our notary announced.

The emergence of diaries as a literary genre needs some explanation. It has been argued that the earliest diaries in European culture were written in the fourteenth century not as a conscious decision to record one's experiences in a narrative form in order to reveal aspects of the writer's personality to him-self/herself and eventually, as it were, to readers. Rather, early Renaissance diaries developed out of booklets recorded by businessmen and were devoted originally to account keeping. Of early examples one may note the *ricordanze* of the Florentine merchant-banker Strozzi and Sassetti families. A variety of information is contained in this sort of domestic chronicle, including details of estate management, records of taxation, land sales, rents, births and deaths, marriages, and family feuds.[11] The earliest diaries in the Italian city-states of the fourteenth century were a product of a "mentality of expenditure."[12] Perhaps to our surprise, Ibn Ṭawq appears as a counterpart of someone like the fifteenth-century Florentine patrician Lapo Niccolini, who recorded the deaths of his family members in the plague, the fate of his son, the food his family ate, and, no less important, the calculation of his finances, all this combined with moral reflections.[13] Or, take the example of Luca Landucci, another Florentine, the owner of an apothecary, whose diary covers the second half of the fifteenth and the early years of the sixteenth centuries.[14] Incidentally, information on the first 30 or so years in his diary is less detailed than Ibn Ṭawq's in his

10 Ibn Ṭawq, *Taʿlīq* 39, 224.
11 Jones, Florentine families.
12 Bayley, *Private life* xxiii, dates its beginning to the fifteenth century. For the view that this genre had emerged already in the fourteenth century, see briefly Lejeune, *On diary* 51.
13 Johnson, *Brief history* 18–22.
14 Jones, Florentine families.

Taʿlīq. Like Niccolini's and similar early diaries, which are a sort of magnifying glass that enables the modern historian to observe the daily life of ordinary people (well, bourgeois, at least) walking, so-to-speak, the narrow streets of Renaissance towns, Ibn Ṭawq, the Damascus notary, enables us to observe those roaming in his city's markets on the eve of its capture by the Ottomans.[15]

That Ibn Ṭawq wrote his diary not much later than Italians wrote the earliest diaries is accidental, added to which, unlike in the European case, he was not followed by other diarists for hundreds of years afterward. Although one can detect some transformation in fifteenth-century Arabic historiography, in the shift of its focus from general affairs to the private experiences of the writers and their circles, and to everyday life,[16] our notary stands apart, and one should not underestimate his uniqueness. Surely, we have nothing comparable to the *Taʿlīq* at that stage in Islamic culture. Earlier so-called diaries that have survived in a most fragmentary form do not come close to it.[17] If indeed unique, and no comparable diaries simply disappeared, then Ibn Ṭawq's diary begs the question of why it was written. Lacking any clue, we must leave this question open.

At this point, it suffices to state that the uniqueness of Ibn Ṭawq's *Taʿlīq* derives not only from its rich details but, no less, from what has already been noted briefly, namely, the use he made of his profession in writing it. As a sort of a clerk in the Islamic legal system, he kept in his possession a great number of copies or drafts of various transactions and agreements he certified (*mustanadāt, waraqat mustanad, nuskha,* [*nuskha*] *wāḥida naẓīr dhālika*), which he then copied into his daily records verbatim or in a paraphrased manner.[18] They constitute the skeleton of the diary and provide us with precious materials that tell us much about the socioeconomic and cultural fabric of the Damascus of his day. To some extent, their importance is on a par with what comes closest to archival records in pre-Ottoman Islam, such as court records from fifteenth-century Granada[19] or the hundreds of so-called Ḥaram documents of Mamluk Jerusalem, especially those 540 issued by or connected with the Shāfiʿī qadi Sharaf al-Dīn ʿĪsā b. Ghānim at the end of the fourteenth century.[20] Like

15 Johnson, *Brief history* 18–22.

16 Elbendary, *Crowds* 91–92, 106. It seems to me that her opinion that an enhanced sense of the self is also reflected goes too far.

17 This may be concluded from Makdisi, Diary. This is not the place to engage in a comparative analysis, but the difference should be evident to anyone comparing Makdisi's examples with Ibn Ṭawq's diary.

18 For these terms, see e.g. Ibn Ṭawq, *Taʿlīq* 242, 363, 422.

19 Shatzmiller, *Her day*.

20 For the most comprehensive analysis, which is based on estate inventories and related

in the latter case, what we have before us is not a systematic archive;[21] yet, it gives us access to a variety of matters. Our notary's private archive, or what is close to that, falls into a recently suggested scheme of Mamluk "decentered archival practices" maintained by a multitude of "archival actors," in fact hundreds of small-scale sites outside the central administration. Their importance is enhanced by the unfortunate disappearance of a central archive that must have existed at least in Mamluk Cairo.[22] Of these, Ibn Ṭawq's is one of the best surviving examples.[23]

Yet, the *Taʿlīq* is not just a collection of documents. It is a mine of many sorts of information, both personal and communal. On personal matters Ibn Ṭawq reports, for example, on some partly sleepless nights, when a strong wind was blowing, to which he reacted as a pious Muslim: "O God, have mercy on us."[24] He also records some of his dreams. In one of them, "a long dream," as he notes, a qadi (? *kabīr*) and a Jew appeared, and the latter, or so it is implied, paid a large sum to escape forced conversion. In another dream, our notary dreams on a dispute involving some deceased men.[25] A daydream may have expressed his anxiety about the moral situation: he saw peasants in a mosque and a scholar playing musical instruments, to which our notary reacted with anger, yet the scholar did not share his negative attitude. As Ibn Ṭawq left the mosque and was about to complain about what he had seen, he woke up.[26]

Another set of notes is about his physical problems. We learn even about which tooth was pulled out on a certain day, or that "the right side" of his back ached. Numerous brief reports on his physical ills—Ibn Ṭawq frequently resorts to the contemporary explanation of "change of balance" (*taghayyur al-mizāj*)—create an image of a hypochondriac.[27]

Another set of many brief notes pertains to the writer's family and involves some intimate details. For example, when his wife entered her second month

---

documents, see Lutfi, *al-Quds al-Mamlūkiyya*. Other work has been more limited in scope. See some articles in Little, *History and historiography*; Richards, Glimpses.

21 This is the thrust of Muller, Ḥaram al-Sharīf collection. The argument is more elaborated in his *Kadi*.

22 For this category of archives, see Hirschler, From archive, esp. 17–26. El-Leithy, Living documents 428–431, discusses the destruction of central archives as a political act of violence. See also Bouden, Mamluk-era documentary studies 17–18.

23 Another example is a thirteenth-century merchant's archive discovered in the Red Sea port of Quṣayr. See Guo, *Commerce*. See also some contributions in *L'autorité*.

24 E.g. Ibn Ṭawq, *Taʿlīq* 751 (translated in Wollina, *Zwanzig* 42), 1792.

25 Ibn Ṭawq, *Taʿlīq* 308, 329.

26 Ibn Ṭawq, *Taʿlīq* 241.

27 E.g. Ibn Ṭawq, *Taʿlīq* 29, 49, 86, 244, 469, 480, 490, 737, 763, 772, 881, 930, 985, 1303, 1308, 1312, 1315, 1316, 1343, 1361, 1362, 1377, 1889.

of pregnancy, she had desire for certain kinds of food (*wiḥām*). We learn about a conflict the two had for an unspecified reason, or one that involved their slave Mubāraka and affected their suckling son.[28] We read quite a lot about the wife's and children's health problems.[29] We learn who was the midwife of one of the couple's children and that she only substituted for the woman who had done it on previous occasions.[30] Details of the birth of one of the daughters are given: pains of labor began at night but, as they disappeared on the next day, Ibn Ṭawq left for a walk in the garden to have some fresh air. Then, another day passed and labor was resumed and lasted from morning to midday. When the baby started to come out, labor stopped and the birth was completed only in the afternoon. Incidentally, the father deems it pertinent to add that, because of the birth, he had not gone to the old city and had missed a lesson.[31] These and similar notes expose the reader to a middle-class Muslim as no other source does. We shall return to the vexing question as to what was on Ibn Ṭawq's mind when recording the most intimate details.

As to communal information, Ibn Ṭawq provides it in abundance, and it may seem occasionally trivial. Of the socio-professional milieu to which he belonged, and especially members of the Ibn Qāḍī ʿAjlūn family, more will be said later. It suffices here to note that he was updated about their minutest news such as, for example, Kamāl al-Dīn's (*mawlānā al-sayyid*, as he constantly refers to him) tumor being removed from his *right* eyelid.[32] Of other acquaintances, he reports, for example, of the death of the uncle of Yūsuf al-Jaramānī's wife (and specifies where he lived), Yūsuf being of Jaramānā, a village not far from Damascus, and our notary's partner in a few agricultural projects.[33] Surely, attending many feasts (*walīma*) was an opportunity to learn of the city news and the latest gossip.[34] One such feast was on the occasion of of his neighbor, a miller, wedding a widowed woman; Ibn Ṭawq adds that the marriage was consummated on the following night.[35] Occurrences in the notary's neighbor-

28 E.g. Ibn Ṭawq, *Taʿlīq* 133, 135, 321.

29 E.g. Ibn Ṭawq, *Taʿlīq* 78, 85, 96, 108, 146, 170, 173, 199, 206, 217, 218, 241, 244, 250, 259, 260, 280, 287, 458, 459, 486, 489, 497, 516, 593, 629, 631, 645, 733, 782, 793, 813, 862, 864, 867, 886, 968, 987, 1040, 1041, 1045, 1054, 1057, 1112, 1113, 1120, 1121, 1221, 1237, 1302, 1388, 1563, 1704, 1838, 1839, 1863.

30 Ibn Ṭawq, *Taʿlīq* 472.

31 Ibn Ṭawq, *Taʿlīq* 992 (translated in Wollina, *Zwanzig* 82).

32 Ibn Ṭawq, *Taʿlīq* 1548.

33 Ibn Ṭawq, *Taʿlīq* 394. For this village see Yāqūt, *Muʿjam al-buldān*, s.v.

34 E.g. Ibn Ṭawq, *Taʿlīq* 228–229, 295. This aspect has been extensively discussed in Wollina, *Zwanzig*.

35 Ibn Ṭawq, *Taʿlīq* 1842.

hood and elsewhere in the city may appear to the modern reader quite trivial but, apparently, were of importance to him and his contemporaries. For example, the second floor of a residence collapsed and all the family members were killed. Also, a roof of a public bath collapsed and the woman who operated it was killed and in the havoc some women's nakedness was exposed. Someone's horse was killed in the collapse of a stable. The Mālikī deputy qadi fell off a ladder at his home and broke his leg. Someone bought a camel to go on the hajj but fell ill and had to sell it and cancel his plans.[36]

Some of the matter-of-fact reports are a real revelation for the modern historian and at times contrast common knowledge. Take, for example, the subject of women's socioreligious role. We read that the lady Sitt al-Quḍāt, so named for being a qadi's daughter, one Friday night hosted a celebration on the occasion of concluding the reading of al-Bukhārī's *Ṣaḥīḥ*. A daughter of the notary's friend is reported reading a legal compendium that the notary gave her as a present. Another woman was known for copying religious texts.[37] One woman was permitted to give testimony when there were conflicting opinions about the beginning of a new month.[38]

Interesting is the report about the journey to Cairo of the widow of the Damascus Shāfiʿī qadi, a few days after her husband had been killed there in an earthquake. Unfortunately for him, less than three months earlier he had been honored by the sultan to occupy the qadi's post in Cairo, an invitation that turned out to be fateful for him. His widow, who now set out to the Mamluk capital, still not knowing her sad status because news about the death had not yet reached her, was accompanied by her husband's successor. He rode in front of her canopy (*maḥmal*) some distance out of the city, a gesture normally reserved to men only.[39] These examples notwithstanding, the intermingling of the sexes was disliked, at least in some sectors, and occasionally the feasting of men and women took place a day apart.[40]

Many pieces of information in the *Taʿlīq* may generate interest. For example, it took about two to three weeks for a letter dispatched from Cairo to reach Damascus and even, occasionally, no less than one month from the Palestinian town of Ramla. Not all mail arrived safely. Letters were wrapped in a piece of

36 Ibn Ṭawq, *Taʿlīq* 36, 58, 209, 286, 405, 661, 855, 933. For other reports of similar nature, see e.g. 66, 75, 95, 107–108, 172, 332, 413, 523, 678, 684, 1372.

37 Ibn Ṭawq, *Taʿlīq* 194, 410, 1595.

38 Ibn Ṭawq, *Taʿlīq* 114. For the complicated process of fixing the beginning of a month on the basis of testimonies, see e.g. 276, 547, 889–890, 1719.

39 Ibn Ṭawq, *Taʿlīq* 44. For the circumstances of his death, see Ibn Iyās, *Badāʾiʿ* iii, 178–179. For the lack of news about his fate, see Ibn Ṭūlūn, *Mufākahat al-khillān* 31.

40 E.g. Ibn Ṭawq, *Taʿlīq* 239, 246, 362.

cloth and tied by a silken thread. Occasionally, also cash was sent in the mail. Mail was often carried by traders in snow (*thallāja*) from the Damascus area to Cairo, where the snow was put to use.[41] In one memorial service held at a mosque, the prayer leader, who happened to be the Shāfiʿī qadi, was dressed in black.[42] During *mawlid* celebrations, popular literature such as *Sīrat ʿAntar* was recited (or perhaps read from a written text), as well as poetry composed by the renowned Sufi Ibn al-Fāriḍ. Disregarding the objection of scholars, the participants used to sing to the sound of musical instruments.[43] With the death of one Shams al-Dīn, a copyist, a specific calligraphic style was no longer mastered in Damascus.[44] At least some of the births, perhaps in leading families, were recorded.[45] When a dead baby was born, three hens were sent to the bereaved parents.[46] A morning prayer (*ṣubḥa*) in honor of a deceased person could be recited also in honor of women.[47] Birth could take place at a hammam.[48] And so on and so forth.

Quite a few reports relate the display of immoral conduct in public. A notary was seen drunk near the Umayyad Mosque. Likewise, Ibn Ṭawq's wife spotted a man sitting in the company of a married woman all night, both sipping wine and singing. At the house of one Ibn Sālim, a performance of a shadow play by "Naʿīṣ and co." had taken place; the rumor was that women and wine had been part of the happening.[49] One ʿAbd al-Qādir al-Qudsī was suspected of intimate contact with a European woman. A European was found drunk—of all places, at a property belonging to the *shaykh al-Islām*—in the company of a married Muslim woman. He was taken to the militant Sufi shaykh Faraj, forced to convert, and underwent circumcision on the following day; the woman and her husband were able to flee.[50] A Ḥanbalī teacher was found hanged in his madrasa cell. Our notary claims to lack further details, but Ibn Ṭūlūn, the renowned chronicler, adds that the dark-skinned man had bought the rope for

---

41 Ibn Ṭawq, *Taʿlīq* 203, 204, 244, 308, 354, 356, 357, 362, 369, 979. This trade is mentioned by the chronicler al-Jazarī (d. 739/1338). It operated from the mountain region, especially Manīn, north of Mt. Qāsyūn. For further details, see Eychenne, Production agricole 593–595, 603–604. See also Braudel, *Mediterranean* i, 28–29.

42 Ibn Ṭawq, *Taʿlīq* 390.

43 Ibn Ṭawq, *Taʿlīq* 470.

44 Ibn Ṭawq, *Taʿlīq* 590.

45 On the birth registration of the *shaykh al-Islām*'s daughter, see Ibn Ṭawq, *Taʿlīq* 688.

46 Ibn Ṭawq, *Taʿlīq* 233.

47 Ibn Ṭawq, *Taʿlīq* 50 and editor's n. 1 for an explanation.

48 E.g. Ibn Ṭawq, *Taʿlīq* 406.

49 Ibn Ṭawq, *Taʿlīq* 109, 316, 325, 398, 503. Ibn Ṭawq considered the shadow play an innovation (*bidʿa*). On the literary genre, see Khayāl al-ẓill, *EI*²; Ibn Dāniyāl, *EI*³; Guo, *Performing arts*.

50 Ibn Ṭawq, *Taʿlīq* 433, 435, 487.

half a dirham and that the death was beyond any doubt a case of suicide; the poor teacher had probably suffered from a problem and "his brain dried up." Some months earlier he had suffered from physical weakness and had been temporarily hospitalized at the Ṣāliḥiyya Hospital. Ibn Ṭawq and Ibn Ṭūlūn disagree about the exact sum of cash he left.[51] There are numerous similar accounts in the *Taʿlīq*.[52]

Some reports reflect the *mentalité* of our notary and his contemporaries, in the sense of "the inert, obscure, unconscious elements in a given world view."[53] In a quarrel between two men concerning a debt, the debtor vowed not to return home if it were revealed that the debt had not been settled. After a while, a wall crushed him.[54] At one scholar's home, a terrifying black snake was discovered and was killed by the black maid. Subsequently, she and the master's son suffered from epileptic seizures and had to be taken to a healer.[55] In another case, a woman from ʿAnāba village claimed that the Prophet had told her about a treasure locked in a box hidden at her home, to which he had given her a large key. This came to the knowledge of some senior Mamluk officers, who could not take such a story lightly. Despite the rough weather, they came and dug quite deeply, but nothing was found and they left disappointed.[56] Similarly, al-Akshar al-Kamālī, known as the "sorcerer," together with a Maghribi man, was summoned to the citadel after claiming a treasure was hidden at some house. Once again, the governor's men dug but could not find anything. Now it was time to blame al-Akshar for being a swindler. In the meantime, in what appears to have been a clear attempt to nail him, it was "revealed" that his mother had spoken confusedly "in the name of the Devil."[57] Others engaged in alchemy (*kīmā*), to the resentment of scholars.[58]

Some dreams generated action. One villager was ordered in his dream to build over a grave, and the site became a popular place of visitation for the

51 Ibn Ṭawq, *Taʿlīq* 1901; Ibn Ṭūlūn, *Mufākahat al-khillān* 193; Martel-Thoumian, *Délinquance* 26. There are numerous accounts of this kind.

52 E.g. Ibn Ṭawq, *Taʿlīq* 29, 61, 172, 668.

53 This is taken from Ginzburg, *Cheese* xxiii, who recognizes the importance of the concept for historical research but is cautious about its use in the case he studied. I use this term in the sense used by the so-called Annales school of history. For a case that reflects medieval *mentalité*, see E. Cohen, Law. For the medieval Islamic scene, see Malti-Douglas, *Mentalités*; Shoshan, Jokes.

54 Ibn Ṭawq, *Taʿlīq* 413.

55 Ibn Ṭawq, *Taʿlīq* 619.

56 Ibn Ṭawq, *Taʿlīq* 1886.

57 Ibn Ṭawq, *Taʿlīq* 961.

58 Ibn Ṭawq, *Taʿlīq* 510, 583.

sick. Another man was shown in a dream the grave of the Prophet near the city (in reality, an absurdity) and erected there a construction that drew "the riff-raff and Satan's followers."[59] Occasional expressions of our notary's beliefs or criticism may reflect those of a wider constituency. A lunar eclipse he considers "portents of the Day of Judgment" (*ashrāṭ al-sāʿa*).[60] Commenting on a dispute, he notes that "order broke down and rules turned to naught; evil prevails and Islam is on the wane."[61] Learning that a corpse had been reburied in the family grave after being buried elsewhere, he laments the prevailing ignorance.[62]

Even some Damascus dignitaries were not spared from our source's ire and criticism. The Shāfiʿī qadi Ibn al-Muzalliq was involved up to his neck in a fraud. He had contemplated purchasing an expensive robe with mongoose fur (an item favored by Mamluk officers and the bourgeoisie). Unable to decide, he had kept the robe for quite a while, until he received a message from the dealer. Declining the purchase, the qadi returned the garment, at which point the dealer suspected that the expensive fur had been replaced by a cheaper one. He confirmed it with the tailor who had done the job. After further inquiry, Ibn al-Muzalliq agreed to pay 60 dinars in compensation, on condition that the affair be kept secret. Concluding the report, Ibn Ṭawq remarks that such a person (i.e., the qadi) occupies an elevated office because of the sins of the Believers.[63] The removal and escape of the "major domo" (*ustādār*) was an opportunity for our notary to refer to the widespread tyranny and pray for a quick salvation and God's mercy; may "the wheel of fortune" turn against this official and his father.[64] Following the release of the "brave but tyrannical" Yilbāy al-Aynālī, the *dawādār al-Sulṭān* (keeper of the royal inkwell, who is in charge of the official correspondence), from temporary arrest, Ibn Ṭawq implies that torture awaits him in Hell.[65] Our notary was glad to learn about the death of Jundar, the viceroy's personal mamluk, an influential man who served in a number of posts. After relating all the damage he had caused, Ibn Ṭawq concludes that "God relieved us from him, as He causes every oppressor to perish."[66] There were a few others about whom he does not fail to express his negative opin-

59 Ibn Ṭawq, *Taʿlīq* 1411, 1622.
60 Ibn Ṭawq, *Taʿlīq* 46.
61 Ibn Ṭawq, *Taʿlīq* 101.
62 Ibn Ṭawq, *Taʿlīq* 116.
63 Ibn Ṭawq, *Taʿlīq* 478.
64 Ibn Ṭawq, *Taʿlīq* 72, 313. He was in charge of the distribution of salaries.
65 Ibn Ṭawq, *Taʿlīq* 45, 64. On his post, see Ibn Ṭawq, *Taʿlīq* 25.
66 Ibn Ṭawq, *Taʿlīq* 1161. See on him, e.g. Ibn Ṭawq, *Taʿlīq* 66, 740.

ion.[67] Here and there, he shows his aversion to the Mamluk elite in general,[68] and even to the sultan. When he reports about Qāytbāy's order to demolish a house because of its expensive woodwork, which he desired, Ibn Ṭawq wishes that God would have punished the ruler and saved the Muslims.[69]

Certainly striking and quite unique are the numerous weather reports.[70] Were these a result of sheer pedantry? Or, can they be ascribed to the writer's peasant origins? In any case, on very cold days he reports putting on a fur.[71] An especially elaborate report tells that Saturday, 3 Rabīʿ II 891/8 April 1486 was a day of thunderstorms in which "the world darkened." Heavy rain with drops as big as chickpeas, the like of which one saw only in the open country, caused flooding. This continued for about 24 hours, and all that time the light of the sun could be seen for short spells only. Then, for a few hours, heavy rain resumed, water dripped into many homes, and rivers and canals flooded.[72] Our notary hoped, as he did on such occasions, that "God would spare [the believers] His ire."[73] Also unique is the attention he repeatedly pays to vegetables and fruits—once again, possibly due to his peasant background.[74]

Although limited to the Hijrī years 885–906, and even that with a lacuna of a few weeks between 22 Rabīʿ II and the beginning of Jumādā II 887,[75] given its coverage of the minutest details pertaining to both its author and the Damascus of his time, one can safely argue that it is impossible to point to a local history that is comparable to the *Taʿlīq*. Albeit with relatively limited interest in politics, Syrian politics included, Ibn Ṭawq's approximately 1,900 pages (in the printed edition) are a unique example of microhistory, or *Alltagsgeschichte*.[76] A comparison with Muḥammad b. ʿAbd al-Bāqī al-Makkī's *Tārīkh Ḥimṣ*, subti-

67 Ibn Ṭawq, *Taʿlīq* 47, 49, 116, 278, 295, 307, 316, 334, 342, 355, 392, 824, 1806.

68 Ibn Ṭawq, *Taʿlīq* 1216.

69 Ibn Ṭawq, *Taʿlīq* 295. For political criticism in Egyptian chronicles, see Elbendary, *Crowds* 117–119.

70 E.g. Ibn Ṭawq, *Taʿlīq* 33, 34, 35, 36, 37, 42, 46, 47, 48, 78, 86, 90, 91, 93, 94, 95, 96, 98, 107, 109, 112, 115, 117, 118, 140, 141, 142, 144, 145, 182, 191, 193, 195, 196, 200, 204, 208, 209, 215, 216, 219, 221, 222, 228, 229, 230, 231, 232, 233, 293, 301, 302, 303, 304, 305, 306, 309, 342, 406, 415, 420, 423, 439, 452, 458, 459, 472, 516, 520, 521, 524, 529, 585, 592, 597, 664, 667, 671, 740, 750, 751, 809, 841, 867, 919, 921, 924, 925, 928, 929, 943, 984, 990, 995, 1020, 1090, 1111, 1233, 1244, 1270, 1321, 1559, 1563, 1824.

71 E.g. Ibn Ṭawq, *Taʿlīq* 278.

72 Ibn Ṭawq, *Taʿlīq* 607.

73 Ibn Ṭawq, *Taʿlīq* 1824.

74 E.g. Ibn Ṭawq, *Taʿlīq* 451, 454, 455, 467, 751, 758, 840, 942, 955, 1012, 1017, 1265, 1284, 1415.

75 Ibn Ṭawq, *Taʿlīq* 166–167. This is most likely due to conditions of preservation.

76 Although not discussed by him, Wollina's use of the term *Alltag* in the title of his book is

tled "Diary" (*yawmiyyāt*) and covering the years 1099–1134/1688–1722 which has recently been the subject of a stimulating literary study, would prove instructive. Striking enough, like Ibn Ṭawq, al-Makkī was a clerk, probably a notary in the local court. However, his diary, although it is occasionally a source of information on marriage contracts, endowment deeds, and transactions and, like the *Taʿlīq*, is concerned with all walks of life,[77] appears to be less detailed, and the amount of documentation in it is inferior to that reproduced by our notary.

The hundreds of names that feature in Ibn Ṭawq's diary, many of men and women who cannot now be identified and who appear only once and then disappear never to be mentioned again, turn his city into an intimate place and his records into a microhistory.[78] Thus, a transaction between the two brothers ʿAlāʾ al-Dīn and ʿAbd al-Raḥmān of the al-Sayūfī family, through "their legally approved agent" (*mutakallim*), and ʿAlā al-Dīn ʿAlī b. Qabbās al-Iqbāʿī ("the hat dealer") is certified by Ibn Ṭawq in his capacity as a *shāhid*. The two brothers purchased 68 velvet-like patched red hats, plus 55 red horse curbs (? *ḥakmiyya*) for 97 ashrafīs (dinars), yet they actually paid nothing, as the seller owed them an almost identical sum for a fountainhead (? *ʿayn mabīʿa*) he had purchased, and for which he had advanced only 7 dinars. At the time of that purchase, he had attested to his ability to pay the whole sum and had had to mortgage his share in his home. Also, his mother had guaranteed the transaction, and the two brothers had "accepted it legally" (*qabūl sharʿī*).[79] In another transaction, Ḥāj Suwaydak al-Turkumānī, a merchant in cattle, purchased a variety of expensive cloths, of which a detailed description is provided, for the enormous price of 500 ashrafīs, of which he paid 50 in cash and for another 90 he had a guarantor (*ḍāmin*); the rest was to be paid within a year.[80] The Ḥanafī deputy qadi Amīn al-Dīn Muḥammad al-Ḥisbānī purchased from the merchant Zayn al-Dīn ʿAbd al-Qādir b. al-ʿAdl a variety of cloths for 18 ashrafīs in cash. The two had concluded an earlier transaction, which had left a standing debt of 26 ashrafīs and which had been transferred (*iḥāla*) to one Ḥāj Muḥammad.[81]

---

justified. The study of *Alltagsgeschichte* was in vogue in German historiography especially in the 1980s and 1990s. See e.g. Mattern, *Leben*. But see also most recently Hitz, *Kampfen*.

77 Sajdi, *Barber* 93–94, 126, 143–144.

78 For the association of microhistory with some late Mamluk chronicles see also Elbendary, *Crowds* 92–98. She rightly argues that, generally, Syrian writers, because of their provincial location, were more interested in local affairs and this is reflected in their chronicles. This tendency would intensify after the Ottoman conquest.

79 Ibn Ṭawq, *Taʿlīq* 369–370. The editor's understanding that interest was charged in this case seems to me erroneous.

80 Ibn Ṭawq, *Taʿlīq* 128–129.

81 Ibn Ṭawq, *Taʿlīq* 1063.

Also, some women are mentioned as active in business. Sitt Fāṭima of Eastern ʿAnāba sold the right to the wood in her grove (the exact borders of which are detailed) to Muḥammad b. al-ʿAṭṭār, the constructor (*miʿmār*), for 120 ashrafīs, on condition that the chopping would be done in the same month. Payment was in three different types of coins, new silver dirhams, ashrafīs, and Manṣūrī dinars. Incidentally, the broker received a strikingly small fee of much less than 1 percent.[82] Another Fāṭima, the wife of qadi Muḥibb al-Dīn, most likely the Ḥanafī known as Ibn Qaṣīf, together with her mother, hired for 500 silver coins, in the presence of her husband, the "tall" camel driver Ibn al-Ṣayfī; the purpose was travelling to Jerusalem and Hebron and selling merchandise (the details of which are provided).[83]

Such information brings to mind the opening pages of a classic of the microhistory genre, Natalie Zemon Davis's *The return of Martin Guerre*, which introduce the sixteenth-century village of Artigat in the French Pyrenees through the records of a notary from the nearby burg of Le Fossat. There, Jean Banquels rented a mare for six years to a peasant from Pailhes; a priest of Le Fossat sold a garden to a merchant, explaining he had to support his old parents for eight years; Antoine Basle of Artigat sold for 35 livres the fourth part of the goods and succession of his father to a man from a nearby hamlet; and so on.[84] All these bits and pieces, when put together, reveal a world in which names, routines, and trivial behaviors come to life. As Davis puts it, "Small and often invisible interactions and structures can be 'seen' and poked at by the historian's pen to find out how they work. If the data is rich, then there is the chance to construct a *dynamic of experience* … to establish a *morphology of thought and experience*."[85]

Like the aforementioned Florentine *ricordanze*, our notary's diary has not only a great deal of microhistory to offer; it also was an account book for recording his various expenses—home repair work, cultivation of agricultural plots, various items bought, gifts he sent to and received from friends and their prices, sums of money owed, and more.[86] At this point we have to return to a question posed earlier: Was somebody expected to see the diary? Here is a puzzle, for although it was clearly intended for private use, one finds it strange that on at

---

82 Ibn Ṭawq, *Taʿlīq* 322–323.

83 Ibn Ṭawq, *Taʿlīq* 138. On Ibn Qaṣīf, see Ibn Ṭūlūn, *Quḍāt Dimashq* 232.

84 Davis, *Return* 10, 11.

85 Davis, Shapes 30 (italics in the original).

86 E.g. Ibn Ṭawq, *Taʿlīq* 35, 44, 45, 62, 91, 92, 98, 99, 101, 105, 106, 107, 112, 121, 130, 131, 132, 136, 140, 142, 144, 146, 149, 166, 176, 216, 227, 254, 274, 292, 356, 371, 403, 405, 410, 419, 420–421, 1694, 1839. On this point, see also El-Leithy, Living documents 412.

least two occasions our notary writes down the initials only of some names.[87] This is unusual, since on all other occasions he identifies people in full, even when he bears a grudge against them. One may recall his criticism of the sultan and local authorities. Were the initials just a technicality? Alternatively, was he apprehensive that another eye might see his diary after all? Did he ever think that his *Taʿlīq* might eventually land in the public domain? We have no way of knowing. However, as we shall soon see, it so happened that Ibn Ṭūlūn, the leading chronicler of Damascus, must have seen at least parts of the *Taʿlīq* not long afterward. What were the circumstances? How did they reach him? We do not know.

In order to better grasp the uniqueness of Ibn Ṭawq's diary as a historical source, it is pertinent to compare it with contemporary histories of Damascus. One is the chronicle by ʿAlāʾ al-Dīn ʿAlī al-Buṣrawī (d. 905/1500), who was a Shāfiʿī deputy qadi, preacher, and holder of some administrative posts.[88] Reported to have covered the years 872–904 H (that is, till shortly before his death), his work has reached us in an incomplete manuscript.[89] Of some 250 pages in its printed edition, it refers briefly to political and administrative occurrences and has obituaries of Damascene dignitaries. One finds in it little on social matters.[90]

Shihāb al-Dīn Aḥmad b. Muḥammad Ibn al-Ḥimṣī's *Ḥawādith al-zamān wa-wafayāt al-shuyūkh wa-l-aqrān* covers the years 851–930 H, that is, until about four years before the author's death. It is an abridgement of a longer version that, according to the author, was devoted to obituaries.[91] Precisely like al-Buṣrawī, Ibn al-Ḥimṣī was a Shāfiʿī deputy qadi, as well as a preacher at the Umayyad Mosque and holder of some other posts.[92] Also, this work has survived incomplete; the year 892 H and the early part of 893 H, as well as most of 895 H and 901–902 H, are missing in the available manuscript.[93] Fur-

---

87 Ibn Ṭawq, *Taʿlīq* 358, 979.

88 On his illness and funeral, see Ibn Ṭawq, *Taʿlīq* 1818–1819. On his posts, see editor's introduction to al-Buṣrawī *Tārīkh*, 28–29.

89 For lacunae, see al-Buṣrawī, Tārīkh 92–93, 152–153.

90 At least on one occasion Ibn Ṭawq copied from al-Buṣrawī. See Ibn Ṭawq, *Taʿlīq* 188. As regards a report about a major water dispute, our notary notes that al-Buṣrawī did not mention it; he refers to the *ṣaḥāʾif*, but it remains unclear if by this he means the history book or the judicial records. See Ibn Ṭawq, *Taʿlīq* 957.

91 Ibn al-Ḥimṣī, *Ḥawādith* i, 82, 83, 99, 163. Some years appear incomplete. See e.g. Ibn al-Ḥimṣī, *Ḥawādith* i, 201. Petry, *Criminal underworld* 20–21, errs about the precise coverage of the work. Also, his characterization of this work should be qualified.

92 Ibn al-Ḥimṣī, *Ḥawādith* i, 133, 262. See on him editor's introduction, 23–24, 29–36. His father was a muezzin in the Umayyad Mosque.

93 Ibn al-Ḥimṣī, *Ḥawādith* i, 307, 308, 323; ii, 9–10.

thermore, between 900 H and 914 H the author was in Cairo, probably serving there as a *khaṭīb*,[94] and his information on Damascus for these years is minimal.

Shams al-Dīn Muḥammad Ibn Ṭūlūn (d. 953/1546), a native of Damascus and Ibn al-Ḥimṣī's pupil, wrote a history of Damascus covering the years 880 H–951 H, which is rightly considered the best for that period.[95] Its good access to information notwithstanding,[96] the author occasionally copied from Ibn al-Ḥimṣī's abridged history and here and there from al-Buṣrawī's.[97] Given the similarity between Ibn Ṭūlūn's and Ibn Ṭawq's reports in a few instances, the former clearly copied, though unsystematically, from the latter directly, abridging some of his reports.[98] Some personal assessments and expressions by Ibn Ṭawq that Ibn Ṭūlūn repeats leave little doubt about that.[99] But, for a few exceptions, the *Taʿlīq* is much more informative than Ibn Ṭūlūn's book. This can be easily demonstrated quantitatively: while for the years 886–902 H the *Taʿlīq* has about 1,000 pages, Ibn Ṭūlūn's book has only 40.

For information recorded in his diary, Ibn Ṭawq relied on dozens of informants, some identifiable, such as Muḥibb al-Dīn, a deputy qadi and member of the Ibn Qāḍī ʿAjlūn family; the notary Shihāb al-Dīn b. ʿAbd al-Ḥaqq; Mubārak Shāh, a servant of the wealthy Ibn al-Muzalliq family; and many more. He also mentions many unidentified informants, such as a man of the village of Jarūd,

94 Ibn al-Ḥimṣī, *Ḥawādith* i, 32–34, editor's note.

95 For a biography of Ibn Ṭūlūn, see editor's introduction to Ibn Ṭūlūn, *Ḥawādith* 62–68; al-Ḥaṣkafī, *Mutʿat al-adhhān* i, 166–167. See also Conermann, Ibn Ṭūlūn; Elbendary, *Crowds* 111–112. The surviving manuscript of Ibn Ṭūlūn's history, which covers the years 880–926 H, is incomplete. The reports on the years 927–951 H have been reconstructed from later works. See Ibn Ṭūlūn, *Ḥawādith* 74–92 (editor's introduction).

96 E.g. Ibn Ṭūlūn, *Mufākahat al-khillān* 31, 39, as regards the Ottoman Mūrād. See also 55, 56–62.

97 For copying from Ibn al-Ḥimṣī, compare, e.g., Ibn Ṭūlūn, *Mufākahat al-khillān* 45, 46–52, 52–56, 131–132 to Ibn al-Ḥimṣī, *Ḥawādith* i, 265–266, 269–280, 281–296, 350, respectively. For copying from al-Buṣrawī, compare the unsystematic copying in Ibn Ṭūlūn, *Mufākahat al-khillān* 72–74, 95–96, 110, 119–120, to al-Buṣrawī, *Tārīkh* 117–122, 131–137, 140–144, 145–149, respectively.

98 For direct (though unsystematic) copying, see Ibn Ṭūlūn, *Mufākahat al-khillān* 35, 36, 45, which terminates in Ramadan. Reporting on a certain transaction, the author notes that Ibn Ṭawq, who most likely was his source, served as a (professional) witness. In Ibn Ṭūlūn, *Mufākahat al-khillān* 32, our notary is actually identified as the source. For abridging, compare the report on the construction of a bridge in Ibn Ṭūlūn, *Mufākahat al-khillān* 34 to Ibn Ṭawq, *Taʿlīq* 50. See also Ibn Ṭūlūn, *Mufākahat al-khillān* 80 and Ibn Ṭawq, *Taʿlīq* 778.

99 Compare, e.g., the expression as regards Yilbāy by Ibn Ṭūlūn, *Mufākahat al-khillān* 38 to Ibn Ṭawq, *Taʿlīq* 64.

or "one informant."[100] On a substantial number of days he did not come to Damascus, or he passed through the city quickly (*ʿābir ṭarīq*), which he notes as a matter of careful recording or possibly to remind himself of the reason for the empty space left in his records.[101] On one occasion he does not go to the city, because he has to wash his clothes and, five days later, because he has to do some computation concerning a waqf.[102] And yet, one may characterize Ibn Ṭawq's mode in keeping his diary as extremely devoted, if not obsessive. For many days he gives just the precise date but nothing more.[103] At times he explicitly notes that there is nothing to report.[104] For an unclear reason he moves in Jumādā I 903/January 1498 to Maʿlūlā, a village northeast of the city, the majority of whose inhabitants are Christian. This happens about three years before the diary terminates abruptly. Thereafter, it is in the village that he regularly receives information on Damascus, either from his esteemed friend Taqī al-Dīn Ibn Qāḍī ʿAjlūn, or from others who visit and update him.[105] During his stay in Maʿlūlā he goes to Damascus infrequently.[106]

Ibn Ṭawq may have written his notes at the end of each day or a few days afterward. There are instances of information reaching him considerably later than the event he reports.[107] On several occasions he corrects or updates notes he has written on a previous day, which he discovers to be wrong. Here and there he repeats the same note. According to the manuscript's editor, the notary occasionally added notes in the margin of the diary.[108] Here and there he interrupts the continuity of a report and inserts some unrelated information.[109] All this evidences that he did not edit the diary. As one would expect, quite a few of his notes are cryptic or formulated in such a way that they make interpretation

---

100 E.g. Ibn Ṭawq, *Taʿlīq* 197, 287, 312, 314, 316, 317, 321, 381, 397, 498, 679, 903.

101 E.g. Ibn Ṭawq, *Taʿlīq* 348, 349, 353, 355, 357, 363, 365, 373, 392, 393, 407, 417, 461, 480, 484, 495, 623, 691, 772, 794, 888, 893, 894, 986, 1106, 1149, 1155, 1186, 1210, 1297, 1354, 1385, 1393, 1412, 1462, 1536, 1539, 1632, 1633.

102 Ibn Ṭawq, *Taʿlīq* 1729, 1730.

103 E.g. Ibn Ṭawq, *Taʿlīq* 28, 52, 56, 61, 64, 76, 77, 79, 85, 86, 87, 167, 178, 180, 250, 264, 272, 277, 281, 285, 386, 393, 421, 677, 689, 707, 714, 715, 718, 720, 721, 722, 788, 791, 803, 898, 983, 1067–1068, 1149, 1171, 1186, 1767.

104 E.g. Ibn Ṭawq, *Taʿlīq* 1502, 1515, 1566.

105 E.g. Ibn Ṭawq, *Taʿlīq* 1576, 1578.

106 E.g. Ibn Ṭawq, *Taʿlīq* 1585, 1586, 1590, 1594, 1596, 1598, 1600, 1601, 1602, 1607, 1608, 1609, 1611, 1612, 1615, 1617, 1619, 1620, 1627, 1628, 1651, 1665, 1671, 1678, 1690, 1729, 1730.

107 E.g. Ibn Ṭawq, *Taʿlīq* 211, 221, 373, 797, 823, 841.

108 E.g. Ibn Ṭawq, *Taʿlīq* 56, 72, 84, 199, 204 and n. 2, 230, 237 and n. 3, 264, 747, 783, 785, 834, 873, 889, 958, 1087, 1104, 1105, 1107, 1125, 1228, 1360–1361, 1469 (see also Wollina, *Zwanzig* 41–42), 1478, 1533, 1550, 1554, 1557, 1559, 1600, 1827, 1839, 1841.

109 E.g. Ibn Ṭawq, *Taʿlīq* 1787–1788.

difficult.[110] As far as language and style go, the diary is at times influenced by some Damascus-specific vocabulary, and the grammar and syntax are far from perfect.[111]

Chapter 1 introduces Ibn Ṭawq, on the basis of the autobiographical data in his diary. Although by no means an autobiography, the diary tells us a great deal about his professional activities, as well as about his various acts and contacts, some of which intended to supplement his income as a notary. Some information is provided on his cultural world. The second part of this chapter turns to his family and household. All in all, the material in this chapter offers not only an exceptionally detailed portrait of a lower middle-class individual at the end of the Mamluk period but also sheds further light on related issues.

The aim of the following chapters is to provide, mainly on the basis of Ibn Ṭawq's immense materials, what comes closest to a microhistory of the approximately 20 years that the diary covers. The chapters are organized around the main subjects one may gather from the many thousands of items in the *Taʿlīq*. The overall picture emerging out of the rich data is a complex one. There is definitely a sense of crisis. That is to say, the Ottoman conquest of Damascus in 1516 does not look totally unexpected—perhaps, even, it was not a complete surprise to the city's residents; instead, it came after some critical years during which the local Mamluk government faced difficulties and the local people were at the mercy of natural disaster, corrupt and ruthless rulers, and ravaging bedouins and criminal elements. This comes out clearly in Chapter 2. Ibn Ṭawq's diary enables us to reconstruct the historical context much better than has been possible thus far. We learn about the demographic situation resulting from the frequent epidemics and the high death tolls. And we learn also about the poor situation of the Damascenes and of the villagers in the vicinity, who, in addition, suffered from heavy taxation and pillage. It is also argued that the structure of the city, which was based on quarters, demonstrates a lack of cohesion or a real sense of urban community.

Chapter 3 is about the ulema and bureaucrats, some of whom were acquaintances of our notary. The beginning of this chapter tells a story of many conflicts among them, evolving out of both legal and personal issues. Somewhat contrary to the received wisdom that the ulema were a homogeneous body of scholars who worked as intermediaries between ordinary Muslims and their

110 E.g. Ibn Ṭawq, *Taʿlīq* 141, 146, 211, 212, 380.

111 For colloquialisms, see e.g. Ibn Ṭawq, *Taʿlīq* 65, 112, 141, 146, 154, 163, 165, 174, 200, 201, 253, 265, 434, 525, 836, 850, 882, 1380. For grammatical errors, such as *raddaytu*, or *tuwuffiya* (for feminine), see 406, 726. See also briefly Elbendary, *Crowds* 92.

governors, this chapter reveals a great deal of internal rifts that subjected the ulema to Mamluk manipulation. In a way, this factor may be seen as part of the larger crisis. In contrast to it emerges the towering figure of Taqī al-Dīn Ibn Qāḍī ʿAjlūn, the Shāfiʿī mufti, also known as *shaykh al-Islām*, who features in the *Taʿlīq* frequently and about whom we learn a great deal as regards not only his position but also his personal life. He appears as a most influential figure and at the same time is involved in a number of legal and personal controversies.

Chapter 4 brings unique details about transactions, loans, and other topics related to the bourgeoisie and middle class. We learn here especially about the assets and endowments in the city and the neighboring regions. These details, like many others that the diary provides, help us identify the leading bourgeois individuals and families, as well as the less prominent ones, who were active on the economic scene. Of special interest is the information on women's activities as investors and founders of waqfs.

Chapter 5 is a study of the functioning of the law in the context of the disputes and criminal scene. It opens with financial disputes and the procedure by which they were resolved. It then turns to the criminal scene—notably homicide, theft, and religious transgression—and the system of punishment. The emerging picture is of a city beset by constant criminal activity, which most likely resulted from the difficult prevailing conditions. In such a context, the Mamluk rulers collaborated with the jurists, and perhaps also vied with them, to control the legal system, and one can discern an encroachment by the regime at the expense of the qadis and scholars.

Chapter 6 discusses the data that the diary provides on marriage and divorce and on domestic female slaves and concubines. The marriage contracts reproduced by our notary teach us a great deal about gender relationships and the status of married women. The information Ibn Ṭawq provides on his own family, on the family of the *shaykh al-Islām*, and on the family of some other friends is unique for studying the pre-Ottoman family situation.

The book ends with a brief outline of the fate of the city in the approximately 20 years between the abrupt termination of the *Taʿlīq* and the Ottoman conquest of Damascus.

CHAPTER 1

Ibn Ṭawq, His Family, Household, and Close Friends

Having almost nothing on Ibn Ṭawq from other sources, what we can say about him must come from his diary. We first meet him, so to speak, when he is about 50 years old, and we learn only indirectly bits and pieces about his earlier life.[1] His origins, as far back as his grandfather, were of a peasant family of the Jarūd village in the Ghūṭa region, northwest of Damascus and about half-a-day's horse ride from that city. He kept in contact with people of this village and on occasion visited and stayed there overnight—whether at his relatives' homes or at those of others, we do not know.[2] Surely, he knew well many Jarūdīs and thus, on one occasion, he reports on a raid by the viceroy's troops, after which men of the village were marched in fetters along the streets of Damascus, of whom he recognized 20 and also the severed head of a man who had been wounded during the raid, so had been slow to march, with the result that an angry soldier had chopped off his head.[3]

Most of the years during which he kept a diary (or at least, the part that survived), Ibn Ṭawq lived in Damascus. We learn only indirectly about the location of his residence. Perhaps this should not surprise us, since it was obvious to him, so there was no need to write down the details. From his reference to "our quarter" (*ḥāratunā*), we may conclude that his home was near the al-Qaṣab Mosque at the Ṣārūjā Market, outside the northwest section of the city wall.[4] He also had a share in land (perhaps a waqf) at Maʿlūlā, a Ghūṭa village the majority of whose residents were Christian. He disputed with his relatives, the Banū Nabhān, about this share. The issue came before a Shafiʿī court, but the decision was not to his liking, and, despite being a Shafiʿī, he turned to the Ḥanbalī qadi to review the case. In the event, the dispute was resolved in an agreement rectified by no less than seven fatwas by scholars adhering to three of the four Sunnī legal schools. It remains unclear why such a complicated procedure was required.[5]

---

1 For the time it took to reach the city from the village, see e.g. Ibn Ṭawq, *Taʿlīq* 272.

2 E.g. Ibn Ṭawq, *Taʿlīq* 804, 897, 988, 1579, 1581, 1634, 1636–1637.

3 Ibn Ṭawq, *Taʿlīq* 670.

4 Ibn Ṭawq, *Taʿlīq* 599. The editor's note at 1377 n. 1 seems erroneous. On this mosque, see briefly al-Nuʿaymī, *al-Dāris* ii, 265.

5 For his share in the estate, see Ibn Ṭawq, *Taʿlīq* 699. For the dispute, see 702, 706, 736, 741–742, 743, 828, 847–848. See briefly Wollina, *Zwanzig* 48.

 | DOI:10.1163/9789004413269_003

Ibn Ṭawq's contact with Maʿlūlā appears to have been a close one, and in 903/1498 he even moved there, for how long is not stated, but a year and a half appears likely. Initially he resided at Ilyās's, the local priest's son, whom he employed as a land cultivator. A pious Muslim's staying at a Christian home may raise an eyebrow, especially since Ibn Ṭawq at times displays in his diary little tolerance for Christians. In that, our notary was by no means an exception. However, as we shall see, his daily contact with Christians was not that simple (or simplistic). During his residence in the village, his wife stayed in the city, and he reports little on her, but it appears that his two mature sons were with him—about one of them, Muḥammad, we know that at that point he was a widower. From Maʿlūlā, Ibn Ṭawq would come to Damascus only occasionally. However, his friends visited him and updated him about things in the city. Surely, residing in the village provided Ibn Ṭawq with far fewer opportunities to work in his profession as a notary, and whenever he did, he worked mainly in the service of Christians of the village and of neighboring villages.[6] Whether his income during that year and a half was supplemented by the proceeds from his aforementioned property in Maʿlūlā remains unclear.

Ibn Ṭawq was a notary/witness (*shāhid*) in the sharʿī judicial system, an office for which there was need whenever official certification was required. We do not know the qualifications for this job, but one would assume that no systematic madrasa education was required. However, to acquire the know-how of the many technicalities involved one might need some apprenticeship and training. Ibn Ṭawq was not the only Damascus *shāhid* known to have come from peasant stock; some of similar background were promoted to the post of deputy qadi (*nāʾib*).[7] Our notary mentions at least a dozen of his professional colleagues by name, as well as the location of their "offices," usually in a central place in the city.[8] As a *shāhid* he drafted and kept documents (*mustanadāt*) and

---

6 For his occasional visits and stays in the village, see e.g. Ibn Ṭawq, *Taʿlīq* 788, 790, 803, 907, 983, 1068, 1082, 1172. For a possible reference to the move to Maʿlūlā, see 1574. For his stay there, see 1640, 1666, 1671. For arriving at the city, see e.g. 1621, 1634, 1691. For "passing through the city," see e.g. 1632, 1633. For not coming to Damascus, see e.g. 1598, 1600, 1601, 1602, 1608, 1611, 1615. For friends visiting him, see e.g. 1641, 1707, 1871. For his activity as a notary for Christians, see 1666–1667, 1668–1669, 1670, 1671, 1768–1769. For a peasant he employed at Maʿlūlā, see 1915.

7 See Shāid, *EI*^{2}; Tyan, *Notariat*. See now further information in Muller, *Kadi*, esp. 56–80, 268–319; Martin and Zomeno, Identifying. For promotion in Damascus, see Miura, *Dynamism* 142–143. For two notaries of suspicious background in 915/1509, see Ibn Ṭūlūn, *Mufākahat al-khillān* 270; Miura, *Dynamism* 144.

8 For the location of notarial "shops" near some of the city gates and elsewhere, see e.g. Ibn Ṭawq, *Taʿlīq* 153, 174, 235, 371, 457, 851, 857, 876, 1062, 1254, 1414. See also Miura, Urban society 166 n. 44.

receipts (*wuṣūl*), and signed his name at their bottom when certifying them.[9] He testified that someone had received his share as specified in a will, that a waqf register (*sijjil*) had changed hands, that there was a standing debt or that a debt had been paid, that a settlement had been reached, and so forth. He signed rent agreements and ascertained the payment of rent and certified property sales.[10] He approved some financial balances that others were unable to do or preferred him to do.[11] He drafted a waqf document (*jarīda*) for a high-ranking mamluk.[12] Normally, after a draft (*musawwada*) was approved by the parties, by their stating that "it is correct (*saḥīḥ*)," a final version (*mubayyaḍa*) would be issued.[13] On occasion, a document "completely wrapped up" was sent to him to be certified.[14] He put the document of the aforementioned family property at Maʿlūlā in "a white sack made of cotton."[15] When, on another occasion, he transferred a document from one man to another, he attached a piece of paper stating: "What appears on the fifth line [of the document], that is: [the sum] owed [is correct]."[16] He wrote a receipt on behalf of a miller for the proceeds of a waqf known as the Mill of the Church (*ṭāḥūn al-kanīsa*) outside the Bāb Tūmā gate. Later he witnessed at the Umayyad Mosque, "[standing] before the ʿUthmānī [Quran] copy (*muṣḥaf*)," that someone had received his share in this waqf.[17] For one lady he testified the sale of her books and furniture, and for his friend and colleague Abū l-Faḍl al-Qudsī when selling one-third of the teaching position he occupied at some madrasa. Although normally charging fees,[18]

9 E.g. Ibn Ṭawq, *Taʿlīq* 242, 410.

10 E.g. Ibn Ṭawq, *Taʿlīq* 139, 141, 149, 156, 219, 220, 228, 229, 289, 320, 409–410, 417, 422, 426, 438, 447, 480, 488, 517, 581, 660, 745, 886, 887, 898, 916, 1032, 1046, 1063, 1181–1182, 1619, 1727. Debts had a certain date of remittance, and on occasion a guarantee (*ḍamān*) or a pawn was required, usually in the form of some jewelry pieces. Upon repayment, a note was made on the original loan document and copies were handed to all those involved. See e.g. Ibn Ṭawq, *Taʿlīq* 128–129, 177, 198, 269, 390. 475. For loans and security in legal theory, see Hallaq, *Sharīʿa* 266–268.

11 For his writing at the residence of the Mālikī qadi at some madrasa a three-year balance concerning a mill, see Ibn Ṭawq, *Taʿlīq* 316. For another example, see 511.

12 Ibn Ṭawq, *Taʿlīq* 1915. For the role of *waqf al-usarāʾ* in releasing prisoners, see Dahmān, *Dimashq* 22; Frenkel, *Fikāk al-asīr*, esp. 154–155. I thank Professor Frenkel for drawing my attention to his article.

13 E.g. Ibn Ṭawq, *Taʿlīq* 139, 146, 156, 320, 438, 772, 898, 1660. For *nuskha thābita, masṭūr thābit, waraqa thābit aṣluhā*, see 517, 1727.

14 E.g. Ibn Ṭawq, *Taʿlīq* 1881.

15 Ibn Ṭawq, *Taʿlīq* 847.

16 Ibn Ṭawq, *Taʿlīq* 665.

17 Ibn Ṭawq, *Taʿlīq* 125, 140, 700 (on the location of this mill, see also 61, editor's note 1), 1131, 1132, 1133.

18 For the small fee of 5 dirhams paid to a few notaries in two cases, see Ibn Ṭawq, *Taʿlīq* 156,

at times our notary did not charge anything, for example, when sent by Taqī al-Dīn Ibn Qāḍī ʿAjlūn as an *amīn* (incidentally, against his own will) to certify the details of some estate.[19] The policy of foregoing fees was probably normal among notaries when doing some service for one another.[20]

Ibn Ṭawq performed other jobs, by which he most likely supplemented his income as a notary. These were legion, and only some may be listed. He was in charge of a waqf supporting the Bādirāʾiyya madrasa, where he also kept a cell (*khilwa*), as well as of the nearby Dawlaʾiyya madrasa.[21] Earlier he quit the post of Quran reciter for six ashrafīs.[22] To put this sum in context, this was the average price of 100 kilograms of wheat.[23] He quit from the Ḥalabiyya madrasa for the considerable sum of 50 ashrafīs the post of the leader of communal prayer (*imām*), preacher (*khaṭīb*), and part-time Quran reciter of one specific chapter, the *sūrat al-Kahf*, every Friday.[24] In favor of a colleague, he quit for the price of 4 ashrafīs half of the post of inspector (*nāẓir*) and imam that he shared with him at a mosque in the Kharāb neighborhood. From the fact that a document of this act was sent to the sultan's archive in Cairo (*dīwān Miṣr*), we may conclude that for some reason it was of interest to the Egyptian authorities. As to the joint ownership with that colleague of a hall (*murabbaʿ*), which was also terminated on this occasion, Ibn Ṭawq insisted on a clause stating that any expenses incurred in the future would fall on that colleague only.[25] Another temporary job he held, of reading from al-Bukhārī's *Ṣaḥīḥ*, was financed by an agricultural waqf.[26] It seems that our notary was entitled to it after receiving, about a dozen years earlier, an authorization (*ijāza*) to read al-Bukhārī's compendium in public from Badr al-Dīn b. Nabhān, his relative, and later also from

200. See, however, 764, where he reports that he received two dinars for his work to settle debts. His colleague received 1 ashrafī and 40 dirhams in two different cases. See 365, 539. For some details on fees, see also Miura, Urban society 165 n. 43; Miura, *Dynamism* 142 and n. 31.

19 Ibn Ṭawq, *Taʿlīq* 269. For another example, see 1727.

20 E.g. Ibn Ṭawq, *Taʿlīq* 226.

21 Ibn Ṭawq, *Taʿlīq* 167. For his cell, see 144. On the Bādirāʾiyya, see al-Nuʿaymī, *al-Dāris* i, 154–161. On the Dawlaʾiyya, see al-Nuʿaymī, *al-Dāris* i, 182–190.

22 Ibn Ṭawq, *Taʿlīq* 35.

23 For relevant prices see Appendix under, e.g. Jumādā II 889 H.

24 Ibn Ṭawq, *Taʿlīq* 350. Since his successor in these positions appears to have lacked the necessary amount in cash, he had to borrow it through a certain procedure that is not entirely clear. See also El-Leithy, Living documents 413, who misses some elements and questionably considers the case as an example of interest. For the Ḥalabiyya, see al-Nuʿaymī, *al-Dāris* i, 175–176; Badrān, *Munādama* 96.

25 Ibn Ṭawq, *Taʿlīq* 427. For the Kharāb, see 114 n. 6. For al-Ḥarīrī, see 35, 113, 127.

26 Ibn Ṭawq, *Taʿlīq* 1593.

the imam of one of the local mosques.[27] Further posts that Ibn Ṭawq occupied are mentioned in the diary.[28] And yet, despite all these jobs, his financial situation appears to have been unstable, and occasionally he was short of cash. At one point he repaid Umm Yūsuf three ashrafīs he had borrowed from her, for which he had deposited some jewelry as a guaranty.[29] On another occasion he notes that the list of those to whom he owed money "became longer."[30]

Ibn Ṭawq appears to have been also quite active in performing almost daily jobs for which it is unclear whether he was financially compensated. To three partners, apparently on behalf of its owner, he sold a hall (*qāʿa*) in the al-Sharaf al-Aʿlā, a neighborhood of high social status between the city and Mount Qāsyūn.[31] He was frequently asked to inspect cultivated fields and waqf land and to see to the sale of their proceeds, as well as supervise property owned by friends or men of the scholarly circles.[32] Considered trustworthy, he was entrusted from time to time with cash or money orders (*ḥawāla*) for delivery. Two merchants entrusted him with 278 dinars (3 of which, as specifically mentioned, were rather Italian florins) and 390 dirhams and, in addition, considerable sums from two more merchants, to deliver to one Sulaymān in a commercial agreement (*muḍāraba/qirāḍ*) similar to the Western *commenda*. The purpose was trade in sheep, and the expected profit was to be divided between the investors and the agent.[33] In other instances he was asked to write down a

---

27 Ibn Ṭawq, *Taʿlīq* 389–390, 620. See Idjāza, *EI*²; Mahamid, *Waqf* 301–309.

28 For serving as a *qārī* at the Zinjīlī (or Zinjarī) Mausoleum, see Ibn Ṭawq, *Taʿlīq* 197, 204. See on it al-Nuʿaymī, *al-Dāris* i, 404–406, who lists a Ḥanafī Zinjāriyya/Zinjiliyya madrasa, established in 626/1229 outside the St. Thomas Gate; the preacher there received funding from the Umayyad Mosque. For serving as inspector of a Sufi lodge (*zāwiya*) at Marj al-Shaykh, southeast of the city, see Ibn Ṭawq, *Taʿlīq* 26, 241 (a document is drafted). For serving as inspector of a mosque at Jarbā in the Marj, see 240. For the post of imam he shared at the Dār al-Ṭuʿm al-ʿAtīq (see Chapter 4) and transferred to his friend, the notary Abū l-Faḍl al-Qudsī, see 363. For the posts of imam, preacher (*khaṭīb*), and muezzin that he shared at the mosque of Jarūd, see 638. He also quit for 750 dirhams another Quran-reciting position, which he shared and which was funded by waqf land at the Ghūṭa village of Ḥammām al-Saṭrā. See 584; Wollina, *Zwanzig* 50 (details are missing). For the job of a *qārī* at the Mashhad al-Muaʾdhdhinīn, see Ibn Ṭawq, *Taʿlīq* 1816.

29 Ibn Ṭawq, *Taʿlīq* 274.

30 Ibn Ṭawq, *Taʿlīq* 829.

31 Ibn Ṭawq, *Taʿlīq* 32. For its location, see al-Shihābī, *Muʿjam Dimashq* ii, 66; Dahmān, *Dimashq* 119 n. 1. For its prestige, see Miura, *Dynamism* 103 n. 67.

32 E.g. Ibn Ṭawq, *Taʿlīq* 117, 169, 209, 210, 240, 431, 501, 543, 707, 877, 897, 923, 955, 1050, 1134, 1162, 1447.

33 Ibn Ṭawq, *Taʿlīq* 1217. For other examples, see 113, 177, 189, 232, 241, 267, 353, 397, 403, 409, 427, 428, 436, 470, 474, 519, 651. See Ḳirāḍ, *EI*² and Muḍāraba, *EI*²; Hallaq, *Sharīʿa* 254–256. The use of promissory notes (*ḥawāla*), whereby money expected by the debtor to be

protocol of a session devoted to some financial settlement, or to make some computation.[34] He worked to reconcile parties disputing financial or other matters.[35] Together with the Ḥanbalī deputy qadi he was appointed to perform the duties of a jurist or educator (*faqīh*) at his ancestral village, Jarūd.[36] It is almost impossible to follow all the jobs he did day in and day out.

Then there was business in agricultural land. From an orchard (*bustān*), most likely at Maʿlūlā, in which he employed Christian peasants whose names he specifies, our notary received dates and other fruits. With a man named Ibn Shārid, he signed a long-term *ḥikr* contract, which gave the renter of a waqf land special rights, including to repair dilapidated elements, and thus, under certain circumstances, to become its owner.[37] From a lady relative he rented for two years her share in an orchard and a two-story house that stood on it for 100 dirhams a year, excluding additional expenses.[38] Incidentally, the low profit received from land property, as reflected in this specific agreement, appears to have been a widespread phenomenon (which will be further discussed in Chapter 4). Together with his close friend Abū l-Faḍl al-Qudsī, also a notary, he owned in equal shares a garden (*junayna*) in the village of Ḥammām al-Saṭrā in the Ghūṭa, in which they grew fruits and which was cultivated by one Ibrāhīm "the baker" (*khabbāz*) and later by Yūsuf al-Jaramānī, with whom our notary cooperated for quite some time. He cultivated the garden on the basis of *ḍamān*, according to which the renter paid a lump sum, regardless of the future profit or loss. In 892/1487 the two partners sold the orchard for 3,000 dirhams to Muḥammad, the son of the wealthy merchant (*khawājā*) ʿĪsā al-Qārī. Ibn Ṭawq received 350 dirhams in cash; the rest apparently was paid later.[39] A few years earlier, together with Zayn al-Dīn Khiḍr al-Ḥisbānī, who acted as administrator of various waqfs, he had rented for two years from the lady Bt. al-ʿAdl half a plot at Barza, in the Ghūṭa region, to grow on it wheat and fruits. The total rent was 320 dirhams, 200 dirhams of which was paid immediately and the rest deferred;

---

received from a third party would go directly to the creditor, is frequently noted. See e.g. Ibn Ṭawq, *Taʿlīq* 107, 113, 118, 231, 281, 288, 308, 312, 326, 434, 474, 1063, 1727. For *ḥawāla*, see Hallaq, *Sharīʿa* 260–261.

34 E.g. Ibn Ṭawq, *Taʿlīq* 359, 374, 543–544, 1381.

35 E.g. Ibn Ṭawq, *Taʿlīq* 338, 407, 431.

36 Ibn Ṭawq, *Taʿlīq* 199.

37 Ibn Ṭawq, *Taʿlīq* 88, 196, 240, 470, 803. On the nature of such agreement, see Ḥikr, *EI*²; Contract law, *EI*³. According to Muller, Legal instrument 190, 191, one should be cautious in suggesting that a long-term *ḥikr* contract alienated waqf property and led to its cessation.

38 Ibn Ṭawq, *Taʿlīq* 206; Wollina, *Zwanzig* 102.

39 Ibn Ṭawq, *Taʿlīq* 94, 652, 696. For the location of this village, see 94, editor's n. 1; Yāqūt, *Muʿjam al-buldān*, s.v. For the nature of the contract, see Ḍamān, *EI*²; Guarantee, *EI*³.

land (*kharāj*) tax of 60 dirhams a year was also demanded.[40] About the same time, together with his aforementioned partner Yūsuf of Jaramānā, our notary leased a garden located near the Bādirā'iyya madrasa for 50 dirhams annually. The lease agreement included a clause about constructing a fence (*tasīj*).[41]

As regards other sorts of information on our notary, we learn about some of the books he read or consulted. In his cell at the Bādirā'iyya madrasa he kept one part of an endowed copy of *Qāmūs* ("The dictionary"), most likely Fīrūzabādī's.[42] He read Ibn Sayyid al-Nās's (d. 734/1334) biography of the Prophet,[43] and appears to have borrowed cash to purchase Muslim's and al-Bukhārī's two *Ṣaḥīḥs*. He also read Ibn Ḥajar al-ʿAsqalānī's *al-Fatḥ al-bārī* [*bi sharḥ al-Bukhārī*], a commentary on al-Bukhārī.[44] From Sīdī Ibn al-Bānyāsī he borrowed the third (last) volume of *Maqbūl al-Manqūl* [*min ʿilmay al-jadal wa-l-uṣūl*] by his contemporary, the prolific Ḥanbalī scholar Yūsuf ʿAbd al-Hādī, better known as Ibn al-Mibrad (d. 909/1503).[45] From Shams al-Dīn al-Kafrsūsī, at one point the qadi of the hajj convoy, he borrowed a volume on Tamīm al-Dārī, the renowned Companion, as well as Ibn al-Jawzī's *Faḍā'il al-Quds* ("The merits of Jerusalem") and Ibn ʿAsākir's *Faḍā'il Ibrāhīm al-khalīl* ("The merits of Abraham the Patriarch").[46] He kept Ibn Saʿd's *al-Ṭabaqāt al-kubrā*, of which he gave ten parts (*karārīs*) of the second volume to someone to copy.[47] He sent to Kamāl al-Dīn Ibn Qāḍī ʿAjlūn the *Shifā*, most likely Taqī al-Dīn al-Subkī's *Shifā al-siqām fī ziyārat khayr al-anām*,[48] as well as the *al-Burda al-sharīfa* by al-Būṣīrī.[49] From this list of books one learns of Ibn Ṭawq's interest in a variety of religious sub-

40 Ibn Ṭawq, *Taʿlīq* 113, 158 (the woman's agent in this transaction was her grandson). For Barza, see 110 n. 6. For Zayn al-Dīn, an administrator (*mutakallim*) of Ibn al-Muzalliq's waqf (for which see Chapter 4), see also e.g. 225, 245, 290, 358, 543, 862, 1063.

41 Ibn Ṭawq, *Taʿlīq* 291. For Jaramānā, see Yāqūt, *Muʿjam al-buldān*, s.v. The details of another sojourn the two made to Kafr Baṭnā in the Ghūṭa do not clarify whether it was for another shared lease. See Ibn Ṭawq, *Taʿlīq* 117. See briefly also Wollina, *Zwanzig* 123.

42 Ibn Ṭawq, *Taʿlīq* 337. See al-Fīrūzābādī, *EI*[2].

43 Ibn Ṭawq, *Taʿlīq* 1098. See Ibn Sayyid al-Nās, *EI*[2].

44 Ibn Ṭawq, *Taʿlīq* 427, 633. For the purchase, see 220–221.

45 Sīdī Ibn al-Bānyāsī was the grandson of the Sufi shaykh Ibn Dā'ūd. See Ibn Ṭūlūn, *al-Qalā'id* i, 300, and Chapter 2.

46 Ibn Ṭawq, *Taʿlīq* 1556. For Ibn ʿAbd al-Hādī, see Yūsuf b. ʿAbd al-Hādī, *EI*[2]. For his biography, see also ʿAbd al-Hādī, *Imām*; see also editor's introduction to Ibn al-Mibrad, *Sayr al-hathth* 9–14. In addition to a few dozen printed works, no less than 160 are listed as manuscripts, most of which were kept at the Damascus National Library. See al-Salāma, *Muʿjam mu'allafāt*. For Tamīm al-Dārī, see Tamīm al-Dārī, *EI*[2]; Frenkel, *Volksroman*; Frenkel, *Ḍaw' al-sārī*. For Kafrsūsī, see Ibn Ṭawq, *Taʿlīq* 25.

47 Ibn Ṭawq, *Taʿlīq* 350.

48 For a detailed analysis, see Taylor, *In the vicinity*, chap. 6.

49 Ibn Ṭawq, *Taʿlīq* 905. For further information on books, see e.g. 1090, 1098.

jects and that some of the books were by Syrian authors. These books circulated within "a network of readers who overcame the obstacle of their meager financial resources by passing books to one another." Although this has been said of the sixteenth-century miller Domenico Scandella, called Menocchio, of the Friuli region, it seems to have applied also in our notary's case.[50]

Ibn Ṭawq's orthodoxy and all that went with it may be deduced from occasional notes. At the beginning of one of the Ramadan fasts he is sick, so is "hesitant about his fast (*mutaraddid fī l-niyya*)," but carries on nevertheless.[51] He is averse to the mingling of women and men at public events and outside mosques, wishing that "their number would not increase" and that God would not punish the believers for that.[52] He dislikes musical instruments and singing, not to speak of the smell of wine which, quite surprisingly, comes out of the vestibule (*dihlīz*) of Taqī al-Dīn Ibn Qāḍī ʿAjlūn's residence. Surely, this must have occurred when the house was rented.[53] He also bemoans the large quantities of wine consumption that the viceroy (*ṣāḥib*) allowed—as we shall see in Chapter 2, he has quite a lot to report about wine—and that "the reprehensible (*maʿāṣī*) is widespread and no one condemns it." He prays to God not to hold it against the people and to destroy only those responsible for it.[54] On the occasion of a funeral of someone originally from Iranian land (*aʿjamī*), which was attended by many, originally non-Damascene, he condemns the reprehensible and novel customs (*manākīr, bidaʿ*), which he details and for which he asks for the Almighty's forgiveness.[55]

Ibn Ṭawq was averse to a man who claimed to have dreamt of the Prophet instructing him to construct a minaret at some mosque and, in another dream, was ordered by the first two caliphs to invite the viceroy to pray there. He concludes his report stating: "May God guard us from such innovations and from the erring governors."[56] He dismisses the popular romance *Sīrat ʿAntar* as "nonsense."[57] That he despised the Shīʿīs is implied in his report on the death of a *rāfiḍī* (a term synonymous for a Shīʿī) in prison whereby, unlike the verb normally used for death, he writes *halaka* and, to remove any doubt, he adds: "May God destroy (*yuhliku*) this sect (*ṭāʾifa*)."[58] He hated the gangsters known as *zuʿr*

50 Ginzburg, *Cheese* 30.
51 Ibn Ṭawq, *Taʿlīq* 86.
52 Ibn Ṭawq, *Taʿlīq* 259, 395, 1224.
53 Ibn Ṭawq, *Taʿlīq* 1687.
54 Ibn Ṭawq, *Taʿlīq* 1697.
55 Ibn Ṭawq, *Taʿlīq* 1609, with some peculiar details.
56 Ibn Ṭawq, *Taʿlīq* 1184.
57 Ibn Ṭawq, *Taʿlīq* 268. See ʿAntar, Sīrat, *EI*[2]; ʿAntar, Sīrat, *EI*[3].
58 Ibn Ṭawq, *Taʿlīq* 1021.

(see Chapter 2) and wished that God made them vanish.[59] Toward Christians he appears to have had an ambivalent attitude. On the one hand, as already mentioned, he was amiable with Christians on an individual basis, employed Christian peasants, and served as a notary in their transactions.[60] Christian villagers dined with him occasionally, and Ilyās, the son of the clergyman (*qaṣṣ*) of Maʿlūlā, whom he visited at his home and vice versa, was also his informant about news in the city, as were other Christians.[61] On the other hand, he was annoyed when informed about a Christian provocation in Jerusalem,[62] or seeing Muslims mixing with Christians in the Christian Quarter, for which he asked for God's mercy.[63] In a dispute he had with a Christian he expected God to help him "against those [Christians]."[64] On one occasion of Corpus Christi (*khamīs al-bayḍ*) he avoided entering the Old City because of the large crowds and ended his brief note with apparent anxiety: "May God protect us from the evil of our souls and our bad deeds."[65] As for Jews, it so happened that his cousin was married to a man with some Jewish connection.[66] At one point he was informed that the waqf inspector al-Ḥisbānī, with whom he conducted business, was possibly of Jewish origin, but he states it dryly without further comment.[67] And, yet, when reporting the death of the Jewish doctor Yūsuf Baydara (?) he uses the verb *halaka* and notes that "God relieved the Muslims from his presence."[68]

Ibn Ṭawq records on many days his daily routine, starting with a note on the gate through which he entered the Old City after leaving home and where he performed the morning prayer.[69] Take, for example, Friday, 4 Rabīʿ I 894/5 February 1488, when he prayed in the company of one ʿUmar al-Fākhūrī, whom he paid the equivalent of three ashrafīs in silver coins, which was al-Fakhūrī's share with his brothers-partners in that year's unspecified profit. Then, he spent some time at the residence of the Ḥanbalī qadi—he describes the route—to

59 E.g. Ibn Ṭawq, *Taʿlīq* 1516.
60 Ibn Ṭawq, *Taʿlīq* 267, 416, 789, 1621–1622, 1867.
61 For two Bukhʿā men having a meal at his home, see Ibn Ṭawq, *Taʿlīq* 429. For Ilyās, see 1574, 1577, 1637, 1644, 1666, 1871. For Ibn Sawāq of Maʿlūlā, see 1227.
62 Ibn Ṭawq, *Taʿlīq* 54.
63 Ibn Ṭawq, *Taʿlīq* 602.
64 Ibn Ṭawq, *Taʿlīq* 1315.
65 Ibn Ṭawq, *Taʿlīq* 854.
66 Ibn Ṭawq, *Taʿlīq* 1457.
67 Ibn Ṭawq, *Taʿlīq* 310.
68 Ibn Ṭawq, *Taʿlīq* 244.
69 For entering through Bāb al-Salāma, see e.g. Ibn Ṭawq, *Taʿlīq* 1571. For praying at al-Qaṣab Mosque, see e.g. 1333, 1512, 1563, 1634. For praying at the Zinjīliyya, apparently identical with the Zinjīlī Mausoleum (see n. 28 above), see e.g. 1558, 1560, 1565, 1782. For praying at the Umayyad Mosque, see e.g. 1571, 1741. For praying at al-Jawza Mosque, see e.g. 1785, 1815.

whom he presented a rental document. Then, as he was near the house of Shihāb al-Dīn al-Ḥamrāwī, one of his colleagues, it came to his mind that he had kept dinars in a piece of cloth, some of which he had given to al-Ḥamrāwī, but now he was unable to recall where he had kept the rest. This was important because, as he divulges, he was at that point in financial stress.[70] He provides a detailed report on his journey in Shawwāl 891/September 1486 with Taqī al-Dīn Ibn Qāḍī ʿAjlūn and two more men of their circle, to Beirut and Baʿalbek. Under light rain they set out to Manīn, where they stayed at least one night at the house of one Ḥāj Yūsuf b. Ghanī. At the nearby ʿAyn al-Fīja they took a meal and spent the night at the house of a peasant with whom Ibn Ṭawq made business. Then they continued to the Zabadānī region and spent the night at a local *khaṭīb*'s. The next morning, after prayer, they continued (again, we are informed about the route) and performed the noon prayer at the Bawārish village in the Biqāʿ. (Details on the house where they spent the night are effaced in the manuscript.) Finally, they entered Beirut, where they stayed at a local madrasa and met those who had come to honor Taqī al-Dīn. After a few days they continued to Baʿalbek and, after an absence of 20 days, returned to Damascus. It would be pointless to detail all the places and people they met during that journey.[71]

Ibn Ṭawq recorded accusations directed at him. Thus, ʿAlī b. ʿUmar al-Fākhūrī's widow and his son claimed he owed them about 5 ashrafīs. The claim was submitted to the Shāfiʿī qadi, who appointed a notary to look into the matter. It was decided that Ibn Ṭawq had to pay within a few days, yet he had difficulties to do so at such short notice. Here, the qadi came to his aid. Ibn Ṭawq notes that the widow insisted that the debt be paid to the last dirham.[72] Another embarrassing situation occurred when he was required by Taqī al-Dīn's son to deliver several ashrafīs that had been generated from a transaction in alkali and had been deposited with him. However, by that point our notary seems to have used most of the money. Assistance from a friend was delayed, so he had to ask for 14 ashrafīs from his son and wife. As he admits, his wife was reluctant to cooperate, and a fight between the two reached such a point that he swore to divorce her; in any case, he promised to guarantee the loan. In the event, there was no need to do so, because the friend did help partly after all,

70 Ibn Ṭawq, *Taʿlīq* 828–829. On al-Ḥamrāwī, see 38, 105, 146–147, 226, 407.

71 Ibn Ṭawq, *Taʿlīq* 662–663. For the location of Bawārish (modern Bawārij), see 158 editor's n. 1.

72 Ibn Ṭawq, *Taʿlīq* 1152–1153. For his involvement in the deferred marriage gift after the man's death, see 682.

and the rest came from his son.[73] Perhaps no less embarrassing was his summons by the Shāfiʿī qadi on the grounds that he had served as a witness in a dubious procedure. When pressed by the qadi as to whether he had recorded the case in writing, he had to admit he had not. When further pressed, he confessed that he had consulted the Ḥanbalī qadi, which enraged the Shāfiʿī qadi even more.[74] There were further disputes in which our source was involved.[75]

Ibn Ṭawq's first wife—it is not stated for how long they were married—is mentioned in the diary only once, as "Abū Bakr's daughter."[76] One supposes he divorced her at least some time before he began writing the diary (or, at least, the part preserved) and that by that time she was completely out of his life. From this marriage he had three children. Khadīja was divorced from her husband, a peasant, after which she moved to her father's home. She must have remarried, as a year and a half later she gave birth to a son.[77] From his first marriage, Ibn Ṭawq had also a son, Aḥmad, and another daughter, Sāra, who mothered a son or a daughter.[78]

Ibn Ṭawq's social aspirations must have risen after his second marriage. He never refers to his second wife by her name but, occasionally, as Umm al-Sitt Āmina. Āmina not being one of their daughters, we may infer that she had been born from this wife's previous marriage. Most frequently, the second wife is mentioned as "my spouse" (*zawjatī*) and "the mother of my children" (*umm awlādī, umm al-awlād*).[79] She was the daughter of the *shaykh al-Islām* Muḥammad b. ʿAbdallāh Najm al-Dīn (d. 876/1471), of the Ibn Qāḍī ʿAjlūn family, an older brother of Taqī al-Dīn, Ibn Ṭawq's esteemed friend.[80] Socially, the second marriage was successful and, as we shall see in Chapter 6, deviated somewhat from the model of social equality. What, we may ask, enabled a peasant's grandson, who had developed a career of limited potential, to marry into one of Damascus's most distinguished scholarly families? Was it Umm Āmina's infatuation with him, although at the time of their marriage he was already married or divorced? Of course, one should note that also Umm Āmina had been married

73 Ibn Ṭawq, *Taʿlīq* 1723, 1724.
74 Ibn Ṭawq, *Taʿlīq* 1891–1892.
75 Ibn Ṭawq, *Taʿlīq* 461, 805, 1083, 1661, 1906.
76 Ibn Ṭawq, *Taʿlīq* 486.
77 Ibn Ṭawq, *Taʿlīq* 1861.
78 Ibn Ṭawq, *Taʿlīq* 1673, 1678, 1679.
79 Ibn Ṭawq, *Taʿlīq* 1032. This is a term he uses throughout for a wife married by law, to distinguish from a concubine (*umm walad*). See e.g. 341, 492, 524, 616, 618, 737, 888, 982, 1056, 1217. On occasion, *zawja* and *umm awlād* are used by him as identical terms. See e.g. 524.
80 See on him al-Nuʿaymī, *al-Dāris* i, 263.

before. Be that as it may, in Ṣafar 890/March 1485 this marriage was temporarily terminated by a *khulʿ* agreement (the nature of which will be discussed in Chapter 6), although the wife was pregnant and gave birth to a daughter less than three months later. Ibn Ṭawq dryly notes that she asked for it because of his repeated "oaths of divorce" (for which see also Chapter 6), and "things he did and things he neglected."[81] Two years earlier Umm Āmina had rented a house (or a section of it) for a monthly rent of 100 dirhams, two months of which, according to the custom, were free of charge.[82] Although it is not stated in the diary, the couple probably reunited; circumstantial evidence for that is our source being *au courant* about her state of health.[83] Furthermore, less than three years after the *khulʿ* came into effect, she gave birth to a daughter.[84] Ironically, the husband reverted to his bad habits and pronounced the "oath of divorce" on a few other occasions.[85] We also learn that because of his sojourns in the countryside, which, on occasion, may have lasted some weeks, he sent to his wife financial support (*nafaqa*). There are also indications, one of which came up earlier, that she had her own budget, of which she could make use according to her own decision.[86]

The fate of Ibn Ṭawq's children from his second marriage is tragic. The couple had five daughters and a son. Fāṭima Umm al-Faḍl died aged less than 14 in the plague. Obviously unaware of the true symptoms, the father reports that she contracted "smallpox (*judūr*) in her throat." Five weeks later he noticed a sort of a red-colored sting (*qarṣa*) between her throat and her neck. Five days later she died.[87] Muḥammad Raḍī al-Dīn Abū l-Faḍl was born two years after Fāṭima.[88] ʿĀliya Umm Hānī was born about two years after him; she was ill most of her short life, which lasted barely a year.[89] The father mentions the fact of her death dryly and records the burial expenses. Was the reserved reaction a reflection of his personality? Was it the norm? Was it somehow connected with the

81 For the separation, see Ibn Ṭawq, *Taʿlīq* 449; Rapoport, *Marriage* 1–2. For the birth, see Ibn Ṭawq, *Taʿlīq* 472. Rapoport, *Marriage* 95, speculates about the couple's stratagem for remarriage. He thinks that the relationship between the two appears to have been good, but this is hard to know from the diary. In fact, as we shall see, there are indications to the contrary.

82 Ibn Ṭawq, *Taʿlīq* 230, where further terms of this rent are mentioned.

83 E.g. Ibn Ṭawq, *Taʿlīq* 516.

84 Ibn Ṭawq, *Taʿlīq* 782.

85 Ibn Ṭawq, *Taʿlīq* 1425, 1449.

86 Ibn Ṭawq, *Taʿlīq* 1446, 1915.

87 Ibn Ṭawq, *Taʿlīq* 1113, 1120, 1121. The terms he used should not be taken as a trustworthy diagnosis, and the symptoms could have been plague "bubus."

88 Ibn Ṭawq, *Taʿlīq* 28.

89 Ibn Ṭawq, *Taʿlīq* 195, 280.

impression one gets (we shall come back to it) that Ibn Ṭawq would have liked to have fathered sons rather than daughters? Following his wife's miscarriage—Ibn Ṭawq was carried away to believe that the fetus was a son[90]—and shortly after the couple's separation, ʿĀʾisha, also named Umm Hānī, most likely after her deceased sibling ʿĀliya, was born. After a couple of months she became ill, and the father once more details the symptoms. He notes that a grown-up could have died of it, let alone a baby. She died barely one year old. Before her death she refused suckling, and the father suspected that this was due to the coming out of teeth but then realized that she had fallen victim to the plague.[91] Baraka came two years after ʿĀʾisha's death—when he heard the strong voice of the crying newborn, the anxious father thought, or at least hoped, that this time he had a son. About Baraka he has trivial things to report; for example, a tooth came out when she was eight months old. She was destined to die only three months later. For three weeks after Baraka's death the father does not mention any activity of his. Was his grief the reason for that? Was it just a coincidence? We do not know.[92] Death in this family was not over, and in Muḥarram 896/November 1490 a daughter was born after a painful delivery but lived only 22 months.[93]

All in all, apart from the two daughters and son who survived from his first marriage, and the son from his second marriage, Ibn Ṭawq's five daughters from his second marriage died in infancy. There also were a few miscarriages. Such a family situation is terrible by any standard but was not necessarily unique.[94] And, yet, our notary does not express his emotions. Thus, when the 14-year-old Fāṭima dies, he writes what a believing Muslim was expected: "We belong to God and to God we return." He adds the hope that when his day came he would join her in "God's benevolence without prior suffering … May God render [her spirit] a treasure for me and her mother."[95]

Of all his children, Ibn Ṭawq appears to have been most concerned with his son from his second marriage, Muḥammad Abū l-Faḍl, "the boy," as he frequently refers to him. Whereas Aḥmad, his son from the first marriage, is only rarely mentioned, we are much better informed on Muḥammad—who his wet

90 Ibn Ṭawq, *Taʿlīq* 340, 341.

91 Ibn Ṭawq, *Taʿlīq* 472, 497 (he erroneously refers to her as Fāṭima Umm Hānī, apparently confusing her with the aforementioned Fāṭima Umm al-Faḍl), 631; Wollina, *Zwanzig* 85.

92 Ibn Ṭawq, *Taʿlīq* 782, 835, 862, 863, 864, 865, 866.

93 Ibn Ṭawq, *Taʿlīq* 992, 1136; Wollina, *Zwanzig* 82, 98.

94 For the death of the daughters of al-Sakhāwī, the fifteenth-century Egyptian chronicler, see Musallam, Ordering 197.

95 Ibn Ṭawq, *Taʿlīq* 1121.

nurse was, that he weaned at about 15 months and shortly later had his first haircut, that he started walking at about two and a half. Barely aged four he entered a boys' school (*kuttāb*), and on that occasion the father, unusually emotional, expresses his wish for him to reach the age of 40 (either this was a standard wish or, otherwise, due to low life expectancy, one did not dare to ask for more). In fact, our notary adds his hope that, God willing, Muḥammad would enjoy good health and not suffer any hardship (*miḥna*). This was also an occasion to wish all the best to Fāṭima, Muḥammad's older sister; one cannot miss the gendered wish for her to become a pious mother, nothing else. Alas, as already noted, it did not happen.[96] A year later, now five years old, together with his father's young cousin, Muḥammad underwent circumcision (*ṭuhūr*), and the father describes the anxiety of the two boys before undergoing the procedure.[97] At age 12, Muḥammad is reported reading the first Quran *sūras* and the Shāfiʿī legal compendium *Minhāj*, probably al-Nawawī's.[98] At age 21, he rented a shop in the Silk Market, in the environs of the Umayyad Mosque.[99]

Even with death as a frequent visitor, the notary's family must have had its moments of joy, such as in 901/1496 when, at age 16, Muḥammad married ʿĀ'isha, a "virgin who reached puberty," the daughter of the deceased Fatḥallāh al-ʿAjamī, a name which may indicate that the family was not originally Damascene. The groom's marriage gift was 69 ashrafīs, of which he paid 50 at the time of betrothal; the remainder, as was the custom, was deferred indefinitely. The groom's representative (*wakīl*) was his father, and for the orphaned bride the *mutawallī* was her uncle, who hosted the ceremony. Among those present was the *shaykh al-Islām*, Taqī al-Dīn. Our notary details the various kinds of food they sent to the bride's mother.[100] ʿĀ'isha died exactly two years later in the plague, one day after her brother.[101] After less than a year and a half, the young widower betrothed Khadīja, a daughter of the deceased Ḥāj ʿUthmān al-Qāqawī. Once again, various kinds of food were sent to the bride's family upon learning the news.[102] The marriage contract was signed five months later, and, like in the first marriage, the son was represented by his father and the bride by her uncle. This time the marriage gift was 60 ashrafīs, of which 40 were paid

96 Ibn Ṭawq, *Taʿlīq* 28, 147, 162, 260, 401, 454. For further information on his son's education, see e.g. 670, 733, 949.

97 Ibn Ṭawq, *Taʿlīq* 542.

98 Ibn Ṭawq, *Taʿlīq* 1117. On the author, see al-Nawawī, *EI*².

99 Ibn Ṭawq, *Taʿlīq* 1904. According to Wollina, *Zwanzig* 99, he was a notary as well, but I did not find any information on that.

100 Ibn Ṭawq, *Taʿlīq* 1415, 1419, 1422; Wollina, *Zwanzig* 99.

101 Ibn Ṭawq, *Taʿlīq* 1604.

102 Ibn Ṭawq, *Taʿlīq* 1694.

immediately (*muʿajjal*); allowance (*kiswa*) in the amount of 8 ashrafīs possibly indicates that Khadīja was either widowed or divorced, which is further supported by the note that the groom moved to her residence. The bride's trousseau (*ḥawāʾij*) was in the considerable value of 15,000 dirhams (about 300 dinars).[103]

This marriage suffered from a bad start, and Ibn Ṭawq's notes allow a glimpse at the relationship between two lower middle-class families. It so happened that on the night on which the marriage was expected to be consummated, Khadīja had her monthly menstruation, so that female relatives had to clean her with alkali.[104] This created tension between the two families, and the bride's mother confronted Ibn Ṭawq, telling him that they had been warned against entering into this marriage bond. Our notary notes that he wished God gave him respite from her.[105] About a month later the groom reported to his father euphemistically that "the problem was solved during the previous night."[106] That tension continued may be gathered from the note taken three months later about Khadīja's mother and brother coming to reconcile the young husband.[107] This was not the end to the problems between the two families. Later, "malice existed," and Khadīja used "harsh words" toward her husband and her in-laws. On this occasion Ibn Ṭawq does not shy away from condemning her "lack of manners." It came to the point that she locked herself in her room refusing to eat. Later, following another of the couple's quarrels, Khadīja spent the night on the neighbor's roof. The next day her stepfather and brother came to work out a reconciliation. However, tension between the young couple and between Khadīja and her mother-in-law continued.[108]

In Ibn Ṭawq's household there was a slave (*mawlā*), Mubārak,[109] and several female slaves. One, Mubāraka, is mentioned doing errands.[110] A female slave named Shahdiyā was sold for 2,000 dirhams to a "dark-colored" educator (*faqīh al-awlād*), of which he paid 1,700 in cash. As the notary relates, Shahdiyā was reluctant to go with her new master and was screaming and crying to the point that Ibn Ṭawq's relative, who was present, had to apply physical force and drag her—apparently with little success, though, for on the same day the new master showed up with the slave because she had refused to eat and had threatened to take her own life. He asked Ibn Ṭawq to annul the transaction, and our notary

103 Ibn Ṭawq, *Taʿlīq* 1736, 1854, 1855. See also Wollina, *Zwanzig* 59.
104 Ibn Ṭawq, *Taʿlīq* 1855, 1856.
105 Ibn Ṭawq, *Taʿlīq* 1858; Wollina, *Zwanzig* 75.
106 Ibn Ṭawq, *Taʿlīq* 1863.
107 Ibn Ṭawq, *Taʿlīq* 1882.
108 Ibn Ṭawq, *Taʿlīq* 1901, 1907–1908, 1910, 1915; Wollina, *Zwanzig* 75–76.
109 Ibn Ṭawq, *Taʿlīq* 850, 1023.
110 He uses the form *mawlāt*. She died in 888/1483. See Ibn Ṭawq, *Taʿlīq* 274, 277.

had to return the money.[111] A couple of months later he sold Shahdiyā for the same price, this time to a lady who bought her for her grandson, a perfume dealer. Apparently, most of the payment was deferred.[112] A few years later, the notary reports selling his black slave (*jāriya*) Nawfara at the slave market (*fī l-raqīq*) for the somewhat low price of 1,100 dirhams, "because of her faults" and following his wife's demand. The next day he purchased a white slave, who had lived in the household of the Mamluk family Manjak.[113] A week later, in his absence—and this may be interpreted as a sign of independence—his wife paid 1,130 dirhams for Mubāraka, whom she purchased from an official in the service of a high-ranking mamluk.[114] Four months later Ibn Ṭawq reports on the purchase of the *jāriya* Mubāraka-Jawhara for 1,160 dirhams. It appears to have been an unfortunate deal, for less than a year later our notary reveals that he hit one of his female slaves with a stick because of her "lack of manners." He does not specify which of the two, but it must have been Jawhara—he adds that he regretted it afterward. However, a couple of days later he put Jawhara on sale, and she was examined at the house of the merchant Zayn al-Dīn ʿAbd al-Qādir. Perhaps the transaction was not finalized, as a couple of months later he hit a slave (whose name is unspecified) once again.[115] Be that as it may, he sold a female slave to Jalāl al-Dīn al-Buṣrawī, the historian's son and later a qadi.[116] He did not hide from the buyer her faults, being a lack of piety ("she did not say the prayers"), a tendency to mess things up, bad manners, and also some physical problems, such as weak eyesight and easily catching a cold. All that did not affect her price of 1,230 dirhams, of which he received 546, the rest being deferred.[117] A month afterward, Ibn Ṭawq bought the dark-skinned

---

111 Ibn Ṭawq, *Taʿlīq* 96, 97. The computation is unclear, and apparently he did not return the full sum.

112 Ibn Ṭawq, *Taʿlīq* 118.

113 Ibn Ṭawq, *Taʿlīq* 288, 289. For the death of her owner, see 254. He was a descendant of the emir Sayf al-Dīn Manjak (d. 776/1334), who was at one point the viceroy. Nāṣir al-Dīn Muḥammad Ibn Manjak (or his father?) established in the early fifteenth century a mosque also known as al-Qaṣab Mosque, in which our notary frequently prayed. See Ibn Ṭawq, *Taʿlīq* 229; Badrān, *Munādama* 386. For his death in 844/1840, see al-Nuʿaymī, *al-Dāris* ii, 82. For the family's holdings in the sixteenth century, see El-Zawahreh, *Religious endowments* 182–183.

114 Ibn Ṭawq, *Taʿlīq* 290. For his posts, see 47, 205, 313.

115 Ibn Ṭawq, *Taʿlīq* 334, 411, 431. Note the use of the name Mubāraka for two different slaves. Incidentally, a year earlier, the same Zayn al-Dīn bought a white slave for his son. See 292.

116 See on him editor's introduction to his book, 18. On him as a deputy qadi, see Ibn Ṭawq, *Taʿlīq* 53, 72, 109–110, 126 and editor's note on 848. For Jalāl al-Dīn al-Buṣrawī's marital history, see Chapter 6. For him as a qadi, see 1516.

117 Ibn Ṭawq, *Taʿlīq* 594, 595; Wollina, *Zwanzig* 65.

Ghazzāl from a silk merchant, who authorized the female slave dealer Ḥujayja to conclude the transaction on his behalf and receive about half the price of 1,300 dirhams. Later our notary sold either Ghazzāl or the aforementioned Mubāraka, by then already a few years in his household. He also mentions a slave and her child (? *bi-walad*), whom he inspected (? *ʿaraḍtu*) shortly afterward.[118] Altogether, Ibn Ṭawq refers in his diary to at least seven or eight female slaves, probably more than one serving at one and the same time. He did not have children from any of them.[119]

Other than his immediate family and the slaves in his household, Ibn Ṭawq refers to some relatives, such as a cousin in the Ṣāliḥiyya Quarter and the aforementioned Nabhān family.[120] As to friends and acquaintances, they were from his social and professional milieu. The most distinguished was Taqī al-Dīn of the prominent Ibn Qāḍī ʿAjlūn family, seven years his junior, the Shāfiʿī *shaykh al-Islām* (i.e., formally, and at least according to our source, also practically, the leader of his *madhhab* in Damascus).[121] Our notary refers to him routinely as *sīdī al-shaykh*. He reports about countless visits he paid him, occasionally taking meals and staying overnight.[122] Quite frequently he reports visiting the shaykh's two homes (*baytayn*) in the old city.[123] At one point, on the eve of the marriage of Taqī al-Dīn's son, according to a local custom, and perhaps also as a token of friendship, Ibn Ṭawq slept in the groom's bed.[124] The shaykh repaid visits and stayed at the notary's overnight as well.[125] Ibn Ṭawq gave him gifts on

---

118 Ibn Ṭawq, *Taʿlīq* 604, 619, 629; Wollina, *Zwanzig* 65–66, who interprets the verb as perforce indicating a sale and raises the possibility that the son was Ibn Ṭawq's. This, of course, is not the only possible meaning of *ʿaraḍtu*; "I inspected" would indicate an intention to purchase. Also, the speculation about Ibn Ṭawq's fathering another child is out of place; what is intended is a child born to her of marriage with a male servant. See further the following note.

119 Contrast Wollina, "Ego-document," 356 and n. 106; Wollina, *Zwanzig* 49, 63–64, 66–69, based on a misinterpretation of the term *umm al-awlād* that actually refers to his wife. See e.g. Ibn Ṭawq, *Taʿlīq* 1032, where *zawja* is synonymous with *umm awlādī*. See also n. 79 above.

120 E.g. Ibn Ṭawq, *Taʿlīq* 4, 407, 411. For his children visiting the Khātūn on the occasion of her birthday, see 243.

121 al-Ḥaṣkafī, *Mutʿat al-adhhān* i, 186. See further on him Chapter 3.

122 E.g. Ibn Ṭawq, *Taʿlīq* 439, 552, 583, 584, 647, 1010, 1011. Below I use the attribute "shaykh" for him frequently.

123 E.g. Ibn Ṭawq, *Taʿlīq* 462, 466, 467, 469, 470, 490. See also Wollina, "View," 289, and Chapter 3 below.

124 Ibn Ṭawq, *Taʿlīq* 580, and editor's n. 3. The report has *fī bayt Sīdī Muḥammad*, which leaves somewhat unclear the precise location. Did the shaykh's son own a residence? Perhaps what is meant is his space at his father's home.

125 E.g. Ibn Ṭawq, *Taʿlīq* 34, 38, 115, 149, 550, 788, 796, 1107, 1362.

special occasions, such as on the birth of one of his children. When the shaykh was away for an extended period, they corresponded.[126] And yet, it appears that the relationship was not between equals, and the shaykh's superior status could come to the fore. On one occasion Taqī al-Dīn suspected that Ibn Ṭawq was a party to some plan against him and reprimanded him for that. On another, after the notary advised him on some matter, he reacted angrily: "Your mind is fragile." Ibn Ṭawq had to accept the insult and notes stoically in his diary: "I told him my opinion and he told me his and everything is according to God's desire."[127]

Our notary appears to have been *au courant* with his friend's almost daily activities and deemed these worthy of being documented meticulously in his diary. He notes that the shaykh's *red* horse—he knows who gifted it to him—died, or that his esteemed friend had fallen off a horse he was riding on his way to a hammam. He knows about his health, even that he needed to clean his bowls, or that because of back pains he rode with friends on some peasant's mule, sitting on a special seat to avoid pain. He notes when the shaykh's children start their studies and the price paid for that. Also intimate details are occasionally provided, for example, when precisely he visits his concubine.[128] Only seldom he confesses that some details concerning the shaykh escape him.[129] Taqī al-Dīn's sojourn to Cairo for an extended period at the end of 888/1483, to which we shall return in Chapter 3, is considered no less than a watershed in the diary: "[Following are] reports about what happened after the journey of *sīdī al-shaykh* to Cairo."[130] The departure is reported in detail, as well as his return to Damascus two years later.[131] Ibn Ṭawq joined the shaykh on journeys to villages in the Damascus region and beyond.[132] Noteworthy is their journey for 17 days at the end of 894/1488. It took place after one of the frequent quarrels the shaykh had with his so-called Egyptian wife, for whom Ibn Ṭawq did not have much sympathy and at one point did not conceal it: "Let Allāh save us from her evil and from all evil doers."[133] Following the notary's abortive attempt to bring about some reconciliation, the two friends decided to set out to the Biqāʿ region in order to distribute the proceeds of some waqf that the shaykh supervised. Then, they continued as far as Karak, where they

126 E.g. Ibn Ṭawq, *Taʿlīq* 326, 327, 1815.
127 Ibn Ṭawq, *Taʿlīq* 1765, 1793.
128 Ibn Ṭawq, *Taʿlīq* 25, 91, 92, 95, 122, 123, 126, 132, 133, 140, 142, 162, 207, 541, 590, 828, 834, 917, 1108, 1009, 1110, 1013, 1158.
129 E.g. Ibn Ṭawq, *Taʿlīq* 1418.
130 Ibn Ṭawq, *Taʿlīq* 298.
131 Ibn Ṭawq, *Taʿlīq* 298–299, 331, 521.
132 Ibn Ṭawq, *Taʿlīq* 167. See also, e.g. 36, 154, 804–805.
133 Ibn Ṭawq, *Taʿlīq* 587.

were received, among others, by one Ḥāj Jaʿfar and the *dawādār al-ḥājib*.[134] Over the years Ibn Ṭawq performed numerous jobs for the shaykh, such as seeing through some transactions, making for him computations, inspecting his property, and transferring payments owed to him.[135]

Next in rank among Ibn Ṭawq's friends was Kamāl al-Dīn Muḥammad b. Ḥamza ʿIzz al-Dīn al-Ḥusaynī (d. 933/1527), about 15 years his junior and another prominent member of the Ibn Qāḍī ʿAjlūn family by virtue of being both the son of Taqī al-Dīn's sister and a son-in-law of Muḥibb al-Dīn, another member of the family and a Shāfiʿī deputy qadi.[136] Kamāl al-Dīn rose to the office of mufti—he had been qualified to issue fatwas by the famous Badr al-Dīn Ibn Qāḍī Shuhba—by succeeding his uncle Taqī al-Dīn.[137] He also had many other jobs.[138] Ibn Ṭawq refers to him as *sīdī al-sayyid* and, although the contact between the two appears to have been not as close as with Taqī al-Dīn, he reports taking meals at Kamāl al-Dīn's home, giving him gifts on special occasions, riding with him to Jarūd—apparently, to inspect Kamāl al-Dīn's cultivated land and sell on his behalf its fruits—journeying to see a waqf he was in charge of, and more. When Kamāl al-Dīn was jailed at the citadel as a suspect of embezzling an inheritance, Ibn Ṭawq sent him books.[139]

Our notary also had a close relationship with another member of the family, the aforementioned Muḥibb al-Dīn.[140] Before the latter's death he notes how he was shattered seeing him in his poor situation.[141] With Abū l-Faḍl al-Qudsī, a notary as well, he enjoyed such a close friendship that the latter's daughter was nursed by his wife (which of Ibn Ṭawq's two wives is unclear).[142] We may learn about further acquaintances from the list of guests at his son's wedding, among whom we find the emir Qurqumās (? al-Tanamī).[143]

---

134 Ibn Ṭawq, *Taʿlīq* 901, 902, 903, 904.

135 E.g. Ibn Ṭawq, *Taʿlīq* 57, 111, 112, 141, 189, 268, 375, 796, 799, 1246, 1475, 1603, 1727.

136 Ibn Ṭawq, *Taʿlīq* 41, 223, 523. For a daughter born, see 223. For a son, see 1015. For an obituary of his father, see al-Buṣrawī, *Tārīkh* 40–41.

137 al-Ḥaṣkafī, *Mutʿat al-adhhān* ii, 642. For a detailed biography, see al-Ghazzī, *Kawākib* i, 40–46. See also al-Nuʿaymī, *al-Dāris* i, 131–132.

138 For his involvement in Khān Julbān, see Ibn Ṭawq, *Taʿlīq* 40. For his office at al-Shāmiyya, see 264–265.

139 E.g. Ibn Ṭawq, *Taʿlīq* 41, 76, 178, 242, 253, 261–262, 270, 364–365, 384, 420, 452, 606, 802, 903, 905, 909, 913, 926, 936.

140 For a brief report on one of their meetings, see Ibn Ṭawq, *Taʿlīq* 457.

141 Ibn Ṭawq, *Taʿlīq* 615. For his biography, see also al-Buṣrawī, *Tārīkh* 111.

142 Ibn Ṭawq, *Taʿlīq* 1350. For Abū l-Faḍl (b. Abī Luṭf) al-Qudsī, see 34 editor's n. 3.

143 Ibn Ṭawq, *Taʿlīq* 1854–1855. For his rank as *muqaddam alf*, see 36, 43.

CHAPTER 2

Damascus ca. 1480–1500: A City in Crisis

A study of Damascus in the period under consideration should begin with the size of its population. The problem is that nowhere in Mamluk records do we have a clue for that. One is forced to begin with the earliest figure in Ottoman archives, which suggests anywhere between 40,000 and 60,000 inhabitants in 1535.[1] Now, one has to bear in mind that this was a period of recurrent epidemics, mainly caused by the *Pasteurella pestis*, in Syria, as well as in Egypt and other Near Eastern regions. It must be regarded as the most critical factor not only in demographic terms but in its overall repercussions.[2] Of course, we know nothing about other demographic factors, such as birth rate or a movement of population into and out of Damascus. To go by the Ottoman figures, then, an estimate of 45,000 to 65,000 in the period under consideration is plausible.[3]

In 873–874/1468–1469 an epidemic outbreak is reported to have taken a daily toll of 1,000 dead. Obviously, this is an impossible figure in the light of the estimated total. Whatever the correct figure, although there were somewhat less people to feed after an outbreak, grain prices shot up due to the anarchy normally caused under such circumstances in the short term. Prices were five times higher or even more than in normal years, and hunger prevailed to the point that, as the chroniclers are in the habit of stating on such occasions, perhaps using a literary topos, people resorted to cannibalism.[4] Add to it the devastat-

1 Archival figures for 942/1535 are 8,278 households. See Miura, *Dynamism* 62, 86, 145, who reasonably assumes 6 persons per household, which makes a total of about 50,000. For the calculation of households in ca. 1600, see Pascual, *Damas* 25–27.

2 For plague recurrence in the 150 years after 1348 CE, see Shoshan, Notes. For a most recent treatment of the plague in the Middle East, see Varlik, *Plague and empire*. I find it odd that Miura disregards the plague in his recent book on the Ṣāliḥiyya Quarter; there is not even an entry for it in his index. His single (uncritical) reference to the plague, *Dynamism* 62 n. 52, is in citing Ibn al-Ḥimṣī's report for 919/1513–1514 of 75,000 deaths, which is an imaginative figure and is much above Miura's own estimate of the total population.

3 This estimate takes into account a possible decline in the decades before the Ottoman conquest, due to continuous epidemics, as well as wars in Syria and migration. Wollina, View 271, estimates between 60,000 and 100,000 in the fifteenth century, but the latter figure is much too high. The figure of 100,000 in Petry, *Criminal underworld* 206, is unrelated by him to any specific time after 1348.

4 Ibn al-Ḥimṣī, *Ḥawādith* i, 188, 189; al-Buṣrawī, *Tārīkh* i, 38.

 | DOI:10.1163/9789004413269_004

ing fire that broke out in the Umayyad Mosque, and we have a picture of a city in a disastrous situation.[5] After less than ten years of respite, toward the end of 881/1477 a new outbreak caused (here is another exaggerated estimate) 1,500 daily deaths.[6] A third cycle started in 896/1491 and lasted no less than three years. By that point we have Ibn Ṭawq's detailed information; actually, there are months for which the only details provided in the *Taʿlīq* are on those stricken by the pandemic. One of the symptoms our source notes is the spitting of blood, probably an indication of a pneumonic plague. In 902/1497 there began another epidemic cycle that lasted three more years.[7] According to one source, in some villages less than 20 inhabitants survived.[8] In sum, in the last quarter of the fifteenth century the plague ravaged for at least a total of seven full years.

Ibn Ṭawq specifies the identity of many dozens of persons who perished, including cases of sudden death, such as of a woman who succumbed to the plague barely three months after her wedding, or the *ḥājib*'s son who collapsed while in the public bath, or one ʿAlāʾ al-Dīn al-Talīlī, aged less than 20, who returned with his father to the city and died on the same day.[9] In many families there was more than one death on a single day or within a few days. Thus, Shihāb al-Dīn [b.] al-Muḥawjib lost his two children.[10] Taqī al-Dīn Ibn Qāḍī ʿAjlūn, the *shaykh al-Islām*, lost three of his teenage sons, as well as a granddaughter, two of his concubines, and a male slave. Muḥammad al-Qubaybatī died before being able to implement his marriage contract, one month after the death of his two daughters—clearly, from an earlier marriage. The Ḥanafī qadi suffered deaths in his family, and even the viceroy Qanṣūh al-Yaḥyāwī lost no less than five children in the plague of 897–898/1492.[11] At Maʿlūlā a family of eight perished. Similar cases are recorded.[12]

---

5 al-Buṣrawī, *Tārīkh* i, 70, 85, 88–92; Ibn al-Ḥimṣī, *Ḥawādith* i, 223, 232–237.

6 al-Buṣrawī, *Tārīkh* i, 81, 82, 83. See also Dols, *Black Death* 313; Shoshan, Notes.

7 Ibn Ṭawq, *Taʿlīq* 1040, 1041, 1044, 1051–1067, 1069, 1082–1087, 1090, 1105, 1111–1113, 1116, 1126, 1137, 1578, 1607–1608, 1640, 1642, 1799. For deaths, see 1602, 1681, 1754. Ibn al-Ḥimṣī first notes this cycle under Rajab 897/May 1492 and has about 25 obituaries. See *Ḥawādith* i, 333–339.

8 Ibn Sibāṭ, *Tārīkh* ii, 904–906. The author lost his brother and son in this plague.

9 Ibn Ṭawq, *Taʿlīq* 1511, 1535.

10 Ibn Ṭawq, *Taʿlīq* 1120. For his political activity, see al-Nuʿaymī, *al-Dāris* ii, 19.

11 Ibn Ṭawq, *Taʿlīq* 1121, 1123, 1127, 1128, 1132, 1135, 1145. For the governor, see also Ibn Ṭūlūn, *Iʿlām* 101.

12 Ibn Ṭawq, *Taʿlīq* 1169, 1170, 1172, 1177, 1183. For the plague and deaths, see also 1187, 1188, 1190, 1197, 1309, 1313–1315, 1336–1337, 1359, 1363, 1510, 1530, 1538, 1542, 1543, 1544, 1566, 1567, 1572, 1576, 1583.

Occasionally, people attempted to avoid the terrible fate by escaping from the city, a controversial step from a legal point of view, but even this proved to be to no avail. Thus, the *naqīb al-ashrāf* was criticized (unjustly, as Ibn Ṭawq seems to opine) for moving together with his two sons to his childhood village by Jūsīy, near Ḥimṣ, because of his trust in the better conditions of the countryside. Yet even thus he was unable to prevent the death of one of his sons. Embarrassed, the bereaved father tried to keep it secret and did not wish any of his acquaintances to attend the funeral. Another man escaped to al-Khiyāra, a village southeast of Damascus and, after the astrologers predicted that the epidemic would come to a halt, returned with his family, but one of his sons died.[13] Infant mortality is a phenomenon generally assumed, but our source gives it concreteness by identifying more than 100 children of his friends and other inhabitants as victims.[14] When the six-month-old daughter of the qadi Ibn Farfūr died, many attended her funeral, and even the viceroy, who himself would lose five of his own children, prayed for her soul.[15] Little is known about the situation in the nearby rural area. One report tells of the disappearance of more than 200 villages, from 300 to 42, in the Ghūṭa, but its reliability is unclear.[16]

One should add to this context an environmental problem—fires that broke out at least once every few years on average, causing a great deal of material loss, as well as chaos and pillage. Noteworthy is the fire on the night of 26–27 Rajab 884/13–14 October 1479 that left the Umayyad Mosque in ashes. Restoration work lasted more than six years, and the costs were enormous.[17] Two fires in 888/1483 destroyed some city sections and were followed by looting; among

13 Ibn Ṭawq, *Taʿlīq* 1496; Ibn Ṭūlūn, *Mufākahat al-khillān* 144 (where the editor erroneously reads the name as Ḥanāra), 146. For other attempts at escape, see Ibn Ṭawq, *Taʿlīq* 1601, 1624. For the early Ottoman period, see Ibn Ṭūlūn, *Quḍāt Dimashq*, 311.

14 E.g. Ibn Ṭawq, *Taʿlīq* 27, 62, 72, 106, 175, 189, 238, 262, 370, 371, 418, 492, 498, 522, 534, 599, 607, 644, 667, 679, 685, 694, 699, 710, 712, 881, 882, 883, 885, 889, 905, 969, 989, 994, 1045, 1047, 1055, 1120, 1127, 1129, 1130, 1132, 1267, 1271, 1305, 1307, 1331, 1350, 1376, 1428, 1431, 1490, 1498, 1500, 1502, 1503, 1504, 1505, 1566, 1567, 1580, 1582, 1585, 1588, 1590, 1598, 1601, 1646, 1691, 1733, 1749, 1827, 1829, 1854, 1878, 1881, 1884, 1887, 1905, 1910. On this topic in general, see Giladi, *Children of Islam* 69–93.

15 Ibn Ṭawq, *Taʿlīq* 930; Ibn al-Ḥimṣī, *Ḥawādith* i, 322.

16 Lapidus, *Muslim cities* 39, 254 n. 71. For a figure of about 80 percent decrease in the number of villages in the Jordan Valley between the Mamluk period and the sixteenth century, see Walker, *Jordan* 217–230. However, according to Walker it is unclear whether it reflects demographic decline or rather shifts in settlement distribution and the merger of previously separate villages.

17 al-Buṣrawī, *Tārīkh* 88–91; Ibn al-Ḥimṣī, *Ḥawādith* i, 232–233, 235–237, 239; Behrens-Abouseif, Fire.

the burnt sites was Khān Julbān.[18] A fire also broke out in Rabīʿ I 890/March 1485 and another at the end of that year for a whole day, resulting in "a terrifying sight." In 894/1489, apparently a result of arson, fire caused much damage. A couple of months later fire spread from the "European depots" to the depot established by the Ibn al-Muzalliq family, causing loss of property valued in the thousands of ducats (*aflūrīn*). A few more fires are reported for the following years.[19]

Damascus was the major Syrian city and the seat of the sultan's viceroy (*nāʾib al-Shām, malik al-umarāʾ, kāfil*)[20] in that Mamluk province (*al-Shām*), which stretched from Beirut eastward to Baʿalbek, then to the village of Jūsīy (or Jūsīya), about 20 miles south of Ḥimṣ, then eastward to the desert. Southward, the boundary went from Beirut to Sidon, and from there along the Ḥāṣbānī River and the Jordan Valley, down to the Dead Sea.[21] The viceroy's authority extended to Ḥimṣ, Aleppo, Tripoli, Ḥamā, and Safed. Although he did not appoint the governors there, he could be authorized by the sultan to imprison them and confiscate their property.[22] Next to the viceroy operated a bureaucratic machinery, and among the officeholders one can point out the *nāʾib Dimashq* or *nāʾib al-qalʿa*, who controlled the citadel, which, like in many cities, was the center of power.[23]

Despite the distance from Cairo, the sultan's authority in Damascus was considerable. Appointment to some offices in its administration, especially of the four qadis, was made in Cairo.[24] Surely, the sultan might be expected to object to an appointment without his authorization, or to punish those refus-

---

18 Ibn Ṭawq, *Taʿlīq* 40, 276, 284; Ibn al-Ḥimṣī, *Ḥawādith* i, 287, 288, 304. The *khān* was possibly endowed by Shādī Bek al-Julbānī, a high-ranking officer.

19 Ibn Ṭawq, *Taʿlīq* 554, 555, 869–870, 871, 906–907, 1277, 1353, 1748; Ibn al-Ḥimṣī, *Ḥawādith* i, 304, 316, 354; al-Buṣrawī, *Tārīkh* 135–136, 137, 195–196, 199; Ibn Ṭūlūn, *Mufākahat al-khillān* 58, 90, 94, 167, 182, 183, 196.

20 E.g. Ibn Ṭawq, *Taʿlīq* 31, 32; Ibn al-Ḥimṣī, *Ḥawādith* i, 230–231; Ibn Ṭūlūn, *Mufākahat al-khillān* 29, 30. The term *kāfil* is shorthand for *kāfil al-salṭana al-sharīfa bi-l-Shām al-maḥrūs*. See Dahmān, *Dimashq* 16.

21 Tarawneh, *Province* 19.

22 For authority over Ḥims, see Ibn Ṭūlūn, *Mufākahat al-khillān* 118; Ibn Ṭūlūn, *Iʿlām* 124; for Aleppo, see Ibn Ṭawq, *Taʿlīq* 1294, 1660–1661, 1850, 1852, 1862; for Tripoli, Ibn Ṭawq, *Taʿlīq* 1827; Ibn Ṭūlūn, *Iʿlām* 126–127; for Ḥamāt, Ibn Ṭawq, *Taʿlīq* 1853; for Safed, Ibn Ṭūlūn, *Mufākahat al-khillān* 63.

23 For *nāʾib Dimashq*, see e.g. Ibn Ṭawq, *Taʿlīq* 1517; Ibn al-Ḥimṣī, *Ḥawādith* ii, 25. For *nāʾib al-qalʿa* and *naqīb al-qalʿa*, see e.g. Ibn Ṭawq, *Taʿlīq* 39, 225; Igarashi, *Land tenure* 173. For citadels as a Mamluk symbol of authority, see Luz, *Mamluk city* 151–156.

24 E.g. Ibn Ṭawq, *Taʿlīq* 1594, 1819–1820. See also Petry, *Protectors?* 36.

ing to accept an office about which he had decided.[25] Occasionally, officials were called upon from the Syrian city to serve in Cairo. Orders to confiscate the property of those suspected or accused of mismanagement, or just falling out of favor, were sent from Cairo to Damascus. Of special notice is the case of al-ʿAdawī, the sultan's personal agent (*wakīl al-sulṭān*), who apparently was in charge of most of the sultan's financial assets in Syria. For unspecified reasons he had to pay (provided we are willing to accept the figures) 10,000 dinars in Damascus and thrice as much in Cairo.[26] Shādī Bek al-Julbānī, a Mamluk officer, was released only after paying 10,000 dinars plus 2,000 standard measures (*gharāra*) of grain and a few other items.[27] Orders (*marsūm*) to place Syrian emirs and other officeholders under arrest, or even execute them, or, at best, to send them to Cairo for interrogation, were quite common. Al-Aslamī, a converted Samaritan who was the *kātib al-kizāna*, was summoned to the citadel following the sultan's order, denigrated by one of the viceroy's bodyguards (*khāṣṣakī*), beaten and cursed, and forced to pay an enormous sum. He was released only after the Shāfiʿī qadi interceded on his behalf.[28] Another case reported in some detail is what might be called the Nābulusī affair, named after Shihāb al-Dīn al-Nābulusī, who served as the *wakīl al-sulṭān* and comptroller (*nāẓir al-jaysh*). Here, one has to begin with Burhān al-Dīn, Shihāb al-Dīn's father, who had preceded his son in these posts and had been active in Syria, where he had collected, as the report has it, over 120,000 dinars. His son also collected huge sums. In 882/1477, following complaints about his misconduct, Shihāb al-Dīn was summoned to Cairo. The rumor was that an enormous sum of 100,000 dinars he had embezzled had been found hidden in different places. He was paraded in an act of shaming and eventually died after torture. The aftereffects of this affair seem to have lingered, as seven years later someone complained to the sultan that several men, among them Shams al-Dīn, the *khaṭīb* of the Saqīfa

---

25 E.g. Ibn Ṭawq, *Taʿlīq* 28, 31; Ibn al-Ḥimṣī, *Ḥawādith* i, 252–253.

26 Ibn al-Ḥimṣī, *Ḥawādith* i 305–306; Ibn Ṭūlūn, *Mufākahat al-khillān*, 62. Al-ʿAdawī (d. 908/1502), originally from Balqāʿ in the Jordan Valley, grew up in Damascus and served in administrative jobs before becoming the Shāfiʿī qadi in 886/1481. He was replaced after three days. See Ibn Ṭawq, *Taʿlīq* 39, 66; Ibn Ṭūlūn, *Quḍāt Dimashq* 179–180; al-Anṣārī, *Nuzhat al-khāṭir* ii, 142. For the post of *wakīl al-sulṭān*, see Igarashi, *Land tenure* 162–163. For the confiscation of the estate of the deceased viceroy Qujmās, see Ibn Ṭūlūn, *Iʿlām* 98, 99.

27 Ibn Ṭawq, *Taʿlīq* 109, 110, 136; Ibn al-Ḥimṣī, *Ḥawādith* i, 267; Ibn Ṭūlūn, *Mufākahat al-khillān* 45, 46. Miura's opinion, in *Dynamism* 123–124, that confiscation was not an arbitrary imposition, seems to me untenable. After all, apart from its disregard for private property, what was confiscated did not go for the benefit of the public but to support the sultan's and viceroy's needs (and whims).

28 Ibn Ṭawq, *Taʿliq* 608–609.

Mosque, and his father, had in their possession a huge sum of 50,000 dinars of the "Nābulusī's money."[29] Another case was of Aḥmad b. Ṣubḥ (or Ṣubayḥ), characterized as a *rāfiḍī*, who in Jumādā I 893/May 1488 returned to Damascus after soliciting in Cairo a job that involved taxing merchants. Complaints were addressed against him and against a notary with whom he cooperated, and both were jailed in the citadel. The sultan ordered that Ibn Ṣubḥ be flogged and shamed in public. Escaping from being lynched, he died a few days later; the notary was forced to pay 2,000 dinars.[30]

The political situation in Damascus during the last decades of the fifteenth century was instable. Since Khushqadam's days (865–872/1461–1467) tension had existed between the sultan and the viceroy, Janim, who had been forced out of the city. A few of his successors did not serve long and died soon after taking office. Bardabak, who ascended in the summer of 871/1466 and was considered pious, was dismissed barely a year later for his passive policy toward the rebel Turkmen Shāh-Suvār of the Tulghādir (Dhū l-Qādir) principality in Anatolia, then reinstalled but poisoned a short time later. Similar was his successor's fate in 877/1473.[31] Ibn Ṭawq refers repeatedly to a feeling of insecurity that required locking the city gates after sunset and imposing a curfew. The reasons for that were many. For example, in Ramaḍān 900/June 1495 there was a confrontation between Qanṣūh al-Yaḥyāwī, now eight years into his second term as viceroy, and the commander of the citadel, about which we have at least four different versions. Al-Buṣrawī writes that the commander, who had quarreled with one of the viceroy's officers, closed the gates and placed catapults ready to bombard the viceroy's palace. The viceroy himself took shelter in the stable and had to go to prayer in the mosque on foot instead of riding his horse. Markets closed and "chaos prevailed." The conflict was resolved after emirs arranged a meeting the details of which are uknown; however, in the end the viceroy bestowed on the rebel a robe of honor. Ibn Ṭawq, who is quite reserved about the informa-

29 Ibn Ṭawq, *Taʿlīq* 323–324, 325, 326–327; Ibn al-Ḥimṣī, *Ḥawādith* i, 212–217, 218, 220, 222, 223; al-Buṣrawī, *Tārīkh* 81–84; Petry, *Protectors?* 36–37.

30 al-Buṣrawī, *Tārīkh* 127–128, who seems quite content with Ibn Ṣubḥ's sad end. Ibn Ṭawq, *Taʿlīq* 780, has a different version, according to which he was summoned to Cairo and later received 600 (!) lashes (? *rawtan*) for an unspecified reason. Ibn Ṭūlūn, *Mufākahat al-khillān* 80–81, has his version, with further details. The fullest version is in Ibn al-Ḥimṣī, *Ḥawādith* i, 308, 310. For other instances, see e.g. Ibn Ṭawq, *Taʿlīq* 44, 62, 69, 247, 795, 864–865, 872, 912, 981, 1059, 1151, 1348, 1354, 1363–1364, 1480–1481; Ibn al-Ḥimṣī, *Ḥawādith* i, 260, 266, 267, 274, 276, 282, 285, 319, 324, 364, 389; Ibn Ṭūlūn, *Mufākahat al-khillān* 94, 128; Igarashi, *Land tenure* 163.

31 For the viceroys, see Ibn Ṭūlūn, *Iʿlām* 83–89. For insecurity, see Ibn Ṭawq, *Taʿlīq* 1433, 1469, 1473, 1474, 1480, 1545, 1549, 1629. See also Dhu'l-Ḳadr, *EI*²; Aḳ Ḳoyunlu, *EI*².

tion he has ("I believe and don't believe it"), places the incident nine days later and writes that the reason for it is unclear. He quotes the viceroy's instruction to his men to keep a low profile ("Do not carry even a club! Whoever disobeys, I'll cut his hand off") and has some further details. There is a totally different and shorter version of this event in Ibn al-Ḥimṣī's book, which agrees with Ibn Ṭawq's on the date but otherwise relates that the cause of the conflict was that the rebel planned to decorate the city on the occasion of the sultan's recovery from illness, but the viceroy objected because of the Ramadan fast and was anxious about "women going out." According to this version, the people (*ʿāmma*) deserve credit for preventing further deterioration. Our fourth source, Ibn Ṭūlūn, devotes more space to the rumor about the sultan's grave illness and concludes by pointing out that the event demonstrated the rebel's stupidity but also the little prestige that the viceroy enjoyed.[32]

Two years later, in 902/1497, Qanṣūh al-Yaḥyāwī died aged 80. On the evaluation of his relatively long reign in the city the writers differ. Ibn Ṭūlūn states that he was beloved by the people, but others blamed him for neglecting and oppressing them. Al-Buṣrawī ascribes to him the daring wish to become sultan and reports of a fortune he amassed to this end, even employing an "infidel" (*shakhṣ min al-zanādiqa*), who embezzled money from the generously funded Umayyad Mosque. Following al-Yaḥyāwī's death, no successor was appointed, and the grand chamberlain served as a temporary viceroy (*nāʾib al-ghayba*). He tried to suppress the criminals and even, so we are told, inspected the streets at night in person. After a couple of months, he also died. The appointment at the beginning of 903/1497 of a new viceroy, Ināl al-Faqīh, who prior to that had ruled in Aleppo, coincided with a revolt against the sultan in Egypt. It was led by Āqbirdī the *dāwadār* (secretary) and proved detrimental for Damascus. After the rebelling emir had been defeated on Egyptian soil, he fled with his army to the Syrian city, where he hoped to join forces with the viceroy, Ināl, and his subordinate governors of other Syrian towns and resume his attempt to seize the sultanate by advancing to Egypt from the north. Barely one month in office, Ināl was suspected of conspiring to join forces with the rebel and, in a unique showdown, the Damascenes forced him out of the city. He was haphazardly replaced by Kurtbāy "the red" (*al-aḥmar*), though without any ceremony; that had to wait for better days. Governors of some Syrian towns refused to be part of the conspiracy and came to Kurtbāy's help. The rebel's siege of the city lasted almost 50 days, with grave effects, of which Ibn Ṭūlūn gives the minutest

32 Ibn Ṭawq, *Taʿlīq* 1351; al-Buṣrawī, *Tārīkh* 161; Ibn al-Ḥimṣī, *Ḥawādith* i, 385; Ibn Ṭūlūn, *Mufākahat al-khillān* 135.

details that are on occasion difficult to follow, yet even so provide in this case a more coherent account than the piecemeal details in Ibn Ṭawq's diary.[33]

A reconstruction of the events reveals that Āqbirdī made a few attempts to enter the city by deceit. On one occasion he pretended to retreat, but then his troops laid an ambush at a market outside the Jābiya Gate, causing deaths and injuries. Some residential sections were set ablaze. The rebels even set guns (*makāḥil*) on the roof of one mosque, causing fire and disrespecting the sacredness of a nearby cemetery. There were rumors of the rebel army pillaging the agricultural vicinity; according to one report, possibly exaggerated, 100 villages were set on fire. The inhabitants of Damascus were ordered to mend the city gates and block the quarters in order to make it difficult for the hostile troops to penetrate. Each of the city's main gates was manned by troops of one of the viceroy's subordinate governors. The ditch around the city was filled constantly with water to counter Āqbirdī's attempt to cut off the water supply from the neighboring canals; his plan was subverted by the Almighty, who caused an exceptionally heavy rain that lasted 15 days.[34] A delegation headed by Taqī al-Dīn Ibn Qāḍī ʿAjlūn was sent to meet the rebel, but, despite his promise not to harm the inhabitants, they would not let him enter. There is a claim that Ināl, the deposed viceroy and now in the opposite camp, tried to deceive the delegates, claiming that Āqbirdī was not really a rebel. The latter's attempt to subdue the city by force first concentrated on the Ṣāliḥiyya Quarter in the northwest and left there about 40 dead; their heads were gruesomely hung on fences. According to another report the rebel's troops violated dozens of women. Ibn Mibrad, a renowned Ḥanbalī scholar and a resident of the quarter, cites a letter in which Āqbirdī demanded 100 local men be put at his service. Ibn Mibrad was asked to write an answer, which, of course, rejected the demand.

Other quarters suffered similar damage. There was much looting, including of a 1,000 volumes stored at one of the madrasas. As Āqbirdī realized his failure to break his way into the old city, he retreated but took the sayyid of

33 Ibn Ṭūlūn, *Iʿlām* 101, 103–105; Ibn Ṭawq, *Taʿlīq* 1498–1499, 1530, 1537–1538, 1545, 1548, 1549, 1550–1551, 1552, 1553, 1554, 1555, 1560, 1561, 1567, 1568–1569; al-Buṣrawī, *Tārīkh* 218–219; Ibn al-Ḥimṣī, *Ḥawādith* ii, 33. Contrast Ibn Ṭawq, *Taʿlīq* 1567, with Ibn Ṭūlūn, *Mufākahat al-khillān* 159–160. See also Miura, *Dynamism* 153–154.

34 The largest volume of the city's water was drawn from the Baradā River and its six branches, wherefrom it was diverted through canals for irrigating fields and providing water to drink. Yazīd and Tūrā were the northern branches that irrigated the Ṣāliḥiyya Quarter. Banyas and Qanawāt watered the old city and the Marj, a pastureland east of the city. See generally Lapidus, *Muslim cities* 70, and the references he cites; Khayr, *Madīnat Dimashq*. For the situation of water supply and some of its problems in the city in later periods, see Grehan, *Everyday life* 125–132.

the ʿAbbāsid family as a hostage, with the hope—at least this is what was claimed—that he would bestow on him the title of sultan. Reportedly, the resistance put up by the city's inhabitants was a major factor in making the rebel and his army withdraw; according to Ibn Mibrad, Āqbirdī was surprised at their stamina. Ibn al-Ḥimṣī sums up his report of the events by noting that they resembled Tīmūr's attack exactly 100 years earlier, and that the fate of the city "was mourned by all." A confrontation near Aleppo, to where Āqbirdī continued his flight, between his forces and a coalition of Syrian governors loyal to the sultan and joined by an expedition force from Egypt, resulted in a defeat of the rebel troops. But the region was not totally free of their menace till Āqbirdī's death from natural causes about a year later.[35]

The end of the siege was not the end of the problems, for barely a year had passed before viceroy Kurtbāy died. He was succeeded by Jānblāṭ, another governor transferred from Aleppo, who, after less than a year in office, was summoned to Cairo to be installed as the grand atabek and was succeeded by Qaṣrūh, who, like his predecessor, came from Aleppo. Contrary to Jānblāṭ's draconian measures, Qaṣrūh tried to bring things under control and ordered that no one should carry arms, that the special tax (*mushāt*, for which see below) should be abolished, and that everyone should return to their routine. Soon a conflict between him and Qanṣūh al-Ghawrī, the sultan (newly appointed in late 903/1498), involved also leading emirs. At some stage, when the sultan faced revolt, Qaṣrūh entertained the idea of becoming sultan himself. The successive coup attempts generated a chaotic situation in Cairo, with repercussions in Syria. Each day had its new rumors and its political turnabout. When the anxious Ṭūmān Bāy, the short-lived sultan, came to Damascus in Jumādā I 906/December 1500, he was received by the viceroy and proclaimed there as sultan, and some of his opponents in Damascus were instantly arrested. A gesture proclaimed by the new sultan during his stay in the city was to abolish the collective fine in case of murder (for which see Chapter 5). Qaṣrūh left his post as viceroy and was nominated as the sultan's atabek, only to be murdered in Cairo a short time later. His successor was Dawlatbāy of Aleppo, but shortly afterward, facing problems with the regime in Cairo, he fled. Three more governors ruled Syria in the remaining years before the Ottoman conquest, of whom Sībāy, who, except for a brief intermission, served the relatively long term between 911/1506 and 922/1516, was destined to be killed on the battlefield. During his office the situation in Damascus was chaotic, many rivalries

35 Ibn Ṭūlūn, *Mufākahat al-khillān* 148–163, 167, 168, 178; Ibn al-Ḥimṣī, *Ḥawādith* ii, 23–24, 26, 28–33, 35, 44, 72, 77. See also briefly Miura, *Dynamism* 107 and n. 79 (for Ibn al-Mibrad's answer), 164.

within Mamluk ranks plagued the government, and the control of subordinate towns in Syria was minimal.[36] From what has been said so far on the political situation, clearly, the Ottoman conquest came after at least two decades of continuous instability in Syria.

Prior to the Ottoman conquest, military conflicts with this great enemy were sporadic. Here and there, the Mamluks were even able to gain limited victories in small-scale fighting in southern Anatolia. For example, in 893/1488 the skulls of 30 Ottoman soldiers were displayed in public, and 3 years later qadis in the service of the Ottomans came to sign a truce agreement.[37] Still, the Mamluk state was increasingly threatened by political developments north of its Syrian domain. The Aqquyunlu, a Turkmen principality in southeast Anatolia led by Uzun Ḥasan, became embroiled with the Mamluk state in a crisis on the Upper Euphrates frontier between 868/1464 and 870/1466. After 872/1467 the Aqquyunlu, having progressed from the status of a clan to an agrarian empire, were a power to be reckoned with. In 877/1472 they reached the outskirts of Aleppo, and in 886/1481 they captured the viceroy Qānṣūh al-Yaḥyāwī. But "my enemy's enemy is my friend," and a clever policy required a good relationship with the Aqquyunlu against the Ottomans. This is the context for the arrival of a giraffe in Damascus one day in 900/1495. As Ibn Ṭawq implies, the giraffe and predatory animals were a gift from Sultan Qāytbāy to Rustam, one of Uzun Ḥasan's successors, and the consignment made a stop in the city on the way north.[38]

The bedouin clans, who not only roamed in the neighboring regions but also could reach the city gates, posed a perennial problem. For example, in 897/1492 bedouins executed 12 inhabitants in the Qubaybāt Quarter, and the following year they captured some of the viceroy's property. The Lām/Mafārija

36 The best source for the last dozen years is Ibn Ṭūlūn, *I'lām* 110–231. For some specific reports, see e.g. Ibn Ṭawq, *Ta'līq* 1830. See also Tarawneh, *Province* 29. For further details see the epilogue to this book.

37 Ibn Ṭawq, *Ta'līq* 594, 602, 603, 623, 768, 973, 1081, 1089; al-Buṣrawī, *Tārīkh* 110, 115, 147; Ibn al-Ḥimṣī, *Ḥawādith* i, 302, 304, 306, 308, 311–312, 314, 317, 325, 327, 331. See also briefly Lapidus, *Muslim cities* 38; Petry, *Protectors?* 51–53.

38 On the Aqquyunlu and their relationship with the Mamluk state, see Woods, *Aqquyunlu*, esp. 10, 92, 115–116; Petry, *Protectors?* 44–49. On the gift, see Ibn Ṭawq, *Ta'līq* 1335. Such gifts were exchanged between rulers as a routine. For a note on Qāytbāy's consignment of a giraffe to Lorenzo de Medici in 1486 and for Muḥammad 'Alī's to the French king in the 1820s and the giraffe's voyage, see the fascinating story in Allin, *Zarafa*. Incidentally, the stop in Damascus raised the question whether the meat of a giraffe was allowed. See al-Buṣrawī, *Tārīkh* 157.

clan ravaged frequently and occasionally even murdered officials.[39] Jarūd, Ibn Ṭawq's ancestral village, as well as a number of other villages, all a few hours' ride from Damascus, suffered from the clans of ʿAlī and Faḍl, the latter emerging from relative marginality in the fourteenth century.[40] Also in more distant regions, especially in the Ḥawrān, the Mafārija/Lām, occasionally supported by bedouins from the Nāblus area, pillaged cultivated land and caused the migration of peasants. The Ibn Muqallad clan controlled the hajj caravan route, and between 900/1494–1495 and 918/1513 hardly a year passed without an attack. Pilgrims returning from the Hijaz at the beginning of 900/1494 were exposed naked in the Jordan Valley. Among those held and their goods confiscated was the qadi Ibn al-Muzalliq, who had to pay 100 dinars as ransom, and similar was the case of a few wealthy merchants, such as ʿAlī al-Qārī. A year later the number of pilgrims decreased, and no qadi (a qadi normally joined the pilgrims) agreed to take part in the caravan.[41]

Here and there, campaigns against the bedouins were successful, and at one point Mamluk troops captured thousands of camels, and the heads of their defeated riders were stuck on javelins.[42] Punitive measures could be brutal, as demonstrated by the Mamluk officer in charge of the Ḥawrān killing of about 30 of the Haytham clan, disregarding their claim that they had a guarantee of safety from one of the viceroys. The report has it that even the bellies of pregnant women were ripped open and that atrocities that were not even done against "infidels" (*ahl al-ḥarb*) occurred. Anti-bedouin campaigns were occasionally conducted as far as Nāblus, in which Mamluk troops were occasionally defeated. The regime also applied a policy of "divide and rule" and employed loyal bedouins (*ʿashīr, al-ʿurban al-ṭāʾiʿūn*) against rebel bedouins (*al-ʿāṣīyūn*).[43]

It was not only bedouin clans who challenged the Mamluk regime in Damascus and its environs; the rulers' weakness was manifested in their failure to

39 Ibn Ṭawq, *Taʿlīq* 61, 353, 483, 484, 489, 797, 1103, 1202, 1205, 1444, 1546, 1635, 1761; al-Buṣrawī, *Tārīkh* 217–218, 221.

40 Ibn Ṭawq, *Taʿlīq* 484, 511, 512, 606, 670, 715, 860–861, 897, 1899; Ibn al-Ḥimṣī, *Ḥawādith* i, 243, 275; Ibn Ṭūlūn, *Mufākahat al-khillān* 14; Drori, Role. For these villages, see Yāqūt, *Muʿjam al-buldān*, s.v.; Tarawneh, *Province* 20.

41 Ibn Ṭawq, *Taʿlīq* 1084, 1312, 1542, 1654, 1725, 1745, 1756, 1856, 1904, 1907; al-Buṣrawī, *Tārīkh* 177, 223, 232; Ibn al-Ḥimṣī, *Ḥawādith* i, 368–369, 371–372; Ibn Ṭūlūn, *Mufākahat al-khillān* 105; Ibn Ṭūlūn, *Iʿlām* 129, 135. For the process of "bedouinization," especially in Egypt, see Elbendary, *Crowds* 48–54. See also briefly Lapidus, *Muslim cities* 39.

42 Ibn Ṭawq, *Taʿlīq* 1451, 1797–1798, 1889. See also 98, 353, 456, 904, 952, 1733; al-Buṣrawī, *Tārīkh* 206; Ibn al-Ḥimṣī, *Ḥawādith* i, 243, 275.

43 Ibn Ṭawq, *Taʿlīq* 172, 487, 499, 638, 642, 1012, 1061, 1200, 1334, 1481, 1531, 1628, 1654, 1730, 1830, 1757, 1831. For further examples, see Ibn al-Ḥimṣī, *Ḥawādith* i, 242, 243, 275; Ibn Ṭūlūn, *Mufākahat al-khillān* 8, 10, 61–62, 74–75, 83, 88, 134–135; Ibn Ṭūlūn, *Iʿlām* 115.

curb the rising power of regional strongmen (*muqaddam*). Although, curiously enough, other sources are completely silent about him, the case of Sharaf al-Dīn Ibn ʿAlūṭa, the *muqaddam* of Jubbat al-ʿAssāl, appears in the *Taʿlīq* like a telenovela. Originally of the Nabk village, and possibly a manumitted slave, Ibn ʿAlūṭa first comes to our attention *sub anno* 888/1483, competing for and subsequently gaining the post of *muqaddam* at Jubba. He appears to have abused it, extorting money from the locals, especially Christian peasants at Maʿlūlā; in one instance he executed a Christian who was suspected of having an affair with a Muslim woman. Ibn ʿAlūṭa was dismissed and reinstated a few times. What brought him back to office each time is unclear, but bribes cannot be excluded. Occasionally, he was at the viceroy's service in confronting bedouins. However, in the aforementioned Āqbirdī revolt he joined the rebels. From our notary's notes we learn that he terrorized the region under his control for no less than 15 years.[44]

The case of the al-ʿAzqī gang is not much different. Like Ibn ʿAlūṭa in Jubbat al-ʿAssāl, their leader served as a *muqaddam* in the Zabadānī region, and his men used their service for filling their pockets. In 885/1480 one member of the gang attacked a large convoy of merchants. Some years later there was a fight between the al-ʿAzqī and the Bāklū gang in the Sāliḥiyya Quarter, and there are further references to their activities. A highway robber of Safīra village in the Zabadānī deserted the al-ʿAzqī, joined their rivals, and was responsible for many cases of murder. In return for bribes, the viceroy alternated in his support of both gangs. At one point their leaders were ordered to share the office of *muqaddam*, but, as our source notes, it was "like mixing fire with water." In the fighting that resulted from this manipulative policy, 40 of the Bāklū gang perished. Less than a year later, the leader of the al-ʿAzqī bribed the powerful Samaritan official Ṣadaqa (on whom see Chapter 4), but the plan was foiled by the viceroy, who sent assassins to get rid of the gangster. The latter's mutilated corpse was left on the Ṣāliḥiyya White Bridge and then hung for a few days on a tree. Six more members of the gang were also executed. Later in the year, the al-ʿAzqī are referred to once again as "rebels." However, not dissimilar to Ibn ʿAlūṭa's case, members were still appointed as *muqaddam* at the Zabadānī. One of them suffered a gruesome end; his severed head was displayed at the gate of the governor's stable. At the beginning of 905/1499 we find members of

44 Ibn Ṭawq, *Taʿlīq* 277, 505, 703, 772, 773, 786, 909, 914, 915, 919, 972, 976, 1007, 1042, 1044, 1052, 1053, 1069, 1094, 1095, 1128, 1144, 1158, 1169, 1171–1172, 1176, 1209, 1214–1215, 1219, 1221, 1224, 1229, 1230, 1232, 1233, 1241, 1261–1262, 1280, 1285, 1318, 1319, 1324, 1444, 1446, 1448, 1545, 1644, 1684–1685, 1720, 1735, 1737, 1744, 1779, 1821, 1907, 1914; al-Buṣrawī, *Tārīkh* 178; Ibn al-Ḥimṣī, *Ḥawādith* ii, 29–31.

al-ʿAzqī and Bāklū still holding the post of *muqaddam*, and one of the al-ʿAzqīs is mentioned holding it as late as 916/1510.[45] Like Ibn ʿAlūṭa, they practically controlled villages north of Damascus in the two decades before the Ottoman conquest, with the Mamluk regime largely powerless in curbing their authority.

The political problems that the Mamluk regime faced, coupled with the personal expenses of viceroys and high-ranking officers, required huge expenditure, which had to be financed.[46] Here, a note is in order on a structural economic change detrimental to the Mamluk fisc. It is assumed that in the course of the fourteenth and fifteenth centuries the *iqṭāʿ* system (that is, the system of granting cultivated land of specified boundaries to the military not as property but for extracting revenues from the right to taxes[47]) was alienated from the state by practically becoming private land through the waqf mechanism. The flexibility that earlier regimes had enjoyed by reallocating *iqṭāʿ*s, their control of land in their territories and of the flow of cash from taxes to the treasury, all were now significantly reduced. The reasons for this process are complex, but Mamluk sultans and the Mamluk elite cannot be considered innocent in this regard. They often transferred state land directly to their own waqfs without compensating the treasury. Surely, rulers' preferring their own selfish interests at the expense of public welfare was no Mamluk invention. What was specifically Mamluk, however, is that the last sultans transferred state property on a large scale into the ruler's personal trust. The result was that by the end of the Mamluk era possibly about 40 percent of agricultural land in Egypt was waqf land over which the treasury had no direct control and from which it enjoyed no financial gain. According to scholars' calculations, by the time of the Ottoman conquest the treasury was practically emptied.[48]

Some contemporary observers in Damascus (and in Egypt) saw the problem evolving before their eyes. One of them, Muḥammad al-Asadī, who possibly was a Syrian clerk, completed in 855/1451 his *al-Taysīr wa-l-iʿtibār*, which contains criticism of the financial (mis)management in the late Mamluk period. The author presents a model process whereby a village previously assigned as an *iqtāʿ* to an emir now remains, contrary to the old policy, as a source of income

45 Ibn Ṭawq, *Taʿlīq* 642, 720, 770 and n. 1, 776, 824, 847, 897, 902, 958, 1045, 1155, 1158, 1169, 1199, 1200, 1214, 1303, 1359, 1361, 1561, 1575, 1744; Ibn al-Ḥimṣī, *Ḥawādith* ii, 31; Ibn Ṭūlūn, *Mufākahat al-khillān* 9, 19, 79, 85, 93, 280.

46 For a figure of 1,000 dinars as daily expenses in 904/1498–1499, see Ibn Ṭūlūn, *Iʿlām* 131.

47 See Iḳṭāʿ, *EI*².

48 Petry, *Protectors?* 198–208, provides details of the process in Egypt which are culled from waqf documents. See also Walker, *Jordan* 241 (citing Abū Ghāzī, *Taṭawwur al-ḥiyāza al-zirāʿiyya fī Miṣr*, 16–22), 264–267.

for the same emir and his descendants after his retirement. Then, in later generations, the village passes through many hands and is divided, and its taxes cease to reach the treasury (*bayt al-māl*). Another process al-Asadī describes is the purchase of state land from the treasury and turning it into waqf.[49]

Another writer in the same vein was the Shāfiʿī scholar Taqī al-Dīn Muḥammad al-Balāṭunusī (851–936/1447–1529), a pupil of the Ibn Qāḍī ʿAjlūn brothers. In his book, compiled at the early age of 20, he relies on his father ("our shaykh") Shams al-Dīn (d. 863/1458) and many earlier Shāfiʿī authorities, and he gives expression to their and his own misgivings about the sale of state land as private property or turning it into waqf. He cites a fatwa issued by the prominent fourteenth-century Shāfiʿī Taqī al-Dīn al-Subkī, who apparently disapproved of a sale of a waqf endowed in 720/1320 to a certain Mamluk by an ʿAbbāsid descendant in his capacity as a *ḍāmin*. Like al-Asadī, al-Balāṭunusī's conclusion is that in his own time the sale of land and turning villages into endowments are invalid acts that, "to a great surprise (*kullul-ʿajab*)," not only are committed by the Mamluk establishment but also are approved by qadis reputed for their knowledge and who should have known otherwise. In fact, the qadis and scholars are among those who take possession of waqfs without having the right to them.[50]

While al-Asadī and al-Balāṭunusī discuss the problem in general, other sources provide some figures about how things worked in reality. According to Ottoman archives, by the 1580s about 80 percent of all villages in the Damascus province were in the status of waqf, which may suggest that around the year 1500 waqf lands in Syria were proportionately even more widespread than in Egypt. Entire villages were declared of such status, some located even at a considerable distance from the city. The proceeds of vast areas of cultivated land declared as waqf supported both religious and nonreligious institutions in the city. Thus toward the end of the sixteenth century, 75 percent of the waqfs supporting religious institutions in the Ṣāliḥiyya Quarter were farmland.[51] From Ibn Ṭawq we learn that the Nūrī Hospital received at the end of the

49 al-Asadī, *Taysīr* 79–82 (for the date of finalizing his book, see 175). See also Walker, *Jordan* 24; Igarashi, *Land tenure* 179, 181–182. For Ibn Humam's observation a generation earlier, see Cuno, Was the land? 126–127.

50 al-Balāṭunusī, *Taḥrīr* 256–261. For details on his biography see editor's introduction. For a fatwa he issued in 930/1524 permitting the mass killing of Druze in the Shūf region, see Ibn Ṭūlūn, *Ḥawādith* 171. For his posts in Damascus, see al-Nuʿaymī, *al-Dāris* i, 221, 355. For his reliance on his father, see e.g. al-Balāṭunusī, *Taḥrīr* 170. On his father, see al-Sakhāwī, *al-Ḍawʾ* viii, 86–88. See also Walker, *Jordan* 251–252; Igarashi, *Land tenure* 186.

51 Miura, Ṣāliḥiyya quarter 279–280, 287–288; Miura, *Dynamism* 178–195; Igarashi, *Land tenure* 177–182; Frenkel, *Awqāf* 157–158.

fifteenth century the proceeds of a waqf land in the Ghūṭa villages of Quṭayfa and Muʿaẓimiyya.[52] The kitchen (*maṭbakh*) that stood by Bāb al-Barīd received the proceeds of orchards at Jawbar, northeast of the city, and at Dayr al-Sarūrī, which in 891/1486 were leased for four years for 1,100 dirhams (more than 20 dinars annually).[53]

Thus the Mamluk state lost a substantial proportion of its traditional source of income, and in Damascus, like in Cairo, the Mamluk government resorted to means other than legally sanctioned taxes to make up for the deficit in the treasury and the depletion of private funds. In the absence of other resources to tap, it had to do so both short-sightedly and at the expense of the local population.[54] One means was the sale of offices, which, needless to stress, was bound to have a corrupting effect and damage the quality and stability of the administrative apparatus. As one might expect, offices were often sold to the highest bidder rather than granted to the most qualified. The sale of offices was also an incentive for a quick turnover of officeholders. Thus the number of those serving in a post in the last decades of the Mamluk era could reach a few dozen.[55] Only a couple of the legion of available examples is needed. When Timarbughā, the sultan's interpreter (*tarjumān*), purchased the office of comptroller (*naẓr al-jaysh wa-l-jawālī wa-l-qalʿa*), interestingly enough, 10,000 dinars out of the 16,000 were collected for him by foreign merchants. Apparently, they expected him to open doors for them in his new position.[56] The grand chamberlain (*ḥājib al-ḥujjāb*) Yilbāy became the governor of Safed in return for 20,000 dinars.[57]

52 Ibn Ṭawq, *Taʿlīq* 76, 825.

53 Ibn Ṭawq, *Taʿlīq* 585. I am unable to locate Dayr al-Sarūrī.

54 Since Walker, in her otherwise extremely interesting work, shares in the interpretation of the process outlined above, it is unclear on what basis she finds long-term motivation and innovative measures in Mamluk policy in the fifteenth century. See Walker, Popular responses, esp. 51; Walker, *Jordan* 233–235. At least for Damascus during the period under consideration, one is struck by the lack of any long-term policy due to a variety of reasons, some suggested in the present chapter.

55 The sale of offices in the late Mamluk era is discussed with some general conclusions and tables in Martel-Thoumian, Sale. The author appears more interested in counting figures than in evaluating the wide-ranging aspects of this phenomenon. For Damascus she relies on Ibn Ṭawq's first volume only, other volumes being unavailable to her at the time. See also briefly Elbendary, *Crowds* 34–35; Miura, Urban society 160; Miura, *Dynamism* 115–120, where he gives a precise count of cases and other relevant data. One should note that even though certain offices, such as qadi, depended on educational qualifications, the regime could still increase its financial benefit by the process of bidding when there were a few candidates for one post.

56 Ibn Ṭawq, *Taʿlīq* 940.

57 Ibn Ṭawq, *Taʿlīq* 639; Ibn Ṭūlūn, *Mufākahat al-khillān* 63. For other examples, see e.g. Ibn Ṭawq, *Taʿlīq* 64, 756, 794, 1194, 1224, 1619, 1889.

Confiscation of property and cash was another common measure for supplanting the depleting treasury. An intellectual giant, and a man with practical experience, Ibn Khaldūn had well known that "chicanery and confiscation are always to be feared from royal authority."[58] Things in Damascus some decades after his writing proved him correct, as the wealthy bourgeoisie and high-ranking officials were the first to be targeted and ordered to pay enormous sums. ʿĪsā al-Qārī had to pay 10,000 dinars (as we have seen, perhaps a typological figure) and, on another occasion, 1,000 loads (*ḥiml*) of spices. Upon his death in 895/1490 the enormous sum of 100,000 dinars (once again, if we are to believe this figure) was confiscated from his estate, and his son was subjected to harsh measures. The sum of 8,000 dinars was confiscated on the sultan's order from the estate of the wealthy merchant (*khawāja*) Ibn al-Kharīzātī. With that, his family's saga did not come to an end, and less than a year later 10,000 dinars were demanded from his son after it had allegedly been revealed that he had plans to flee to Aleppo. The estate of Shihāb al-Dīn al-Shāghūrī, another deceased *khawāja*, was confiscated and also a few thousands dinars of the estate of *khawāja* Shihāb al-Dīn b. ʿAlwān al-Shuwaykī. Especially harsh measures were taken in 894/1489 against merchants in pepper, whereby 11,000 ashrafīs were levied against them.[59]

Among those subject to confiscation were prominent men of the minority communities. About 3,000 dinars were taken "for an unknown reason" from two money changers, one of whom, the Jew Faraḥ (or Faraj?), was also a fur dealer. From the estate of the deceased Jew Yaʿīsh, 600 ashrafīs were taken. Yūsuf al-Aslamī, most likely a Samaritan (or a convert), was jailed and flogged at the citadel, his assets were demanded, and he was probably executed. Two other high officials of Samaritan origin were forced to give a loan of 10,000 dinars. Some years later, one of the two was jailed and flogged, and from the other 5,000 dinars were demanded. The viceroy was about to declare him a criminal (*tajrīm*), then backed down after intercession, yet kept him incarcerated.[60] Enormous sums were transferred from Damascus to Cairo from a variety

---

58 Cited in Igarashi, *Land tenure* 184.

59 Ibn Ṭawq, *Taʿlīq* 1681, 1755; al-Buṣrawī, *Tārīkh* 142; Ibn al-Ḥimṣī, *Ḥawādith* i, 373. For the governor surveying the stores of the pepper merchants, including that of ʿAlī, ʿĪsā's son, see Ibn Ṭawq, *Taʿlīq* 753, 1059, 1808. For the confiscation of property of another family member, see Ibn Ṭawq, *Taʿlīq* 286. For the confiscation of mamluks, see 348, 398, 776, 1189, 1538, 1627, 1681, 1755.

60 Ibn Ṭawq, *Taʿlīq* 111, 523, 831, 1002, 1436, 1540, 1574, 1617, 1711. For other cases of auditing and sealing (*ḍabṭ, khatm*) and of confiscation (*ḥawṭa, kabs*) of the property of deceased persons, see e.g. 259, 269, 286, 287, 647, 921, 1258, 1434, 1505, 1506, 1537, 1543, 1546, 1805, 1806,1851, 1891; al-Buṣrawī, *Tārīkh* 111, 139, 153, 168, 173, 241; Ibn al-Ḥimṣī, *Ḥawādith* i, 258,

of sources. The sum of 100,000 dinars specified under Muḥarram 902/September 1496 may be inflated but could serve as a clue to the traffic in cash to the Mamluk capital.[61]

Acts of confiscation were not initiated exclusively by the viceroy. There were cases of troops putting their hands on property at their whim. One instance is related in detail. In Ṣafar 905/September 1499 mamluks broke into the former Ibn al-Muzalliq residence (see Chapter 4), where the family of the *shaykh al-Islām* now resided. They even threatened to invade the harem (*ḥarīm*). Although the viceroy's men later apologized for not knowing it was the shaykh's residence, at least so they claimed, a message came from the viceroy that the women should leave. Najm al-Dīn, the shaykh's son and himself a qadi, sought repeatedly an audience with the ruler, yet the mamluks insisted on executing the order, even to the point of demanding the entire family leave for Beirut, where Taqī al-Dīn was at the time. After a couple of days, some demolition work began in order to enable access to horses. It took another day before there was a turnabout and an order was issued to the troops to vacate the hall. The incident came to an end when allegedly the viceroy's demand to receive a pearl kept at the estate residence was answered. Apparently, the dismal situation of the spacious residence continued, and the mamluks (*atrāk*) continued "residing at, constructing and demolishing" the place, without paying any rent. Apparently frustrated, Taqī al-Dīn decided to turn part of its hall (*līwān*) and stable into a bath and another section into a garden.[62]

One further means of tapping financial resources to the benefit of the treasury was taxing waqfs. Ironically, under dire financial conditions the very ploy that worked against the Mamluk fisc was now to pay a price. Although waqfs should have been immune from intervention, reality dictated otherwise. The Umayyad Mosque, the most important and by far the best endowed public institution in Damascus, is a case in point. This is an institution about whose funding we lack basic details; however, it must have come from both Mamluk and civilian sources. In 894/1489 the viceroy intervened in its budget and ordered that the income of its approximately 100 hundred beneficiaries be reduced. Protest from those with vested interest in this huge waqf, such as the

---

374; Ibn Ṭūlūn, *Mufākahat al-khillān* 62, 70, 92, 112–113. On the confiscation of the property of Jews, Christians, and Samaritans, see Ibn Ṭawq, *Taʿlīq* 988. For Salamī or Aslamī indicating conversion, see Martel-Thoumian, Converti 172–173.

61 Igarashi, *Land tenure* 172 and n. 97.

62 Ibn Ṭawq, *Taʿlīq* 1746, 1747, 1748–1749, 1750, 1916. See also a brief note in Ibn Ṭūlūn, *Mufākahat al-khillān* 197.

shaykh al-Islām, was not of much help.[63] Especially severe measures were taken in 903/1498, following the siege on the city by the rebel forces. The viceroy, who was enraged because the mosque's waqf document could not be located, also found out that the supervisor was unknown; hence he decided to take charge. He demanded that the funds of the previous 15 years (according to another version, of the previous year only) be audited. Subsequently, he exacted the enormous sum of 1,500 ashrafīs (only 600 in another version) from beneficiaries and others and punished some of them. Less than a couple of years later, we learn that one of the viceroy's close officers was the waqf's *nāẓir* and in charge of the distribution of its proceeds. Their magnitude is indicated by the note that, after deducting various expenses, 70,000 dirhams (about 1,400 dinars) were distributed among those entitled (*mustaḥiqqūn*).[64]

As in Cairo, so in Damascus, also other endowments for the public benefit were targeted. Thus 600 (? dinars), including florins, which most likely were derived from international trade in pepper and hence known as "the pepper for captives," were deposited with Ibn Ṭawq as a waqf devoted to the release of captives, most likely from the hands of the Ottoman and Turkmen forces. However, our notary was later instructed to divert the money elsewhere.[65] Another waqf established on agricultural land was meant to finance the burial of the poor (*waqf al-ṭuraḥāʾ*), especially those many dying in the plague. However, at one point its proceeds in the amount of 12,000 dirhams had to be funneled to Mecca. Occasional surveys of waqfs in Damascus were an excuse for extorting money.[66] Also, private waqfs were not immune. When the *khawāja* Shams al-Dīn b. Naḥḥās died in 902/1496, his residence, which had been declared by him as a waqf and valued in the enormous sum of 30,000 dirhams (about 600 dinars), was nevertheless offered for sale by the sultan's order. Quite significant is the fact that to sanction this act the Mamluk ruler had to turn to the Ḥanafī qadi of Tripoli, most likely because no Damascus qadi would approve it.[67]

63 Ibn Ṭawq, *Taʿlīq* 831, 832.

64 Ibn Ṭawq, *Taʿlīq* 1617–1618, 1620, 1623, 1628, 1630, 1755.

65 Ibn Ṭawq, *Taʿlīq* 99. For this waqf, see also 112, 113, 127–128.

66 Ibn Ṭawq, *Taʿlīq* 1002, 1055, 1649. On this endowment, see Dols, *Black Death* 176–177. For general notes on confiscation, see e.g. Ibn Ṭawq, *Taʿlīq* 622, 629, 1780, 1821; Ibn al-Ḥimṣī, *Ḥawādith* ii, 89 (exacting 7,000 dinars). For confiscation and sale, see Miura, Urban society 159. For a waqf survey, see e.g. Ibn Ṭawq, *Taʿlīq* 1502; Ibn Ṭūlūn, *Mufākahat al-khillān* 145. For the deterioration of the waqf system and further useful material see Mahamid, *Waqf*, esp. 115–129. For tampering with waqfs in Egypt in the second half of the fifteenth century, see Petry, Class solidarity 128–129.

67 Ibn Ṭūlūn, *Mufākahat al-khillān* 139, who describes the act as "filth." For the ruling of

The Dīwān al-Mawarīth al-Ḥashriyya, whose task was reviewing the estates of the heirless, appears to have been quite active in putting its hands on financial resources, yet not always acting within its sharʿī boundaries. There were instances of withholding property and cash despite the existence of relatives.[68] Occasionally, steps to evade the *dīwān* were taken, such as specifying names in a will even when not of immediate heirs, or relatives transferring property to their custody before the *dīwān* entered the scene.[69]

Not just the rich but also ordinary people suffered. In Jumādā I 895/March–April 1490 the people were hard-pressed by troops from Egypt and the viceroy's local army, and no one dared to ride a donkey out of fear of confiscation; even qadis were worried about their horses. Shops were shut down; one mamluk stole money from people in the public bath. Those forced to loan money to soldiers were officially informed that they would not be repaid.[70] About a year later a tax on each loom was imposed by the sultan. After some protest the viceroy changed the terms but still imposed a global sum of 15,000 dirhams (or 200 dinars in another version). The governor also surprised the participants in a horse race at al-Maydān al-Akhḍar ("Green Hippodrome") and took their horses "to the very last." Only after payment were the horses released. Especially harsh measures were taken in 904/1499, under viceroy Jānblāṭ, who forced peasants of the Qābūn village to sell sheep for a very low price and, when they refused, their servants were taken as hostages. Others in Damascus were forced to buy camels captured in raids against bedouins for a price twice as high as the market price. Administrators in rural regions (*muqaddams*) were demanded to raise enormous sums. Also Europeans residing in Beirut had to raise large amounts of silver, and their property was audited.[71]

In addition to the legally sanctioned land tax (*jawālī*), which, on occasion, was collected through intermediaries such as deputy qadis on the basis of con-

the Ḥanbalī school that a dilapidated waqf can be sold, see Ibn Ṭūlūn, *Naqd al-ṭālib* 148; Rapoport, Royal justice 78.

68 For this *dīwān*, see Dols, *Black Death* 175–181. For its operation in Jerusalem at the end of the fourteenth century as reflected in the Ḥaram documents, see Muller, *Kadi* 398–400. For "coercion and wrongdoing" approved by the *nāʾib al-qalʿa* and some notaries, see Ibn Ṭawq, *Taʿlīq* 293. For the *dīwān* exacting from Lady Khātūn's estate 1,600 dirhams, more than a quarter of its value, see Ibn Ṭawq, *Taʿlīq* 91–92, 92–93 (the calculation is unclear, see also editor's note), 200. Apparently, the Shāfiʿī school allowed it in case of only female heirs. See Ibn Ṭūlūn, *Iʿlām* 181 n. 2.

69 Ibn Ṭawq, *Taʿlīq* 398, 410, 1128, 1787.

70 Ibn Ṭawq, *Taʿlīq* 101.

71 Ibn Ṭawq, *Taʿlīq* 1080, 1683, 1837; Ibn Ṭūlūn, *Mufākahat al-khillān* 121–122; Ibn Ṭūlūn, *Iʿlām* 115–116.

tractual obligation or guarantee (*ḍamān*),[72] a new tax termed the "Dirham of the Infantry (*mushāt*)" was levied by 889/1484 at the latest for the upkeep of soldiers drafted in Damascus and formed into units outside the regular Mamluk corps. The military quality of these units may be considered questionable, since training city inhabitants with no prior military experience was not an easy task.[73] In any case, the tax was calculated on the basis of a few dinars for the maintenance of each infantry man, the exact sum fluctuating from time to time. Once again, in the first place the wealthy were those who had to shoulder the burden. Thus in 891/1486, following the news about Ottoman troops advancing toward the Anatolian town Malaṭiya, 15 ashrafīs for the upkeep of each infantry man were levied. Qadi Ibn al-Muzalliq had to pay for no less than 60 soldiers (i.e., 900 ashrafīs). According to one report, the number of infantry drafted on this occasion was a trifling 100, yet its cost should have been 15,000 dinars. In 895/1490, when ordered to pay the tax once again, the same qadi refused, was threatened with flogging, detained, and eventually had to agree to finance 15 infantry. In another instance, the Ḥanafī deputy qadi, who refused to pay, was severely beaten. Other than targeting individuals, this tax was meant to gather money from wide sectors and was calculated in lump sums. When 10,000 dinars were demanded by the sultan, the inhabitants of the Maydān al-Ḥaṣā Quarter objected and protested till the viceroy exempted them. At one point, 3,000 dirhams were demanded of the Shāghūr Quarter, and similar sums were imposed on other quarters. Abolition of this tax in 905/1499–1500 did not last long.[74] Another tax in lieu of military service, about which we lack details, was *māl al-aʿwāḍ*.[75]

---

72 For *jawālī*, see Ibn Ṭawq, *Taʿlīq* 1768; Ibn al-Ḥimṣī, *Ḥawādith* i, 248; Ibn Ṭūlūn, *Mufākahat al-khillān* 18, 25. For qadis as tax collectors, see Ibn Ṭawq, *Taʿlīq* 75, 78, 151; al-Buṣrawī, *Tārīkh* 49; Ibn Ṭūlūn, *Quḍāt Dimashq* 173, 222. For *ḍamān*, see Hallaq, *Sharīʿa* 258–260.

73 There was at least one merit in infantry troops. Whereas the mamluks refused to use firearms, the infantry had no qualms about it. See also Miura, Urban society 170–171. The reasons for Mamluk rejection of firearms were argued by David Ayalon in some of his publications. More recent views challenge his thesis, but the debate, important as it is, does not belong here.

74 Ibn Ṭawq, *Taʿlīq* 373, 622, 624–625, 627–628, 635, 639, 642, 647, 765, 766, 767, 768, 774, 781, 938, 1175, 1177, 1178, 1180, 1187 (the editor has Ibn Ḥarīrātī, but the name is most likely Ibn Ḥazīrātī, as transcribed elsewhere in the edited text), 1190, 1197, 1431, 1588, 1617, 1620, 1624–1625, 1680, 1718, 1830; al-Buṣrawī, *Tārīkh* 113, 180; Ibn al-Ḥimṣī, *Ḥawādith* i, 308, 322; Ibn Ṭūlūn, *Mufākahat al-khillān* 79, 100, 101, 102 (refers to Qaysiyya after the eponym Qays); Ibn Ṭūlūn, *Iʿlām* 97–98. Miura, Urban society, has 891/1486 as the earliest date, but Ibn Ṭawq's information seems more complete. On Maydān al-Ḥaṣā, see Roujon and Vilan, *Fabourgs*.

75 Ibn Ṭawq, *Taʿlīq* 532.

The pillaging of villages by various Mamluk elements was a common phenomenon. Al-Mizza, a few miles west of the city, was devastated at least a couple of times, allegedly for neglecting to pay the sultan's secretary (*dawādār al-sulṭān*) his share in the *kharāj* and *ʿushr* taxes.[76] At least in one instance an exchange of population was ordered, whereby the people of Dāriyā, southwest of the city, were expelled to other villages, and others, among them of the Druze faith, were settled in their place after promising to raise large quantities of grain to the benefit of the regime.[77] In Muḥarram 899/October 1493, while in Maʿlūlā, our notary learned that the Mamluk bureaucrat (*kāshif*) intended to pillage the produce and that anxious Christians vacated their homes. In the summer of 903/1498 the viceroy ordered all peasants, especially of Adhriʿāt in the Ḥawrān, to return to their land; implied is an earlier massive migration. The rumor was—it might have been not entirely fabricated—that the order had been issued just for the purpose of extortion.[78] Individuals and groups were subject to frequent mistreatment and severe punishment, possibly with no due process.[79]

The financial problems were also reflected in the monetary situation. The fragmentary picture we have for Damascus has similarities but also differences when compared to that available for Cairo. One noteworthy phenomenon is the occasional scarcity of silver currency. Whereas gold was used mainly for making calculations or for business among the elite, in many transactions, perhaps the majority, prices fixed in gold terms (dinars) were actually paid in silver currency (dirhams) or a mixture of both.[80] Dirhams being most frequently used, certainly by most of the city inhabitants, they were occasionally scarce because of wear and tear and other reasons. One common way to tackle the scarcity was to tamper with the contents of coins and issue low-quality coins.[81] As a result, at the end of 885/1481 the dirham reached an extremely low point in its value

---

76 Ibn Ṭawq, *Taʿlīq* 636, 900, 1155, 1179, 1227, 1291, 1383, 1627, 1630, 1635, 1636, 1642, 1683, 1759, 1802, 1820, 1882; al-Buṣrawī, *Tārīkh* 225; Ibn al-Ḥimṣī, *Ḥawādith* i, 319–320; Ibn Ṭūlūn, *Mufākahat al-khillān* 137.

77 Ibn Ṭawq, *Taʿlīq* 1395.

78 Ibn Ṭawq, *Taʿlīq* 1227, 1627.

79 One viceroy sent his men to capture the son of the former governor of Ḥamā, who disappeared, and instead about 20, among them some elderly men and women, who had nothing to do with this matter, were detained. See Ibn Ṭawq, *Taʿlīq* 214. For ten of al-Mizza inhabitants detained by the viceroy for unexplained reasons, see Ibn Ṭawq, *Taʿlīq* 780. For other cases, see 1183, 1676, 1818; Ibn Ṭūlūn, *Mufākahat al-khillān* 80–81.

80 E.g. Ibn Ṭawq, *Taʿlīq* 96, 261, 323 (also Manṣūrī dinar), 760, 969.

81 Ibn Ṭūlūn, *Mufākahat al-khillān* 108.

and had an exchange rate of 1:52 per the ashrafī. At this point the government attempted to salvage it by recalling the silver coins to the mint in order to issue "renewed" ones (*mustajadd*), of better quality, to be rated at a much higher value of 1:12.5. The feasibility of such a reform would be questioned to begin with and, as with many other reforms, also this one was rejected by the market, and the viceroy had to give in.[82] The reissued dirhams were only slightly increased in value, and less than three years later the dinar:dirham rate was once again at the level of 1:50. At that point, in what appears to have been an attempt to save face, the circulation of the old dirhams was banned. Also this, of course, could not be expected to see the light of the day. Other measures also failed.[83] One may note that despite the silver problems, for some reason the use of copper coins appears to have been minimal when compared to Cairo, for it is hardly mentioned in our sources.[84] Transactions were concluded also on the basis of barter.[85]

As to the price situation, a sharp increase in grain prices occurred in the early months of 873/1468, most likely caused by the outbreak of the plague sometime earlier. Hunger prevailed to the point that, as the chroniclers are in the habit of stating on such occasions, people resorted to cannibalism. Prices went down by at least 50 percent in the following year, albeit still a year of plague, most likely because the market was able at that point to readjust itself by resuming supply now needed for less mouths to feed. Following a gap in the data, we have one more adequate set of figures from 888/1483 onward, whereby we can see that, as a general trend, prices stayed close to their 874/1469 level. The stability of grain prices in the last quarter of the fifteenth century suggests a balanced supply and demand. Excepting the chaos immediately following an epidemic outbreak, or temporary supply problems, such as in the second half of 899/1494, or in 911/1506,[86] reduced grain production by peasants was most likely offset by the urban mortality rate, and thus equilibrium was preserved. This is why attempts by the authorities to intervene in the grain market appear

82 Ibn Ṭūlūn, *Mufākahat al-khillān* 24, 28; Ibn Ṭawq, *Taʿlīq* 26, 27. For the devaluation, see Ashtor, *Histoires des prix* 390. For ordering foreign merchants to bring silver to the mint in the 1470s and 1480s, see Ashtor, *Métaux précieux* 47, 53.

83 Ibn Ṭawq, *Taʿlīq* 96, 198, 199, 233, 239, 247, 264, 265, 280; Ibn Ṭūlūn, *Mufākahat al-khillān* 55.

84 Ibn Ṭūlūn, *Mufākahat al-khillān* 75; Ibn Ṭawq, *Taʿlīq* 65. For the widespread use of copper coins in Cairo in that period, see Shoshan, From silver.

85 For an example of exchanging a donkey for cloth, see Ibn Ṭawq, *Taʿlīq* 1149.

86 Ibn Ṭawq, *Taʿlīq* 1297; Ibn Ṭūlūn, *Mufākahat al-khillān* 235. For the Ḥawrān as a source of grain, see e.g. Ibn Ṭawq, *Taʿlīq* 88.

to have been sporadic.[87] This is also presumably why, in contrast to Cairo, no grain riots are recorded in Damascus for this period.[88] It is only in the last years of the Mamluk regime, when political menace became immediate, that one observes a considerable rise in grain prices.

In the 15 years between 885/1480 and 900/1495 the price of mutton (*laḥm*) remained stable, around 4 dirhams per *raṭl*, which would indicate that, by and large, demand was fixed, most likely because it was limited to only certain (i.e., elite) groups in the population. The rest, those who could afford meat, at least occasionally, had to satisfy themselves with beef. Surely, there were exceptions, such as on ʿĪd al-Aḍḥā of 890/1485, when the mutton price per *raṭl* reached 10 dirhams. Ibn Ṭawq, who bought "boneless meat" for 30 dirhams, and thus could be an example of someone buying meat just on a holiday, notes that he failed to recall such a high price. From his notes about fixed prices, forced sale (*ṭarḥ*), and attempts to bribe the viceroy in order to reduce prices, we may conclude that the meat market was regulated.[89]

Although normally subject to price regulation through the mechanism of forced sale, and perhaps undergoing a decline in production, sugar is mentioned by our notary only once.[90] In Rabīʿ II 886/June 1481, 1 *raṭl* fetched a market price of 14 dirhams. Employing the measure of *ṭarḥ*, the *ustādār* doubled the price of sugar coming from the "valleys" (*aghwār*) to 28–30 dirhams and punished disobedient dealers. This generated resentment and, as a result, the viceroy fixed the price at 22 dirhams, with which the *shaykh al-Islām* was still dissatisfied. In letters he dispatched to some leading scholars and officials

87 Ibn Ṭūlūn, *Mufākahat al-khillān* 57. For the notorious *ṭarḥ* imposed by the market inspector on two millers and a grain dealer, see Ibn Ṭawq, *Taʿlīq* 598; al-Buṣrawī, *Tārīkh* 110. For other cases, which appear to be of marginal importance, see Ibn Ṭawq, *Taʿlīq* 1189, 1806, 1808. For a general statement about price control in the late 1490s, see Ibn Ṭūlūn, *Iʿlām* 99. For Cairo see Elbendary, *Crowds* 147–149.

88 In a single case, when the sultan imposed tax (*maks*) to be paid to wheat dealers, the angry mob caught his messenger and murdered him. See Ibn Ṭawq, *Taʿlīq* 781 (not entirely clear); Ibn al-Ḥimṣī, *Ḥawādith* i, 310; Ibn Ṭūlūn, *Mufākahat al-khillān* 81. In Cairo, there appears to have been some correlation between a price increase and grain riots in the second half of the fifteenth century. See Shoshan, Grain riots, esp. 473–478.

89 Ibn Ṭawq, *Taʿlīq* 157, 262, 547, 548, 929, 1007, 1098, 1118, 1164, 1201, 1201–1202, 1711, 1802. For other examples of scarcity, see 27, 287, 332, 432, 495, 689, 747, 1007, 1101, 1260, 1326, 1462, 1466, 1688, 1694, 1697, 1711, 1771, 1773, 1779, 1895. For regulation, see Ibn Ṭūlūn, *Iʿlām* 98, 188. The *raṭl* equalled 1.85 kg. See Ashtor, *Histoire des prix* 247. The term used for beef is *baqar*. See e.g. Ibn Ṭawq, *Taʿlīq* 1694.

90 For scattered data on sugar in Syria and on the Mamluk sugar industry in general, see Ashtor, Levantine sugar industry. For sugar plantations in the Jordanian Ghūr in the fourteenth century and their possible disappearance thereafter, see Walker, *Jordan* 200–201, 229–231.

in Cairo, he demanded their intervention to influence the sultan to fix a lower price. It proved successful, and the ruler ordered a price only 3 dirhams above the market level, that is, 17 dirhams, including all extra expenses. A session at the viceroy's ended in fixing the price even lower, at 16 dirhams.[91] Is the only reference to sugar an indication that by and large there was no problem? Given Ibn Ṭawq's systematic information on such matters, one is tempted to answer in the affirmative. Be that as it may, this case shows the vectors that might at times operate in the food market.

Damascus consisted of many quarters, of which a few are known by name, each having a leader (*shaykh*) and a "chief of police" (*walī*), the latter normally appointed by the authorities.[92] Although our information on the composition of the quarters is extremely meager, the scholarly assumption about the ethnic or religious homogeneity of quarters in Islamic towns in general appears to apply to Damascus in the late Mamluk era.[93] The quarters come up in Ibn Ṭawq's diary, especially in the context of their opposition to the authorities and their conflicts with one another, thus questioning the unity of Damascus as a city on the one hand, but suggesting the existence of a quarter identity and of shared interests on a narrow basis on the other hand. The picture emerging is of a disintegrating "city"—if there ever had been one in the accepted sense—that at the end of the fifteenth century was engulfed by inner conflicts.

Ṣāliḥiyya, the quarter located about 2 kilometers northwest of the old city wall and established by Ḥanbalī immigrants some 300 years before Ibn Ṭawq's time,[94] was notorious not only for its many homicide cases but also for being an enclave of opposition to the government, especially to the appointed *walīs*.[95] In one instance, when a lady fell from the second floor under dubious circumstances, and her corpse was dumped somewhere in the quarter, the *walī* arrested the dead lady's son, as well as the man who was seen carrying the corpse. The arrest enraged the inhabitants, who planned to murder the offi-

91 Ibn Ṭawq, *Taʿlīq* 62, 63, 66, 70–71, 74, 75, 80; Ibn Ṭūlūn, *Mufākahat al-khillān* 38, 40; Elbendary, *Crowds* 127.

92 For *kabīr al-ḥāra*, see Ibn Ṭawq, *Taʿlīq* 626, 1537. For *shaykh*, see 1181, 1737. For *ʿurafāʾ*, see Ibn Ṭūlūn, *Mufākahat al-khillān* 76; Ibn Ṭūlūn, *Iʿlām* 100. For *walīs* of several quarters, see e.g. Ibn Ṭawq, *Taʿlīq* 726, 1207, 1215, 1497. For names of quarters and discussion of terminology, see Miura, *Dynamism* 83–86.

93 For a summary of this assumption, see Luz, *Mamluk city* 85–89.

94 For this quarter, see Miura, Urban society 132, now superseded in *Dynamism* 50–110.

95 E.g. Ibn Ṭawq, *Taʿlīq* 713, 823, 1265, 1508; and see Chapter 5 below.

cial and set fire to his home.[96] In 896/1491 the viceroy allowed the residents of the quarter to choose a *walī*, but later a black eunuch was appointed and was blamed for extorting money to satisfy his superiors. When one of his assistants was murdered, a collective fine (for which see Chapter 5) of 500 dinars was imposed. A couple of years later, Bashīr "the evil," the "head of the quarter," was murdered and his corpse burnt. After another leader was murdered, the authorities demanded 10,000 dinars, or that the perpetrators be surrendered, or else the quarter would be destroyed and its residents massacred. This was a serious threat to many of the high-level residents, who were caught between the governor and the quarter's gangsters. Apparently, the affair was resolved by the *shaykh al-Islām*'s intervention, as well as with the capture of the perpetrators. Three months later, a man known as Jāmūs and his gang killed two of the *walī*'s men. The Ṣāliḥiyya people protested against taxes and clashed with the authorities on other economic issues.[97]

Also other quarters had their share of problems with the authorities. Al-Fawwāz, the shaykh of the al-Ḥāritha Quarter, referred to as "the rebel" and a *khārijī*, was reported drunk at the beginning of 891/1486 at his friend's residence and was executed on the same day. The severe punishment was explained by his long-time misconduct. His corpse remained on the gallows for five days, till one ʿAlī al-Daqāq, allegedly following the Prophet's order, requested its removal. After negotiating with the authorities and paying 5 ashrafīs, he took the corpse and buried it in the presence of no less than 400 residents, apparently admirers of the victim. The amazing epilogue to this affair is that about a week after al-Fawwāz's burial, women came to his grave for a "visit" (*ziyāra*), and the deceased was proclaimed a "saint" by the "riffraff." The Shaghūr and other quarters also had conflicts with the government.[98]

There were quite a few inter-quarter confrontations, such as between Qubaybāt and Maydān al-Ḥaṣā. Our notary ascribed it to "Jāhilī ideology," allegedly going back to the pre-Islamic conflict in Arabia between the tribes of Qays and

96 Ibn Ṭawq, *Taʿlīq* 279. The Ḥanbalī qadi was asked to intervene, but he declined. It is not reported how the case was resolved.

97 Ibn Ṭawq, *Taʿlīq* 722, 1003, 1007, 1041, 1160, 1166, 1507, 1632, 1633, 1642–1643, 1669, 1671; Ibn al-Ḥimṣī, *Ḥawādith* i, 352; Martel-Thoumian, *Délinquance* 91, 161, 285. The name "Jāmūs" appears common among quarter gangsters. See further this chapter below. The collective fine imposed for murder is discussed in Chapter 5.

98 Ibn Ṭawq, *Taʿlīq* 595, 596, 599, 722. Martel-Thoumian, *Délinquance* 285, 304, and Wollina, *Zwanzig* 178, bring this case briefly in different contexts. For conflict with the *dawādār* and causing damage to a bridge, see Ibn Ṭawq, *Taʿlīq* 488. For killing a *walī*'s slave, see 1549. For Qubaybāt clashing with black (infantry) troops (*ʿabīd*), see 1537.

Yaman.[99] The "Peace of Ḥudaybiyya," famously concluded between the Prophet and the Meccan pagans, is invoked in an agreement achieved in 890/1485, apparently as a metaphor for its shaky foundation.[100] The recurrent mention of the village of Dāriya in inter-quarter conflicts attests to the bonds between certain quarters and neighboring villages. In one instance, about 200 horse riders of that village are reported attacking the Qubaybāt Quarter at night, and there were deaths on both sides. In that case also the Shāghūrīs, who had a strained relationship with the Qubaybāt inhabitants, were ready to intervene. Further information on conflicts between quarters abounds.[101]

Ibn Ṭawq and Ibn Ṭūlūn imply that the fact that in each quarter were active gangs, which are referred to as *zuʿr*, added to the tension, as these not only took part in the inter-quarter conflicts but also inflamed them.[102] The *zuʿr* are an intriguing phenomenon in the Mamluk urban scene, and historians have tried to decipher their social significance. Lapidus describes them as "bands of young men," "young toughs," "paramilitary youth gangs," and successors of the Syrian militias (*aḥdāth*) that had been active in earlier periods. He further maintains that some *zuʿr* were shopkeepers, that they probably were bachelors, that their hairstyle was distinctive (*qarʿanī*), and that they wore a uniform. Lapidus further discusses their recruitment and inner fights. As he sees it, they struggled for the benefit of the city residents, and were both *lumpenproletariat* and representatives of the community in, inter alia, acting against taxation.[103] According to Petry the *zuʿr* were disciplined militias with well-defined chains of command who fought other militias and the city governor.[104]

Against a somewhat romanticized view, a reexamination of the available data, especially of Ibn Ṭawq's numerous references, depicts the *zuʿr* as more of the criminal type and outlaws who were an element in the general scene of

---

99 For this conflict in the Syrian context, see Lapidus, *Muslim cities* 88.

100 Ibn Ṭawq, *Taʿlīq* 23, 462, 488, 491 (the text is somewhat unclear, and some words are missing). See al-Ḥudaybiya, *EI*².

101 Ibn Ṭawq, *Taʿlīq* 489, 1514, 1555–1556, 1560, 1561, 1562, 1567, 1568–1569, 1569. See further 503, 504, 520, 1507, 1508, 1513, 1533, 1535, 1536, 1540, 1554; Martel-Thoumian, *Délinquance* 55, 134.

102 For *zuʿr* as the plural form of *azʿar* and for derived verb, see e.g. Ibn Ṭawq, *Taʿlīq* 202, 1282, 1515, 1567–1568, 1623, 1906; Ibn Ṭūlūn, *Mufākahat al-khillān* 79, 93, 147, 178, 182. For *ahl al-zaʿāra* (? "people of malice"), see Ibn Ṭūlūn, *Mufākahat al-khillān* 138, 164. For further explanation of the term and for their participation in inter-quarter conflicts, see Miura, *Dynamism* 156, 160–161.

103 Lapidus, *Muslim cities* 42, 88, 143, 154–162, 175 (he transcribes the term as *zuʿar*). See also Aḥdāth, *EI*² and *EI*³.

104 E.g. Petry, *Criminal underworld* 28, translates occasionally as "mob," which is misleading. See also Miura, Structure, esp. 417–424.

crime (to be discussed in Chapter 5), a symptom of a city gradually getting out of control in the twilight of the Mamluk era. Arguably, our sources, members of the petite bourgeoisie and of the scholarly circles, could be assumed to be biased against the low-life *zuʿr*. However, in the absence of any set of alternative data, there is nothing that could support a different picture, and one must be wary of reading into the available information some "socialist" ideology of the Robin Hood type. Perhaps in this case the *zuʿr* were simply as reported—a criminal urban element exploiting an increasing political vacuum to their benefit.[105]

Ibn Ṭawq and Ibn Ṭūlūn report abundantly about the criminal activity of the *zuʿr*. Our notary states that the term applied to "rebels" or "youngsters" (*maradat al-nās*) and devotes a whole paragraph to "the so-called *zuʿr* … whose number has increased and their evil grown." Ibn Ṭūlūn refers to them occasionally as "criminals."[106] We learn about quite a few acts of murder perpetrated by the *zuʿr*. A certain group identified as "the sons of al-Ḥamrāwī" murdered a few people and terrorized merchants, with hardly anyone daring to oppose them. ʿAbd al-Salām, one of the al-Ḥamrāwīs, killed a Christian for dealing in wine. Ironically, together with the "Hashish's son" (we shall come back to their nomenclature), he was himself involved in the sale of wine. At the end of 902/1497, *zuʿr* of Ḥārat al-Mazābil stole money and property, and one of the viceroy's bodyguards (*khāṣṣakī*) executed two of them. One night *zuʿr* attacked the dark-skinned Ibn al-Zuhūrī and stabbed him, and his corpse remained in the street till the next afternoon. Further instances of murder[107] and taxing the commoners are reported.[108]

Noteworthy were the *zuʿr* of the Shāghūr Quarter. In 887/1482 Jāmus ("Buffalo") was murdered; Ibn Ṭawq does not conceal his satisfaction and implies that this gangster deserved it, for he had killed many people and had pillaged homes. His murder "passed without any uproar (*wa lam yantaṭiḥ fīhā ʿanzān*)."[109] As to the name Jāmus, it indicates the existence of a special "zoo-

105 For the decline, see also Lapidus, *Muslim cities* 155. Petry duly discusses them in his book on crime. My assessment is similar to that in Miura, *Dynamism* 157–158, 165.

106 Ibn Ṭawq, *Taʿlīq* 1910; Martel-Thoumian, *Délinquance* 40–41. For *mujrimūn*, see Ibn Ṭūlūn, *Mufākahat al-khillān* 218. See also Lapidus, *Muslim cities* 154.

107 Ibn Ṭūlūn, *Mufākahat al-khillān* 93, 166, 193–194, 232; Ibn Ṭawq, *Taʿlīq* 1437, 1491 (Martel-Thoumian, *Délinquance* 30, 193), 1511, 1512, 1516, 1536 (referred to as *shuṭṭār*), 1567, 1626, 1658.

108 Ibn Ṭawq, *Taʿlīq* 1515; Ibn Ṭūlūn, *Mufākahat al-khillān* 292–293, 314, 316; Miura, *Dynamism* 161.

109 Ibn Ṭawq, *Taʿlīq* 202, 1370, 1373.

logical" gangster nomenclature, to which one can add "water dog" (*kalb al-māʾ*). Another leader of the Shāghūrī *zuʿr*, Abū Ṭāqiya ("the hat owner"), took hold of private property and left the government helpless.

Some of the *zuʿr*'s activity was directed against the authorities and their agents. In Ṣafar 890/February 1485 the viceroy sent troops to the Shāghūr Quarter against the "villain (*fussāq*) *zuʿr*." Sayūr (also written Sayyūr), another gangster, originally of the Maghrib, was involved in several cases of theft and murder. His comrade ʿAlī b. Bulghān was murdered, apparently by someone sent by the governor, and the victim's brother retaliated by killing the quarter's *walī*. Ibn Ṭūlūn adds that, in the chaos that followed, a woman, who was about to be married, fled with her trousseau to her sister and, upon arriving, collapsed dead. In another incident, *zuʿr* of the same quarter confronted some dark-skinned (*ʿabīd*) infantry in the service of the governor, and a couple of days later, for obscure reasons, murdered a notary's son and left his corpse in a nearby valley. Sayyid Quraysh (or ʿArīsh), another gangster of this quarter, was arrested, but his comrades were able to release him, and he gained a lease of life for a few more months before being captured again and executed. Also the *zuʿr* of the Ṣāliḥiyya Quarter appear to have been active. A gang known as "al-Dhahabī's Sons" attacked the governor's dark-skinned troops and killed the quarter's *walī*. One of the gang members was then killed and, a year later, another executed. The brothers Banū ʿAṭā, originally of Nāblus, murdered a *walī* and another official; eventually, they were executed by the governor of Ḥamā.[110] At one point, in 902/1497, some scholars even instigated the *zuʿr* to get rid of hateful officials and offered a prize for that. There were many fatalities in the Ṣāliḥiyya Quarter as a result. Ibn Mibrad, a leading Ḥanbalī scholar and resident of that quarter, wrote afterward that the *zuʿr* must not be encouraged.

His objection to their activity reflects the ambivalent attitude shared by many people. It was not only the scholars who were divided in their opinion about them; given the problems in the city, there was a need to placate them by different means and curb their criminal activity. As in the case of local strongmen discussed earlier in this chapter, the governor and his officials were ready to conclude a temporary truce with the gangs, and both sides must have benefited from that. The *zuʿr* could even be recruited to a *walī*'s

---

110 Ibn Ṭawq, *Taʿlīq* 283, 295, 441, 1091, 1146, 1150, 1176, 1210, 1217, 1281, 1300, 1376, 1478, 1500, 1541, 1564–1565, 1578, 1616, 1623, 1631, 1710, 1731, 1759, 1774, 1824, 1894, 1912; Ibn Ṭūlūn, *Mufākahat al-khillān* 127, 144, 145 (implies indecent behavior on the part of the victim), 148 (citing Ibn Mibrad), 165–166, 178, 182–183, 199, 200, 209, 258–259; Martel-Thoumian, *Délinquance* 117, 137 ("voleurs"), 271–272.

entourage or to the service of a Mamluk officer. Occasionally, they joined the local leadership in welcoming a newly appointed viceroy or were guests at receptions for an Ottoman envoy.[111]

Toward the end of the fifteenth century, Sufis appear to have played a significant role in the public sphere. By that time, they had been able to establish many institutions and had become an essential part of the religious scene in Damascus.[112] Some Sufi shaykhs were especially active. Qāsim al-Jayshī (d. 874/1469), the author of a guide for Sufis, resided in the *zāwiya* of the Dāʾūdiyya[113] at Mt. Qāsyūn, which had been constructed in the first half of the fifteenth century as a large complex with a variety of services.[114] Shaykh Ḥasan (d. 886/1481) resided with his Jamāʿat al-ʿAddās ("ʿAddās Group") at al-Qaṣab Mosque. Saʿd al-Ḥawrānī (d. 895/1490), who was known for his blessing (*mubārak*), was affiliated with these Sufis.[115] Aḥmad b. Shāh (d. 888/1483), known as *al-ʿajamī* probably for his Iranian origin, was the leader of the Ṣawābiyya, who most likely derived their name from a certain shrine. Every Wednesday night he conducted a special session (*waqt*) to which arrived throngs of followers. He was widely respected, and qadis attended his funeral.[116] Regular *mawlid* sessions to celebrate the Prophet's birthday took place at the *zāwiya* of shaykh Ibrāhīm al-Iqbāʿī, to which also scholars arrived. Poetry by Ibn al-Fāriḍ, the prominent Sufi poet, was recited on these occasions, and a woolen robe was bestowed on the group's leading shaykh.[117] *Mawlid* celebrations also took place at the *zāwiya* of Shaykh Faraj, in the course of which traditions on the Prophet's ascent to

111 Ibn Ṭawq, *Taʿlīq* 713, 1592, 1894; Ibn Ṭūlūn, *Mufākahat al-khillān* 205, 211; Ibn Ṭūlūn, *Iʿlām* 127; Miura, Urban society 171; Miura, *Dynamism* 159–160. For Ibn Mibrad's opinion, see Miura, *Dynamism* 164–165.

112 For Sufis in Damascus in the early Mamluk era, see the detailed discussion in Pouzet, *Damas* 208–243. See also Geoffroy, *Soufisme*, esp. 216–239; Ephrat and Mahamid, Creation.

113 For the *zāwiya* in general and how it differed from other Sufi institutions, see Geoffroy, *Soufisme* 167–175.

114 Ibn al-Ḥimṣī, *Ḥawādith* i, 189–190. It was named after Abū Bakr b. Dāʾūd (d. 806/1403) and was established by his son. For its construction, see Ibn Ṭūlūn, *al-Qalāʾd* i, 300; al-Nuʿaymī, *al-Dāris* ii, 158; Miura, Urban society 157; Geoffroy, *Soufisme* 22–26, 94–95, 156, 169, 174, 226–227.

115 Ibn Ṭawq, *Taʿlīq* 105, 945.

116 Ibn al-Ḥimṣī, *Ḥawādith* i, 281–282; Ibn Ṭūlūn, *Mufākahat al-khillān* 52. For the *turba*, see al-Nuʿaymī, *al-Dāris* ii, 197–198. For *waqt*, see Geoffroy, *Soufisme* 408.

117 Ibn Ṭawq, *Taʿlīq* 346, 455. See on them Ibn Ṭawq, *Taʿlīq* 36 n. 3. The Iqbāʿīs were possibly a group of Sufis whose craftsmanship was producing hats. For *mawlid* in Syria and elsewhere, see Geoffroy, *Soufisme* 105–107. For Ibn al-Fāriḍ's prestige and the controversy about him in the late Mamluk period, see Geoffroy, *Soufisme* 439–443.

Heaven (*miʿrāj*) were at the center of recitation. Among those attending was the *shaykh al-Islām*.[118] Further information on Sufi shaykhs and their circles abounds.[119]

One may note in this context that, by the fifteenth century, the gulf between mainstream scholars and Sufis, previously seldom bridgeable, had narrowed. The foremost call for reconciliation between the two camps was voiced by Zakariyyāʾ al-Anṣārī (d. 926/1520), the leading Shāfiʿī of his generation, who is known, among other things, for his fatwa in which he accepted the sincerity of Sufi exclamations during their sessions.[120] Also a few Damascus scholars may be noted for providing examples of rapprochement with the Sufis. Abū l-Fatḥ al-Mizzī (d. 906/1501) is described as both a scholar and a Sufi.[121] The Shāfiʿī qadi Quṭb al-Dīn al-Khayḍarī (d. 894/1488) arranged for the maintenance of Sufis.[122] The wedding of Shaykh Mubārak was attended by qadis.[123] The funeral of ʿAlī b. al-Sumaykātiya (d. 873/1468), the *ṣāḥib al-karāmāt*, was attended by the viceroy, qadis, and scholars. His benevolence was such that Ibn al-Ḥimṣī "did not have enough space to relate." Incidentally, as if to add to his exceptional gifts, the gravedigger (*ḥaffār*) reported that ʿAlī had been able to predict exactly the day of his death a couple of days before it actually happened.[124]

Of Sufi activity in the period under consideration, one may refer to their occasional initiatives to confront the local government. Sufis became the leaders of popular opposition. One, the "blessed" and miracle performer Yūsuf al-Bahlūl (d. 906/1500), of Maydān al-Ḥaṣā, instigated worshippers at the Umayyad Mosque against the policy of confiscation. He was soon supported by other Sufis and commoners, and the resulting small-scale riot led to some deaths and injuries. In another instance, in Ṣafar 899/November 1493, there was a *fitna*

118 Ibn Ṭawq, *Taʿlīq* 1167, 1240.

119 al-Buṣrawī heard from a real-estate agent a dream in which he saw Taqī al-Dīn al-Ḥiṣnī (d. 829/1426) standing on Jabal Qāsyūn, a torch in his hand, lighting up all of Damascus. See al-Buṣrawī, *Tārīkh* 79. See on him Geoffroy, *Soufisme* 216–217, 447–448. Shihāb al-Dīn b. ʿAjlān, who had been appointed by the sultan as *naqīb al-ashrāf*, is mentioned some years later as the shaykh of the Rifāʿiyya, one of the most prominent orders. It seems that Ibn Ṭawq met him one night at the residence of another Sufi, wherefrom, together with some friends, he went to the Arslān Mosque and attended a special session (*waqt*). See al-Buṣrawī, *Tārīkh* 142, 153, 161, 1116. For this Sufi order, see Aḥmad al-Rifāʿī, *EI*[2]; al-Rifāʿiyya, *EI*[2]. For this order in Syria in the early Mamluk period, see briefly Geoffroy, *Soufisme* 223–224.

120 See al-Anṣārī, Zakariyyāʾ, *EI*[3]; Geoffroy, *Soufisme* 149–152.

121 Ibn Ṭūlūn, *al-Muʿizza* 67–71. The author was his disciple. See also Geoffroy, *Soufisme* 201.

122 Badrān, *Munādama* 8–9. For his biography, see Ibn Ṭūlūn, *Quḍāt Dimashq* 177–179.

123 Ibn Ṭawq, *Taʿlīq* 1190; Wollina, *Zwanzig* 71.

124 Ibn al-Ḥimṣī, *Ḥawādith* i, 227.

between Sufis and the *dawādār al-sulṭān* after the arrest of men from the Abū ʿUmar madrasa in the Ṣāliḥiyya Quarter. In retaliation, the Sufis besieged the Umayyad Mosque.[125]

Sufis were active in their efforts to remove immorality from the public sphere. Hashish was one major target. Aḥmad al-ʿAddās (d. 865/1461), who was known for his assaults on all kinds of reprehensible conduct, led a campaign against a building infamous for "immoral affairs," to curb there the consumption of hashish and turn it into a mosque. One incident involving his followers 20 years after his death is provided in some detail: a man passed by the *zāwiya* of the ʿAddāsīs, carrying food which was said to contain hashish. The Sufis forced him to declare that it was not for sale. The man went to the citadel to complain, and the shaykh of the *zāwiya* was arrested, and even the *shaykh al-Islām's* intercession on his behalf was to no avail. However, on the next day a crowd pressured for the release of the Sufi, and the threat of violence proved effective. In another incident, a Mamluk official was spotted by Sufis with hashish in his sleeve; he was suspected of trading in it, and the material was burned.[126] There are further references to acts against the sale and consumption of hashish.[127]

But Sufi activity was directed primarily against the production of and trade in wine by Mamluks and Christians.[128] This set the Sufis and the Mamluks on a collision course, since quite a few Mamluk officers operated wine presses (*khammāra*). According to al-Buṣrawī there were no less than 100 of these in the city.[129] Confrontations between Sufis and Mamluk soldiers, who accompanied wine dealers to protect them, could become quite violent.[130] Also Christians and Jews were confronted. One "European" who was caught drunk was led to the Sufi Faraj and converted, and then underwent circumcision.[131] A Jew was detained for wine found in his possession and brought before Taqī al-Dīn. He

---

125 Ibn Ṭawq, *Taʿlīq* 951, 1884; Ibn Ṭūlūn, *Mufākahat al-khillān* 104–105, has a somewhat different version; Martel-Thoumian, *Délinquance* 161. For the treatment of this incident and a comparison between the two Damascus sources, see Elbendary, *Crowds* 130. For the *fitna*, see Ibn al-Ḥimṣī, *Ḥawādith* i, 345–346. For this madrasa, also known as the ʿUmariyya and named after Abū ʿUmar, the alleged founder of the Ṣāliḥiyya Quarter, see Miura, Urban society 135–136, 156–160, 172; Miura, *Dynamism*.

126 Ibn al-Ḥimṣī, *Ḥawādith* i, 153–154; Ibn Ṭūlūn, *Mufākahat al-khillān* 12, 14.

127 Ibn Ṭawq, *Taʿlīq* 275, 431, 1039, 1141, 1197. See also Geoffroy, *Soufisme* 185–187; Stilt, *Islamic law* 95–97.

128 For the early Mamluk period, see briefly Lapidus, *Muslim cities* 106.

129 al-Buṣrawī, *Tārīkh* 205.

130 Ibn Ṭawq, *Taʿlīq* 236–237, 459.

131 Ibn Ṭawq, *Taʿlīq* 487.

was then taken to Shaykh Faraj and flogged, after which he testified that the wine, unsurprisingly, belonged to an official in the viceroy's service.[132]

Shaykh Mubārak "the Ethiopian," and member of the al-ʿAddās circle, emerges as the most militant Sufi in the campaign against wine during the couple of years between 897/1492 and 899/1494, whereby he was involved in more than a dozen attacks on wine consumers. In Rabīʿ II 898/January–February 1493, his removal of two wine presses led to a confrontation with some mamluks, after which Mubārak's associates were arrested. About a year later, his continuous activity provoked the authorities and brought about his downfall. Our sources relate it in detail. On Friday, 2 Ramaḍān 899/6 June 1494, the *dawādār* detained Mubārak and two of his associates and sent them to the viceroy, who ordered their flogging, before parading them on their way to prison. Following intercession by Taqī al-Dīn and the Shāfiʿī qadi, Mubārak was released. According to one version, no less than 2,000 people gathered to celebrate his release. However, his companions remained incarcerated, and on the next day Mubārak was joined by the "riffraff," and all went to release them, in the course of which other prisoners broke out of prison. The governor sent soldiers, who indiscriminately killed about 60 (100, and even 150, in other versions); it is claimed that these were mostly spectators who had nothing to do with the affair. The governor also ordered a raid on Mubārak's complex in the village of Lower Qābūn. Furthermore, mamluks tried, unsuccessfully, to break into Taqī al-Dīn's nearby residence for his contact with the Sufi. They also shot arrows into the Shāfiʿī qadi's residence, where Mubārak was suspected of sheltering. However, the Sufi disappeared, and the rumor spread that he was conscripting bedouins and peasants to continue his struggle. Those rumors turned out to be false, and later he was seen escaping southward, met by shaykhs in Palestine, who provided him with supplies and urged him to address the sultan. About a week later Mubārak was seen in Gaza, and finally he arrived in Cairo. There, he was able to receive an audience with the sultan and convince him of the injustice done to him. The ruler instructed his viceroy in Damascus to return to Mubārak his confiscated property.

Mubārak stayed at al-Azhar, where he was respected. At some point he returned to Damascus but now remained there, inactive. Furthermore, his presence in the Lower Qābūn, once his stronghold, became a nuisance to its inhab-

---

132 Ibn Ṭawq, *Taʿlīq* 96–97. Upon his release he complained to the viceroy about the official who had detained him and who, so he claimed, also had pressured him to divulge things about Shamla the Jew (for which case see Chapter 5). The *shaykh al-Islām* was involved in this case (however, the text is not entirely clear). See also Martel-Thoumian, *Délinquance* 289 (only part of the text is discussed).

itants, who appear to have suffered enough. In fact, a couple of years after the tumult of 899/1894, we still learn of one of Mubārak's men who killed someone, was captured by the victim's son, and sentenced to death. When it came to his execution, as in a good story, the gallows broke down. At the beginning of 903/1497 the anxious residents of Qābūn demanded that Mubārak move out, and one of them even planned to destroy his *zāwiya*. He died many years later, in 944/1537, by then perhaps largely forgotten. The only information about him is that in the last stage he was affiliated with the Dā'ūdiyya Sufis.[133]

To sum up, this chapter has presented the contours of Damascus in the last decades of the fifteenth century as they feature mainly in Ibn Ṭawq's diary. The emerging picture is that life was difficult for "ordinary people," but also that the bourgeoisie paid their price, both financially and otherwise. The decimation of thousands of the city's inhabitants over the years by plague outbreaks was coupled with the atrocities of Mamluk viceroys and quite a few of their officers and officials, who were temporarily stationed in the city and bereft of genuine concern for local affairs. Any of their alliances with the people was short-term and was motivated by limited concerns. The burden of their taxes and arbitrary acts, the confrontation among their own ranks, the Ottoman threat, bedouin invasions, and the fear imposed by the town gangs, all these and more cast their shadow over Damascus at the end of the fifteenth century and created a situation of crisis. Two elements especially stepped into the vacuum, the *zu'r* and the Sufis. Although to some extent representing the people's needs, they largely had their own agendas and acted accordingly.

---

133 Ibn Ṭawq, *Ta'līq* 1112, 1114, 1115, 1129, 1141, 1146, 1157, 1160, 1167, 1173–1174, 1179, 1198, 1235, 1265, 1272, 1273, 1280, 1282, 1287–1290, 1291, 1292, 1294, 1296, 1299, 1461, 1513, 1531; Ibn al-Ḥimṣī, *Ḥawādith* i, 357–359, 360–361 (the additional details that he provides about Mubārak in Cairo may derive from information he received during his stay in the Egyptian city at the time; see the Introduction to this book); Ibn Ṭūlūn, *Mufākahat al-khillān* 130; Ibn Ṭūlūn, *Ḥawādith* 307, 308; Ibn Ṭūlūn, *al-Qalā'id* i, 301; Wollina, *Zwanzig* 180–182.

CHAPTER 3

The *Shaykh al-Islām*: A Giant in an Embattled World of Scholars

Since the reign of Nūr al-Dīn in the twelfth century, the Shāfiʿī school had been the predominant school of law (*madhhab*) among the Sunnīs of Damascus. Under the Mamluks, Ḥanafī scholars tried to change the situation; especially active in that was Najm al-Dīn al-Ṭarsūsī (d. 758/1357). His *Kitāb tuḥfat al-turk fī mā yajib ʿan yuʿmal fī l-mulk* was a compendium of advice to the ruler in a genre enjoying a long tradition in the Islamic world. What was special about it was the author's polemics against the three other legal schools, the Shāfiʿī school in particular, and the focus on Ḥanafī opinions as regards a whole range of issues, from waging Holy War (*jihād*) to the support of orphans. Al-Ṭarsūsī stressed the merits of his *madhhab* and by that urged the Mamluk regime to prefer Ḥanafīs in the legal-bureaucratic apparatus.[1] To what extent he succeeded in the long run remains an open question. As to the Ḥanbalīs, although in the course of the Mamluk era there emerged among them some intellectual giants such as Ibn Qudāma, Ibn Qayyim al-Jawziyya, and, above all, Ibn Taymiyya, this school occupied a marginal place in Mamluk Damascus. Still, one should not underestimate its occasional role.[2] Even more marginal was the Mālikī school, its bastion being in the Maghrib; Mālikīs active in late fifteenth-century Damascus were mostly immigrants from that region.[3] In late fifteenth-century Damascus, but certainly not only there, affiliation to different schools cut across even one and the same family. This was the case of the prominent Shāfiʿī family of Ibn Qāḍī ʿAjlūn. In another leading family of the same school, the Ibn Farfūr, Shihāb al-Dīn was the Shāfiʿī qadi, while his nephew, Badr al-Dīn Muḥammad, occupied the Ḥanafī *qaḍāʾ*.[4]

Some general observations about the relationship between the Damascus circles of scholars (*ʿulamāʾ*) and the civilian and religiously trained bureau-

1 Guellil, *Damaszener Akten*. For al-Ṭarsūsī and his book, see Winter, Inter-madhhab competition.

2 Thus, when appointing a Ḥanbalī qadi in 732/1332, it was proclaimed that he was the only one who could authorize specific kinds of transactions. See Rapoport, Royal justice 77–78, 81.

3 For the history of the legal schools in Damascus till the early Mamluk era, see Pouzet, *Damas* 24–105.

4 Ibn Ṭūlūn, *Quḍāt Dimashq* 227. For another member of the family, Bahāʾ al-Dīn Muḥammad, see Ibn Ṭawq, *Taʿlīq* 377. On this family, see also Miura, Urban society 161–164.

 | DOI:10.1163/9789004413269_005

crats, on the one hand, and the Mamluk regime in Cairo and Damascus on the other hand, are pertinent. Generally, as already pointed out in Chapter 2, civilian officeholders depended on the regime in a number of ways. To begin with, the appointment of qadis of all four *madhhab*s and to bureaucratic offices was decided by the sultan in Cairo, the viceroy in Damascus, or other high-ranking Mamluks. In the second half of the fifteenth century the number of qadis who came in succession was more than half a dozen for each of the four schools. At times they were forced to alternate and thus played one against another in a matter of a couple of years or even less. This generated rivalry (*khaṣāma*) between contenders to one and the same office.[5] Also the routine of "purchasing" offices, at times for enormous sums, had a considerable effect on the situation, not only financially but also morally, in that it generated corruption and spread incompetence.[6] Since extremely high sums were occasionally demanded of the contenders, even if these sums are inflated and should not be accepted at face value, one would have to assume that a large investment in offices was worthwhile either politically (i.e., for gaining influence) or economically (for the returns after the initial investment), or both. An example of an exceptionally high sum that should raise doubt is the 30,000 dinars allegedly paid by Shihāb al-Dīn Aḥmad Ibn Farfūr (d. 911/1505), the Shāfiʿī qadi, who held other administrative offices as well. He was appointed after his predecessor had served barely four days; a recommendation that the sultan received on his behalf from the *shaykh al-Islām* was probably of some help. After being appointed and then replaced a few times, toward the end of his life Ibn Farfūr became qadi in Cairo, which was an exception, since the office was reserved for Egyptians.[7] Another qadi, the Ḥanafī Muḥibb al-Dīn b. Qaṣīf, paid 3,000 dinars, but this was not to his credit when replaced a couple of years later. His successor suffered a similar fate and, in addition, was incarcerated for about a year for an alleged debt, and only after his mother went to Cairo to beg for him was he released after paying 7,000 dinars. Also his successor was at some point

5 Ibn Ṭūlūn, *Quḍāt Dimashq* 172–184, 222–239, 258–269, 300–305. For details on the frequent changes in the post of the Ḥanafī and Mālikī qadis in the last decade of the fifteenth century, see al-Nuʿaymī, *al-Dāris* i, 491–498, ii, 16–22.

6 For the "clear predominance" of Damascus with respect to the sale of religious and administrative posts, see Martel-Thoumian, Sale 54. For one example, see Miura, *Dynamism* 143.

7 Ibn Ṭawq, *Taʿlīq* 54; al-Ṣayrafī, *Inbaʾ al-hasr* 514. For his buying offices, see also Ibn Ṭawq, *Taʿlīq* 480. For biographical details, see 49, 73, 126, 379; Anṣārī, *Nuzhat al-khāṭir* ii, 143–146; Miura, Urban society 161–164 (reproduced in Miura, *Dynamism* 138–141). While serving in Cairo, Ibn Farfūr received 100 dinars for approving the appointment of a qadi in Baʿalbek, but this must have been only the tip of the iceberg of his returns. See Ibn Ṭawq, *Taʿlīq* 1514. For further examples, see Ibn Ṭawq, *Taʿlīq* 33, 40, 84, 252, 370, 535, 584, 694, 725, 832, 1086, 1100, 1135, 1713.

summoned to Cairo and was forced to pay a higher sum.[8] The appointment of another Ḥanafī was conditional on paying the debt of an officer, and he was detained in the citadel for no less than nine months.[9] These examples are sufficient in order to demonstrate that the purchase of offices could on occasion generate heavy loss and appears to have been a gamble—one was not guaranteed to stay in office, even after spending much money; added to which, the sums, even if exaggerated by our sources, were not entirely available to the candidates, so they were forced to take loans. Here is the place to point out that, if this was the case, then it indicates that the wealth of the high bourgeoisie and the financial resources it could mobilize for attaining office were considerable. Where these funds came from is difficult to answer, but we shall return to that question in the next chapter.

Established as a system under the late Mamluk sultans, the sale of offices was just one aspect of the control exerted by the regime on the civilian elite. Mamluks of various ranks, from the sultan via his viceroy to lesser officials, were generally in a position to impose their wish and whim and inflict on their civilian subordinates severe punishment. The property of a few qadis was confiscated.[10] Others underwent shaming in public.[11] Thus, the Mālikī qadi left the city in fetters "so that all could see him," and the same was repeated some years later as regards Muḥibb al-Dīn al-Aslamī, the *kātib al-khizāna*. When one preacher was summoned by the sultan "because we long for him," one presumes it to be a sarcastic explanation and that the summons did not bid him well.[12] The Ḥanafī al-Ḥisbānī was incarcerated by a high-ranking emir for two months and was forced to ride dressed and equipped like a mamluk, thus serving as a laughing stock. He was urged to drink wine and, ironically, blemished for his neglect of prayer. What was the reason for that? We do not know.[13]

Turning to the ulema and bureaucrats, as well as various bourgeois and petit bourgeois entrepreneurs, many of them derived their income from waqfs established mostly by the Mamluk elite for the public benefit. Although earlier analysis of the waqf system has emphasized its negative role in the pre-

---

8 Ibn Ṭawq, *Taʿlīq* 28; al-Nuʿaymī, *al-Dāris* i, 495, 496; Ibn Ṭūlūn, *Quḍāt Dimashq* 233–237.

9 Ibn Ṭawq, *Taʿlīq* 890–891; al-Buṣrawī, *Tārīkh* 136; Ibn Ṭūlūn, *Mufākahat al-khillān* 92; al-Nuʿaymī, *al-Dāris* i, 495. For other examples of venality, see Ibn Ṭawq, *Taʿlīq* 30, 56, 82, 83, 110, 195, 312, 370, 414, 636, 664, 720, 725, 823, 1034, 1086, 1088, 1156, 1316, 1387, 1713.

10 E.g. Ibn Ṭawq, *Taʿlīq* 50–51, 1480, 1846, 1877; Ibn al-Ḥimṣī, *Ḥawādith* i, 306; Ibn Ṭūlūn, *Mufākahat al-khillān* 134.

11 E.g. Ibn Ṭawq, *Taʿlīq* 1492; al-Buṣrawī, *Tārīkh* 215.

12 Ibn Ṭawq, *Taʿlīq* 1305, 1317, 1719. For al-Aslamī's career and private life, see Martel-Thoumian, Muḥibb ad-Dīn.

13 Ibn Ṭawq, *Taʿlīq* 845; Martel-Thoumian, *Délinquance* 290.

modern economy, a more balanced view (although we must not lose sight of the adverse results of the widespread waqf system) should consider some of its positive aspects.[14] One such aspect was employment—the administrative apparatus of waqfs was an important source of income for many. In fact, there were those who became quite rich through endowments. This must have been the case of Shams al-Dīn al-Kafrsūsī, who held no less than ten posts financed by waqfs, which at some point went to his brother, and which were valued at a total of 22 ashrafīs (per month?). Another held about half a dozen posts, for one of which, at the Yalbughā Mosque, he received 170 dirhams a month.[15] The Dār al-Tuʿm al-ʿAtīqa, an institution that appears to have supplied victuals and was located opposite the citadel's main gate, was operated in absentia by Zayn al-Dīn al-Ikhnāʾī, the Shāfiʿī qadi in Cairo, through his relative, the Damascus deputy Shāfiʿī Muḥyī al-Dīn al-Ikhnāʾī. It was leased to three brothers, the sons of Jumʿa al-Iqbāʿī. In 890/1485 the rent was as high as 10,000 dirhams, of which one brother paid 1,100 in gold and silver currency and the rest in installments in the following months. Maintenance expenses were the inspector's responsibility. At the end of that year the same brother paid on behalf of his two brothers another 1,200 dirhams. The lease was extended to the end of the year for another 4,500 dirhams, to which a debt of 1,500 dirhams for the first four months was added; the total of 6,000 dirhams was divided into four installments. A few years later, following the death of one brother and the failure of his widow to handle the property, it was leased to two partners for four years, for the price of 8,000 dirhams a year, of which 1,500 dirhams were paid at the beginning of each year and the rest at its end. The two partners were allowed to spend whatever was necessary for the upkeep, knowing, however, that most of the property was dilapidated (*kharāb dāthir*). In Jumādā I 905/December 1499 the property was supervised by al-Ikhnāʾī's son and the notary al-Qudsī.[16]

Also urban property, such as rented houses, warehouses, halls, public baths, inns, bakeries, mills, and more, all supported endowed institutions through their returns. However, from data from the early Ottoman period, we learn that

14 Miura, *Dynamism* 63; Luz, *Mamluk city*, 111–147. For the role of waqfs in supporting educational institutions in Mamluk Syria, see Mahamid, *Waqf* 55–129.

15 Ibn Ṭawq, *Taʿlīq* 832, 1764–1765. For this mosque, see al-Nuʿaymī, *al-Dāris*, index.

16 Ibn Ṭawq, *Taʿlīq* 46, 474, 547 (unclear calculations), 614, 992, 1053, 1789, 1790. For this institution, see al-Nuʿaymī, *al-Dāris* i, 404. For Muḥyī al-Dīn al-Ikhnāʾī, see Ibn Ṭawq, *Taʿlīq* 34 n. 5, 126, 1825. As I understand, it should not be confused with the "new" Dār al-Ṭuʿm, which was endowed in 703/1303. Its location was outside Bāb Tūmā opposite the Zinjiliyya. See Eychenne, Production agricole 602–603.

its share was less than 10 percent compared to land property.[17] One may suggest that investment in land was much cheaper than in urban property.

Ibn Ṭawq provides unique information about a dozen institutions supported by endowments, mostly mosques and madrasas, but also about a few nonreligious ones, some of which were established long before his time.[18] At least some of the beneficiaries must have been ulema. Most important by far was the Umayyad Mosque. Its restoration after the fire of 884/1479 kept it the most generously funded institution in the city, and it sustained many officeholders.[19] Although we lack information on the sources of its funding, we do know of income derived from an orchard that at one point was supervised by the *shaykh al-Islām* and leased to a peasant known as "the Ḥanbalī." The extent of the finances involved in this mosque is indicated by a report drawn up in Rabīʿ I 905/October 1499. According to the waqf's inspector and the board that was convened, after deducting various expenses, no less than 70,000 dirhams (about 1,400 dinars) were distributed among those entitled (*mustaḥiqqūn*), whose number could reach over 100 at any given point. It may not come as a surprise that the viceroy set his sights on this mosque's funds, occasionally examining its financial balance and trying to decrease the number of its affiliated positions. This led to a clash with the religious establishment. In 903/1498, following the siege on the city, the temporary viceroy charged a total of 600 ashrafīs from the mosque's beneficiaries and diverted it to the treasury.[20]

We have details on the funding of only a few madrasas, mostly Shāfiʿī and Ḥanafī.[21] Obviously, Ibn Ṭawq was mainly interested in the Shāfiʿī ones. The Bādirāʾiyya appears to have benefited from a lucrative endowment. At one

17 Miura, *Dynamism* 195; Mahamid, *Waqf* 70–71.

18 Lapidus, *Muslim cities* 198, lists without further explanation details about ten religious institutions presumably established in the period under consideration. Mahamid, Mosques 189, notes that several (medieval) historians estimate that there were 1,000 mosques of different levels by the end of the fifteenth century. Given the size of the city's population, and the possible number of those going to mosques, the figure appears inflated.

19 Ibn al-Ḥimṣī, *Ḥawādith* i, 241–242, 244–245, 249–250, 252, 255, 257, 263, 273, 275, 313. Other sources have only brief reference. See Ibn Ṭawq, *Taʿlīq* 40, 69; al-Buṣrawī, *Tārīkh* 147; Ibn Ṭūlūn, *Mufākahat al-khillān* 56. See further Behrens-Abuseif, Fire.

20 Ibn Ṭawq, *Taʿlīq* 326, 831, 832, 835, 1617, 1630, 1755; ʿIlabī, *Khiṭaṭ* 331–332. For an unclear reference to *muḥākara ʿalā waqf al-Atābik* associated with the "burnt" (*maḥrūq*) al-Qaṣab Mosque, see Ibn Ṭawq, *Taʿlīq* 916. For a special endowment for muezzins, see 742.

21 al-Nuʿaymī's survey lists 152 madrasas. About 85 percent were either Shāfiʿī or Ḥanafī. See Miura, *Dynamism* 21, 25, 34, 39–49. However, how many of these functioned at the end of the fifteenth century is a different question. Hence the conclusion that in Damascus their number was twice or thrice as many as Cairo needs some qualification.

point fields for its benefit were leased for a period of 20 months for 12,000 dirhams (240 dinars); also fixed measures (*ḥiml*) of wheat were assigned to it. As in such transactions, the renter was exempted in the two first months.[22] As to the adjacent Dawlaʿiyya, land for its upkeep was leased by Taqī al-Dīn, most likely in his capacity as its administrator, to four mutually guaranteeing (*mutaḍāmmin*) partners for 8,700 dirhams. In addition, they had to supply 60 *raṭls* of peaches. It was agreed that in case they stood by the agreement, a discount of at least 700 dirhams would be granted.[23] Part of the support for the Rukniyya came from the proceeds of Khān Julbān, which at one point was rented by Kamāl al-Din Ibn Qāḍī ʿAjlūn to two partners for 700 dirhams annually, the Ramadan month considered *gratis* (*muṭlaq*); also wheat had to be supplied. Among the beneficiaries was the notary Abū l-Faḍl al-Qudsī, whose income over the course of three years was 2,160 dirhams (more than 40 dinars). To this madrasa also belonged 11 feddans of cultivated land in Jarūd village. In Rabīʿ II 890/April 1485 one Aḥmad b. ʿAbdallāh vouched to deliver a quantity of 97 *gharāra* of wheat and barley to this institution.[24] Al-Shāmiyya al-Juwāniyya, located near the Nūrī Hospital and established by Saladin's sister, received proceeds from a *khān* which at the beginning of 891/1486 amounted to 6,000 dirhams (about 120 dinars).[25] Details on other madrasas and religious institutions are few and far between.[26] Endowments were plagued by a great

22 Ibn Ṭawq, *Taʿlīq* 745–746. For its location, see 1264.

23 Ibn Ṭawq, *Taʿlīq* 1194. Apparently, a notary was financed by this waqf. See 153. For further details on its finances, see 156.

24 Ibn Ṭawq, *Taʿlīq* 40, 156, 288, 465. The Shāfiʿī Rukniyya was established by Rukn al-Dīn al-Falakī in ca. 620/1223. See al-Nuʿaymī, *al-Dāris* i, 190–199. Two feddans were leased for four years to Kamāl al-Dīn and the Shāfiʿī deputy qadi Burhān al-Dīn b. al-Muʿtamid for the annual sum of 1,200 dirhams, to be paid at the beginning of each year.

25 Ibn Ṭawq, *Taʿlīq* 586, 590. For this madrasa, see al-Nuʿaymī, *al-Dāris* i, 227–236; Mahamid, *Waqf* 71. For the description of its fourteenth-century endowment, see Melcak, Reconstruction. Much more modest financially was the Saqīfa Mosque, which stood outside the St. Thomas Gate. Our notary reports on a waqf document drafted in 881/1476 about its proceeds from land at Barza. Exactly ten years later a small wasteland near the mosque, the exact borders of which are detailed, was leased for 20 years for the small price of 5 dirhams annually. The total rent was paid in advance. See Ibn Ṭawq, *Taʿlīq* 610, 1133, 1264. The rent was "to be counted by number (*ʿadadiya*)," that is, not by the total weight of the coins.

26 A long-term agreement (*ḥikr*) around 890/1485 stipulated financial support by agricultural proceeds to the Ṭāwawusiyya madrasa (or *khanqāh*) in the annual sum of 140 dirhams. See Ibn Ṭawq, *Taʿlīq* 447. For its location, see al-Nuʿaymī, *al-Dāris* ii, 129; al-Shihābī, *Muʿjam Dimashq* ii, 66. For the Āmidiyya, see Ibn Ṭawq, *Taʿlīq* 536. For the ʿImādiyya, near Bāb al-Farādīs, built by Nūr al-Dīn's son, and its financial support in 865/1460–1461, see al-Nuʿaymī, *al-Dāris* i, 312–313. A lucrative "waqf of the Mālikīs," which in 891/1486 was val-

deal of corruption. In one instance, a Ḥanafī qadi, who served in a number of posts, was fined with his aides in the sum of 10,000 dirhams after being accused of embezzlement.[27]

Surely, political weakness and financial dependence created a strong incentive to curry favor with the Mamluk elite and maintain cordial relations with the sultan, the viceroy, and their associates. The notary Shihāb al-Dīn al-Ṣumaydī gifted the viceroy a set of copperware filled with out-of-season fruits. He also composed poetry in praise of the ruler and read it to him, to his utmost satisfaction. The Mamluk was given the written version as a souvenir. In reward he treated al-Ṣumaydī generously and even guided him to his private chamber, where they spent the evening till late, all the time the ruler making al-Ṣumaydī drink wine.[28] In another instance, the Shāfiʿī qadi hosted the viceroy at a madrasa for a whole day.[29]

Being aware of the situation, and perhaps of the balance tilting in their favor, viceroys worked constantly to broaden their sphere of influence and encroach on the scholars' traditional domain. This meant intervening in legal and religious issues that had not been subject to their authority yet had been disputed among scholars and thus created some room for outside infiltration. Another factor working in the viceroys' favor was the frequent lack of shared interest and cohesion among the ulema and the bourgeoisie in general.[30] They were divided on both ideological and personal grounds. The picture painted by our sources, especially by Ibn Ṭawq, contradicts to some extent what has been generally maintained by modern scholars concerning the cohesion enjoyed by the religious establishment, which allowed it to function wisely and negotiate power vis-à-vis the more powerful. As our notary repeatedly reports, the scholars and bureaucrats exposed and perhaps even enhanced their internal conflicts by requesting that the Mamluks intervene or letting them do so.

ued at 10,000 dinars (!) and was at that point disputed, appears to have involved shops (*ḥawānīt*) and land at Qarʿūn village in the Biqāʿ; the *ḥājib* had a protection (*ḥimāya*) agreement. See Ibn Ṭawq, *Taʿlīq* 403, 629, 759–760. Part of the proceeds of endowed land at Dimās, together with similarly endowed land at al-Marj al-Qibli, southeast of the city, belonged to seven different waqf owners and accordingly was identified as "the waqf of the seven." It went to the Ghazāliyya, which was inside the Umayyad Mosque. See Ibn Ṭawq, *Taʿlīq* 1191–1192. See on it al-Nuʿaymī, *al-Dāris* i, 313–323.

27 Ibn Ṭawq, *Taʿlīq* 1617–1618, 1620, 1623, 1630, 1706–1707; al-Buṣrawī, *Tārīkh* 106; Ibn al-Ḥimṣī, *Ḥawādith* i, 304.

28 Ibn Ṭawq, *Taʿlīq* 124.

29 Ibn Ṭawq, *Taʿlīq* 762.

30 See also the statement in Elbendary, *Crowds* 125.

A few examples may be mentioned. A controversy surfaced in 884/1479 in a session convened by Taqī al-Dīn at the Umayyad Mosque, following an unspecified statement made by another prominent Shāfiʿī, Burhān al-Dīn al-Biqāʿī, during his stay in Damascus, whereto he had come from his permanent residence in Cairo, and where he died a year later. It is implied that al-Biqāʿī objected to one of al-Ghazālī's opinions expressed in his famous book *Iḥyāʾ ʿulūm al-dīn* ("The revival of religious sciences"). Taqī al-Dīn ruled that al-Biqāʿī's objection amounted to apostasy (*takfīr*). Perhaps because in this case two of the most distinguished Shāfiʿīs were at odds, and the accusation leveled at one of them was severe, the viceroy got himself involved but then decided to defer the hearing till the qadis of all four schools were present in the city. Al-Buṣrawī, whose intention was to bring further information on this case, left for that a blank space in his manuscript but, unfortunately, failed to return to it.[31]

Further cases may be noted. One viceroy got himself involved in a difference of opinion between the Shāfiʿī qadi (and chronicler) Ibn al-Ḥimṣī and Ḥanafīs as to the legitimacy of some phrases recited by muezzins. According to one version, the Mamluk supported the Ḥanafīs and, according to another, due to Taqī al-Dīn's objection, he convened a session in which a compromise was reached and each of the two schools was entitled to its own decision.[32] A dispute about the legitimacy of a certain statement connected with the *ʿaqīqa*, the ritual of the earliest hair shaving of infants, over whether it ought to be considered a blasphemy, resulted in another instance of a viceroy's involvement and in Taqī al-Dīn's fatwa.[33] The same viceroy approved of the validity of a marriage bond when a question about the woman's divorce from her former husband was raised. The Mamluk ruler convened a session and ordered that witnesses be summoned.[34] Another viceroy banned women from wearing certain clothes and went even further than the Ḥanbalī qadi, who, as one might suspect, was not a libertine on such issues.[35] During one of the regular hearings (*majlis ḥukm*) held by a viceroy, a parcel fell off the roof, and there was a com-

---

31 al-Buṣrawī, *Tārīkh* 87–88. For a few further details, see Geoffroy, *Soufisme* 443–446. Al-Biqāʿī (d. 885/1480) authored the *ʿUnwān al-zamān fī tarājīm al-shuyūkh wa-l-aqrān* and *Iẓhār al-ʿaṣr li-asrār ahl al-ʿaṣr*. See, e.g. the obituary in Ibn al-Ḥimṣī, *Ḥawādith* i, 245–248.

32 Ibn Ṭawq, *Taʿlīq* 1016–1017; al-Buṣrawī, *Tārīkh* 147, clarifies some puzzles. Ibn Ṭūlūn, *Mufākahat al-khillān* 119, who relies on the latter, gives a fuller version. Curiously, the case is not mentioned by Ibn al-Ḥimṣī.

33 Against the opinion of two of his colleagues, the shaykh rejected the ruling of blasphemy. See Ibn Ṭawq, *Taʿlīq* 268. On the ritual, see ʿAqīqa, *EI*³.

34 Ibn Ṭawq, *Taʿlīq* 693, 694, 695.

35 Ibn Ṭawq, *Taʿlīq* 1618.

plaint against the Shāfiʿī deputy qadi; clearly, someone intended it to reach the ruler. Indeed, he sent a warning to the deputy's superior, namely, the qadi.[36] Quite ironical, not to say hypocritical, were the occasional measures taken by governors against wine producers and dealers, even those among the Mamluk establishment, when at the same time viceroys themselves were notorious wine consumers.[37]

Conflicts between members of different schools of law made it easier for viceroys to manipulate the scholarly establishment. For example, the Shāfiʿī qadi Ibn al-Muzalliq complained against the deputy Mālikī for employing a slave contrary to the legal consensus (*ijmāʿ*).[38] Najm al-Dīn, Taqī al-Dīn's son, refused to say a blessing for the qadis in sermons he delivered. Furthermore, he complained about the widespread bribery that influenced legal decisions. As it turns out, the Ḥanbalī qadi played a role in instigating Najm al-Dīn against his Ḥanafī colleague.[39] One conflict was stirred by a group of "low-life Ḥanbalīs" at the al-Ṣāliḥiyya madrasa, which served as an important Ḥanbalī center. They hit shaykh Zayn al-Dīn al-Zuhrī, known as "the blind" (*ḍarīr*) preacher, who was a Shāfiʿī and employed at that institution, and blamed him for characterizing Aḥmad b. Ḥanbal as an innovator (*mubtadiʿ*). According to Ibn Ṭawq, this was only a pretext and what actually enraged them was the man's discussing in the Friday prayer at the Umayyad Mosque the theological question of anthropomorphism (*tanzīh*).[40] After being attacked, "the blind" preacher turned to Taqī al-Dīn, who enquired among the Ḥanbalīs, but they denied the allegation. A couple of days later two leaders of that school came to him, and a heated debate ensued. However, the meeting was concluded in a positive atmosphere, as the two promised to provide the names of the attackers. In fact, a list of names was given to the Shāfiʿī qadi, which he submitted to the viceroy. One of those on the list was even arrested at the notorious *ḥabs al-dam* of those waiting for execution, and was released only after intercession. How the affair ended is not reported, but, in any case, on the following Friday "the blind" preacher resumed his job.[41] In yet another case, the son of *shaykh al-maṣṭaba* and his

36 Ibn Ṭawq, *Taʿlīq* 839, where the accused double-dealer reaction and Ibn Ṭawq's criticism of it are noted. For Shuʿayb, see 147 n. 4, 213. See also Miura, *Dynamism* 140.

37 E.g Ibn Ṭawq, *Taʿlīq* 1622 and Chapter 2 above.

38 Ibn Ṭawq, *Taʿlīq* 448.

39 Ibn Ṭawq, *Taʿlīq* 1589.

40 See Tashbīh wa-tanzīh, *EI*[2].

41 Ibn Ṭawq, *Taʿlīq* 131, 132, 133. On *al-ḍarīr*'s will, see 296. In another instance the Shāfiʿī qadi sent envoys to his Mālikī colleague with a message, part of which they refused to read to him because of the shame involved. The enraged Shāfiʿī also argued that there were Mālikīs who claimed that their qadi owed them money or abused them. Hearing that, the

relative escaped from the detention imposed on them by the Ḥanbalī qadi for their unpaid debt. The two turned to the shaykh of some mosque to whose clan they belonged, and he addressed the Shāfiʿī deputy qadi. The latter decided that, since they had no means to repay the debt, they were not to be detained. Obviously, the Ḥanbalī qadi objected to that. Later, things deteriorated into a physical struggle and news came to the aforementioned shaykh, who advised the two to turn to the Mālikī qadi. Also the Shāfiʿī supported them. One can see how quite a trivial case drew in at least three of the four schools of law into some conflict.[42]

The *madhhab*s had their own frictions. Among the Shāfiʿīs, two deputy qadis were summoned to Cairo after one of them, supported by the testimony of the qadi of Jubbat al-ʿAssāl, was able to prove that his colleague had taken 5,000 dinars that were found in some residence and had not delivered them to the treasury.[43] No love was lost between the Ibn Farfūr and the Ibn Qāḍī ʿAjlūn families. Upon the appointment of Ibn Farfūr to the qadiship, Muḥibb al-Dīn, Taqī al-Dīn's cousin, delivered a sermon, the first part of which was in praise of the incumbent qadi and a critique of his predecessor. However, when addressing issues such as "commanding the right and forbidding the wrong," the speaker appeared to allude negatively to Ibn Farfūr. Kamāl al-Dīn, another leading family member, intimated to our notary that, although he had urged Ibn Farfūr to ban various expressions of public behavior during the celebration in his honor, the qadi had ignored the request. He was responsive to female singers who asked his permission to divorce. Ibn Ṭawq, certainly no sympathizer of Ibn Farfūr, comments on the latter's hypocrisy in neglecting to pay his tailor yet preaching from the pulpit about justice.[44] Less than three years into his term, in Rajab 893/July 1488, Ibn Farfūr and his 14 deputies (one assumes they were an important financial resource for him by the money they paid him) were

latter defamed his Shāfiʿī colleague and accused him of embezzling thousands of dinars. See Ibn Ṭawq, *Taʿlīq* 582, 583.

42 Ibn Ṭawq, *Taʿlīq* 104. For the Ḥanafī ruling that arrest has to precede any decision of bankruptcy, see Rapoport, Royal justice 83. The *maṣṭaba* was a stage constructed for celebrations and located north of the city wall.

43 Ibn Ṭawq, *Taʿlīq* 976; al-Buṣrawī, *Tārīkh* 142; Ibn Ṭūlūn, *Mufākahat al-khillān* 108. For the leading merchant (*khawājā*) Shams al-Dīn al-Qārī, a Shāfiʿī, debating with the deputy qadi al-Buṣrawī whether playing chess against a Ḥanafī was permissible, see al-Buṣrawī, *Tārīkh* 183–184, 50 (for al-Buṣrawī's opinion as regards a dietary question), 186 (for the question of beating the drum during Sufi *dhikr*s), 221–222 (for another issue discussed by the qadi Ibn Farfūr), 168 (for al-Buṣrawī reporting on the imam Burhān al-Dīn al-Muḥibbī, who, on his way to Cairo, stopped in Damascus and discussed under which circumstances a waqf should be renovated).

44 Ibn Ṭawq, *Taʿlīq* 499–500.

lampooned and accused of apostasy in a pamphlet discovered in the Umayyad Mosque. Suspicion about the pamphlet's authorship fell on a young man who it was assumed wanted to take revenge on the qadi for rejecting his candidacy for some job.[45] A dispute between one of the qadi's deputies, who served as a preacher at the Umayyad Mosque for about 40 years, and another deputy, the frequently mentioned al-Buṣrawī, resulted in a physical encounter, after which the two were summoned to the viceroy.[46]

The Ḥanafīs had their own share of conflicts. A notary addressed the qadi Burhān al-Dīn b. Quṭb against Yūsuf b. Ṭūlūn, the mufti of his school (and the chronicler's relative), concerning an unspecified legal matter. The qadi issued some ruling, which the mufti disregarded. Subsequently, intending to shame Ibn Ṭūlūn, the qadi ordered him to arrive, his head uncovered as a token of humiliation. In revenge, the latter preempted by uncovering the qadi's head. The qadi now instructed his associates to hit the rebellious mufti and forced his dispatch to the citadel, where he was imprisoned. In a session convened by the viceroy, in which the qadis of the four schools were present, the Ḥanafī insisted that the mufti stay uncovered, to which the Shāfiʿī qadi objected, leaving the session in anger.[47] In another case the two brothers Ibn Qaṣīf disputed about a certain post, one blaming the other for falsifying a document. One of the brothers turned to the Shāfiʿī qadi, who decided about the need to present the relevant document.[48]

As to the Mālikīs, a man originally of Medina, whose request was not answered, confronted the qadi of his school. The latter decided on his arrest at the prison of those condemned to death. At this point Taqī al-Dīn intervened (once again, the conflicting interests of prominent men of the four schools came to the fore) and worked for his release. In another instance, ʿAlī al-Miknāsī, who appears to have been an aggressive type and to have had good contact with the leading Shāfiʿīs, disputed the qadi of his *madhhab* about a

45 Ibn Ṭūlūn, *Mufākahat al-khillān* 82; Miura, *Dynamism* 140.

46 Ibn Ṭawq, *Taʿlīq* 67, 81, 83, 976; al-Buṣrawī, *Tārīkh* 142; Ibn al-Ḥimṣī, *Ḥawādith* i, 361–362; Ibn Ṭūlūn, *Mufākahat al-khillān* 108. For the case of Ibn Abī Khālid, a scholar (*faqīh*) as well as a notary and administrator at the (? Nūrī) Hospital turning to the Ḥanafī qadi, who was only too happy to intervene in the internal Shāfiʿī dispute, see Ibn Ṭawq, *Taʿlīq* 1378–1379. For Sirāj al-Dīn's involvement in another personal conflict between scholars, see Ibn Ṭawq, *Taʿlīq* 1799–1800.

47 Ibn al-Ḥimṣī, *Ḥawādith* i, 334. In his *Quḍāt Dimashq* 233, Ibn Ṭūlūn mentions that there was a conflict but does not say anything else. Perhaps the reason was his family ties to Ibn Ṭūlūn.

48 Ibn Ṭawq, *Taʿlīq* 164–165. One gets the impression that the document was in fact falsified. See further 377, 478–479, 970, 1212, 1685. For the Ibn Qaṣīf family, see 1381.

teaching position in some endowed mosque. After insulting the qadi ("Dealer in hashish! Eater of forbidden meat!"), the latter initiated a hearing at the viceroy's. Al-Miknāsī presented a report on the excellent financial balance of the waqf and also a fatwa in his support by the Shāfiʿī *shaykh al-Islām*, who perhaps was quite happy to intervene again in a dispute raging within another school of law. In fact, it led to the rejection of the qadi's claim.[49] Also the Ḥanbalīs were not immune to internal problems.[50]

Operating on the margins of the Damascus milieu of scholars and bureaucrats at the end of the fifteenth century, the figure of Taqī al-Dīn Abū Bakr b. ʿAbdallāh Walī al-Dīn, of the Ibn Qāḍī ʿAjlūn family loomed large for Ibn Ṭawq.[51] Excepting himself, this is the man whom he mentions in his diary more than any other. The author of the *Taʿlīq* provides much information on the man he admired, his personal life, and his activity as the leading authority, both legally and morally, among the Shāfiʿīs, and among the Damascus people in general. Compared with the divided circles of local ulema, the *shaykh al-Islām* (hereafter, shaykh) was as solid as a rock.

The Ibn Qāḍī ʿAjlūn family originated in ʿAjlūn in Transjordan and migrated from there to Damascus at the beginning of the fifteenth century, making a stop at Zarʿ in the Ḥawrān for some years. In the Syrian city, in a matter of a few decades, family members rose to prominence. Leaving ʿAjlūn as a child, Taqī al-Dīn's father (d. 865/1461) became in Damascus late in his life deputy qadi. His eldest son (Ibn Ṭawq's father-in-law), Najm al-Dīn Muḥammad (d. 876/1472), excelled as a scholar and wrote a few *fiqh* books. The second son, ʿAbd al-Raḥmān Zayn al-Dīn, also a deputy qadi, as well as a madrasa teacher and a preacher, was on friendly terms with the sultan. He died barely a year after his older brother, both prematurely in their 40s. Another family member, Burhān al-Dīn Abū Isḥāq Ibrāhīm (d. 872/1467), was also a deputy qadi, and his son Muḥibb al-Dīn Muḥammad was a madrasa teacher. ʿAlī ʿAlāʾ al-Dīn b. Aḥmad Shihāb al-Dīn (d. 882/1477) crossed the lines to the Ḥanafī *madhhab* and occupied the post of qadi.[52]

---

49 Ibn Ṭawq, *Taʿlīq* 578, 579, 580 (al-Buṣrawī, *Tārīkh* 108–109, has a slightly different report), 650, 690, 691; Martel-Thoumian, *Délinquance* 29.

50 al-Buṣrawī, *Tārīkh* 109. For another case, see Ibn Ṭawq, *Taʿlīq* 879.

51 For his biography see, e.g. al-Ghazzī, *Kawākib* i, 114–118. For various assessments by other writers, see briefly Wollina, View 275.

52 Ibn al-Ḥimṣī, *Ḥawādith* i, 153, 179, 202; al-Buṣrawī, *Tārīkh* 28, 52–53, 57–59, 111; al-Sakhāwī, *Ḍawʾ* iv, 87–88, 143; v, 24–25; viii, 96; al-Nuʿaymī, *al-Dāris* i, 168, 263. For the Ḥanafī, see al-Sakhāwī, *Ḍawʾ* viii, 493; Ibn Ṭūlūn, *Quḍāt Dimashq* 226–228.

Taqī al-Dīn was born in Damascus in 841/1438 and died there in 928/1522 at the advanced age of 84. We first meet him in Ibn Ṭawq's diary aged 45 and already the *shaykh al-Islām*, that is, one of the muftis (jurisconsults) appointed to the Dār al-ʿAdl ("Hall of Justice"), which had been established in the second half of the twelfth century for attending to the grievances of the local Muslims.[53] The mufti's importance lay in his authority to issue opinions in response to questions posed about legal rulings, even such that would never be adjudicated in court. His fatwas represented a statement of law that courts routinely would uphold and apply.[54] At the beginning of 893/1488, on a single day, Taqī al-Dīn is reported to have issued no less than 40 fatwas to ʿAbd al-Raḥmān al-Ṣafūrī, a preacher at the Umayyad Mosque, which were read at the al-Shāmiyya madrasa in the presence of the historian (and deputy qadi) al-Buṣrawī and his son, as well as others who frequented sessions held at that institution.[55] What precisely was the occasion and what were the contents of these fatwas we do not know. But we do learn of some fatwas he issued. One, for example, concerned the "left over" water (*min faḍalāt*) of the river water, with none's right to it, which appears to have operated a mill adjacent to the al-Shāmiyya al-Barrāniya madrasa. Although not all the details of the report are clear, it appears that the shaykh approved of the use of this water for some kind of construction, a decision to which, incidentally, a Ḥanbalī shaykh objected.[56] Some other fatwas he issued will be taken up in Chapter 5. As already noted, a collection of his fatwas (which has not reached us) was compiled by Ibn Ṭawq. Among his books one can single out *Iʿlām al-nabīh mimā zāda ʿalā l-minhāj min al-ḥāwī wa-l-bahja wa-l-tanbīh*, a commentary on three Shāfiʿī legal books.[57] Another book in the same field is *al-Zawāʾid ʿalā l-minhāj al-farʿī*.[58] He

53 See Dār al-ʿAdl, *EI*³; Rapoport, Royal justice 84–85; Rabbat, Ideological significance.

54 For the mufti in premodern Islam, see Masud, Messick, and Powers, *Islamic legal interpretation*, esp. chapters 1 and 2; Hallaq, *Sharīʿa* 176–179.

55 Ibn Ṭawq, *Taʿlīq* 1426; Ibn Ṭūlūn, *Mufākahat al-khillān* 75. For al-Ṣafūrī see, e.g. Ibn Ṭūlūn, *Mufākahat al-khillān* 131; Ibn Ṭawq, *Taʿlīq* 491, 493; Ibn al-Ḥimṣī, *Ḥawādith* i, 350. For two different madrasas under this name, the "inner" and "outer," see al-Shihābī, *Muʿjam Dimashq* ii, 187. See further details in Melcak, Reconstruction.

56 Ibn Ṭawq, *Taʿlīq* 1533.

57 There is a printed edition (Beirut 2005). The three books are as follows: (1) Najm al-Dīn ʿAbd al-Ghaffār al-Qazwīnī's (d. 665/1266) *al-Ḥāwī* ("Compendium"; on the author, see al-Ḳazwīnī, *EI*²); (2) Ibn al-Wardī's (d. 749/1349) *al-Bahja* ("Splendor"), a rendering of al-Qazwīnī's "small" *al-Ḥāwī* (*al-ṣaghīr*) in 5,000 verses (on the author, see Ibn al-Wardī, *EI*²); and (3) Abū Isḥāq Ibrāhīm al-Fīrūzābādī/al-Shīrāzī's (d. 476/1083) *al-Tanbīh fī l-fiqh*, a treatise on *fiqh*, one of the major works of the Shāfiʿī school, which has been the subject of more than 70 commentaries (on the author, see al-Shīrāzī, *EI*²).

58 Ibn Ṭawq, *Taʿlīq* 1006, 1084; al-Buṣrawī, *Tārīkh* 58.

also wrote a short book on *aḥkām* (juridical decisions and rules of positive law on subjects such as purification, prayer, pilgrimage, commercial transactions, marriage, and divorce).[59]

As far as his private life goes, Taqī al-Dīn's first wife, Fāṭima, the daughter of Tāj al-Dīn al-Umawī, also referred to as Sitt Ḥāj Mālik,[60] the "ancient wife" (*al-zawjat al-ʿatīqa*) and "the grand lady" (*al-sitt al-kabīra*), appears to have been considerably younger than her husband. Her first-born was Muḥammad Najm al-Dīn, after whom she was also named Umm Sīdī Muḥammad. Twelve years later she miscarried.[61] Another 6 years passed and, in the seventh month of pregnancy, she gave birth to a daughter about 18 years younger than her brother.[62] Ibn Ṭawq hardly mentions the Sitt except for the note that, for some reason, about 10 years later (i.e., after 30 or so years of marriage), she asked for divorce.[63] Possibly, by then she was fed up sharing with the shaykh's second wife, Saʿādāt, known as "the Egyptian," the daughter of Zayn al-Dīn ʿAbd al-Raḥmān al-Malījī.[64] The shaykh was Saʿādāt's third husband. Before that she had been a divorcée of ʿUbayd al-Ṭanāzī, with whom she had a son, Abū l-Faḍl.[65] Still earlier, she had been the widow of Zayn al-Dīn ʿAbd al-Raḥmān, one of Taqī al-Dīn's brothers, who, to remind, died in his 40s. From that marriage was born Fāṭima.

Apparently, each of the shaykh's two wives had a residence in the old city, and Ibn Ṭawq notes his frequent visits to "the shaykh's two residences."[66] The "old" or "large" residence is where the first wife resided and was in the neighborhood of the Bādirāʾiyya madrasa.[67] His "new" home, in which the "Egyptian" lived, was near the Qaymariyya, east of the Umayyad Mosque.[68] His home was in Qābūn village, slightly north of the city.[69] On a few occasions the two wives are reported running into one another, exchanging harsh words (*ḥaṣala kalām*),

59 See Aḥkām, *EI*².
60 Ibn Ṭawq, *Taʿlīq* 249.
61 Ibn Ṭawq, *Taʿlīq* 102, 479, 617.
62 Ibn Ṭawq, *Taʿlīq* 685.
63 Ibn Ṭawq, *Taʿlīq* 1478. On her exclusion from her father's will, see 249, 250–251, 617.
64 Ibn Ṭawq, *Taʿlīq* 747.
65 Ibn Ṭawq, *Taʿlīq* 519.
66 E.g. Ibn Ṭawq, *Taʿlīq* 350.
67 Ibn Ṭawq, *Taʿlīq* 37, 250.
68 E.g. Ibn Ṭawq, *Taʿlīq* 103, 148, 218, 236. The "large" Qaymariyya, located east of the Umayyad Mosque, was named after its founder, Nāṣir al-Dīn Qaymar (d. 665/1266–1267). For this madrasa, see al-Nuʿaymī, *al-Dāris* i, 335–339; al-ʿAlmāwī, *Mukhtaṣar* 69–70; al-Shihābī, *Muʿjam Dimashq* ii, 205; Badrān, *Munādama* 140, 142.
69 E.g. Ibn Ṭawq, *Taʿlīq* 1483, 1532.

and even fighting each other.[70] The shaykh alternated his nights between the two wives. Ibn Ṭawq refers repeatedly to quarrels between Taqī al-Dīn and "the Egyptian." There were instances when she did not let him enter and he had to spend the night in the courtyard (*ḥawsh*) or at his mother's home. The quarrels caused him health problems.[71] Even upon his return from a two-year forced absence in Cairo, to which we shall return, she "displayed anger and insanity as has been her habit." A few days later, after another quarrel, the shaykh "seemed strange" and fell ill, and the worried Ibn Ṭawq and another of his friends spent the night with him.[72] Things continued to deteriorate for several years afterward, and at one point the shaykh and his son Muḥammad sought a place to stay for two to three days. Then, Ibn Ṭawq began urging his friend to initiate a divorce by a *khulʿ* procedure (for which see Chapter 6). It came after the shaykh had announced his intention to divorce by the usual procedure (*ṭalāq*), but he stated it only once and not thrice, as legally required. Subsequently, following his decision about separation (*firāq*) as a first step toward actual divorce, he vacated the "new" home. Ibn Ṭawq found there only a few pieces of furniture, and he does not miss the opportunity to blame the "Egyptian" for putting her hands on other pieces. He further reports that at that point nothing had any effect on her, and that she was actually glad about the prospects of divorce.[73]

Following their separation the shaykh sold immediately part of the "new" home for 500 ashrafīs and another part for 100, plus the equivalent of 200 more dinars in silver currency, to the *kārim* merchant (*al-saffār*) ʿAlāʾ al-Dīn ʿUmar of the al-Qārī family.[74] For some reason the divorce procedure was prolonged, and it was agreed that till its completion Taqī al-Dīn would keep providing his estranged wife with 20 dirhams daily to cover all expenses; other than that, the two would be free of any financial obligation. A draft was signed by the wife's parents. However, only a few months went by before Saʿādāt permitted her representative to ask for reunion in return for a marriage gift of a token 1 ashrafī. Ibn Ṭawq reports that, following the new engagement, Taqī al-Dīn spent the night with her, and it is implied that to make the reunion legally binding intercourse was required. But this turned out to be a failed reunion, and, barely a year later, problems started anew and, once again, Taqī al-Dīn had to spend his

70 Ibn Ṭawq, *Taʿlīq* 834, 1462.
71 E.g. Ibn Ṭawq, *Taʿlīq* 25, 100, 162, 170, 521, 522, 523, 526.
72 Ibn Ṭawq, *Taʿlīq* 521, 522, 523, 524, 526, 528.
73 Ibn Ṭawq, *Taʿlīq* 553, 554, 583, 742, 747.
74 Ibn Ṭawq, *Taʿlīq* 743, 748–750, with further details about the payment; a goldsmith (*ṣāʾigh*) had to examine the coins.

nights elsewhere.[75] During one of their quarrels he told his son-in-law to take his wife (apparently both lived in a section of the Egyptian's residence) and move to his cousin's residence.[76] Possibly, he felt uncomfortable with the young couple being exposed to his marriage situation. The following years did not see any improvement, and at the end of 904/1499, after further attempts at reconciliation, Ibn Ṭawq succeeded in persuading his friend to initiate a *khulʿ*.[77] From what has been mentioned, clearly, he did not have much sympathy for this woman. "Let Allāh save us from her evil and from all evil doers." This and similar unfriendly notes recur in the diary.[78] The "Egyptian" wife fell ill shortly after the divorce. Ibn Ṭawq notes that she suffered from melancholy (*malikhulya*), and her medical situation deteriorated to the point that she was unable to recognize her visitors. Despite his ill feelings toward her, he expresses his wish for her recovery and notes that his wife went to visit her. Saʿādāt died in Rabīʿ II 905/November 1499.[79]

More than a year before his second divorce, aged 62, Taqī al-Dīn married Sāra, a widow, the daughter of the *kārim* merchant (*khawājikī*) Shihāb al-Dīn Ibn al-Muzalliq, one of Damascus's wealthiest individuals.[80] Two weeks after signing the marriage contract the shaykh received a message defaming her for immoral conduct (*ṭaʿn*). Possibly, it had to do with an incident with Sāra's cousin, a young man originally from Aleppo, who became a prominent merchant in Damascus and headed one of its markets. A few years earlier he had been spotted under suspicious circumstances by the doorman at Sāra's house and had been able to escape after the latter snipped some of his clothes and reported him to the viceroy. Following an inquiry, the man was sentenced to be castrated, but he then paid 500 dinars in lieu. Sāra was fined 1,000 dinars.[81] The shaykh was also blamed for his involvement in the death of Sāra's former husband. However, these insinuations fell on deaf ears.[82] The marriage to Sāra

75 Ibn Ṭawq, *Taʿlīq* 801–802, 833, 834, 901, 1049, 1217.

76 Ibn Ṭawq, *Taʿlīq* 1515. For his marriage to Taqī al-Dīn's daughter, see 1532.

77 For their reconciliation, see Ibn Ṭawq, *Taʿlīq* 1591, 1729. For its failure, see 1631, 1636, 1655, 1729.

78 Ibn Ṭawq, *Taʿlīq* 100, 587, 743.

79 Ibn Ṭawq, *Taʿlīq* 1760, 1762.

80 Ibn Ṭawq, *Taʿlīq* 1586, 1587, 1589, 1599. For the terms of their marriage, see Chapter 6. For her father, see ʿAbd al-Bāsiṭ, *Muʿjam* i, 544, and editor's n. 4 with further references. For the *kārim*, see Kārimī, *EI*².

81 Ibn Ṭawq, *Taʿlīq* 1345–1346 (the text is ambiguous and can also be interpreted differently, namely, that the doorman was punished); Ibn al-Ḥimṣī, *Ḥawādith* i, 382.

82 Ibn Ṭawq, *Taʿlīq* 1591.

was not the shaykh's last one, and a couple of years later he married in Egypt.[83] Apparently, the bitter experience with "the Egyptian" did not stand in the way.

Of Taqī al-Dīn's children, Muḥammad Najm al-Dīn (d. 935/1528), born in 874/1470 from the shaykh's first marriage, was the oldest.[84] As a young man he taught at the Abū ʿUmar madrasa in the Ṣāliḥiyya Quarter, substituting for his father, who delegated to him other offices as well. For some years he served as a *khaṭīb* at the Yalbughā Mosque and in other posts. At 29 he became a deputy qadi to Shihāb al-Dīn b. Farfūr despite the qadi's strained relationship with his father.[85] Ten years later he succeeded Ibn Farfūr.[86] As to his personal life, at 17 he married his cousin Fāṭima, the "Egyptian's" (i.e., his stepmother's) daughter from her marriage to his deceased uncle.[87] A few years into their marriage problems started. A daughter died aged 18 months, and 3 months later Fāṭima miscarried twin daughters. After one more year another daughter was born, but she died less than two years later. About nine months afterward, a son was born, and after three more years another deceased daughter is mentioned.[88] The young couple lost almost all their children. There is no further information on their situation after our notary's diary terminates.

From the shaykh's marriage to his "Egyptian" wife at least six children are mentioned. ʿUmar died in the plague of 1492 aged 17.[89] Also Aḥmad, only slightly younger, died in that plague.[90] ʿAbd al-Raḥīm, a few years younger, married at age 20. Shortly afterward, he had a conflict with his mother-in-law, and a year later the couple hit one another in the course of a game.[91] Another of ʿAbd al-Raḥīm's rifts was with his foster brother Najm al-Dīn. He complained to the Shāfiʿī qadi about the latter's immoral conduct, which allegedly included wine drinking. The Mālikī qadi was glad to get involved, and the case reached the viceroy.[92] After ʿAbd al-Raḥīm, a daughter was born; her name is unspecified, but Ibn Ṭawq implies it was Amīna Zayn al-ʿUlamāʾ; she married her cousin Abū

83 Ibn Ṭūlūn, *Mufākahat al-khillān* 199.
84 Ibn Ṭūlūn, *Mufākahat al-khillān* 268.
85 Ibn Ṭawq, *Taʿlīq* 1267–1268, 1676–1677.
86 Ibn Ṭawq, *Taʿlīq* 1873; Ibn Ṭūlūn, *Mufākahat al-khillān* 268; Anṣarī, *Nuzhat al-khāṭir* ii, 128 n. 5, 148 and see references there. For biographical information, see Ibn Ṭūlūn, *Quḍāt Dimashq* 183–184.
87 Ibn Ṭawq, *Taʿlīq* 536, 539.
88 Ibn Ṭawq, *Taʿlīq* 877, 1213, 1312, 1325, 1490, 1580, 1873.
89 Ibn Ṭawq, *Taʿlīq* 921–922, 1122. For the Egyptian wife referred to as Umm ʿUmar, see 833.
90 Ibn Ṭawq, *Taʿlīq* 1124. For the Egyptian wife referred to as his mother, see 769.
91 Ibn Ṭawq, *Taʿlīq* 1792, 1806, 1818, 1861; Ibn Ṭūlūn, *Mufākahat al-khillān* 12.
92 Ibn Ṭūlūn, *Mufākahat al-khillān* 201–202, 210.

l-Yumn when she was 15.[93] Another son, probably named ʿUthmān, came about three years after her and died aged three. Ibn Ṭawq admits that he was unaware of his death and was not present at the funeral, since the shaykh kept it secret in order for it not to overshadow Najm al-Dīn's coinciding marriage.[94] About half a year following ʿUthmān's death another daughter was born, but she did not survive more than 18 months.[95] Concerning four more children—which of the two wives, or the shaykh's concubines, was their mother is unspecified—Āsya gave birth to a daughter who also, like two of the shaykh's sons, died in the plague of 1492.[96] ʿAbd al-Raḥmān died in the same plague aged less than 15, and an unnamed daughter died 12 years later.[97] During the shaykh's long absence, when he was forced to stay in Cairo, another son was born.[98] Altogether, the shaykh had at least twelve children, including from concubines, of whom no less than four were victims of a single plague that broke out in 1492.

Taqī al-Dīn's household included male slaves (*ʿabd, mawlā*),[99] but it is mainly about female slaves that we are informed. In the course of the approximately 20 years covered in the *Taʿlīq*, the *shaykh al-Islām* is reported to have owned no less than 9 female slaves, 6 of whom bore him children, some of whom, as noted, may have died in the plague.[100]

An important aspect of the shaykh's scholarly activity was teaching at various madrasas.[101] He also held private sessions at his own small mosque, where pupils read to him texts and he examined them before accrediting them with a

93 Ibn Ṭawq, *Taʿlīq* 56, 1436. On this marriage see also Chapter 6.

94 Ibn Ṭawq, *Taʿlīq* 207, 644; Wolina, *Zwanzig* 96.

95 Ibn Ṭawq, *Taʿlīq* 688, 790.

96 Ibn Ṭawq, *Taʿlīq* 1120.

97 Ibn Ṭawq, *Taʿlīq* 1123; Ibn Ṭūlūn, *Mufākahat al-khillān* 215.

98 Ibn Ṭawq, *Taʿlīq* 326, 328. The reference to the "new home" suggests that he was the son of the "Egyptian," who resided there.

99 Ibn Ṭawq, *Taʿlīq* 140, 174, 530. The young *ʿabd* Mubārak died in 903/1498. See 1602. For Salīm, the eight-year-old *mawlā*, who died a few years earlier, see 1127.

100 Ibn Ṭawq, *Taʿlīq* 196, 291, 521, 538, 838, 896, 929, 1119, 1120, 1148, 1240, 1251, 1479, 1578, 1646, 1672, 1752, 1823, 1857.

101 Ibn Ṭawq, *Taʿlīq* 30, 103, 904; Ibn Ṭūlūn, *Mufākahat al-khillān* 19. On the sale of one-third of the job for 600 dinars, see Ibn al-Ḥimṣī, *Ḥawādith* i, 321–322. The Falakiyya was established by Falak al-Dīn, a brother of the Ayyūbid al-ʿĀdil. See ʿAlmāwī, *Mukhtaṣar* 67. The Rukniyya was established by Rukn al-Dīn al-Falakī in ca. 620/1223 near Bāb al-Farādīs, east of the Falakiyya. See ʿAlmāwī, *Mukhtaṣar* 42–43; Badrān, *Munādama* 137. The waqf was administered jointly by Taqī al-Dīn's nephew Kamāl al-Dīn and the Shāfiʿī deputy qadi Burhān al-Dīn b. al-Muʿtamid, who was appointed at one point also to the post of mufti. See on him, e.g. Ibn Ṭawq, *Taʿlīq* 31, 38, 58, 87, 90, 106, 126, 1545, 1597. For his teaching at the al-Shāmiyya al-Barrāniyya, see al-Nuʿaymī, *al-Dāris* i, 223.

permission to read them independently in public (*ijāza*). In one such session, 30 men were present (our notary gives some of the names), and the reading was divided between 4 of them and lasted a few hours. On another occasion, in addition to laymen, quite a number of the city's leading scholars arrived; the precise order of their sitting in relation to the shaykh is provided. The session included discussion of some Quranic verses and a *khuṭba* delivered by the shaykh. Beverages were provided.[102] Ibn Ṭūlūn, although a Ḥanafī, was Taqī al-Dīn's disciple, and he lists the books he read to him. He refers to him in his chronicle as "our master" (*mawlānā al-shaykh*).[103] Ibn Ṭawq reports on the shaykh's gesture, or perhaps an established custom, of gifting the "graduates" with clothes, in one instance in the considerable value of 4 dinars, or giving 100 dirhams to someone who excelled in his reading.[104] In the list of more than a dozen books read to the shaykh, one finds books on *qirā'āt*, Ḥadīth, grammar, logic, and *balāgha*, most of which by Damascus authors, among them members of the Ibn Qāḍī ʿAjlūn family.[105]

Taqī al-Dīn took a few administrative posts from which he was able to generate considerable income. He supervised the waqf of the Rukniyya madrasa, which, in 881/1476, for some reason, he was ordered by the authorities in Cairo to cede to his relative the Ḥanafī qadi. Taqī al-Dīn did not give it up lightly and went to Cairo to argue against the decision. In the event, and according to the custom of his day, he had to pay to be able to retain it together with the supervision of the special endowment for the release of war prisoners (*waqf al-usarā'*).[106] Four years later he decided to cede this post and took one-third of a teaching position at al-Shāmiyya al-Barrāniya. Still later he became supervisor of the waqf supporting the al-Wazīr Mosque in the Ṣārūjā Market and was appointed by the Cairene qadi Walī al-Dīn al-Asyūṭī as supervisor of another endowment, referred to as the Atābikiyya and possibly connected with a madrasa thus named. He also administered other waqfs endowed on cultivated land. He leased 2 feddans for the annual sum of 1,200 dirhams for 4 years through his *wakīl*, the *mubāshir* of the Jarūd village, to his nephew Kamāl al-Dīn and the deputy qadi Burhān al-Dīn b. al-Muʿtamid. He administered part of the large waqf established at the village of Ḥadītha in the Ghūṭa region by

102 E.g. Ibn Ṭawq, *Taʿlīq* 57, 107, 112, 207, 533, 552, 553, 688, 842, 904, 926, 1084, 1094–1095.

103 Ibn Ṭūlūn, *Fulk* 29; e.g. Ibn Ṭūlūn, *Mufākahat al-khillān* 8.

104 Ibn Ṭawq, *Taʿlīq* 57, 533, 651. For *ijāza* see Chapter 1 n. 27 above.

105 For specific books, see e.g. Ibn Ṭawq, *Taʿlīq* 57, 461, 525, 533, 545, 688, 689, 926, 1105, 1122, 1123, 1129, 1171.

106 al-Buṣrawī, *Tārīkh* 76–77, 78. On him as a Ḥanafī, see Ibn Ṭawq, *Taʿlīq* 31, 45. He died a year later. See ʿAbd al-Bāsiṭ, *Nayl* vii, 197.

the wealthy merchant Shihāb al-Dīn b. al-Muzalliq (for which see Chapter 4). There are further posts he occupied.[107]

In addition to these financially rewarding occupations, the shaykh was intensely involved in a variety of public affairs. On occasion, when it was difficult to decide about the beginning of a new year, he was consulted by the Shāfiʿī qadi. The annual commemoration of the Prophet's birthday (*mawlid*) took place at his home and, as a rule, he officiated the collective circumcision of orphans, in which the number of the circumcised could reach more than 100 on a single occasion.[108] Suffice it to note that, for an unclear reason, the years 886–887/1481–1482 witnessed a few water disputes. Their frequency may have been accidental, yet there is no doubt that water constituted a conflictual resource. The cases, as minutely detailed in the *Taʿlīq*, tell of tension generated by contradictory claims of rights and unilateral acts that aimed at changing the status quo. A great deal of personal animosity partly drove these disputes and guided the actors in these mini-dramas. The dynamics of the confrontations and attempts to attain solutions reveal the critical role played by Taqī al-Dīn, the *shaykh al-Islām*, whose actions in order to reach agreements were indispensable. Almost without exception, this prominent Shāfiʿī enjoyed the greatest respect of all involved. Given the viceroy's tendency to react spontaneously, without sufficient information, sometimes also giving contradictory orders, and given the need to bring in legal opinions to the deliberations, the shaykh became an irreplaceable person in these water disputes.[109]

Of the shaykh's public activities, one should also note his struggle for the pursuit of moral standards. As generally put by our source, he campaigned for the "removal of the forbidden," and to that end he repeatedly addressed the viceroy and other high-ranking Mamluks on their obligation in this regard.[110] He instructed the market inspector (*muḥtasib*) to see that women were appropriately dressed.[111] It is especially as regards the campaign to counter the consumption of wine that the shaykh's public activities are reported. In one instance, accompanied by Ibrāhīm, of the association of the Iqbāʿīs, as well as the *ḥājib*, he turned against one of the grand emirs who had a wine press operating at his residence. At first the Mamluk denied it, and only later his servant

107 Ibn Ṭawq, *Taʿlīq* 63, 530, 543, 917, 1097, 1194, 1475, 1835. The Atābikiyya was located in the Ṣāliḥiyya Quarter and was established by Nūr al-Dīn's sister or daughter. See ʿAlmāwī, *Mukhtaṣar* 26–27.

108 Ibn Tawq, *Taʿlīq* 114, 115, 1106; Wollina, *Zwanzig* 89.

109 For analysis, see Shoshan, Mini-dramas.

110 Ibn Ṭawq, *Taʿlīq* 159.

111 E.g. Ibn Ṭawq, *Taʿlīq* 29, 164, 165, 172.

turned in the press. In another instance, together with the active Sufi Shaykh Faraj, three qadis, and, ironically, a leading Mamluk who in all likelihood had his own wine press, the shaykh uncovered a wine storage facility owned by a high-ranking official.[112] Christians, especially those residing in the Nabayṭūn Quarter, were an easy target in that campaign. On one occasion, Sufis broke into a Christian home, claiming that Muslim youths had been seen drinking wine there.[113] On other occasions, at least once following Taqī al-Dīn's instruction, Sufis spilled large wine containers.[114]

In biographical dictionaries of the period, Taqī al-Dīn is reported to have been opposed to the Sufis and their rituals. He also wrote a treatise against the foremost Sufi thinker, Ibn al-ʿArabī.[115] However, from the *Taʿlīq* we learn that his relationship with the Sufis of Damascus was rather complex, and he mobilized them not infrequently in order to implement his policy. The cooperation between the *shaykh al-Islām* and the Sufis was based on a shared interest in imposing norms of proper conduct in the public domain. There were plenty of opportunities for that, even besides the campaign against wine and hashish. Thus, when a group of gangsters, led by a dark-skinned slave, abused Damascenes who were en route to the hajj, Sufis, ordered by the shaykh to put an end to it, attacked the gangsters and brought them to him, and allegedly he made them repent.[116] He dispatched Sufis on other missions against "reprehensible habits."[117] However, not everything between him and the Sufis was rosy. In one instance, together with some leading scholars, he accused the Sufi Muḥammad al-ʿUmarī of sexual promiscuity, of not observing the congregational prayer, and of blasphemy. Yet, the shaykh had to give in because of the support al-ʿUmarī received from the "riffraff." Our notary, his association with the shaykh possibly reflected, criticizes the (mis)management of this case.[118]

Taqī al-Dīn acted against various expressions of popular belief, such as healing Muslims and Samaritans in a mosque,[119] or constructing a mosque at some grave and performing there "miracles." A case described in some detail is of a peasant from the Biqāʿ who had been "instructed" in his dream to go to a cer-

112 Ibn Ṭawq, *Taʿlīq* 36–37, 673; Ibn Ṭūlūn, *Mufākahat al-khillān* 31 (probably copied from Ibn Ṭawq); Martel-Thoumian, *Délinquance* 290.

113 Ibn Ṭawq, *Taʿlīq* 240.

114 Ibn Ṭawq, *Taʿlīq* 1007, 1011. For other instances, see e.g. 236–237, 726, 1190, 1232, 1273, 1631, 1659, 1660, 1662, 1784.

115 For activity against Ibn al-ʿArabī in Damascus, see briefly Geoffroy, *Soufisme* 459–460.

116 Ibn Ṭawq, *Taʿlīq* 141.

117 E.g. Ibn Ṭawq, *Taʿlīq* 159.

118 Ibn Ṭawq, *Taʿlīq* 791. For a few further details, see Geoffroy, *Soufisme* 383–384.

119 Ibn Ṭawq, *Taʿlīq* 135.

tain grave and build a mosque there. The guard at the site claimed that the "miracles" performed by the spirit of the deceased were more numerous than those ascribed to the Prophet. However, even the Sufi shaykh Ibrāhīm al-Dasūqī opposed the ritual. The issue came before Taqī al-Dīn, who told the peasant to demolish the mosque, but since he refused, claiming that it would irritate the believers, the case was brought before al-Buṣrawī in his capacity as the Shāfiʿī deputy qadi. At first he found it difficult to agree to the demolishing, and only after examining all the available precedents did he decide to that the construction should be taken down.[120]

In his campaign to defend orthodoxy, the shaykh found himself entangled in the Bāb Jīrūn affair, which is a good example of what might be called the politics of religion. In local tradition this old city gate was named after its alleged constructor, an imagined figure who, according to one version, descended from biblical Noah and preceded Abraham; in other versions, Jīrūn was a contemporary of King Solomon or Alexander the Great. As Ibn Ṭawq has it, one of the "ignorant"—by which, as we shall see, he means a Shīʿī—with the support of an emir and a Ḥanafī scholar, claimed that a woman named Malika, a descendant of Ḥusayn, ʿAlī's son, was buried near this gate. It was rumored that a slab inscribed with a Shīʿī prayer and the names of the twelve imams was found at the site. Subsequently, the gate was blocked, and in the summer of 1485 one Ibrāhīm al-Kayyāl ("corn measurer") initiated the construction of a mosque there. As one would expect, Shīʿī inhabitants joined him on the pretext that the project would make it difficult for thieves to infiltrate the quarter. Others were enraged and adduced opposing views as expressed by the thirteenth-century Syrian chronicler Abū Shāma and the Shafiʿī scholar ʿAlāʾ al-Dīn b. al-ʿAṭṭār (d. 724/1324). Support from the Shāfiʿī qadi was slow to come, but, subsequently, he ruled that what had been constructed must be demolished. Work stopped, but no demolition followed. A week later a session was convened at the Shāfiʿī's office, and opposition to the project was led by Kamāl al-Dīn, Taqī al-Dīn's nephew. Those supporting it threatened to get the sultan involved.

All that time the *shaykh al-Islām* was away in Cairo, and only upon returning to Damascus did he become involved. At that point one ʿAlī, the dealer in flour, or a worker in the cloth industry (*al-daqqāq*), who was one of the promoters of the project, succeeded in attracting the interest of a Mamluk officer, who hired a constructor. Backed up by his Shāfiʿī colleagues, Taqī al-Dīn sent to ʿAlī a warning, but the latter was not taken aback and sent his own threat to set the shaykh's residence on fire. Once again, work was to be stopped, but

120 al-Buṣrawī, *Tārīkh* 174–176.

ʿAlī did not give up. After a year and a half, he sent a letter to Cairo in which he opened a new front—he blamed the shaykh for embezzling funds from some project. The sultan's order was to have another hearing on the Bāb Jīrūn case in which the history of the site would be reconstructed. It was then claimed that after Tīmūr's invasion and the destruction he had wrought on Damascus in 1400, the site had been left in ruins for some decades, until a Mamluk had initiated construction work. This recovered piece of history disarmed the opposition somewhat. However, after ʿAlī sent "proofs" to the shaykh ("claims of an elephant," thus they are described by Ibn Ṭawq), the latter sat down and wrote a well-argued pamphlet. ʿAlī persevered and even tried unsuccessfully to enlist the viceroy's assistance. A few months later, an order sent from Cairo instructed the four qadis of Damascus to go to the site and examine the issue one more time. If they found traces of a mosque, it had to be built anew, and if they did not, the project ought to be abandoned.[121]

Here, Ibn Ṭūlūn comes to our aid, among whose many works one finds "The utmost satisfaction with the history of Bāb Jīrūn" (which is, incidentally, characterized by its author as a *taʿlīq*). It is a short treatise of about 15 pages (in the printed edition), in which we learn not only about the (pseudo) historical tradition of the site but also about the controversy it generated. In fact, the text consists almost entirely of the report Taqī al-Dīn prepared to counter the promoters of the project. The shaykh puts the blame of the origin of the Bāb Jīrūn affair on the Shīʿīs and "the ignorant and those who deceivingly follow them." Relying on Abū Shāma, who is only sparingly mentioned by Ibn Ṭawq in his account, the shaykh cites from Abū Shāma's (extant) work, in which he had argued that everything started in a dream that a dubious man had had one night in 636/1238–1239. In the dream the Damascene was told that one of ʿAlī's descendants was buried near the gate. In another version, which the shaykh took from a scholar of the previous generation, it was rather "one of the commoners" who had made the claim and been supported by some like types. Subsequently, a mosque was built nearby, blocking the narrow passage. An inscription with the name Malika was then falsified, as if a female descendant of the ʿAlīd family was connected to the place. In his report Taqī al-Dīn also mentions a fatwa issued by Ibn al-ʿAṭṭār, who had been active in Damascus in the first quarter of the fourteenth century. When asked whether there was any basis to the mosque built to honor Malika, he answered that a woman with

121 Ibn Ṭawq, *Taʿlīq* 193–194, 509–510, 511, 514, 516, 522, 523, 534, 717, 718, 723, 728, 832, 834–835, 837–838, 841, 842, 853, 854, 888, 913. On Ibn ʿAṭṭār see a short biography in Ibn ʿImād, *Shadharāt* viii, 114–115.

such a name was unknown and the project was ill intended. During Tīmūr's invasion the mosque caught fire and now, about 80 years later, there came this fraud in the form of a plan to rebuild it. Taqī al-Dīn ends his report expressing his hope that the sultan would not allow the project to be completed. It turns out that his hope came true, as Ibn Ṭūlūn ends his cover story with the note that in his own days (i.e., the first half of the sixteenth century) a storage stood on the site. That is to say, after ten years of confrontation, the shaykh and his circle had the upper hand.[122]

Taqī al-Dīn maintained good contacts with high-ranking emirs, most importantly with the viceroy Qujmās, who ruled for almost seven years starting in 886/1481. Upon his appointment and his arrival in the city, the shaykh went to greet him. The Mamluk returned visits to the shaykh's residence and on one occasion spent with him an hour and "drank water from the [shaykh's] well." A few days later, when Taqī al-Dīn delivered a speech at the Umayyad Mosque, the governor sent his secretary to inform him of the shaykh's arguments. The shaykh also sent him a treatise he had written about the topic of *al-amr bi-l-maʿrūf*. Apparently, Qujmās took it seriously and demonstrated his commitment to implement the norms discussed there.[123] Also other officials frequented Taqī al-Dīn's house. The viceroy and high-ranking emirs occasionally resorted to Taqī al-Dīn's advice and good judgment concerning various matters, from individual appointments through monetary issues and the treatment of European prisoners to conflicts between officials and the city's inhabitants. His opinion was asked also concerning some construction projects, and in one instance he instructed one of the emirs to demolish a second floor (*ṭabaqa*) and latrines (? *murtafiqāt*), on the grounds that "such is forbidden." Similarly, he ordered that a newly established bench (*maṣṭaba*) adjacent to the wall of the al-Mu'ayyidiyya madrasa be taken down.[124]

Taqī al-Dīn was honored also by the low-ranked. Even the *zuʿr* of the Shāghūr Quarter declared at one point that they were at his service.[125] In 902/1497, when the Mamluk government attempted to interfere in the waqf system, the shaykh was addressed by waqf owners and promised to review the policy and, if necessary, to address the sultan on it. A session he convened with some officials led to no result, and the case was transferred to Cairo.[126] Later in that year,

---

122 Ibn Ṭūlūn, *Qurrat al-ʿuyūn*.

123 Ibn Ṭawq, *Taʿlīq* 52, 124, 627, 630, 672.

124 Ibn Ṭawq, *Taʿlīq* 50, 79, 81, 167, 173, 203, 214, 226, 252, 287. The Mu'ayadiyya was located below the citadel. See al-Badrī, *Nuzhat* 37.

125 Ibn Ṭawq, *Taʿlīq* 32, 1006, 1530–1531, 1537, 1635.

126 Ibn Ṭawq, *Taʿlīq* 27, 1502, 1503.

following the death of viceroy Qanṣūh al-Yaḥyāwī, and as the interim period between viceroys was prolonged, the shaykh was involved in a confrontation between the grand emir Yilbāy and the inhabitants of a nearby village concerning the release of prisoners. He also opposed one governor's forced sale of sugar (*ṭarḥ*) and was involved in disputes about grain prices.[127] When he thought that certain persons were unjustifiably detained, he demanded their release. This he did, for example, for a Shāfiʿī youth who had been sentenced to death by the Mālikī deputy qadi for blasphemy. In another case he intervened for the release of the Ḥanafī qadi Tāj al-Dīn b. ʿArabshāh, who had been arrested by a high-ranking Mamluk officer, and of Muḥammad b. al-ʿAjlūniyya, a constructor (*al-miʿmār*), who had been arrested for charges concerning a *muḥākara* agreement.[128] He interceded for 30 peasants of the Upper Qābūn, the village of his residence, who had been arrested by the *ḥājib* on suspicion of theft, as well as for the peasants of Jubbat al-ʿAssāl, who suffered at the hands of their corrupt *muqaddams*.[129] In one further case, after the *dawādār al-sulṭān* sent armed mamluks to the al-Mizza mosque, just at the time when the local preacher was delivering a sermon, to attack the crowd of peasants for not paying their taxes, Taqī al-Dīn protested and sent one of the officer's aides to the Mālikī qadi to put him under arrest. As to the peasants, they were released without paying a single dirham.[130] When his efforts to bring about the release of an arrested man failed and the poor man died in jail, the shaykh paid for the purification of the corpse and the burial.[131] When the prison of those condemned to death collapsed and a few were killed, he took care of preparations for their burial and prayed for their souls.[132]

There were still other aspects of the shaykh's public activities. He was occasionally asked by local people to execute their wills,[133] and on numerous occasions he served as an arbitrator in personal disputes concerning finances.[134] A few examples will be discussed in Chapter 5. The intensity of Taqī al-Dīn's public activity took its toll, as we learn from his occasional announcements about

127 Ibn Ṭawq, *Taʿlīq* 62, 66, 68, 71, 73, 75, 598.

128 For these and other cases, see Ibn Ṭawq, *Taʿlīq* 37–38, 41, 916, 941, 942. For *ḥikr* see Chapter 4.

129 Ibn Ṭawq, *Taʿlīq* 277, 281–282. For further cases of his intercession, see e.g. 650 (two cases), 765, 940, 1203, 1236, 1386, 1421, 1462, 1465, 1510, 1546, 1610.

130 Ibn al-Ḥimṣī, *Ḥawādith* i, 319–320.

131 Ibn Ṭawq, *Taʿlīq* 1203.

132 Ibn Ṭawq, *Taʿlīq* 83.

133 E.g. Ibn Ṭawq, *Taʿlīq* 200 (by a hod carrier, *ṭayyān*).

134 E.g. Ibn Ṭawq, *Taʿlīq* 41, 65, 67, 108, 112, 119, 155, 158–159, 170, 505–506, 619, 652, 682–683, 763, 915, 1058, 1239, 1378–1379. See further Chapter 4.

temporarily leaving the city; in fact, these were false and were meant to give him some respite and take a rest with friends.[135]

Given the shaykh's high public profile, it is no wonder that few were indifferent to him. On the one hand, he surely had his admirers. Thus, when returning from one of his several sojourns, which could take him as far as Beirut or Cairo, he was received by a dozen scholars who waited to greet him outside the city wall.[136] But there were those who, for a variety of reasons, were opposed to him. A complaint addressed to the viceroy against a certain qadi concerning his conduct was directed "with the encouragement of the wicked (*manāḥīs*)" against Taqī al-Dīn.[137] The qadi Ibn Farfūr, who with the shaykh led the Shāfʿīs in the city, criticized him for some dispute in the presence of dignitaries, insinuating that "the ignorant are the enemies of the knowledgeable." Such was the animosity between the two that, when the shaykh's cousin died, Ibn Farfūr and the Ḥanbalī qadi did not pay the shaykh a visit, and later, when the shaykh's "Egyptian" wife died, he forbade the two from attending her funeral.[138] Also no love was lost between the shaykh and the Shāfiʿī deputy qadi and chronicler al-Buṣrawī.[139] And upon the death of a certain professional witness, Ibn Ṭawq notes that, of those damaging the shaykh, he was the third to die, the other two being a Mamluk officer and a member of the wealthy al-Qārī family.[140]

Perhaps the most troubling experiences in this respect were the rifts in the Ibn Qāḍī ʿAjlūn family. The most severe and persistent occurred between Taqī al-Dīn and his nephew Kamāl al-Dīn. It began in 904/1498 about some posts. A few years later the tension between the two resurfaced, this time because of land they shared in the village of ʿArbīl, which the shaykh claimed his nephew had taken over entirely when he was forced to be away in Cairo.[141] Then in 913/1508 a dispute arose concerning a legal matter—scholars were asked whether to demolish a construction built over the grave of the son of the *nāẓir al-jaysh*. Kamāl al-Dīn, now occupying the position of mufti, thought it had to be demolished, and this was in fact done. At that point the father of the deceased addressed Taqī al-Dīn, who had a different opinion. This motivated

135 Ibn Ṭawq, *Taʿlīq* 546, 669.

136 E.g. Ibn Ṭawq, *Taʿlīq* 303, 710, 770, 868, 895, 943.

137 Ibn Ṭawq, *Taʿlīq* 53. As one would expect, Ibn Ṭawq defends his esteemed friend.

138 Ibn Ṭawq, *Taʿlīq* 615, 1134, 1762.

139 Ibn Ṭawq, *Taʿlīq* 218. The issue is referred to in Shoshan, Mini-dramas.

140 Ibn Ṭawq, *Taʿlīq* 207. He adds his hope that others of his ilk would soon find a similar fate.

141 Ibn Ṭawq, *Taʿlīq* 1645, 1751, 1911.

the father to go to Cairo and address the sultan on the matter. As one version has it, he dramatically put before the ruler the remains of his son that he had been able to collect from the demolished tomb. Moved, the sultan summoned Kamāl al-Dīn and other top scholars from Damascus to explain their position; we are told that the sultan was inclined to follow Taqī al-Dīn, who, together with his son, the qadi Najm al-Dīn, was also summoned. The end result was that Kamāl al-Dīn was considered wrong and was treated roughly and underwent "tribulation (*miḥna*)."[142]

Another affair in which the shaykh got himself unwittingly involved had to do with the estate of Shihāb al-Dīn Aḥmad b. Ḥiṣn, a wealthy merchant (*khawājā*), reputed to have been generous and modest and to have invested secretively in projects for the public benefit. In the summer of 888/1483, terminally ill, he dictated his will (on a "European sheet of paper," as befitting a man of his status), and Ibn Ṭawq, who was summoned as a witness, describes the scene in detail. Accordingly, Yāqūt, the man's Ethiopian slave (he is also referred to as Badr, but it could be another slave), as was normally the case, now, before his master's death, received a document of manumission. A draft of the will was presented to the dying merchant, and those present urged him to give further sums to charity, but in a somewhat surprising reaction in light of what was reported about his generosity, he declined. This can be explained by his earlier contributions, or else by his long-time habit of donating in secret. Also, two letters of remittance, one for a loan of 200 dinars and one to his nephew, were now issued. He was further asked whether he owed other sums. About a week later our notary returned to Ibn Ḥiṣn, but the sick man was already in a coma, and he passed away shortly afterward. Many attended his funeral, among them the Shāfiʿī qadi. Even before the burial, when the corpse was purified, the qadi summoned Ibn Ṭawq and other professional witnesses to write down the details of Ibn Ḥiṣn's estate. A few weeks later the team came for another survey, and this time new items (for example, carpets of a lion's skin), which were placed in the reception hall, were added.[143]

Here, we reach the crucial matter which involved Taqī al-Dīn: he was appointed by Ibn Ḥiṣn to execute the will. Two months later a letter from the qadi Nūr al-Dīn b. al-Ṣābūnī, a former Damascene, who now served in the Cairo

142 al-Ghazzī, *Kawākib* i, 41–42; Ibn Ṭūlūn, *Mufākahat al-khillān* 257–258; Ibn Ṭūlūn, *Dhakhāʾir* ii, 662–667. For a conflict for reasons that are unspecified between Taqī al-Dīn and his cousin, the deputy qadi Muḥibb al-Dīn, see Ibn Ṭawq, *Taʿlīq* 210–211, 278, 284. On Muḥibb al-Dīn, see 37, 91, 457, 637, 1673; al-Buṣrawī, *Tārīkh* 44.

143 Ibn Ṭawq, *Taʿlīq* 256, 258, 259, 269. He came only because the shaykh asked him to, and he did not charge for it.

bureaucracy as *nāẓir al-jaysh*, was received.[144] Its content—according to Ibn Ṭawq, it was sheer nonsense—was that the shaykh and his associate Shihāb al-Dīn Aḥmad al-Muḥawjib had embezzled a third of the estate and had pocketed 1,000 dinars. Ibn al-Ṣābūnī would later apologize for this letter, but Ibn Ṭawq thought the apology to be an empty gesture. In any case, in this affair were entangled the shaykh's earlier conflicts, such as with Ibn Shaʿbān, the *sulṭān al-ḥarāfīsh*, who allegedly supported hashish dealers and for which, possibly with the shaykh's encouragement, his home was pillaged by the people. This "sultan" planned to take revenge, and now was the right time to send to Cairo a report defaming the shaykh.

A note of explanation is here in order. Like in Cairo and some other Syrian towns, the *ḥarāfīsh* (s. *ḥarfūsh*) was a group of men perhaps with some connection to Sufis and professional organizations.[145] They were active by the fourteenth century at the latest, and in our notary's day they took part in official ceremonies, parading together with soldiers in front of the viceroy and accompanying Mamluk officials.[146] They had their "sultan"—*kabīr*, also referred to, possibly ironically, as *kabīr al-asqāt* (? worthless) *wa-l-ḥarāfīsh*—who is further identified as Muḥammad Shaʿbān or Ibn Shaʿbān. He occupied some post at the Nūrī *maristān*, in connection with which he once was punished by receiving no less than 500 lashes, and only following the Shāfiʿī qadi's intercession was he released and his robe of honor returned to him.[147] In 888/1483 he got himself involved in the aforementioned affair of the sale of hashish, instigating commoners, perhaps those consuming the stuff, to pelt stones at the Sufis, who, as already noted, were the main opponents of hashish consumption. In retaliation, the "sultan's" residence was attacked by Sufis.[148] Shaʿbān (or Ibn Shaʿbān) died in Cairo in 902/1497. He was succeeded by his son, Sharaf al-Dīn Yūnus (d. 929/1523), referred to as Ibn Shaʿbān as well, who had earlier been a witness/notary and then a teacher at the Umayyad Mosque.[149]

---

144 Ibn Ṭawq, *Taʿlīq* 577; al-Buṣrawī, *Tārīkh* 35, 36, 85; Ibn Ṭūlūn, *Quḍāt Dimashq* 179.

145 See Ḥarfūsh, *EI*²; Brinner, Significance. For their possible connection with Sufis, see Shoshan, Popular Sufi sermons, esp. 107–108.

146 Ibn Ṭawq, *Taʿlīq* 382, 442, 463, 485, 499, 548, 731, 799, 946, 952, 978, 1117, 1600, 1609, 1614, 1615, 1661. There is a curios episode as regards the document of his appointment that was lost on the way to Damascus. See 201, 275, 340, 1487. For some information on earlier periods, see Lapidus, *Muslim cities* 180–182.

147 Ibn Ṭawq, *Taʿlīq* 621. For being flogged again for an unexplained reason, see 1386, 1387.

148 Ibn Ṭawq, *Taʿlīq* 275, 276. Ibn al-Ḥimṣī, *Ḥawādith* i, 287, is more elaborate. See also Ibn Ṭūlūn, *Ḥawādith* 158.

149 Ibn Ṭawq, *Taʿlīq* 1487, 1618; Ibn Ṭūlūn, *Mufākahat al-khillān* 96–97.

To return to the (real) sultan, upon receiving the mock-sultan's letter about Ibn Ḥiṣn's estate, he is reported to have joked: "Each new day has its story; one letter from the viceroy just arrived and another one is already in." Perhaps he was not joking after all and what he learned about the shaykh and his activities was to his disliking. The suspicion of the shaykh's management as the deceased man's trustee was coupled with a conflict with the treasurer of Damascus, who, so the rumor went, intended to raise meat prices. Also here an attempt to pillage his property was associated with the shaykh as the éminence grise, although, at least so thought Ibn Ṭawq, the latter rather tried to calm things down. Be that as it may, the sultan summoned the shaykh to Cairo and, in the meantime, Ibn Ḥiṣn's heirs demanded 2,000 dinars, most likely in compensation for what had allegedly been embezzled. On the eve of the shaykh's departure to Egypt, as the year 888/1483 drew to its end, Ibn Ṭawq spent the night at his esteemed friend's home. The next morning, joined by the shaykh's nephew Kamāl al-Dīn, his agent Zayn al-Dīn ʿAbd al-Qādir, and a few more of the shaykh's associates, he accompanied him for some distance as he started his long voyage to Cairo.[150]

During the first weeks of the shaykh's absence, Ibn Ṭawq took down many notes on his friend's whereabouts. He also described a split within the milieu of scholars, as well as intrigues and contradictory interests, all relevant to the issue considered. For example, one of the deputies of the qadi Ibn Farfūr reported that when it was stated that action against the shaykh would be viewed as directed at all scholars, al-Buṣrawī agreed but added that the shaykh should be held responsible for that. The Ḥanbalī qadi was of the opinion that the shaykh had caused his own troubles when reporting to the sultan on his conflict with the *sulṭān al-ḥarāfīsh*. Our notary ran into the preacher of the Saqīfa Mosque, who suggested that the shaykh should bribe the sultan; such an idea, in Ibn Ṭawq's opinion, was not only absurd but also would imply that Taqī al-Dīn was wealthy and, by extension, that he had in fact embezzled Ibn Ḥiṣn's estate. Suspicion as to who did not support the shaykh was in the air. Curiously, some of his friends and associates, including Ibn Ṭawq, reported of dreams in which he appeared to them. Ibn Ṭawq interpreted one of his own dreams as a "blessing" and an end to the shaykh's saga.

In the meantime, relatives and friends took care of the needs of Taqī al-Dīn's two wives and their children. They regularly delivered to them cooked food and basic items and planned to write to the sultan a letter of intercession. The educator of the shaykh's sons even dared at the end of one lesson

150 Ibn Ṭawq, *Taʿlīq* 275, 276, 278, 280, 282, 283, 286, 295, 296.

to condemn the sultan. Regular correspondence with the shaykh was maintained. At the same time, lists were drawn up of men suspected of embezzling 100,000 dinars from the sultan's share in Ibn Ḥiṣn's estate. It was claimed that al-Buṣrawī collaborated with unspecified men, to whom Ibn Ṭawq refers by the two letters *mīm nūn* (see for that also the Introduction), to dispatch a letter to the sultan, presumably accusing the shaykh. However, the envoy who was asked to deliver it refused and tore it to pieces in front of al-Buṣrawī. Ibn Ṭawq further reports on *mīm bā*, another codified reference to someone who boycotted some of the shaykh's associates. Of the news coming from Cairo, Ibn Ṭawq dwells on one item, according to which, after a few weeks, the shaykh gifted the ruler. Yet another piece of news said that the sultan banned Taqī al-Dīn from returning to Damascus and also from serving at al-Azhar as a Quran reader.[151] The intensity of reports on the shaykh's whereabouts in Egypt peters out with the passage of time. What we know is that the shaykh was forced to stay in Cairo for almost two years, after which the sultan agreed to his return to Damascus, the reason being a letter sent by the shaykh's aging mother, in which she described her difficulties during her son's absence. She emphasized that she had had to stop all activities at the madrasas funded by her endowments. Upon his return on a winter's day, the shaykh was welcomed by his friends near Damascus. He first visited his "Egyptian" wife and afterward went to see his mother, where he spent the first night and ate supper with friends. His long absence and his gesture to the "Egyptian" did not prevent the couple from returning only too quickly to their marital conflict. As to the major issue, namely, the Ibn Ḥiṣn estate, apparently it had not completely vanished even a few years later, when the aforementioned Ibn al-Ṣābūnī requested from the shaykh further documents. According to our notary, by that time a Damascene of the Ḥanbalī school, who suffered from a bad reputation for his involvement in scandals related to estates of the rich, rekindled things when he reached an influential position in Cairo.[152] If all this was not enough, another affair cast its shadow when one al-ʿUmarī complained to the sultan about the shaykh. Only about three years after the end of his forced stay in Cairo, Taqī al-Dīn was summoned to Egypt once again. Other than a laconic sentence about al-ʿUmarī's failure to establish his case, we know nothing, and after three months the shaykh was allowed to return.[153]

---

151 Ibn Ṭawq, *Taʿlīq* 298–299, 300, 302, 303–304, 305, 306, 307, 312, 316, 317, 320, 321, 323, 326, 329, 330, 335–336, 337, 338, 342, 350, 356, 357, 358.

152 Ibn Ṭawq, *Taʿlīq* 517, 518, 521, 536, 1138.

153 Ibn Ṭawq, *Taʿlīq* 808, 812, 813, 817, 819, 868, 869, 874, 895.

This is not the end to our encounter with Taqī al-Dīn Ibn Qāḍī ʿAjlūn. We shall have in other chapters further opportunities to learn more about him. However, at least one thing is clear by now. From Ibn Ṭawq's point of view no one was more important in Damascus than the shaykh. With a divided milieu of scholars and bureaucrats, the shaykh was as solid as a rock. His activities in the public domain were intense and impressive and deserved admiration.

CHAPTER 4

Bourgeois Fortunes

Records from the province of Damascus as registered for the summer of 1516 (i.e., immediately after the Ottoman conquest) reveal precious little on the wealth of the local bourgeoisie.[1] Ibn Ṭawq's diary provides unique information on both urban and land property, and especially about waqfs established by civilians. That not a few bourgeois, as we saw in Chapter 2, were able to purchase their offices for enormous sums, or that their assets were confiscated, indicates their strong financial basis. We can learn of the volume of bourgeois fortunes from the reported taxation on merchants, scholars, and officeholders such as qadis. Also the figures that Ibn Ṭawq occasionally has for the sale or rent of property by the bourgeoisie strike one as evidencing considerable wealth. In addition, some, as we shall see, possessed huge sums in cash or left these upon their death. At the same time, the fortunes amassed by the bourgeoisie had a fragile existence because they were not immune from confiscation. How and where did they protect their money? This is an intriguing question for which we have no answer.

1 High Bourgeoisie

At the top of the list of the bourgeoisie of late Mamluk Damascus features the Ibn al-Muzalliq family, whose ancestor arrived from Aleppo at some point, possibly in the fourteenth century. The first family member known to us, Shams al-Dīn Muḥammad b. ʿAlī (d. 848/1444), is referred to as a grand *khawājā*, which is a term used for wealthy merchants. He established *khān*s in various locations, including in the Golan Heights. Muḥammad b. Muḥammad al-Asadī, whose book on the economic situation in the Mamluk state was written less than ten years after Shams al-Dīn's death, describes him as one of the kings (*mulūk*) whose sons were active in the Yemen and in Kīlān (?) and received great honor, so that "drums are beaten at their gate."[2] One of them, Shihāb al-Dīn Aḥmad (d. 873/1468), was similarly known as a *khawājā*, as well as a *kārim*, a term used

1 Winter, Mamluks 297–298, 298–299, 310, 313–314; Reilly, Rural waqfs 29.

2 Ibn al-Ḥimṣī, *Ḥawādith* i, 184 with further references; al-Nuʿaymī, *al-Dāris* ii, 223–224; Anṣārī, *Nuzhat al-khāṭir* ii, 118, n. 1; al-Asadī, *Taysīr* 85.

 | DOI:10.1163/9789004413269_006

for a merchant engaged in seafaring and global trade. Being associated with the circle of Shihāb al-Dīn Aḥmad b. Qurā (d. 868/1464), a Shāfiʿī and a Sufi, he was viewed sympathetically by both scholars and Sufis; when he died, his funeral was crowded, and a prayer for him was led by the Shāfiʿī qadi.[3] The residence he left, near the Ḥanafī al-Jawhariyya madrasa, included two square halls (*murabbaʿ*), a well, and other amenities (*manāfiʿ wa-marāfiq wa-ghayr dhālika*), and was sold for 50 ashrafis to the merchant Zayn al-Dīn ʿAbd al-Qādir, also known as Ibn al-ʿAdl, who had business contact with Taqī al-Dīn, the *shaykh al-Islām*.[4] Of his close relatives, either Shams al-Dīn Muḥammad, who served as a Shāfiʿī qadi and has been mentioned earlier on a few occasions, or his son, Muḥammad Najm al-Dīn, owned a mill at Manīn, north of Damascus.[5] Jalāl al-Dīn Yūsuf (d. 896/1490), another family member, sold his house, as well as a converted shop and a garden, to Shams al-Dīn Muḥammad, the son of the *khaṭīb* of the Saqīfa Mosque.[6]

It is especially about Shihāb al-Dīn's waqfs that we are informed in the *Taʿlīq*. Here, a short digression is necessary. It is well known that endowments have played an important role in the economies of Islamic societies. Although originally having a social purpose, in the course of time, and in the absence of a notion of property rights, they became an essential means, on the one hand, of securing private property from confiscation and, on the other hand, of guaranteeing income not only to the family and descendants of the endower but also to a large number of officeholders and all sorts of beneficiaries.[7] It is assumed that in the course of the fourteenth and fifteenth centuries in Egypt and Syria the ruling Mamluks of various offices and ranks utilized the waqf system to circumscribe the Muslim ban on the privatization of land—its belonging to the "Muslim nation" (*umma*) or "state"—and to turn land formerly assigned as *iqṭāʿ* (i.e., the right to tax cultivated land as a financial resource) into practically private land that was labeled as waqf land.[8] Now, the prevailing assumption is that in Mamluk Syria waqfs were established by the military elite and that

3 al-Buṣrawī, *Tārīkh* 33; ʿAbd al-Bāsiṭ, *Muʿjam* i, 544; al-Sakhāwī, *Ḍawʾ*, s.v.; Ibn Iyās, *Badāʾiʿ* iii, 18. For the term *khawājikī*, see Ibn Ṭawq, *Taʿlīq* 1586. For Shihāb al-Dīn b. Qurā, see Ibn al-Ḥimṣī, *Ḥawādith* i, 164.

4 Ibn Ṭawq, *Taʿlīq* 1179. On this merchant, see further 427, 447, 748–749, 829–830. For a brief note, see Wollina, View 289; Wollina, *Zwanzig* 145. On this madrasa, established in 676/1277–1278, see al-Nuʿaymī, *al-Dāris* i, 381–383; Badrān, *Munādama* 164.

5 Ibn Ṭawq, *Taʿlīq* 292–293.

6 Ibn Ṭawq, *Taʿlīq* 422, 543–544, where further details are given.

7 The literature on this topic is vast. See e.g. Lev, *Charity*; Deguilhem, Waqf.

8 For a discussion of this process, see Igarashi, *Land tenure* 177–182.

merchants were not among the prominent founders.[9] However, this assumption has suffered from a lacuna in our historical sources. Although it cannot be denied that the Mamluks were the main founders of waqfs, Ibn Ṭawq provides unique material on the role of the bourgeoisie in this context.

To return to Ibn al-Muzalliq's endowments, some were based on his urban property. A Sufi lodge (*zāwiya*) and a caravansary (*qayṣariyya*) carried the name of the Ibn al-Muzalliq family, which may suggest a connection to a waqf.[10] Another possible waqf that Shihāb al-Dīn established was a soup kitchen (? *maṭbakh*) known as al-Ḥashīsha (?) by the Bāb al-Barīd; its inspection was in the hands of the Ibn Qāḍī ʿAjlūn family.[11] From another of Shihāb al-Dīn's unspecified waqfs, 90 dirhams were allocated annually to support a Quran reader in Jerusalem.[12]

Most of Shihāb al-Dīn's endowment consisted of land in the Ghūṭa. This is a tendency confirmed by sixteenth-century Ottoman registers that list land as comprising more than 90 percent of private property. Although the low figure for urban property can be explained technically by the "fiscal orientation" of the registers,[13] another and perhaps more meaningful way to explain the investment in land is the low prices of land as compared to urban property, which encouraged the purchase of land by the city inhabitants of various ranks. This shall become clear later in this chapter.

Some of Shihāb al-Dīn's cultivated fields (*mazraʿa*) were in the Upper Qābūn village slightly north of Damascus. They were leased on the basis of *ḥikr* (or *muḥākara*; i.e., a tenancy involving the permission to make the necessary repair in the estate, which would provide the tenant with special rights). Adjacent land of the same waqf was known as the al-Fayāḍ orchard (*bustān*), and both grew fruit trees, as well as different kinds of grain and vegetables. This was a large, charitable waqf (*mabrūr*) that first provided for the endower's descendants. Part of its proceeds supported also a *zāwiya*, perhaps the aforementioned one that carried the family name, as well as a mosque located in the vicinity. Its administrator (*mutakallim*) was Zayn al-Dīn Khiḍr al-Ḥisbānī, who appears to have been prominent in supervising Ibn al-Muzalliq's waqfs. Asked

9 Ghazaleh, Introduction 4 and n. 8. For some qualifying remarks, see Hanna, Guilds 136. For a general treatment, see Lapidus, *Muslim cities* 59–61, 73–75. For the problems involved in researching Syrian waqfs in the period under consideration, see Waḳf, *EI*², Section II/2. For an example of a waqf document and its analysis, see Reinfandt, Beurkundung. A good treatment of the waqfs established by the Mamluks is by Igarashi, *Land tenure* 182–211.

10 Ibn Ṭawq, *Taʿlīq* 1795, 1908. The latter was damaged in a fire at the end of 906/1501.

11 Ibn al-Ḥimṣī, *Ḥawādith* i, 184.

12 Ibn Ṭawq, *Taʿlīq* 660.

13 Miura, *Dynamism* 195–196.

to calculate the revenues generated from this waqf, Ibn Ṭawq provides some figures. In Rabīʿ I 888/April 1483 four partners purchased the produce for 4,200 dirhams, and a month later Sāra, the daughter of the waqf's founder (and a future wife of the *shaykh al-Islām*), received the sum of 2,000 dirhams. In 890/1485 the produce of the al-Fayāḍ orchard was sold for 2,200 dirhams. The following months, for an unknown reason, were a time of severe crisis, and an extremely small revenue of 80 dirhams, much lower than the 1,000 promised by the cultivators, was generated. However, a few months later there was considerable improvement, and in Jumādā I 891/May 1486, apricot (*mishmish*) and other kinds of fruits were sold for 5,300 dirhams. In Rajab 898/May 1493 its fruits were auctioned, fetching 1,300 dirhams. Then, in Ṣafar 905/September 1499, the Qābūn and Fayāḍ fields were rented for four years for the sum of 4,800 dirhams, 4,000 of which were received in cash.[14]

Another cultivated land that Ibn al-Muzalliq endowed and was likewise administered by al-Ḥisbānī was known as al-Funaydiq and Muzarkil. In 896/1491, 17 of its 24 shares (*sahm*) were rented for 4 years for the annual sum of 1,500 dirhams, to be paid at the end of each year.[15] A third and particularly large and lucrative waqf was established at al-Ḥadītha village and was administered jointly by al-Ḥisbānī and Taqī al-Dīn b. Qāḍī ʿAjlūn, at least from 886/1481. In 895/1489 the proceeds of 113 nut trees were bought by a peasant from ʿArbīl for 3,600 dirhams; the sum was guaranteed by an expert in horse training (*al-muʿallim fāris*). On the same day, additional proceeds were bought for 5,000 dirhams by two partners, and nuts (*lūz*) were bought by a Jaramānā peasant for the considerable sum of 7,500 dirhams.[16] The al-Ruqām orchard, located in the village of Jawbar, was another of Ibn al-Muzalliq's small waqfs and was also administered by al-Ḥisbānī. At the end of 888/1484 a peasant took upon himself to cultivate it for a quarter of the fruit (*thamra*) and half the vegetables (*ʿalā al-arḍ*), apparently a normal arrangement in such contracts. The waqf itself bore the land tax (*kharāj*) and further expenses; the peasant's dues were half a tithe (*ʿushr*). A couple of years later the contract with the same cultivator

14 Ibn Ṭawq, *Taʿlīq* 178, 240, 245 (the editor's rendering that it was "a share of her deceased son [*ibnihā*]" should be corrected to the share of her father, *abīhā*), 358, 438, 472, 543 (Ibn Ṭawq went into the service, *khidma*, of *Sidi al-Shaykh*, but it is unclear in what capacity, as Taqī al-Dīn does not appear to be its administrator), 617, 618, 623, 628, 637–638, 660, 769, 862, 923, 1192, 1337, 1718, 1748, 1192. For the original (*aṣl*) waqf document declared missing, see 1337. For *ḥikr*, see Ḥikr, *EI*²; Reilly, Rural waqfs 30.

15 Ibn Ṭawq, *Taʿlīq* 1063. For his appointment as administrator (*walī al-birr*), see Ibn Ṭūlūn, *Mufākahat al-khillān* 202.

16 Ibn Ṭawq, *Taʿlīq* 148, 628, 743, 827, 883, 917, 918, 927, 1835–1836. For al-Ḥadītha see Yāqūt, *Muʿjam al-buldān*, s.v.

specified 300 dirhams a year.[17] A few more waqfs established by Ibn al-Muzalliq are unidentifiable and appear to have been small.[18]

Next on the list of merchants appears the al-Qārī family, whose origin was in the Qārā village, northeast of Damascus.[19] ʿĪsā (d. 895/1490), a *khawājā* and *kabīr al-tujjār*, renovated the Ḥammām al-Murattab near "the Church (*kanīsat al-naṣāra*)."[20] It was opened in 891/1486, and three men operated it on a *ḍamān* basis for the daily price of 80 dirhams,[21] higher than the daily prices of other public baths, and therefore possibly indicating a higher standard. About a month before his death a complaint was filed against ʿĪsā and his sons, as well as two more men, for developing a large property claimed to be owned by another wealthy merchant.[22] Muḥammad ʿAlāʾ al-Dīn, ʿĪsā's son, owned a residence with a bath in it and an orchard at Ḥammām Saṭrā in the Ghūṭa, which he bought from Ibn Ṭawq and his partner for 2,500 dirhams. ʿAlī, Muḥammad's brother, built houses and a *khān* for the silk trade. He had in partnership a plot watered at ʿAyn Thurmā in the Ghūṭa. Their cousin Muḥammad b. Yūsuf established a madrasa near the Jābiya Gate and owned an adjacent spacious residence.[23] Following the death of ʿAbd al-Wāḥid, another family member, his daughter Maryam leased his residence for 100 dirhams (about 2 dinars a month).[24] The family's property in later time is recorded in seventeenth-century sources.[25]

Other *khawājās* are reported to have established waqfs. Such was the residence of Shams al-Dīn b. Naḥḥās, which was valued at the enormous sum of 30,000 (? dirhams; about 600 dinars). However, as already mentioned in Chapter 2, possibly as a means to counter the widespread phenomenon of diverting private property into waqf, the sultan did not honor its status and ordered its

---

17 Ibn Ṭawq, *Taʿlīq* 301, 482 (editor's reading Bustān al-Rifā is an error). For Jawbar, see Yāqūt, *Muʿjam al-buldān*, s.v.

18 The al-Shihābī (after Shihāb al-Dīn) was a grove (*ghayḍa*) at the Rabwa, near the Baradā River. See al-Shihābī, *Muʿjam Dimashq* i, 326–327. For a waqf of cultivated land, known as ʿAyn Ḥamūs in the Biqāʿ al-ʿAzīzī (unidentified), as well as land in the Qabr Ilyās village, see Ibn Ṭawq, *Taʿlīq* 1179.

19 ʿAlī al-Qārī, who is described as "of the merchants of Qārā," died in that town. See Ibn Ṭawq, *Taʿlīq* 1143.

20 On his death, see Ibn Ṭawq, *Taʿlīq* 970; al-Buṣrawī, *Tārīkh* 142.

21 Ibn Ṭawq, *Taʿlīq* 601.

22 Ibn Ṭawq, *Taʿlīq* 957.

23 Ibn Ṭawq, *Taʿlīq* 696, 968, 1014; Ibn Ṭūlūn, *Dhakhāʾir al-qasr* ii, 649. On the village, see Yāqūt, *Muʿjam al-buldān*, s.v.

24 Taqī al-Dīn gave it in rent for two years; half a year's rent had to be paid in advance. A short time later, the agreement was annulled and instead the house was rented for the same price to a notary. See Ibn Ṭawq, *Taʿlīq* 1651, 1655.

25 El-Zawahreh, *Religious endowments* 184.

sale.[26] Aḥmad Shihāb al-Din al-Dulāmī established in 847/1443–1444 a *dār al-Qur'ān*. The waqf document stipulated as beneficiaries an imam, a reader of al-Bukhari's *Ṣaḥīḥ*, six immigrants from the Maghrib, and the same number of orphans. Oil, candles, and mutton were to be supplied. Aḥmad Shihāb al-Din al-Ṣābūnī established a similar institution in 868/1463–1464 south of Bāb al-Jābiya. One of its preachers was the chronicler al-Buṣrawī. The waqf document stipulated that the preacher must be a Shāfiʿī and the imam a Ḥanafī. The endowment also provided for orphans, and its proceeds came from a large number of villages and from urban property, mostly shops, apparently owned by the endower. Incidentally, al-Ṣābūnī was summoned to the citadel a few years later and died there under dubious circumstances.[27]

Of Damascus scholars the Ibn Qāḍī ʿAjlūn family was most prominent as property owners. To begin with the *shaykh al-Islām* Taqī al-Dīn, from all that has been said about him earlier, it will be of little surprise to learn that he was able to accumulate considerable wealth. His "old" or "large" residence, where his first wife resided, was located in the neighborhood of the Bādirā'iyya.[28] His "new" home, where his second wife lived, was located near the Qaymariyya.[29] After their separation he sold it for no less than 600 ashrafīs, plus the equivalent of 200 ashrafīs in silver currency, to the *kārim* merchant (*al-saffār*) ʿAlā' al-Dīn ʿUmar of the al-Qārī family.[30] This price is similar to that of Ibn Naḥḥās's residence mentioned above, in other words, indicating the residence to have been palatial. The shaykh also had a share in Ḥammām Isrā'īl, located outside the city wall, which he rented for the daily sum of 13 dirhams, hence over 4,000 dirhams (about 80 dinars) a year. He also owned an oven, which, together with the second story above it, was rented for 40 dirhams a month, or 480 dirhams (about 9 dinars) a year. The renter had to supply bread, eggplants, and meat to the shaykh's two households. Later, the oven was rented for 60 dirhams a month and a supply of similar food items for a nine-month period.[31] The shaykh also had a share in an oil press (*miʿṣara*) and a mill near Aleppo in partnership with

26 Ibn Ṭūlūn, *Mufākahat al-khillān* 139.

27 al-Buṣrawī, *Tārīkh* 31, 34; al-Nuʿaymī, *al-Dāris* i, 8–9, 11–12.

28 Ibn Ṭawq, *Taʿlīq* 37, 250.

29 E.g. Ibn Ṭawq, *Taʿlīq* 103, 148, 218, 236. The Qaymariyya, located east of the Umayyad Mosque, was named after its founder, Nāṣir al-Dīn Qaymar (d. 665/1266–1267). For this madrasa, see al-Nuʿaymī, *al-Dāris* i, 335–339; al-ʿAlmāwī, *Mukhtaṣar* 69–70; al-Shihābī, *Muʿjam Dimashq* ii, 205; Badrān, *Munādama* 140, 142.

30 Ibn Ṭawq, *Taʿlīq* 743, 748–750, with further details on the payment. A goldsmith (*ṣā'igh*) had to examine the coins.

31 Ibn Ṭawq, *Taʿlīq* 40 (and n. 5 for location), 56–57, 152, 227, 301, 304, 423. The renter was allowed to keep 2 dirhams, apparently to cover expenses. He was granted one month gratis

his mother. As we shall see shortly, it was extremely lucrative.[32] As to land, a garden near the Kaysān Gate was rented according to "the normal custom" of half of the vegetables (*min al-arḍ*) and a quarter of the fruits (*min al-shajar*) going to the cultivator.[33] There is mention of other cultivated fields he owned.[34] One may point out that, as befitting a luminary with considerable property in his possession, the shaykh owned two precious Quran copies, one (incomplete) produced by the renowned ʿAbbāsid calligrapher Ibn al-Bawwāb, the other by the famous encyclopaedist Yāqūt.[35]

Ibn Ṭawq provides a few examples of transactions in which the shaykh invested. With Ḥāj Qāsim, "the Turkmen," his neighbor in Upper Qābūn, he concluded a commercial agreement (*muḍāraba/qirāḍ*) similar to the western *commenda* on two separate occasions, a year apart, the second being in connection with the upcoming ʿĪd al-Aḍḥā. Qāsim, who played the role of an agent/partner, received 100 dinars, of which he was to keep 22 regardless of the profit, which he was expected to share equally with his subagent, another Turkmen, who was to do the actual traveling for the purchase. In such eventuality, Taqī al-Dīn, the so-called sleeping partner, was to get the other half of the expected profit, in addition to the initial investment of 100 dinars. It was implied that the agents were not expected to bear any loss in case the project failed or no profit was made.[36]

Next among the family members, Kamāl al-Dīn, the shaykh's nephew and a leading Shāfiʿī in his own right, owned considerable property. He rented a hall to a Jerusalemite qadi, although for the unimpressive sum of 40 dirhams annually; in practice, the rent was even lower.[37] Another real estate he rented consisted of two halls, a second floor (*ṭabaqa*), and storage (*makhzan*). The duration was six and a half years, and the total sum 2,430 dirhams (close to 50 dinars). He also had rights (*mustaḥiqq*) in Ḥammām al-Rāhib.[38] He owned

---

(*muṭlaq shahr*). For this ḥammām, see al-Nuʿaymī, *al-Dāris* i, 278. For the oven, see also El-Leithy, Living documents 415.

32 Ibn Ṭawq, *Taʿlīq* 409–410, 1302, 1392, 1464.

33 Ibn Ṭawq, *Taʿlīq* 154, 1046. Its location was east of the Shāghūr Quarter and it was named after caliph Muʿāwiya's *mawlā*. See al-Badrī, *Nuzhat al-anām* 17.

34 Ibn Ṭawq, *Taʿlīq* 155 (and n. 1 for location), 326, 375. See also 141, 580–581.

35 Ibn Ṭawq, *Taʿlīq* 1380–1381. Ibn al-Bawwāb, *EI*². While the prices of these books are unknown, we have a few price quotations for manuscripts, usually when sold in some estate. They range between 100 and several hundred dirhams, that is, a few dinars—incidentally, much less than a good-quality saddle. See Ibn Ṭawq, *Taʿlīq* 263–264.

36 Ibn Ṭawq, *Taʿlīq* 760, 818. See Ḳirāḍ, *EI*²; Muḍāraba, *EI*².

37 Ibn Ṭawq, *Taʿlīq* 138. For its location, see al-Shihābī, *Muʿjam Dimashq* ii, 48.

38 Ibn Ṭawq, *Taʿlīq* 632 (with some further calculation), 1212, 1236.

cultivated land at ʿAyn Thurmā and at the Ṭawāḥīn al-Ashnān neighborhood in the Ṣāliḥiyya Quarter, by the Thawra river, and with two partners, in the Qābūn village, he leased land to a *ḍāmin*. Ibn Ṭawq once arranged for a sale of its produce for the nice sum of 3,400 dirhams (close to 70 dinars). There was also a share (*ḥiṣṣa*) in another land, which two *ḍāmin*s, one of whom was the *khaṭīb* of Jarūd, took for cultivation, and on which grain was grown; the two cultivators had to mortgage their vineyard and an oil press in order to conclude the transaction. At the end of 894/1489 the produce generated the large sum of 8,298 dirhams (or over 150 dinars). Kamāl al-Dīn also leased his share of one-eighth of cultivated land at al-Muḥaydatha and at Shūf al-Bayyāḍ, both at Wādī al-Taym, some distance southwest of the city, for 30 years for the total sum of 19 ashrafīs paid in advance. Further lease contracts of his land are mentioned.[39]

Whether the aforementioned plots of land were turned into endowments is not stated, but we do know that Kamāl al-Dīn willed cultivated land at Qalbīn (location unclear) and stipulated that a fixed sum of its proceeds should be spent on a soup kitchen (*maṭbakh*) on the night of the first Friday of each year, which implies it was a waqf. In addition, a monthly sum would be allocated to the muezzins at the Umayyad Mosque to pay for a nocturnal recitation. A sum of 50 ashrafīs was to support every year one pilgrim to Mecca and an identical sum supply pilgrims with water. In Mecca itself a fixed sum would be allotted to Quran readers. Whatever remained of the proceeds would go to Kamāl al-Dīn's descendants (*ilā ākhir al-sharṭ*).[40] The scholar also endowed his residence and all its specified parts "according to their parameters and what they contain." A stipulation allowed his mother (apparently, in case she outlived him) to reside in the complex wherever she desired. An additional endowment was a renovated covered market (*qayṣāriya*) in the vicinity of Bāb Tūmā.[41]

Another member of the Ibn Qāḍī ʿAjlūn family, the deputy qadi Muḥibb al-Dīn, left real estate valued in the enormous sum of 3,000 dinars. His home was rented for the high sum of 6 dinars a month, on condition that his mother-in-law could stay there.[42] While still alive, he leased for 142 dirhams a year a garden located within the city walls, near the Qaymariya, to the cultivator Yūsuf al-Jaramānī, with whom also Ibn Ṭawq did business. After his death the garden, now a waqf, was leased to Yūsuf's mother for a period of 16 months for a total

39 Ibn Ṭawq, *Taʿlīq* 240, 242, 251, 253, 364–365, 396, 428, 898, 950, 1585, 1586. For receiving 119 (dirhams) from Aḥmad the miller, see 428. For its location east of Damascus, see 253 n. 1.

40 For Syrian waqfs to the benefit of the Holy Places in the Hijaz, see Frenkel, *Awqāf* 162–163.

41 Ibn Ṭawq, *Taʿlīq* 1534–1535. Taqī al-Dīn was appointed *waṣṣī* and *nāẓir* to take care of all remaining debts.

42 Ibn Ṭawq, *Taʿlīq* 688, 690.

of 200 dirhams, to be paid at the end of the period. All future investment for the upkeep was to be borne by the renter; a contract (*musāqāt*) regarding the trees was stipulated.[43]

Also women of the Ibn Qāḍī ʿAjlūn family owned property. Taqī al-Dīn's mother (*al-sitt al-kabīra*)—she died in 901/1495 when he was in his 50s—appears to have been extremely well-off and in this respect on a par with the family's male members. Together with her son's first wife, she sold a house located in the al-Sharaf al-Aʿlā, previously rented for 116 dirhams per month, together with its adjacent garden, for 4,500 dirhams (or about 90 dinars).[44] Later, the two women sold the adjacent property known as the "House of al-Najjār" for 16 dinars.[45] With Taqī al-Dīn she shared a lucrative mill in Aleppo, for which she received from the miller at one point 2,000 dirhams and later no less than 4,481, partly in silver ingots (*ḥajarayn fiḍḍa*) instead of currency. The miller vouched for the huge sum of 15,000 dirhams, partly to be paid in advance, for a ten-year extension. Ibn Ṭawq drafted it in several copies, one of which he kept to himself, the Shāfiʿī qadi authorizing the agreement.[46] Together with the wife of Muḥammad b. al-Suyūrī al-Ḥarīrī (also referred to as Bt. al-Ḥaẓīrī), both established in equal parts an orchard as a waqf, of which she was the inspector, for the benefit of their descendants.[47]

Other ladies of the family are also noted. Kamāl al-Dīn's sister, the "honorable lady" (*al-sayyida al-sharīfa*), willed to her brother the main hall of her residence, for which he had to compensate her husband. Upon her death, goldsmiths valued the jewelry she left, which had to be melted to determine the amount of pure gold and silver.[48] Khadīja, also known as Sitt al-ʿUlamāʾ, who died following birth complications, willed to her husband Abū l-Yumn, Taqī al-Dīn's nephew, her share in a property jointly owned also by him, their three-year-old son, and her mother. It was later sold for 4,000 dirhams (about 80 dinars) to two partners, who added 100 dirhams for the young orphan's "good luck." Khadīja also willed cloths, silverware, and jewelry to her family mem-

43 Ibn Ṭawq, *Taʿlīq* 431, 533, 637. Kamāl al-Dīn, Muḥibb al-Dīn's relative, saw to it, probably as stipulated in the waqf document.

44 Ibn Ṭawq, *Taʿlīq* 130, 152, 189, 447, 479. For an abortive attempt to sell earlier, see 394. For her death, see 1424.

45 Ibn Ṭawq, *Taʿlīq* 834.

46 Ibn Ṭawq, *Taʿlīq* 189, 400, 409–410, 516–517 (where the exact calculation and the paperwork procedure are specified).

47 Ibn Ṭawq, *Taʿlīq* 1242. It was located at the Ṣāliḥiyya Path opposite the "Graves of the Martyrs" and the Orchard of the Prisoners (?). For this path, see al-Shihābī, *Muʿjam Dimashq* i, 298.

48 Ibn Ṭawq, *Taʿlīq* 523, 528, 534–535, 537, 539, 540.

bers. Her husband received a quarter of the sale price of 5,342 dirhams, her son 1,265 dirhams, and her mother one-sixth, valued at 3,561 dirhams. Ibn Ṭawq, who served as a witness, provides details on high taxes and charges that had to be paid. Two years later, Abū l-Yumn and his mother-in-law disputed, presenting mutual claims about their share in the estate. In the event, Abū l-Yumn had to pay her 1,300 dirhams.[49]

Of other prominent ulema, noteworthy are members of the Shāfiʿī family Ibn Farfūr. The deputy qadi Muḥibb al-Dīn (d. 900/1494), who is mentioned in 883/1478 together with his brother, a deputy qadi as well, as tax collectors, and a couple of years later also in charge of *dīwān al-jaysh*, endowed a share in villages near ʿAjlūn in the Jordan Valley. Following his death, 220 dinars were discovered hidden at his home, although a much larger sum was suspected to have remained.[50] Most prominent of this family was the qadi Shihāb al-Dīn Ibn Farfūr (d. 911/1505). Born to a bureaucrat who served Ibn Muzhir, the *kātib al-sirr*,[51] Shihāb al-Dīn joined his father's bureau. He must have excelled, as at the young age of 33 he was appointed to the post of qadi, this in addition to other posts he already held such as *nāẓir al-jaysh*, *wakīl al-sulṭān*, and *nāẓir al-qalʿa*. To recall, he paid for the post of qadi 30,000 dinars—at least, this is the figure provided. Even if we divide it by ten, it was still enormous. How did the young qadi save so much money before he even turned 33? Was it through his earlier jobs? This is most unlikely. Did he take a loan? And if this is the case, from how many did he do so? In any case, upon becoming qadi, and during the 25 years he held this job, he appointed no less than 24 deputies who paid him for their appointment. If indeed he had borrowed money to pay for his post, this could have helped him to repay the loan.

In early Ottoman registers Ibn Farfūr appears as the owner of 13 shops and other assets. These were endowed to his descendants, one of whom, his son Walī al-Dīn Muḥammad, became his deputy at age 15 and succeeded him as qadi shortly after his death, when he was barely 16.[52] No further comment is required after reading such details to understand the low ebb the post reached. To go back to Shihāb al-Dīn's endowment, a stipulation in the deed stated that,

---

49 Ibn Ṭawq, *Taʿlīq* 816, 819–820, 842–843, 915, 916, 1049–1050.

50 For his endowment, see Walker, *Jordan* 253 n. 60. For further information on him, see Ibn al-Ḥimṣī, *Ḥawādith* i, 224, 374; Ibn Ṭūlūn, *Mufākahat al-khillān* 27. For his death possibly in his 70s or 80s, see Ibn Ṭawq, *Taʿlīq* 1319, 1320. However, he maintains that no gold coins were found.

51 See on him Geoffroy, *Soufisme* 441–443.

52 Miura, *Dynamism* 138–139. For the dates of his birth and death, see Ibn Ṭūlūn, *Ḥawādith* 242.

in the absence of heirs, the proceeds would go to the benefit of the Nūrī Hospital and the Umayyad Mosque.[53] Shihāb al-Dīn also owned a cultivated garden and a bath at al-Sharaf al-Aʿlā, which in the past had been the property of Tāj al-Dīn Ibn Qāḍī ʿAjlūn, Taqī al-Dīn's cousin. In the winter of 904/1499 he initiated the construction of an underground canal for drawing water to a certain site in the city where he planned to cultivate an orchard. Our notary was present and has a few further details about the project.[54] One puzzling report is about Shihab al-Dīn's administrative grant (*iqṭāʿ*) near Jizīn.[55] Such grant was not normally associated with civilians, especially since its purpose was the upkeep of troops.[56] If the report is correct, one wonders what precisely the grant implied in this case.

The aforementioned Ḥanafī qadi Burhān al-Dīn b. al-Quṭb appears to have been no less successful economically. Appointed in 896/1491 after paying 2,000 dinars, due to a complaint two years into his term he was summoned to Cairo, not for the first time, where he died. He left real estate and endowments in the enormous value of 4.300 ashrafīs, yet his contenders claimed that his debts were in a similar amount. As so often happened, the large estate was disputed between his widow and his grandson.[57] The property of the deceased Badr al-Dīn, of the prominent family of Qāḍī Adhriʿāt, the precise boundaries of which are detailed, was sold "with all its amenities," including a kitchen, a well, a pond for purification, and an open space, to a Sufi shaykh for 90 dinars. Ten dirhams of the proceeds were allocated every year to a nearby mosque, and an identical sum to the benefit of the Holy Places.[58] The Shāfʿī Ṣalāḥ al-Dīn al-ʿAdawī, who served in various administrative posts such as *wakīl al-sulṭān*, *nāẓir al-qalʿa*, and a *nāẓir* at a madrasa, leased an orchard that must have been especially large since it generated the exceptional sum of 3,750 dirhams (or about 75 dinars)

53 Miura, *Dynamism* 195, 196. For the family's property in later periods, see El-Zawahreh, *Religious endowments* 184–185. For his biography, see Ibn Ṭūlūn, *Quḍāt Dimashq* 180–181.

54 Ibn Ṭawq, *Taʿlīq* 1066, 1309, 1681–1682, 1735.

55 Ibn Ṭawq, *Taʿlīq* 703, 704; Miura, Urban society 163 n. 27 (the reference to the *Taʿlīq* is erroneous). For a laconic reference to Ibn Farfūr's *iqṭāʿ*, see also Ibn Ṭūlūn, *Mufākahat al-khillān* 87, 89, 93. For a few *iqṭāʿ*s and the names of their holders without further details, see Ibn Ṭawq, *Taʿlīq* 361, 698, 743, 1057. One about which he does elaborate was granted to Kurtbāy, the *khāzindār* and *ustādār*, as a contractor (*ḍāmin*), in return for the enormous annual sum of 9,500 ashrafīs. In 897/1491 he failed to raise it and was punished with severe flogging and imprisonment. He was soon replaced. See Ibn Ṭawq, *Taʿlīq* 1084, 1087, 1293.

56 See Iḳṭāʿ, *EI*². For specialized studies see, e.g. Rabie, Size.

57 Ibn Ṭawq, *Taʿlīq* 1293; Ibn al-Ḥimṣī, *Ḥawādith* i, 282; Ibn Ṭūlūn, *Quḍāt Dimashq* 232–233.

58 Ibn Ṭawq, *Taʿlīq* 1181–1182. On the proceeds of this estate to the benefit of the mosque, see also 610.

annually.[59] The Shāfiʿī qadi Quṭb al-Dīn Muḥammad al-Khayḍarī (d. 894/1489) endowed in 878/1473–1474 a madrasa or a *dār al-Qurʾān* by his residence near the Jābiya Gate. In the past it had been a small mosque. Al-Khayḍarī enlarged it and provided it with amenities. In addition, he established a *maṭbakh* at Bāb al-Farādīs.[60]

Of high-echelon officials, the Samaritan clerk (? *mutasharrif* ? *mutaṣarrif*) Ṣadaqa strikes the reader as having been of unparalleled wealth. He and his father each owned a residence in the Samaritan Quarter. Ṣadaqa's house is reported as having been valued at 16,000 dinars, a sum that, if of any basis, was 30 times higher than a normal bourgeois residence. Ṣadaqa worked at the viceroy's *dīwān* and was a money changer for the sultan. He was much respected (or feared), to the point that even a deputy of one of the Ḥanafī qadis was spotted kissing his hand. After his conversion, he moved from the Samaritan Quarter. He was granted an *iqṭāʿ*, for which he should have advanced the enormous sum of 7,000 dinars a month, were not the contract abrogated on the next day for unspecified reasons. There were further ups and downs in his career till his final downfall, after being accused of embezzling 24,000 dinars. In 900/1495 he was punished by the sultan after being accused of deceitful conversion (*taqiya*) to save his life. His spacious residence in the Samaritan Quarter was confiscated and demolished. In the poetic expression of our source, "It turned into yesteryear." What was behind its demolition? Was it sheer revenge? At least the furniture of the two houses, his and his father's, was sold for the enormous sums of 1,100 and 900 dinars respectively. He died eight years later.[61]

2 Middle Class and Lower Middle-Class

Below the prominent bourgeois families one finds several men and women who would largely fit into the category of middle class and lower middle-class. Some were able to amass considerable fortunes. Thus a Quran reader at the

59 Ibn Ṭawq, *Taʿlīq* 512–513, 515. See on him 30, 39, 49, 51, 126; al-Buṣrawī, *Tārīkh* 116.

60 al-Buṣrawī, *Tārīkh* 62; al-Nuʿaymī, *al-Dāris* i, 7. For a biography, see Ibn Ṭūlūn, *Quḍāt Dimashq* 177–179; Ibn Ṭawq, *Taʿlīq* 64, 69, 133–134; Ibn al-Ḥimṣī, *Ḥawādith* i, 315 and references there. Another Shāfiʿī qadi, Jamāl al-Dīn al-Bāʿūnī, willed 600 (? dirhams) to support the prisoners' waqf (*waqf al-usarāʾ*). See Ibn Ṭawq, *Taʿlīq* 99.

61 Ibn Ṭawq, *Taʿlīq* 523, 743, 990, 1047, 1059, 1151, 1200, 1203, 1213, 1238, 1253, 1284, 1293, 1600; al-Buṣrawī, *Tārīkh* 126; Ibn al-Ḥimṣī, *Ḥawādith* i, 355, 363–364, 380–381; Ibn Ṭūlūn, *Mufākahat al-khillān* 129, 218.

Shāfiʿī Taqwiyya madrasa sold his share in the so-called Ustādār's Residence for 70 ashrafīs, received in cash.[62] About most we learn from the estates left upon death. One of the Maghribi community (*shaykh al-maghāriba*) left no less than 20,000 dinars—if we are to believe the figure.[63] One named al-Ḥuwayrī (? al-Ḥarīrī) left 18,000 dirhams (rated at 360 dinars) and 300 dinars to support teachers at one madrasa and a Sufi institution.[64] Also the shaykh ʿAlī al-Ḥallāq, who resided at the Bādirāʾiyya and was considered to have been in a dire situation, left upon his death 500 dinars and some other property.[65] The father of Shams al-Dīn al-Ḥimṣī, a prominent notary, whose estate was surveyed by Ibn Ṭawq, established a waqf, and upon his son's death sacks full of dinars and dirhams were discovered. A large sum of 2,500 dirhams (about 50 dinars) was willed to cover the burial costs, and the remainder was to remain in a safe, most likely for the inheritors.[66]

The estate of Tāj al-Dīn al-Umawī, Taqi al-Dīn's father-in-law, consisted of a library in which one could find a copy of al-Bukhārī's *Ṣaḥīḥ* inscribed in gold and valued at 10,000 dirhams, utensils valued at 1,208 dirhams, and a chess set. Part of the future proceeds of the sale he willed to his wife and her son and daughter, and the rest was all endowed.[67]

These appear to have been exceptional cases, however. Most middle-class and lower middle-class Damascenes who feature in the *Taʿlīq* owned real estate or kept savings on a smaller scale. Ibrāhīm Burhān al-Dīn b. Tāj al-Dīn al-Ṣaltī, possibly a *naqīb al-ashrāf* as well as a deputy qadi, sold an oven at Eastern ʿAnāba to a descendent of a leading Sufi shaykh for 400 dirhams in cash. He also owned in partnership land north of Bāb Tūmā.[68] ʿUmar "the Blind," when he still was "in good physical health and in command of his senses," willed one year income he received as a Quran reader for renovating a minaret of a certain mosque and 600 dirhams that remain after his death to support pilgrims.[69]

---

62 Ibn Ṭawq, *Taʿlīq* 84. For this madrasa, see al-Nuʿaymī, *al-Dāris* i, 162–169; al-Shihābī, *Muʿjam Dimashq* ii, 179.

63 al-Buṣrawī, *Tārīkh* 69.

64 Ibn Ṭawq, *Taʿlīq* 504.

65 Ibn Ṭūlūn, *Mufākahat al-khillān* 15.

66 Ibn Ṭawq, *Taʿlīq* 168. His widow was suckling a baby. Since, as we are told, there was no consummation of the marriage, she must have been married to al-Ḥimṣī shortly after giving birth.

67 Ibn Ṭawq, *Taʿlīq* 220, 249–250.

68 Ibn Ṭawq, *Taʿlīq* 800–801, 1825. For Ibn al-Ṣaltī's marriage to the daughter of the qadi al-Ikhnāʾī, see 296, 1647. For his father the notary, see 29, 140, 687.

69 Ibn Ṭawq, *Taʿlīq* 234, 296–297. Ibn Ṭawq was appointed to execute the will and received 10 dirhams for drafting it. See on him also 132.

We find reports on investment in urban property, occasionally in partnership. The seventh part of the mill known as al-Rānif was leased by Ibn Ṭawq by permission of the Shāfiʿī qadi to the notary Abū l-Faḍl al-Qudsī for four years for the annual sum of 600 dirhams paid at the beginning of each year.[70] The brothers known as Banū l-Raqqām supervised the Ḥammām al-Zinjīlī (*bi-l-naẓr wa-l-istiḥqāq*) and rented it for the first half of 888/1483 for a day rate of 9 dirhams. Previously, the operator had accumulated a debt of 523 dirhams and also 500 for manure (*zibl*)—probably heating material—that he had bought from them. A year later the daily rent increased to 17 dirhams, to be paid at the end of each day. By the end of the following year the operator's debt reached already 1,760 dirhams. He was dismissed, and the rent went to Fāṭima, of Turkmen stock, and known as "the bath operator" (*al-ḥammāmiyya*). In the past she had proven her skills as the operator of the Burhān al-Dīn Bath in the Ṣarūjā Market. Later the Zīnjīlī Bath was thoroughly renovated by an emir, who leased it to two partners for 16 dirhams a day.[71] At one point the rent was 100 dirhams a month, two months gratis. Still later, a problem with the water supply caused a shutdown for some time. Apparently, by then ownership had changed hands, and the contractor (*ḍāmin*), a man from Baʿalbek, spent more than 1,000 dirhams on renovation and rented it to a couple, who failed to pay in time the rather low sum of 4 dirhams daily and an accruing debt of 800 dirhams. Shams al-Dīn b. Jumʿa, who had been involved in other projects, guaranteed a large part of the debt, and the couple had to repay him within three months. As problems persisted, it was once again the skillful Fāṭima who was contracted to operate the bath for a period of two years for a rent of 200 dirhams a month (about 7 dirhams a day, as compared to the previous daily rent of 4 dirhams). In 904/1498 this bath was purchased by the grand emir Qujmās, who invested in its renovation, and after three months of work it reopened. Qujmās rented it on a *ḍamān* basis for 16 dirhams a day—the price must have reflected the much better condition—to Manṣūr al-Aslamī, originally a Christian or a Samaritan, together with Muḥammad the scholar (*faqīh*).[72]

Lower-middle-class men owned land in the region. An example is Muḥammad al-Ḥimṣī, who received from his wife a share in scattered plots (which are detailed) in the Ghūṭa. After his death this property was inherited by his son and two daughters, who compensated his second wife, originally of Jarūd, with one-eighth of its value. Later the three sold it to a peasant from

70 Ibn Ṭawq, *Taʿlīq* 687.

71 Ibn Ṭawq, *Taʿlīq* 222–223, 1707. For various calculations, see 322, 374, 399.

72 Ibn Ṭawq, *Taʿlīq* 60, 230, 234, 248, 338, 341, 352, 418, 426, 495, 531, 544, 546, 1678, 1707.

ʿIrbīl for 6 ashrafīs and 19 dirhams, from which they deducted 30 dirhams that their father owned the peasant.[73]

Middle-class city dwellers were also engaged in agricultural transactions. In one case, three partners, one of whom was the notary Abū l-Faḍl al-Qudsī, rented two orchards in a Ghūṭa village for two years from the merchant Zayn al-Dīn ʿAbd al-Qādir, a man active in several agricultural projects. The annual rent was 900 dirhams, to be paid at the end of each year "in Damascus currency." Based on the legal formula of "offer and acceptance (*ījāb wa qabūl*)," the rent contract (*musāqāt*) stated, apparently anticipating a contingency of loss, that whatever the crop yields, the partners would share in the tithe (*ʿushr*) on the produce, the *kharāj* tax on the land, and other expenses on irrigation, with no right to step out of the agreement.[74] Land ownership occasionally could generate reasonable returns. Burhān al-Dīn al-Ṣaltī rented to two brothers a *mazraʿa*—it is unclear whether it was a waqf—on which barley was grown. At one point the produce fetched no less than 3,980 dirhams (nearly 80 dinars). His estate was valued at 500 dinars.[75] But this was an exception, and on the whole the lease of land was much less lucrative than urban property. Thus, the notary Shihāb al-Dīn al-Ṣumaydī and his brother Shams al-Dīn leased to al-Shaghrī (or al-Shaʿrī), a gravedigger or baker (*ḥaffār* and *habbāz* are attributes variously given), for four years for the total sum of 188 (dirhams), paid in advance, half of a wasteland they owned, known as the "Ḥanbalīs' Land," which they had inherited from the estate of the perfume merchant Ibn Baʿyūn. It was agreed that the two owners had the right of canalizing (?) the water (*istiṭrāq*) to the lower field (*al-daraja al-suflā*) that had been someone else's property. The two owned also an orchard curiously identified as Muʿizz al-Dīn and located "between the two rivers," possibly the Baradā and the Dāʿīya, the borders of which were detailed. Earlier, it had been cultivated "in accordance to the legal stipulation" (*ʿalā sabīl al-munāṣaba al-sharʿiyya*) by Yūsuf al-Jaramānī in partnership with the aforementioned al-Shaʿrī (or al-Shaghrī). The extra expenses (including *siyāj*) fell on al-Jaramānī. Another man, Muḥibb al-Dīn al-Ḥarīrī al-ʿAjlūnī, a qadi's son, leased his share in a field at ʿAyn al-Kirsh in a *muḥākara* agreement, for which he received in a certain year 100 dirhams.[76] Zayn al-Dīn

73 Ibn Ṭawq, *Taʿlīq* 130–131 (Ibn Ṭawq's calculation has some errors).

74 Ibn Ṭawq, *Taʿlīq* 507–508. For similar projects, see 427, 467, 630, 829–830. For "offer and acceptance," and the legal theory of contracts and lease, see Hallaq, *Sharīʿa* 239–258.

75 Ibn Ṭawq, *Taʿlīq* 972–973, 1050, 1516–1517. On his widow and her business, see 1619, 1766; al-Buṣrawī, *Tārīkh* 231.

76 Ibn Ṭawq, *Taʿlīq* 431, 436, 438, 609–610, 612 (the editor reads the name and occupation inconsistently). On Shihāb al-Dīn, see 30, 84, 99, 103, 543, 746; Ibn Ṭūlūn, *Mufākahat al-*

ʿUmar b. al-Raqqām leased on a long-term basis to Shihāb al-Dīn al-ʿAnbarī, a teacher of Taqī al-Dīn's sons, land to cultivate (the borders are specified) near Zuqāq ʿAlāʾ al-Dīn for 20 years for 300 dirhams annually, the payment advanced every 4 years of the contract.[77]

Cash was not always available, at least not the entire sums required, and taking loans for transactions was common. Thus, at a notary's residence, one Badr al-Dīn b. Ḥiṣn gave two loans to the merchant Zayn al-Dīn ʿAbd al-Qādir, who also acted as an agent for Taqī al-Dīn. The loan documents were drafted by the notary and Ibn Ṭawq, with the qadi Muḥyī al-Dīn al-Ikhnāʾī adding his name near the *basmala* at the head of the document and ascertaining that both parties confirmed the details. The standard formula was that the borrowing person "was present and eye witnessed (*bi-l-ḥaḍra wa-l-muʿāyana*)." Zayn al-Dīn testified that he was capable of remittance. Incidentally, the qadi al-Ikhnāʾī is mentioned a couple of years later purchasing jewelry in the value of 53 dinars from Ibn Ḥiṣn's estate that was left to his minor heirs. The transaction was carried out through the minors' representative, with only half a dinar paid in cash and the rest deferred for one year; the qadi had to vouch for his ability to remit the loan.[78]

Occasionally, loans were taken at exorbitant interest. Thus the notary Abū l-Faḍl paid 2,000 dirhams, partly in dinars, to a Jerusalemite man, for books he bought from the estate of his deceased cousin. The original price was 1,750, of which 1,000 was a loan. That is to say, an additional 250 dirhams were charged, which makes it a 25 percent interest and about 15 percent price increase.[79] In another instance Ibn Ṭawq took in the service of someone a loan of 3,000 dirhams for 26 days from qadi Najm al-Dīn al-Ṭarābulusī. Not only was the sum to be repaid fixed in gold terms, but it would appear to have involved no less than 37 percent interest, albeit for a short period. Our notary was anxious about the terms, as he states: "I trust in God's help in remitting this loan."[80] Also Muḥammad b. Ramaḍān b. al-Muʾmin deferred payment of 35 ashrafis for about three months to a peasant of Jarūd from whom he bought "three marked camels haltered for travel." For that he had to leave a pawn (*rahn*). Najm al-Dīn

---

khillān 15. One may add Muḥammad the butcher or land surveyor (*qaṣṣāb*), also known as Ibn al-Rawās, who leased to a peasant his land at the Ṣabūra village. See Ibn Ṭawq, *Taʿlīq* 1271.

77 Ibn Ṭawq, *Taʿlīq* 488, 800. For its location outside Bāb Tūmā, see 1181. For al-Iqbāʿī, see 36 n. 3. For al-ʿInbarī, see 25, 195, 213, 854, 861.

78 Ibn Ṭawq, *Taʿlīq* 359, 360, 361, 634. For another case, see 476.

79 Ibn Ṭawq, *Taʿlīq* 146.

80 Ibn Ṭawq, *Taʿlīq* 94 and n. 9; El-Leithy, Living documents 416 (with some errors). On Juhaynī, see Ibn Ṭawq, *Taʿlīq* 298.

Muḥammad, Taqī al-Dīn's son, bought a horse from a peasant for 92 (? dirhams), for half of which he paid cash; the rest was a four-year loan.[81]

As to endowments, Yūsuf Aybak al-Nājī and his wife al-Sitt Kamsar (?) endowed land at Dimās, which together with similarly endowed land at the Marj al-Qibli, southeast of the city, belonged to seven different waqf owners and was accordingly identified as "the waqf of the seven." It was administered by Shihāb al-Dīn Aḥmad b. al-Sirmīnī, probably a notary, on the basis of *ḥikr*, and some of its proceeds went to the Ghazāliyya madrasa in the Umayyad Mosque. A somewhat confused account suggests that for the years 896–898/1491–1493 a revenue of 1,100 dirhams was generated.[82] Rashīd, a Christian convert, endowed a house that was mortgaged (*marhūn*). This raised a legal query and, according to at least one opinion, the act was permissible. Shams al-Dīn Muḥammad al-Sukkarī appeared to be poor but, surprisingly, left large sums, property, and waqfs. A third of his money he willed to the Lodge of the Maghribīs, another third to a certain *khān*, and a third to a relative.[83] Khalīl, the scholar (*faqīh*) of al-Bajdaliyya (?) endowed two Quran copies, one new, with red binding and apparently some marks of reading versions (*qirā'āt*) on it. It was later sold to a young man of the al-Bajdaliyya. The other copy was "old," with an old binding, and similarly with *qirā'āt* and was sold to one Zurayq, a shaykh of a market in the Ṣāliḥiyya Quarter. The sale price (including the dealer's fee of 4 dirhams) of the two copies was 121 and 144 dirhams respectively.[84]

Also peasants in the Damascus region endowed property. ʿAlī, the (Ḥanafī) *khaṭīb* of Jarūd, stipulated in his will that a third of the money left should be used to purchase real estate to become an endowment administered by Kamāl al-Dīn, of the Ibn Qāḍī ʿAjlūn family, for the support of a Quran reader. In addition, an amount of 100 dirhams annually should be spent on inmates at the Bāb al-Barīd prison. Shortly afterward, ʿAlī changed the will and endowed for the same purpose the proceeds of a plot of land he owned opposite his residence. However, his neighbors of the Jumʿa family claimed that the newly established

81 Ibn Ṭawq, *Taʿlīq* 402, 403–404, 1273.

82 Ibn Ṭawq, *Taʿlīq* 1191–1192. For al-Sirmīnī (rendered as Sirbīnī), see 229. For the location of Dimās west of Damascus, see Yāqūt, *Muʿjam al-buldān*, s.v. For a mill of the "waqf of seven" and a dispute about related calculation, see Ibn Ṭawq, *Taʿlīq* 290, 351–352, 932, 1164–1165, 1224, 1681 (apparently editor's error), 1811–1812. For the Ghazāliyya, see al-Nuʿaymī, *al-Dāris* i, 313–323. I thank Professor A. Layish for some clarification concerning this report.

83 Ibn Ṭawq, *Taʿlīq* 457, 792.

84 Still later, the two copies were purchased by Muḥsin "the Turkmen," of Qābūn village. See Ibn Ṭawq, *Taʿlīq* 1659.

waqf infringed on their property rights, and they rushed to Kamāl al-Dīn and complained. The dispute generated some violence and was referred to a qadi, but we have no further details.[85] Tāj al-Dīn, a peasant from ʿArbīl, established a land waqf, a third of whose proceeds was to finance a reader of al-Bukhārī's compendium.[86] Kawthar al-Fāmī and his wife of Eastern ʿAnāba endowed two shops and a residence, as well as a platform (*basṭa*), the revenue from which supported a Quran reader.[87]

Ibn Ṭawq provides information also on urban property and large sums of cash of some Damascus women. Only a few examples out of many more will be listed. Khadīja, a notary's wife and a sister of qadi Muḥyī al-Dīn al-Ikhnāʾī, owned a house and used its renovated hall for teaching children.[88] A woman identified as ʿAbd al-Qādir's spouse inherited a bath, a second-story (*ṭibāq*), and some cultivated land.[89] Sitt al-Minā, Ibn Ṭawq's relative, inherited from her mother a third of a house outside the city walls. Our notary's mother-in-law sold the upper floor of her residence and the stable for over 800 dirhams.[90] A widow known as Umm Hānī willed the enormous sum of 13,950 dirhams (about 280 dinars) to her daughter and other women.[91] Zaynab, of the al-Ṭarābulusī family (originally of Tripoli), a granddaughter of "the Ḥanbalī baker," willed to her brother a portion of 1,800 dirhams in cash, cloth, and jewelry. In addition, she left about 50 dinars. A document detailing the division of her property was drafted by Ibn Ṭawq and certified by the heirs.[92] Umm ʿAlāʾ al-Dīn willed cash for furnishing the Ikhnāʾiyya madrasa, and the sale of some of her fancy clothing for supporting shaykh Abū l-Faḍl (a Sufi?), as well as a soup kitchen (*maṭbakh*) at the Bāb al-Barīd.[93] A lady known as Bt. Ḥarzallāh willed that a third of her cash should be spent by Taqī al-Dīn on a defense tower (? *burj*) near Beirut.[94]

---

85 Ibn Ṭawq, *Taʿlīq* 384–385, 385–386. It is unclear whether the latter part is related to the same report.

86 Ibn Ṭawq, *Taʿlīq* 1593. Ibn Ṭawq was appointed for the job for three months.

87 Ibn Ṭawq, *Taʿlīq* 124. Kamāl al-Dīn's son was among the beneficiaries. For further examples based on archival material, see Miura, *Dynamism* 196–197, 200–201.

88 Ibn Ṭawq, *Taʿlīq* 188, 1110.

89 Ibn Ṭawq, *Taʿlīq* 192–193.

90 Ibn Ṭawq, *Taʿlīq* 400. For land possibly inherited by the same woman, see 320. For her divorce, see 1517. On Bt. Najm al-Dīn b. al-Zamān, who married into the al-Qārī family and left upon her death "large" yet unspecified property, see 1733.

91 Ibn Ṭawq, *Taʿlīq* 537–538.

92 Ibn Ṭawq, *Taʿlīq* 139.

93 Ibn Ṭawq, *Taʿlīq* 378. For its location, see al-Shihābī, *Muʿjam Dimashq* ii, 168. Most likely, it was named after a member of the al-Ikhnāʾī family of qadis.

94 Ibn Ṭawq, *Taʿlīq* 1754.

Exceptionally detailed is the report on Khātūn (an honorary title), Ibn Ṭawq's relative and a resident of Maʿlūlā. Khātūn established a land waqf, in which her daughter Fāṭima had a share of 11 parts (of 24). However, for some reason—most likely a family dispute—her rights had to be rectified in fatwas issued by no less than eleven Egyptian scholars, including the famous Zakariyyāʾ al-Anṣārī. To recall, also Ibn Ṭawq claimed a share in this waqf.[95] Khātūn's will specified the availability of cash in the amount of 10 dinars. However, further sums such as 450 dirhams (9 dinars) were found at her relative, and 5,000 dirhams (about 100 dinars) were placed with some peasants. Under such circumstances, the *dīwān al-mawarīth* became involved. A survey of Khātūn's property revealed that the value of her belongings was 1,200 dirhams. Altogether her property was valued at 7,000 dirhams (about 140 dinars). From this, charity to orphans and payment to the Ibn Farfūr family, as well as some other expenses, were deducted. At the end, the *dīwān* settled for 1,600 dirhams (more than a quarter of her estate). One year after Khātūn's death, the renter of some of her property filed a claim against Fāṭima, Khātūn's daughter. Following deliberation, a settlement was reached whereby the renter would receive 200 dirhams, his rent would be terminated, and Fāṭima's husband would take over the property.[96]

As to land owned by other women, Ibn Ṭawq's mother-in-law bought a plot at Ḥammām al-Saṭrā in the Ghūṭa, in which our notary also had a share. Araj (?), the wife of Rajab al-Fāmī, had the right to land for the growing of reeds (? *maqṣaba*; reeds were used for construction, among other uses) at Sikkat al-Ḥammām.[97] Bt. al-ʿAdl leased to Zayn al-Dīn Khiḍr al-Ḥisbānī, a waqf supervisor, and to Ibn Ṭawq, both in equal shares, half of the land referred to as *bustān al-dawr* in Barza, which grew olives and wheat; the lease was for a period of two years for 320 dirhams, of which 200 dirhams were an immediate payment (*ḥāll*); the remainder was to be paid in two installments of 60 dirhams in each of the two years. Ḥalīma's daughter, who was Ibn Ṭawq's relative, together with a few other women, leased to our notary her share in an orchard and a house for a period of two years for 100 dirhams a year. He had to bear the expenses involved in cultivating the land.[98] Marḥabā bt. Yūsuf b. Sulaymān, a Christian woman known as Bt. Dījā, of ʿAyn al-Tīna in Jubbat al-ʿAssāl, purchased in her village cultivated land (its borders are detailed) from Muḥammad b. Shihāb al-Dīn

95 Ibn Ṭawq, *Taʿlīq* 847–848. See also Chapter 1.

96 On the will, see Ibn Ṭawq, *Taʿlīq* 91–92, 92–93 (the calculation is unclear; see also editor's note). For the dispute, see 200.

97 Ibn Ṭawq, *Taʿlīq* 667, 1850.

98 Ibn Ṭawq, *Taʿlīq* 113, 158, 206; Wollina, *Zwanzig* 102.

Aḥmad al-Ḥimṣī (known as al-Sinī). The price was 750 dirhams, of which 200 dirhams were to be paid immediately, another 200 dirhams after two months, and the rest ten months later. In addition, a fixed amount of grain was to be delivered to the seller's home, probably in lieu of further cash. Marḥabā's husband rectified the agreement and guaranteed it. The relatively low sum of the down payment—only the equivalent of 4 dinars—may indicate that Marḥabā entered the transaction at the lower limit of her financial ability and needed further resources.[99] In another instance, Nājiba bt. Ibrāhīm b. Yūsuf al-Ḥimṣānī sold to another Christian woman, Maryam bt. Sulaymān, whose father was also known as Ibn Shabāna, both of Maʿlūlā, a quarter of a vineyard for 175 dirhams.[100]

Women also established rural waqfs. Khadīja bt. al-Bustānī and her sister leased in the "nether valley (*al-wādī al-taḥtānī*)," also known as the "asparagus valley," an orchard (*bustān*) for a period of two years and four months. Part of it was Khadīja's and her two sisters' waqf, which was administered by the *shaykh al-Islām*, Taqī al-Dīn, together with Shams al-Dīn b. al-Sukkar al-Farrā. Another part (the borders of which are specified) was leased to the "scholar (*faqīh*) of ʿArbīl" and Muḥammad al-ʿArbīlī, presumably of the same village, for two years for 200 dirhams. The lease was extended later to five more years for half of this sum, to be paid twice during the term. The cultivators paid 150 dirhams in advance.[101]

Finally, on transactions concluded by women, Fāṭima, a resident of Eastern ʿAnāba, sold wood from her plot (the boundaries of which are provided) for an impressive 120 dinars. Fāṭima bt. Muḥammad al-Ḥarīrī sold to Kamāl al-Dīn, of the Ibn Qāḍī ʿAjlūn family, five books on religious subjects, some with "Persian binding" and some without leather binding, all of them part of the estate of her deceased husband. Following negotiation, the price was fixed at 1,300 dirhams.[102] Bt. Ibn Ḥumayd gave a huge loan of 8,000 ducats—it is unclear why in foreign currency, how it came into her possession, and what the sources were—to a member of the wealthy al-Qārī family on a *commenda*

---

99 In the event, apparently the payment was arranged differently, so that only half of the immediate price (namely, 100) was paid, and the rest had to be pawned (*ruhinat*). See Ibn Ṭawq, *Taʿlīq* 1668–1669. For Shihāb al-Dīn b. al-Ḥimṣī as a Shāfiʿī deputy qadi and muezzin, see 126, 213, 249, 1107.

100 Ibn Ṭawq, *Taʿlīq* 1769.

101 Ibn Ṭawq, *Taʿlīq* 155, 384, 580–581, 587. On its location near the Baradā, see editor's n. 1. See also 384 n.

102 She and her two mature sons, who testified to the validity of the sale, and two minor daughters, were represented by her brother-in-law, who was authorized for that by the Shāfiʿī qadi. See Ibn Ṭawq, *Taʿlīq* 322–323, 1213.

(*qirāḍ*) basis.[103] Fāṭima, Khātūn's aforementioned daughter, borrowed 2,400 dirhams for some purpose. Significantly, her female servant Tharyā became a "Muslim pawn" (*rahnan musliman maqbūḍan bi-l-idhn nafādh al-yadayn*) and probably went to serve the loaner till the full repayment.[104] Bt. al-Daqīq purchased the house of the deceased al-Ḥisbānī, whose son, Amīn al-Dīn, a future qadi, she later married.[105]

Finally, the involvement of the Damascus high bourgeoisie and middle class in property holding appears parallel to what Walker has concluded as regards the Jordan Valley in the same period. On the basis of both archaeological and textual data, she suggests that there, the collapse of the imperial state made economic conditions no longer conducive to large-scale production, generating an increase in private property in gardens, orchards, and small grainfields.[106] This is where the savings and loans of many Damascenes were also invested.

103 Ibn Ṭawq, *Taʿlīq* 1264.

104 Her husband was her agent (*wakīl*). See Ibn Ṭawq, *Taʿlīq* 198–199; El-Leithy, Living documents 416, provides only a fraction of this report. For slaves subject to being pledged, see Hallaq, *Sharīʿa* 268. For further cases, see Ibn Ṭawq, *Taʿlīq* 220, 417, 1516–1517, 1619, 1766.

105 Ibn Ṭawq, *Taʿlīq* 313.

106 Walker, *Jordan* 231–232. However, her view that this development marked an opportunity for local people and a progress toward systems of the early modern period appears to me to read too much into the historical records.

CHAPTER 5

The Court: Dispute and Crime

Numerous volumes of sharʿī literature have been meticulously studied for over a hundred years now, with impressive results. Much less is known on the actual implementation of the sharīʿa in the long history of Muslim societies prior to the Ottoman period. How were legal decisions taken on a daily basis? How did legal sessions work in practice, and which channels of dispute resolution, both formal and informal, were taken? Who were the legal authorities in charge? What was the nature of cases they handled? Except for limited archival material, or what comes close to it, and extrapolation based on the vast literature of fatwas,[1] medieval chronicles provide extremely dispersed information on such questions.[2] Surely, daily life in Damascus involved all sorts of disputes, some of a personal nature, with limited consequences, and some of wider public concern. Ibn Ṭawq and al-Buṣrawī, the latter not only a chronicler but also a Shāfiʿī deputy qadi, shed some light on such questions in several interesting reports. Elsewhere, I discussed in some detail Ibn Ṭawq's unique information on communal water disputes and the mechanism that succeeded, at least to some extent, in attaining solutions.[3] In this regard, our notary may be considered a forerunner of reports preserved in Ottoman archives.[4] In the present chapter we shall examine our notary's reports on cases of arbitration dealt with outside the court. They sustain the argument that in premodern Islamic societies, disputes were resolved by informal mediation, with a minimum of legislative intervention.[5]

---

1 For analysis of the Jerusalem juridical system based on the Ḥaram documents, see Muller's masterful *Kadi*. For homicide and injury cases, see most recently Muller, Crimes. For the use of fatwa literature, see the impressive output by Powers, e.g. *Law, society, and culture* and *Development*.

2 For a good survey of the history of Sunnī legal theory and the formation of legal schools, see Hallaq, *Sharīʿa*, esp. 60–113. For references to the Mamluk period in particular, see Muller, Mamluk law 267–274. For the lack of studies on the functioning of law in the Mamluk context, see Muller, Mamluk law 263. For a discussion of one case in the presence of the sultan in 760/1359 on the basis of a chronicle's account, see Fernandes, Between qadis 101–104. For another example in Egypt in 854/1450, see Petry, *Criminal underworld* 176–177.

3 Shoshan, Mini-dramas.

4 For water disputes in Ottoman Egypt, see Mikhail, *Nature and empire* 46–66.

5 Hallaq, *Sharīʿa* 159. For a discussion of mediation and arbitration, see 160–164.

 | DOI:10.1163/9789004413269_007

We may begin with Ibn Ṭawq himself, who, as already mentioned in Chapter 1, was involved in a dispute with a widow and her son, who claimed he owed them about 5 ashrafīs. It went to the Shāfiʿī qadi, who appointed another notary to look into the matter, and he decided in their favor. Another case of dispute involved Ibn Ḥamza Ibn Shāṭī and Ḥājja Baraka, his deceased uncle's widow, concerning her late husband's estate turned into a waqf. It included clothing and furniture in the approximate value of 4,000 dirhams (80 dinars), plus an unspecified rent for an indefinite duration (*fī ḍamīr mudda*) that had generated 300 ashrafīs, of which Ibn Ḥamza acknowledged to have received 5. The widow claimed that the sum was the share of a few (specified) persons. Ibn Ṭawq, who was present, reports that the issue was discussed at Baraka's house in the presence of half a dozen men. A compromise was reached whereby Ibn Ḥamza received 10 dinars and the two declared that no further claims were now possible.[6]

Most of the arbitration cases about which we are informed by our notary were presided by Taqī al-Dīn Ibn Qāḍī ʿAjlūn, the *shaykh al-Islām*. Thus the merchant ʿAbd al-Qādir b. Ḥarfūsh took a loan from Tāj al-Dīn al-Ṣaltī when both were in the Hijaz and left a precious stone as a guarantee. Later he accused al-Ṣaltī of tampering with it. The two came before the *shaykh al-Islām*, but al-Ṣaltī denied the charge. In the event, it turned out that part of the stone in fact had been sold to a European merchant, who was summoned to the shaykh and confirmed it. He was asked to return the missing part of the gem.[7] In another case, Zayn al-Dīn Ṭāhir owed Bahāʾ al-Dīn 24 dirhams, a sum that, although trivial, became a bone of contention. When the two came before the *shaykh al-Islām* to settle the matter, they insulted each other—the phrase "a piece of Shīʿī (*qiṭʿat rāfiḍī*)" is mentioned—to the shaykh's embarrassment. The meeting ended with no result, but on the next day the loaner apologized and brought 4 dinars, a sum much higher than the disputed one; the reason for that remains unclear.[8] Taqī al-Dīn was also asked to decide in a dispute over the borders of some cultivated land.[9]

Yet there were cases that the shaykh declined to take. Such was the case of Salmā, a *ḥājja* of Baʿalbek, and her two brothers-in-law, who had received from her some valuable items such as pearls and copper vessels to be used as a pawn, which they had deposited in Beirut. Now Salmā demanded the items be returned, and for that she sent as an envoy to Baʿalbek a camel driver; he

6 Ibn Ṭawq, *Taʿlīq* 1152–1153, 1245.
7 Ibn Ṭawq, *Taʿlīq* 619.
8 Ibn Ṭawq, *Taʿlīq* 112.
9 Ibn Ṭawq, *Taʿlīq* 1770–1771.

charged her 150 dirhams for this service. It is implied that her relatives did not cooperate, and she told the *shaykh al-Islām* about her problem when she met him in Cairo. To Salmā's annoyance, for some reason the case was not convincing enough for him to interfere. A year later, the shaykh being still in Cairo, the issue came up during a meeting at his residence in Damascus in the presence of his son, his nephew Abū l-Yumn, and the aforementioned brothers-in-law. It was decided that Salmā was entitled to a compensation of 500 dirhams, which she received from the two men's agent in a special session at a Shāfiʿī madrasa. Ibn Ṭawq drafted a document that needed a qadi's approval and in which the woman stated she had no further claims.[10]

One case involving arbitration, the importance of which is in shedding light on the situation of Christians coming before a Muslim court, was reviewed in a session (*majlis*) following a written order (*marsūm sharīf*) from Cairo. A Christian, serving as a clerk for the Shāfiʿī qadi—this in itself can be regarded an item of some interest—collided while riding his horse with an elderly man and caused his death. It is implied that some compensation had been paid, but the son of the deceased was not content. In the course of considering his appeal, three witnesses testified that the victim's son had no further claim (*la yastaḥiqqu … ḥaqqan wa la diya wa la qaṣāṣan wa la irthan*). The arbitrator accepted the testimony, and the decision was approved by the Mālikī qadi in the presence of both parties.[11]

Surely, many cases were not resolved by arbitration, nor did they go to arbitration in the first place, and required submission to court. Some were adjudicated in a qadi's session (*majlis*). Unlike the viceroy's (to be discussed shortly), it had no single venue and could be convened at different locations, be it the qadi's residence, a mosque, or another locale.[12] A qadi's session was normally recorded in a protocol or judicial attestation (*maḥḍar*)[13] and had certain prerequisites. For example, a claim issued by a notary with no draft could be regarded deficient, therefore not binding and even requiring the payment of a considerable sum in compensation to the other party.[14] Falsification of

10 Ibn Ṭawq, *Taʿlīq* 505–506.

11 Ibn Ṭawq, *Taʿlīq* 682–683. He notes that for an unspecified reason he did not write the draft or perhaps did not add his signature to it (*wa lam aktub khaṭṭī bi-l-musawwada*). Perhaps the reason was simply technical, and his signature was unnecessary.

12 E.g. Ibn Ṭawq, *Taʿlīq* 932, 1891.

13 Ibn Ṭawq, *Taʿlīq* 1099, 1114, 1314, 1610, 1622, 1834. This supports the argument in Hallaq, Qāḍī's dīwān, about the systematic keeping of records prior to the Ottoman period.

14 Ibn Ṭawq, *Taʿlīq* 1692.

documents was punishable.[15] A qadi could appoint someone to represent the claimant (*yaddaʿī ʿalā*). Qadis had the authority to order detention at the prison located by Bāb al-Barīd.[16]

The category of cases judged by qadis (or their deputies) that is most frequently mentioned is of financial matters: debts, property disputes, or waqf. Ibn Ṭawq himself was summoned to the Shāfiʿī Ibn Farfūr because of a dispute concerning a will. What further inflamed the case was the rivalry between the qadi and Taqī al-Dīn, the *shaykh al-Islām*, whom the qadi blamed (in his absence) for approving of an act that Ibn Ṭawq witnessed.[17]

Property disputes also reached the viceroy's tribunal (*majlis ḥukm*) following an appeal (*qiṣṣa*) made on a qadi's decision. That tribunal was regularly convened at the Dār al-ʿAdl ("Hall of Justice"). The composition of the body that sat is unclear, but there were times when the viceroy presided over the four qadis. An appeal to Mamluk authority was occasionally followed by a summons to the citadel and detention.[18] In Jumādā I 896/March 1491 the bourse of speculations about how many were detained at the citadel was thriving, and the numbers ranged between 30 and 130.[19] We have examples of appeals. In one case the Shāfiʿī Quṭb al-Dīn al-Khayḍarī detained one of the two sons of a leader (*kabīr*) of the al-ʿUqayba al-Kubrā neighborhood, north of the city wall, following a claim that he had failed to make an annual payment out of his proceeds from a waqf land he cultivated. The man appealed, but the viceroy's intervention implied that he had to sell his share.[20] In another case the status of a mill—whether to be considered a private property or a waqf—was not resolved by the qadi and, for an unclear reason, even divided the Mamluk elite. Surprisingly, the case remained open for about seven years, at which point the viceroy made some arrests and ordered the Mālikī qadi to travel to

15 For one case see Ibn Ṭawq, *Taʿlīq* 392; al-Buṣrawī, *Tārīkh* 96–97; Ibn al-Ḥimṣī, *Ḥawādith* i, 293–294, has a brief report. For an accusation directed at an ʿArbīl peasant for falsifying a waqf document and his humiliation, see Ibn Ṭawq, *Taʿlīq* 688–689.

16 E.g. Ibn Ṭawq, *Taʿlīq* 102, 434, 435, 436–437, 932, 1258, 1740, 1810, 1811, 1851.

17 Ibn Ṭawq, *Taʿlīq* 1891–1892.

18 E.g. Ibn Ṭawq, *Taʿlīq* 54, 670, 885, 887, 930, 1051, 1105, 1108, 1109, 1465. There were instances of viceroys initiating detention for unspecified reason as, for example, when one sent 20 of his mamluks to detain in the midst of a party a "go-between (*mutakallim*)" for the qadi Najm al-Dīn, Taqī al-Dīn's son. See Ibn Ṭawq, *Taʿlīq* 1721. For al-Ṭawāqī serving as a *mutakallim* to a certain emir, see 1058. For the viceroy's involvement, see also Martel-Thoumian, *Déliquance* 83–86.

19 Ibn Ṭawq, *Taʿlīq* 1019.

20 Ibn Ṭawq, *Taʿlīq* 102 and n. 1 for al-ʿUqayba. Ibn Ṭawq adds his criticism of the custom to detain with no legal basis.

Cairo, apparently to clarify matters with the sultan.[21] Similarly, two men disputing about a *muḥākara/ḥikr* contract on an orchard in Baʿalbek met before the qadi but, apparently, without a solution, so the case continued to the viceroy, but we do not know what the result was.[22] A woman who was the beneficiary of some waqf land claimed against a member of the Ibn Qāḍī Zarʿ family, who had bought part of it with the approval of the Ḥanafī qadi. The basis for that was it had fallen out of use, which was permissible according to the Ḥanafīs. Now the woman, who denied the existence of such basis, demanded that the four qadis convene, but, since the Ḥanafī objected to any change, the case went to the viceroy. Under his supervision fatwas from some leading Ḥanafīs were solicited, and apparently these provided leeway for annulling the sale on the pretext that the situation was incongruent with the stipulation in the waqf.[23] Another case is of a son of a renowned Shāfiʿī who encountered one night at the Umayyad Mosque another youth, who forced on him a sodomite act. The victim reported it, and it was claimed that witnesses were to testify, so the matter was turned over to the sultan's representative in the city. The protocol of the hearing stated that the attacker repented, but the victim's father was not satisfied with the decision and brought the case to the viceroy. The latter ordered that the accused be flogged, and incarcerated in the section of those sentenced to death. At this point, one of the leading Shāfiʿīs, supported by muezzins, interceded on behalf of the young man, and his sentence was commuted to life in prison.[24] The intervention of Mamluk authorities in cases of assault on female slaves will be dealt with in the next chapter.

Even the sultan was occasionally involved, though, understandably, much less so than in cases in Egypt.[25] In one case a hearing convened by the viceroy reviewed the estate of the deceased qadi Muḥibb al-Dīn, of the Ibn Qāḍī ʿAjlūn family, the value of which in the city alone was estimated at 3,000 dinars. A complaint against Kamāl al-Dīn, a prominent family member, who managed the estate, reached the sultan, and he ordered Kamāl al-Dīn to pay 100 dinars as a special payment (*tasfīr*), but the latter refused. He was arrested at the citadel and was instructed to take an oath that his conduct was faultless and thus, it seems, the issue came to an end.[26] In another case a complaint was filed

---

21 Ibn Ṭawq, *Taʿlīq* 232, 665, 1207, 1213. The editor is inconsistent in transcribing the name of the mill.

22 Ibn Ṭawq, *Taʿlīq* 691. Ibn Ṭawq admits he lacked further details.

23 al-Buṣrawī, *Tārīkh* 186.

24 Ibn Ṭawq, *Taʿlīq* 212–213; Martel-Thoumian, *Délinquance* 168.

25 For Egypt, see Martel-Thoumian, *Délinquance* 77–83.

26 Ibn Ṭawq, *Taʿlīq* 688, 913, 922, 936.

against the wealthy merchant ʿĪsā al-Qārī, his sons, and some others for a large development project that, so it was claimed, was not on their own land but on land of another wealthy merchant. Al-Qārī was summoned to Cairo, imprisoned there for a year and a half, and released after forfeiting a huge load of spices.[27] In another case the "riffraff" of the ʿArbīl and Jawbar peasants objected to the sale to Samaritans of water of a canal (? *kuwwa*) of the Thawrā/Thūrā River, and one qadi allowed them to block it. Some months later, the three other qadis, together with the *ḥājib*, the *nāʾib al-qalʿa*, and the *khāzindār*, went to the Samaritan Quarter because of the water taken. A protocol was drafted and five Samaritans were arrested. An order in this regard was sent from the sultan, and some Samaritans were summoned to Cairo. In an enquiry in Damascus it was revealed that the Samaritans had taken more water than they had the right to.[28]

Some cases were reviewed by various high-ranking Mamluks. Prominent among those addressed was the chamberlain (*ḥājib al-ḥujjāb*).[29] Ibn Ṭawq himself and his relatives turned to him in a dispute they had with someone about their agricultural land at Maʿlūlā; however, the official sympathized with their rival and told them to present their claims before a qadi.[30] In another instance Christians of the Maʿrūbā (or Maʿrubiyya) village, north of the city, complained against inhabitants of some quarters, among them the Ḥanbalīs of the Ṣāliḥiyya Quarter, for stealing cloths they had purchased from foreign merchants, and even causing death. An investigation by the *ḥājib* came to the viceroy's attention and was later delegated to the qadis but did not lead anywhere.[31] A laconic statement about a session in which the *nāʾib al-qalʿa* and the qadis were present, and in which the issue of coercively diverting water from the Manshiyya canal was discussed, provides us with only a faint echo about water conflicts.[32]

Some imprecision is involved in the use of "crime" and "criminal law" in a premodern Islamic context. It has been argued that these are terms and concepts symptomatic of an epistemic transformation in Europe between the seventeenth and nineteenth centuries. To consider the treatment in the sharīʿa of

---

27 Ibn Ṭawq, *Taʿlīq* 957, 1059. See also 753.

28 Ibn Ṭawq, *Taʿlīq* 358, 391; Ibn al-Ḥimṣī, *Ḥawādith* i, 293; Ibn Ṭūlūn, *Mufākahat al-khillān* 56 (copied from the former verbatim).

29 For punishment he inflicted, see e.g. Ibn Ṭawq, *Taʿlīq* 279 (two cases). See also Martel-Thoumian, *Délinquance* 86–88.

30 Ibn Ṭawq, *Taʿlīq* 1619.

31 Ibn Ṭawq, *Taʿlīq* 1168.

32 Ibn Ṭawq, *Taʿlīq* 41.

offenses against life, body, morality, property, and more under the category of crime not only subsumes them under modern notions but also misses fundamentally different categories in the Islamic system.[33] It is with this qualification in mind on the one hand, and with awareness of the usefulness of some simplification on the other hand, that we ought to consider the numerous offense cases that our Damascus notary reports about.

1 Homicide

The Shāfiʿī qadi Shams al-Dīn Muḥammad, of the wealthy Ibn al-Muzalliq family, about 60 years old, was in his bed one evening when burglars broke into his residence. Thus begins the most detailed report we have of a homicide case in late Mamluk Damascus. According to one version, the perpetrators were disguised as women and were able to enter the qadi's private section through the bath, to which female slaves in the household led them. They clubbed Ibn al-Muzalliq on his head, knifed him, and, if this were not enough, hit him with an axe. Surely after such treatment he had no chance of survival. In addition the criminals took valuable items—this, presumably, was the main reason for the burglary and murder—although they appear to have been unaware of some copper trays and large amounts of gold and silver coins kept in niches, or perhaps were in too much of a hurry. Subsequently one of the qadi's dark-skinned female servants was interrogated and pointed to the female slave of the Mālikī qadi as a possible source of information. She added that three mamluks were the perpetrators, in the service of two white female slaves. Further investigation of the Mālikī's maid led to nothing. However, later it was revealed that a group of mamluks, two white female slaves, and a European (*ifranjī*) had been involved and that some of them had been able to escape to Beirut. The European consul (*qunṣul al-faranj*) was now summoned to the citadel, but it turned out that the European suspect had had no role in this crime but had been only a witness to it. A couple of mamluks and one of the aforementioned pair of female slaves were detained and scornfully paraded, the men wearing the female head cloth (*ʿaṣāʾib*) and other ludicrous items (*masākhir muqanziʿ*), by which they had disguised themselves when committing the crime. The woman was forced to put on a conical cap (*ṭarṭūr*) and other items to make her a laughingstock. The three were gruesomely executed in the presence of the viceroy. A day later the other female slave, who was rumored to be pregnant, was captured hiding

33 Hallaq, *Sharīʿa* 308–311; Muller, Crimes 143.

in a place that belonged to a Jew and was thrown into the river with a stone tied to her neck. She survived after this torture for four days.[34]

In a recent book on crime in medieval Islamic society, which actually has its focus on Mamluk Egypt and Syria, Carl F. Petry argues that homicide is the crime most frequently cited in the sources, mainly because it figured so vividly in the chroniclers' imagination.[35] Surely the homicide case just related makes for a good story. Yet the many references to homicide that our notary lists in his diary may simply suggest that it was a frequent crime. In fact, this is supported by his note that at a certain point homicide was thought of as a threat to the social fabric of Damascus. To counter it, a ban on carrying weapons was announced in Shaʿbān 891/August 1486. A black slave or one of the dark-skinned troops (*ʿabd*) was found carrying a knife and had a limb amputated, although he claimed to be unaware of the ban. Another measure was taken, for example, in Muḥarram 903/September 1497, when an evening curfew and, once again, a ban on carrying knives were announced. The following year, a "night watcher" (*walī al-layl*) was authorized to execute without interrogation those found armed.[36] Apparently, however, bans on carrying weapons were not a sufficient deterrent, as a year later three men of the Ṣāliḥiyya Quarter had limbs amputated for carrying daggers.[37] This quarter in particular, as we shall see, was a dangerous place.[38]

Excluding cases for which the criminal gangs (*zuʿr*) were responsible, and which have been discussed already in Chapter 2, for the approximately 20 years between 1480 and 1500, Ibn Ṭawq lists more than 150 cases of murder in Damascus and its countryside, a figure equal to that given by Petry for Cairo and Damascus together for the entire Mamluk period of more than 250 years. Admittedly, the aforementioned description of the qadi's murder is exceptional

---

34 Ibn Ṭawq, *Taʿlīq* 1476, 1477, 1478, 1479; Ibn Ṭūlūn, *Mufākahat al-khillān* 141–142; al-Buṣrawī, *Tārīkh* 207–208 (very critical of his personality); Ibn al-Ḥimṣī, *Ḥawādith* i, 339; Martel-Thoumian, *Délinquance* 60. For his dismissal, see Ibn Ṭūlūn, *Mufākahat al-khillān* 60. For a biography, see Ibn Ṭūlūn, *Quḍāt Dimashq* 182.

35 Petry, *Criminal underworld* 203. For the literary aspects of reporting on crime, see the brief remark in Martel-Thoumian, *Délinquance* 32–33. Her book, which appeared simultaneously with Petry's, largely covers similar subjects and is an excellent and comprehensive presentation of the mamluk crime scene. What follows here is not an attempt to emulate it but focuses on a few aspects of that scene in Damascus in Ibn Ṭawq's time.

36 Ibn Ṭawq, *Taʿlīq* 646, 1536, 1696; Martel-Thoumian, *Délinquance* 247. Petry, *Criminal underworld* 331, argues that Damascus was as safe as some major medieval European cities, but it seems that the argument is insufficiently documented.

37 Ibn Ṭawq, *Taʿlīq* 1828.

38 Ibn Ṭawq, *Taʿlīq* 144, 450, 582, 1066, 1187, 1263, 1364, 1370, 1430, 1441, 1461, 1499, 1507, 1669, 1712, 1739, 1743, 1901; Ibn Ṭūlūn, *Mufākahat al-khillān* 57, 168.

in the details it gives, and most acts of homicide that are reported were committed by individuals who remain unidentified, not only because our sources do not mention their names but also because, quite often, the criminals were able to escape the scene without leaving a trace.[39] We also lack details about the motives for most cases.[40] Of those whose circumstances we know, murder resulting from house and shop burglary or highway robbery was the most common.[41] Notorious for this type of homicide was ʿAbdallāh, the highway robber (*qāṭiʿ ṭarīq*) of Safīra village in the Zabadānī district, who had been a member of the Banū ʿIzqī gang and later joined their rivals the Bāklū gang. He is reported to have murdered no less than ten people and to have planned to take the lives of many more, stating the number 100 as his goal. But before he was able to do that, he had been caught in a public bath and ended his life in a sort of

---

39 For Petry's figures, see *Criminal underworld* 207. By way of comparison, Ibn Ṭūlūn refers to less than a dozen of the 150 cases recorded by Ibn Ṭawq but, on the other hand, adds about a dozen more. In other words, not only is Ibn Ṭūlūn's material very far from the historical reality as portrayed by our notary, but it demonstrates that even the detailed *Taʿlīq* does not provide all the cases. Each of the two writers either made his choice or had limits to his information. For the cases noted, see Ibn Ṭawq, *Taʿlīq* 55, 63, 76, 95, 99, 127, 144, 197, 232, 235, 236 (see also Martel-Thoumian, *Délinquance* 144), 285, 394–395, 439, 450, 638 (see also Martel-Thoumian, *Délinquance* 90), 654, 664 (see also Martel-Thoumian, *Délinquance* 147), 687, 700, 710 (see also Martel-Thoumian, *Délinquance* 141), 711 (see also Martel-Thoumian, *Délinquance* 194–195), 719, 722 (see also Martel-Thoumian, *Délinquance* 285), 750, 758, 774, 777, 780, 781 (see also Ibn Ṭūlūn, *Mufākahat al-khillān* 81), 790, 872, 882, 890 (three cases; see also Martel-Thoumian, *Délinquance* 139, 141), 895, 916, 918, 934, 962, 1004 (see also Martel-Thoumian, *Délinquance* 54), 1013, 1015 (see also Martel-Thoumian, *Délinquance* 164), 1018, 1026, 1034, 1052 (two cases; see also Martel-Thoumian, *Délinquance* 158), 1066 (two cases), 1088, 1136, 1146, 1147, 1150, 1159 (see also Martel-Thoumian, *Délinquance* 144), 1160, 1171, 1182 (see also Ibn al-Ḥimṣī, *Ḥawādith* i, 342; Martel-Thoumian, *Délinquance* 140), 1184, 1187, 1207 (see also Martel-Thoumian, *Délinquance* 143), 1244, 1247 (see also Ibn Ṭūlūn, *Mufākahat al-khillān* 128; Martel-Thoumian, *Délinquance* 47), 1263, 1274, 1283, 1307 (see also Martel-Thoumian, *Délinquance* 140), 1323 (three), 1324, 1337, 1354, 1364 (two cases), 1370, 1374 (see also Martel-Thoumian, *Délinquance* 141), 1385, 1407–1408, 1410, 1426, 1429 (two cases), 1430 (two cases), 1431 (two cases), 1435, 1441, 1453 (two cases), 1457, 1461, 1471, 1488, 1491, 1496, 1499 (two cases), 1501, 1506, 1507, 1508 (see also Martel-Thoumian, *Délinquance* 147), 1514, 1517, 1532, 1535, 1538, 1539, 1540, 1541, 1544, 1563, 1566, 1596, 1684 (two cases), 1687 (see also al-Buṣrawī, *Tārīkh* 239), 1708, 1711, 1712, 1737, 1739 (two cases), 1743, 1744, 1750, 1780, 1874, 1884 (two cases), 1897, 1904 (three cases), 1912; Ibn Ṭūlūn, *Mufākahat al-khillān*, 79, 118, 127, 135, 147, 166, 168 (two cases), 184, 190.

40 For a case where a merchant was murdered "for no reason" and the suspect instantly executed, see Ibn Ṭawq, *Taʿlīq* 1136.

41 For Petry's note that, as in other cultures, including contemporary Western culture, homicide converged most prominently with theft or brigandage in a clear attempt at concealing the criminal's identity, see *Criminal underworld*, 211 and n. 8.

a crime-film scene by gruesome execution.[42] A few more cases of burglary that ended in homicide are reported.[43]

The other main reason for homicide as it emerges from the *Taʿlīq* were family disputes. In one instance, after the body of a stabbed woman was found near the Umayyad Mosque, her brother, who had followed her for quite a while because of information he had received about her immoral behavior—allegedly, he had even spotted her once in the company of a stranger—came under suspicion. In another case, after the Samaritan Ibn al-Ṭalsā was found dead at his home, the investigation revealed that his wife and sister had arranged for his murder. In their confession submitted to the viceroy, it turned out that one of the two perpetrators they had hired was a slave (*mamlūk*) of a respected family. The two women were flogged, and the murderer was gruesomely executed. In yet another case, the low-ranking emir Yashbak al-Ḥamrāwī came home only to find out that his wife and daughter had gone to visit the wife of a deposed *walī*. When Yashbak found them drunk, they ran away. Frustrated, he stabbed their host to death and reported himself to the governor. He was imprisoned in the citadel till further instructions from the sultan, but what these were we do not know.[44] Other murder cases of a similar nature are reported.[45]

Other cases followed wine drinking and fights,[46] and there were also murder cases on political grounds, such as the murders of a low-ranking emir and a tax collector at a village near Jizīn by its Shīʿī inhabitants (? *arfāḍ*), or the murder of a mamluk, originally of European stock, by those tired of his tyranny. Dissatisfied with the amputation of his limbs, following the viceroy's order, the people abducted him and burned him alive near the gallows. Similar in motive was the murder of the Ḥanbalī official ʿAbd al-Raḥmān b. Ruzayq, who was notorious for his manipulation.[47]

---

42 Ibn Ṭawq, *Taʿlīq* 847; Martel-Thoumian, *Délinquance* 48.

43 Ibn Ṭawq, *Taʿlīq* 275, 276, 388, 449, 450 (see also Ibn Ṭūlūn, *Mufākahat al-khillān* 57), 483, 493, 521 (see also Martel-Thoumian, *Délinquance* 140–141), 582, 657, 659, 876, 1004, 1045, 1062, 1285, 1313, 1423, 1513, 1516, 1649 (see also Martel-Thoumian, *Délinquance* 134), 1903.

44 Ibn Ṭawq, *Taʿlīq* 532, 764–765, 1034 (Yashbak was *dawādār* or *ḥājib al-ḥujjāb*; see 49, 133); Ibn Ṭūlūn, *Mufākahat al-khillān* 76 (the text is corrupt); Martel-Thoumian, *Délinquance* 84, 123, 167, 243–244.

45 Ibn Ṭawq, *Taʿlīq* 700, 1282, 1374, 1708; Ibn Ṭūlūn, *Mufākahat al-khillān* 126; Martel-Thoumian, *Délinquance* 29, 95, 142.

46 Ibn Ṭawq, *Taʿlīq* 235, 633, 1887; Ibn Ṭūlūn, *Mufākahat al-khillān* 93, 170; Martel-Thoumian, *Délinquance* 142.

47 Ibn Ṭawq, *Taʿlīq* 703–704, 1897; Ibn Ṭūlūn, *Mufākahat al-khillān* 191; al-Buṣrawī, *Tārīkh* 219; Martel-Thoumian, *Délinquance* 32, 121, 141, 158.

For most cases, however, a prior motive is not given. Thus a man from the Shāghūr Quarter entered a shop in which a youth was in the company of his father, a fight started for an unspecified reason, and as the visitor tried to stab the youth, the latter pulled out a knife and preempted. After he ran away, the Shāghūr men gathered and pillaged the market. Soon things deteriorated into an all-out fight in which no less than six people lost their lives.[48]

What was the punishment for homicide? Following the Quran, classical jurists relegated homicide to the secondary category of criminal acts, thus viewing punishment as negotiable rather than absolute. Since the execution of a murderer was permitted only if the offense could be proven to have been intentional, an unintended act of murder was removed from the category of the criminal and should have been subject to the scrutiny of a magistrate. A judge should have rendered a verdict through a court procedure. In practice, as already hinted above, things worked differently. Petry argues that in a city like Damascus, with its multifaceted urban conglomerate, maintaining order was required in order to preserve social cohesion. As widespread homicide threatened to disrupt this cohesion, it could not be left to negotiation at the behest of the victim's relatives.[49] Our notary reports about a relatively large number of executions of those suspected of murder, even though accusations were not always verified. One further impression from the accounts provided is of a minimal reference to the qadi's court in cases of homicide. This could be accidental—that is, it may be that our source did not consider it essential to explain the qadi's role in such cases. Another possibility to explain it is that the qadi was not authorized to investigate a crime whose details were hidden to him but Mamluk officials were those presenting the relevant material to the qadi-court.[50]

Petry found that the death penalty was applied only in slightly more than a third of the homicide cases in Mamluk Egypt and Syria.[51] Yet, as he cautions, one has to take into consideration that many perpetrators were unidentified or escaped. In fact, this is what Ibn Ṭawq notes in a number of instances.[52] As to those suspects who were detained, the deficiencies in the investigation appa-

48 Ibn Ṭawq, *Taʿlīq* 488.

49 Petry, *Criminal underworld* 204–205, 207. On the severity of punishments applied by the authorities for criminal offenses, see also Rapoport, Royal justice.

50 Muller, Mamluk law 266. By comparison, In Palestine a hundred years earlier in a few Ḥaram documents the role of a qadi's court is mentioned. See Muller, Crimes 138, 143–144, 145, 146.

51 Petry, *Criminal underworld* 250 and n. 75 for details. See also Martel-Thoumian, *Délinquance* 185–195.

52 For the escape of unknown suspects, see Ibn Ṭawq, *Taʿlīq* 197, 890, 1066, 1182, 1184, 1307,

ratus might have led to arrest and severe punishment on the basis of unreliable information and irrelevant consideration. A suspect could be turned easily into an accused and punished even without a charge being properly established. The diary provides some examples for that. In one case, a Dāriya peasant known as "the wolf's son" was able to address the sultan—how a peasant succeeded in doing so, we do not know—about his son's murder, allegedly caused by the local preacher. After the sultan issued an order to the viceroy to take action, the latter sent his men to arrest the preacher and execute him, as well as his son and three collaborators; no trial or even inquiry is mentioned. A few more men were arrested later in connection with this case and executed gruesomely.[53] It is astonishing to read how many paid with their lives in this case for the murder of one person.

Public pressure could bring about execution even when no proof was established. In one instance a camel driver (*hajjān*), known as "good for nothing" or just "bad" (*naḥs*), also a suspect in an earlier homicide case, was accused of killing. The public pressed the viceroy to open a trial, and the investigation was in the hands of the Mālikī qadi. As things prolonged, the protestors intensified their activity, and a couple of days later the viceroy executed the man at night without blame being established.[54]

Only in a few reported cases was guilt admitted, apparently following investigation, or when there were witnesses to the crime or circumstantial evidence provided.[55] Not every suspect survived the torture and the severe conditions of the temporary detainment.[56] Rarely do we find details of the criminal procedure. In the case of a man referred to as al-Bayrūtī, the father-in-law of a Shāfiʿī deputy qadi, who was accused of murdering a "respected man," his accuser on behalf of the *ḥājib* came from the victim's village, and the man for the defense was the Shāfiʿī qadi. What was said in the session we do not know.[57]

Ibn Ṭawq notes about 60 cases of capital punishment for homicide, a figure implying that the number of homicide cases exceeded even the 150 he explicitly

1496; Ibn Ṭūlūn, *Mufākahat al-khillān* 118; Martel-Thoumian, *Délinquance* 92 (residence plundered and the wife arrested).

53 Ibn Ṭūlūn, *Mufākahat al-khillān* 124–125 (probably citing al-Nuʿaymī). Ibn Ṭawq, *Taʿlīq* 1101, has a different version; Martel-Thoumian, *Délinquance* 114.

54 Ibn Ṭawq, *Taʿlīq* 120–121; Ibn al-Ḥimṣī, *Ḥawādith* i, 268, is more elaborate but with slight differences; Petry, *Criminal underworld* 217–218; Martel-Thoumian, *Délinquance* 245.

55 Ibn Ṭawq, *Taʿlīq* 63, 127, 633, 750, 758, 764–765, 1323, 1337, 1684, 1708; Ibn Ṭūlūn, *Mufākahat al-khillān* 128; Martel-Thoumian, *Délinquance* 191.

56 For arrest resulting in death, see Ibn Ṭūlūn, *Mufākahat al-khillān* 128; Ibn Ṭawq, *Taʿlīq* 1247, has a brief note on it; Martel-Thoumian, *Délinquance* 47.

57 Ibn Ṭawq, *Taʿlīq* 144. On al-Ramlī, see 110.

reports about. More than 50 of these cases are cited without specifying the reason for the execution.[58] Thus one may suggest that although, legally, homicide was not to be punished with execution unless it was established as intentional, execution does emerge as quite a common punishment in late Mamluk Damascus. This information is in contrast to Petry's findings on the basis of much less data, according to which two-thirds of the accused were set free. Whether punishment in Mamluk Egypt and Syria was selective, lenient, and comparable to that in the contemporary West, as he also claims, requires further data.[59]

Most executions were by hanging (*shanq*).[60] We also have a few cases of gruesomely chopping the body ("cutting in the middle," *tawsīṭ*), beheading, pilling off the skin (*salkh*), and placing the victim on a spit (*ḥawzaq*).[61] Those waiting to be executed were incarcerated at the "blood prison" (*ḥabs al-dam*), a special section in the prison near Bāb al-Barīd. In 886/1481 it collapsed because of nearby construction, killing some prisoners; those fortunate enough to survive, at least temporarily, had to be transferred to the citadel. Till the end of 899/1494 the gallows were located below the citadel, which turned to be distressing and a cause for complaint, so it was moved eastward to the Kharāb. Yet complaints continued, and at some point between 905/1500 and the beginning of 907/1501 the gallows were moved again to the Ṣāḥat al-Shuhadāʾ ("Field of the Martyrs"), in the neighborhood known as Bayna al-Nahrayn ("Between the Two Rivers"); another location had previously been rejected by the Shāfiʿī qadi because it was near a recreation place.[62] This information reveals an interesting dimension to public executions—while many people probably enjoyed being spectators, others, most likely permanent residents, wished to avoid the sight and reported their aversion to the authorities.

58 Ibn Ṭawq, *Taʿlīq* 55, 453–454, 650 (five black slaves), 651, 656 (slave), 758 (bedouin), 902, 990, 998, 1008, 1024, 1026, 1098 (slaves), 1101, 1205, 1209, 1211, 1214, 1216, 1251, 1263 (Maghribis), 1298, 1306, 1359, 1373, 1385, 1386 (four), 1401, 1440, 1447, 1478, 1485, 1536, 1543, 1544, 1570, 1575, 1648, 1659, 1662, 1668, 1696 (two cases), 1712, 1753, 1789 (slave), 1800, 1801, 1828, 1829, 1831, 1864, 1876, 1913, 1915 (two cases), 1916.

59 Petry, *Criminal underworld* 251.

60 Ibn Ṭawq, *Taʿlīq* 63, 99, 121, 127, 633, 750, 759, 918, 934 (five), 962 (also Ibn Ṭūlūn, *Mufākahat al-khillān* 106) (four), 1018, 1019 (five), 1052 (ten), 1062, 1136, 1147, 1207, 1337, 1410, 1461, 1687, 1708 (three), 1744, 1771, 1897. For the Mamluk state in general, see Martel-Thoumian, *Délinquance* 243–256.

61 Ibn Ṭawq, *Taʿlīq* 765, 882, 1045, 1501, 1515, 1544, 1711, 1737, 1897; Ibn Ṭūlūn, *Mufākahat al-khillān*, 126, 184.

62 Ibn Ṭawq, *Taʿlīq* 83, 1307; Ibn al-Ḥimṣī, *Ḥawādith* i, 263, 365; Ibn Ṭūlūn, *Mufākahat al-khillān* 131, 199–200; Ibn Ṭūlūn, *Iʿlām* 128, 159 n. 1; Martel-Thoumian, *Délinquance* 247. For the prison in the Mamluk state in general, see the excellent survey in Martel-Thoumian, *Délinquance* 208–224.

There were cases in which, for some reason, those found guilty were spared their lives. One of the viceroys released at midnight a shaykh of a Ḥawrān village who had been accused of the slaughter of 20 or more people on a Ramadan night, although before that the same ruler had sworn "to peel off his skin." In the event, he was satisfied with a fine that may have gone to his pocket.[63] Petry's conclusion is that more than half of the cases in which military were involved did not lead to any trial or even inquiry.[64] In one instance the governor's tribunal convened in the presence of the four qadis and other dignitaries (*arkān al-dawla*), following the sultan's order to investigate the murder of an associate of the *dawādār al-sulṭān* by the second *ḥājib*. Accused by the Shāfiʿī qadi Ibn Farfūr, the suspect denied his guilt and was told to swear his innocence "50 times." As the tribunal was adjourned, the victim's frustrated brother, who had arrived from Cairo, jumped on the accused and injured him. A second tribunal was then convened, but we are not told what the verdict was. In any case, about a month later, possibly heartbroken, the victim's brother passed away.[65]

Islamic law considers payment by the liable party a means of punishment,[66] but cash indemnity (*qiṣāṣ, gharam*) was imposed only in a small number of cases, usually because a suspect managed to escape. In one case indemnity appears to have generated considerable cash flow into the Ḥanbalī qadi's pockets, or at least it was thus claimed by the public, whereby the qadi was accused of imposing a fine of 100 dinars and then officially cancelling it but keeping the sum nevertheless. In another case, after a murderer confessed to the Mālikī qadi, the viceroy asked the victim's family to accept 200 dinars but surprisingly failed in that. The murderer Ibn Baʿyūn of al-Jubba and his henchman, a man accused of killing several people, including his own brother, were interceded for an indemnity of 2,000 dinars, of which 800 were paid, but the sultan's order to hang them aborted the compromise.[67]

Occasionally, when a suspect escaped, or an investigation was not carried out or failed, collective indemnity was imposed on the quarter where the victim was found, or even on the entire city. Thus, in one instance, when a youth

---

63 Ibn Ṭawq, *Taʿlīq* 740, notes that people talked about it; Ibn al-Ḥimṣī, *Ḥawādith* i, 321; Ibn Ṭūlūn, *Mufākahat al-khillān* 97; Martel-Thoumian, *Délinquance* 146, 186, 260.

64 Petry, *Criminal underworld* 318. For an example, see Ibn Ṭawq, *Taʿlīq* 1687, 1688.

65 Ibn Ṭawq, *Taʿlīq* 1279, 1287. For a different version, see Ibn al-Ḥimṣī, *Ḥawādith* i, 354–355, 357, who promises to relate the second tribunal but leaves it at that. See also 341–342; Ibn Ṭūlūn, *Mufākahat al-khillān* 130.

66 Muller, Crimes 144.

67 Ibn Ṭawq, *Taʿlīq* 23, 394–395, 439, 441, 758, 916, 917, 1019, 1026; Martel-Thoumian, *Délinquance* 143, 191, 194. On collective indemnity, see also Miura, Urban society 172 (with reference to Schacht).

described as "hatcher, son of a hatcher (*ḥayyāk ibn ḥayyāk*)," who resided in the al-Mazābil Quarter, was murdered at the site of a wine press, a collective fine of 1,200 dinars was imposed on the quarter of one of the suspects, and he was let free. The enraged viceroy, who was under pressure from the inhabitants of the nearby al-Qaṣab Mosque, on whom, as well as on other neighborhoods, the fine was imposed, executed an innocent youth. Almost a year later, other suspects were captured and flogged.[68] In another instance, the inhabitants of Jawbar, mostly Jews, were forced to pay a sum of 1,100 dinars after the corpse of a murdered Jew was found.[69] While the sums cited are especially high, at other times collective indemnity was ridiculously low.[70]

Especially prone to it was the Ṣāliḥiyya Quarter, where many homicides occurred. However, its inhabitants occasionally received legal support from qadis and other scholars, not necessarily Ḥanbalīs—at least, a considerable number of the inhabitants of the quarter adhered to the Ḥanbalī school. In one instance they protested against a fine of 1,000 dinars cynically imposed by the chief of police after he himself had killed an Aleppan man in the quarter. The Ḥanafī qadi advised them not to pay "even a *fals*," and in a session before the viceroy the fine was abolished.[71] In another instance, Ṣāliḥiyya men killed one of the *walī*'s assistants and, once again, the quarter was collectively fined. However, the Shāfiʿī qadi Ibn Farfūr objected to that and the people escaped it, though not for long, and later a few more suspects were detained and more indemnity was imposed.[72] In yet another instance, people came to Taqī al-Dīn to ask for help because of 1,000 dinars imposed on them. The viceroy replied that he followed the law, but al-Buṣrawī notes that he actually followed the Ḥanafīs. The same quarter was also fined in other instances.[73] Also other quarters had to pay from time to time.[74] It appears that collective indemnity was to the dislike of Sultan Qaytbāy, as he issued a decree against it. It was renewed by

68 Ibn Ṭawq, *Taʿlīq* 1780, 1781, 1782, 1793, 1859–1860; Ibn Ṭūlūn, *Mufākahat al-khillān* 184; Martel-Thoumian, *Délinquance* 194; Miura, Urban society 171–172.

69 Ibn Ṭawq, *Taʿlīq* 1776, notes that the victim was "bad" (*naḥs*).

70 For 50 dirhams imposed till the killers of the headman of the Quṭayfa village (on the Ḥimṣ-Damascus road) were to be found, see Ibn Ṭawq, *Taʿlīq* 76; Martel-Thoumian, *Délinquance* 43. For this village, see Yāqūt, *Muʿjam al-buldān*, s.v.

71 Ibn Ṭawq, *Taʿlīq* 1067; Martel-Thoumian, *Délinquance* 121, 123.

72 Ibn al-Ḥimṣī, *Ḥawādith* i, 352; Ibn Ṭūlūn, *Mufākahat al-khillān* 131–132 (cites the former).

73 al-Buṣrawī, *Tārīkh* 179, 198, editor's n. 1, citing al-Mawṣilī's Ḥanafī compendium; Miura, Urban society 172. For collective indemnity see also Ibn Ṭawq, *Taʿlīq* 706, 711, 1244, 1263, 1364, 1429, 1430; Martel-Thoumian, *Délinquance* 186, 194–195. For fifteenth-century Palestine, see Muller, Crimes 144.

74 Ibn Ṭawq, *Taʿlīq* 1374, 1407–1408, 1453, 1454, 1491; al-Buṣrawī, *Tārīkh* 197–198; Martel-Thoumian, *Délinquance* 30, 141, 193.

Ṭūmān Bāy after his coronation in Damascus in 906/1500 but appears to have been unsystematically followed.[75]

2 Theft

Theft (*sariqa*) was the second most frequent crime in late Mamluk Damascus. Ibn Ṭawq lists about 100 cases, to which other sources add a few. Burglary of private homes and shops was the most common type of theft; attacks on travelers came second. On several occasions our notary complains about the troubles caused by theft and highway robbery even when not resulting in death.[76] The break-in at Ibn al-Muzalliq's bedroom that resulted in his death was preceded by earlier cases of burglary at his residence with less fatal results. In one of them a group of Europeans and mamluks connived with some of his female servants and stole a few thousand dinars. After an investigation some of the money was allegedly found at the house of a "European," and this was a pretext for confiscating the property of Europeans residing in al-Jubba. The same qadi was also attacked on his way to Ramla.[77] Other cases are reported in some detail. Thus thieves dug a tunnel from a small mosque to the adjacent residence of the waqf inspector al-Ḥisbānī, which they broke into at night and got hold of three boxes full of cloth. As the family woke up and caught one of the thieves, he summoned his comrades' help and they hit the owner severely. In another instance, a group of thieves broke into two residences in the Ṣāliḥiyya Quarter. As the owner cried for help, his brother was hit by an arrow, but from the neighboring home a rock was thrown onto one of the thieves, killing him. In revenge the criminals returned and killed the owner. A case in which a maid played a role in deterring a thief occurred at the house of Ibn Ṭawq's neighbor.

75 For the sultan's decree, see also Ibn Ṭawq, *Taʿlīq* 1878; Ibn Ṭūlūn, *Iʿlām* 143–144. For the viceroy's decree in 914/1509 that no complaint could be discussed without an adversary being present, see Ibn Ṭūlūn, *Iʿlām* 209; Miura, *Dynamism* 143. For a man murdered at al-Mazāz, outside the Small Gate, and the residents, especially a merchant, who lived near the site of the murder, forced to pay, see Ibn Ṭūlūn, *Mufākahat al-khillān* 190 (translation in Petry, *Criminal underworld* 220; error in the date). In Rabīʿ I 910/August 1504 the inhabitants of the Maydān al-Ḥaṣā were ordered to pay for one of the governor's men killed in their quarter. Apparently, the order was disobeyed. A couple of years later, the residents of another quarter protested against the policy. See Ibn Ṭūlūn, *Mufākahat al-khillān* 204, 225–226, 241–242. For further examples, see 216, 221, 232, 235, 256; Ibn Ṭūlūn, *Iʿlām* 198–199.

76 Ibn Ṭawq, *Taʿlīq* 366, 642, 892, 1144, 1205, 1500, 1529, 1905.

77 Ibn Ṭawq, *Taʿlīq* 1136; Ibn al-Ḥimṣī, *Ḥawādith* i, 339. For earlier instances, see Ibn Ṭūlūn, *Mufākahat al-khillān* 26. For an attack on him at Ramla, see Ibn Ṭawq, *Taʿlīq* 799; Martel-Thoumian, *Délinquance* 54, 135.

"Good Blessing (*jā'a al-khayr*)," as the female slave was fittingly named, spotted a man coming out of a house carrying stolen items, jumped on him, and hit him till he was forced to leave the items. Subsequently, some men were able to capture the thief and deliver him to the governor, who ordered that his hand be amputated immediately and that he then be thrown into prison.[78]

Also shops were a target. In one late-night incident, no less than 25 armed thieves, riding and on foot, arrived at a market and, disregarding the security patrol (*'asās*) and the chief of police (*walī*), broke into about a dozen shops, stealing cloth and cash. In the skirmish that followed a few of the security men were killed and also some of the enforcement team sent by the governor. In another instance thieves broke at night into a dyeing workshop and stole silk in the value of 500 dinars. About a month later, a youth was suspected because of silk found with him and was interrogated at the governor's. Ironically, he claimed that the man who gave him the stolen goods was in the governor's service.[79] Some dared to steal even from mosques and madrasas.[80] As to highway robbery, in one instance the deputy qadi al-Buṣrawī was attacked and stripped naked when coming to greet his son on his return from the hajj.[81]

Since theft was regarded as a *ḥadd* (i.e., an offense the punishment for which was fixed by scripture[82]), suspects were incarcerated and occasionally severely flogged, even to the point of death.[83] Amputation appears to have

---

78 Also at the residence of the Samaritan official Ṣadaqa there was a break-in. At that point only his wife was there, and the thieves took whatever they could and disappeared without a trace. See Ibn Ṭawq, *Ta'līq* 366, 582, 914, 1791; Martel-Thoumian, *Délinquance* 59, 92, 137.

79 Ibn Ṭawq, *Ta'līq* 956, 1474, 1483–1484 (it is unclear who was punished); Ibn Ṭūlūn, *Mufākahat al-khillān* 106, is slightly different; Martel-Thoumian, *Délinquance* 284.

80 Ibn Ṭawq, *Ta'līq* 48, 80, 150, 235, 275, 276, 278, 290, 294, 367, 388, 449, 450, 463, 470, 483, 493, 501, 519, 541, 545, 585, 588, 656, 657, 659, 690, 692, 693, 698, 702, 705, 731, 747, 777, 779, 794, 812, 817, 837, 847, 876, 891, 914, 939, 948, 956, 975, 1032, 1065, 1144 (two cases), 1168, 1215, 1233, 1236, 1238, 1346, 1363, 1423, 1436, 1453, 1459, 1463, 1467, 1472 (two cases), 1476, 1497, 1510 (two cases), 1512, 1541, 1600, 1608, 1683, 1757, 1787, 1823, 1839, 1851, 1857, 1859, 1909, 1913. For unspecified cases of theft, see 643, 649, 1013, 1040, 1501. See also al-Buṣrawī, *Tārīkh* 141, 149; Ibn Ṭūlūn, *Mufākahat al-khillān* 24, 33, 44, 59, 89, 90, 99, 106, 112, 189, 195; Martel-Thoumian, *Délinquance* 30, 36, 37, 43, 54, 58, 59, 129, 131, 132, 133, 134, 154, 232, 253, 284, 285, 286; Petry, *Criminal underworld* 60.

81 Ibn Ṭawq, *Ta'līq* 588.

82 Hallaq, *Sharī'a* 311–315.

83 For incarceration, see e.g. Ibn Ṭawq, *Ta'līq* 1233, 1481, 1483–1484, 1688. For flogging, see Ibn Ṭawq, *Ta'līq* 449, 450, 545, 1032, 1184 (causing death), 1233, 1483–1484, 1501, 1510, 1695, 1785; Ibn Ṭūlūn, *Mufākahat al-khillān* 195 (causing death); Ibn al-Ḥimṣī, *Ḥawādith* i, 339 (causing death); Martel-Thoumian, *Délinquance* 54, 57, 129.

been common, even, on occasion, of all four limbs.[84] In one instance no less than three men and two women had limbs amputated, a search of their place having revealed stolen property, and after allegedly having confessed.[85] However, in 891/1486 it was announced that thieves would be hanged or hooked (*shankala*).[86] Ibn Ṭawq provides a total of more than 50 people who were executed for theft by hanging or other means. A few of them had had limbs amputated before but had not been deterred from continuing with their criminal activity.[87] One may argue that, as in the case of homicide, severe punishment for theft indicated the ubiquity of this crime and that the regime's attempt to conduct a policy of deterrence resulted in measures far beyond those envisioned by the sharīʿa.

Other crime categories are less frequently mentioned.[88] Of sexual offenses, castration was the punishment for a former governor of Baʿalbek accused of a large number of offenses associated with his "treatment of a woman." In another case, Ibn Ṭawq's neighbor was suspected of what appears to have been a homosexual relationship with a good-looking youth from Ḥamā. A huge fine was imposed on him.[89]

3 Religious Offenses

At the end of the Mamluk period Damascus served as a stage for a few theological debates, some of which were between scholars and Sufis.[90] Like other cities in the Mamluk state, it had a tradition of bringing to court cases of religious offense that sometimes resulted in execution. Ibn Ṭawq's reports reveal that religious offenses remained under the jurisdiction of qadis. All in all, although taken seriously from a legal point of view and categorized as *ḥadd*, punishment

---

84 Ibn Ṭawq, *Taʿlīq* 60, 453–454 (seven), 633 (two), 649, 750 (five), 777, 837 (three), 876, 1024, 1147 (five), 1329, 1340, 1395, 1400 (black female slave), 1403 (several), 1406 (two), 1407, 1478, 1644, 1791.

85 Ibn Ṭawq, *Taʿlīq* 837.

86 Ibn Ṭawq, *Taʿlīq* 646; Martel-Thoumian, *Délinquance* 272.

87 For the death penalty, see Ibn Ṭawq, *Taʿlīq* 150–151, 294, 453–454, 501, 595, 642, 644 (three), 646, 649 (following amputation), 777, 779, 795, 796, 812, 1024, 1045 (two), 1062 (twenty black slaves), 1149, 1215 (two), 1329, 1340, 1372–1373 (four), 1478, 1510, 1547, 1743, 1785, 1904 (three), 1908; al-Buṣrawī, *Tārīkh* 111; Martel-Thoumain, *Délinquance* 29, 44, 45, 54, 135, 285.

88 For issuing forged coins, see Ibn Ṭawq, *Taʿlīq* 588, 589.

89 Ibn Ṭawq, *Taʿlīq* 897, 1330–1331. In Chapter 3 above we saw the case of the enormous fine imposed on Sāra, Taqī al-Dīn's third wife, and the relative spotted at her doorway.

90 See the interesting discussion based on a variety of sources in Geoffroy, *Soufisme* 437–476.

of those accused of blasphemy and related crimes tended to be lenient. With one exception there are no reports of execution for religious offense.[91]

Of the cases in this category listed in the *Taʿlīq* and our other sources, one may begin with a complaint that was filed against a man who claimed to have seen in a dream that the Prophet was buried near the city, and who turned "the grave" into an attraction to visitors, whom our notary characterizes as "followers of the Antichrist (*dajjāl*)." A qadi called for a session in which proofs were established against the man, and a *maḥḍar* was written, after which the man was arrested.[92] In another instance a broker was jailed for stating, "I shall not go to so-and-so even if he were a prophet." A review of his statement—to decide whether it should be considered apostasy (*kufr*)—followed, and the question was brought before the authorities in Cairo. In the end, the man was released for the enormous sum of 4,000 dinars.[93] One cannot avoid the thought that such a case was a means to add cash to the treasury or private pockets. In yet another case a blind man, Egyptian by origin, stood up and recited poetry to one preacher's marvel. However, the preacher became infuriated when informed that the lines had been composed by the prominent Sufi Ibn al-Fāriḍ (d. 632/1235). A session was convened by the Shāfiʿī deputy qadi, and it was decided that the man should be flogged. How many lashes? Opinions differed.[94] One Yūnus, a camel driver (*jammāl*) of the Shāghūr Quarter, was blamed for drinking in the company of Christians and for admitting that their religion was older and that "our prophet stemmed from you." He was overheard by two of his neighbors and brought before Taqī al-Dīn, who reprimanded him, and he was put in fetters. The man denied the accusation and, when sent to the Shāfiʿī deputy qadi, admitted only to having been drunk and was flogged.[95] In a Mālikī seminar (*dars*) led by the school's qadi, a man referred to a statement about "the spirits [that] would be gathered without the bodies." He alluded to the issue as it featured in the *Saḥīḥ*, whereby someone referred to

91 Levanoni, *Takfīr*. For the general situation and a similar conclusion, see Petry, *Criminal underworld* 316–317, 328–329. On this topic, see Wiederhold, Blasphemy; Geoffroy, *Soufisme* 381, notes the Shāfiʿīs' lenient attitude.

92 Ibn Ṭawq, *Taʿlīq* 1622.

93 al-Buṣrawī, *Tārīkh* 132–133; Ibn Ṭawq, *Taʿlīq* 826, notes his arrest but not the reason for it.

94 Ibn Ṭawq, *Taʿlīq* 483–484. For Burhān al-Dīn al-Nājī, a Damascus Ḥanbalī scholar, who became a Shāfiʿī and was opposed to Ibn al-ʿArabī's followers, see Ibn Ṭawq, *Taʿlīq* 37, 60, 62, 178, 1052; ʿAbd al-Bāsiṭ, *Majmaʿ* i, 240 (and further references in n. 2), 258. For Shihāb al-Dīn al-Ramlī as a deputy qadi, see Ibn Ṭawq, *Taʿlīq* 110, 126, 509, 848, 1836. For his *Naẓm al-ʿuqyān*, see Ibn Ṭūlūn, *Fulk* 23.

95 Ibn Ṭawq, *Taʿlīq* 642; Wollina, *Zwanzig* 177.

as *al-nabbāsh* instructed his sons to cremate his body and spread the ashes in the river (*baḥr*) for God to gather them on the Day of Resurrection. The man's argument was that his "original organs" were not to be consumed by the fire. The qadi opined that the man should be penalized for his opinion by receiving 80 lashes. Our notary does not hide his disdain for the man's opinion, referring to it as "nonsense" (*khabāṭāt*).[96] In a case starting in Baʿalbek, someone was accused of heresy (*zandaqa*) and of propagating "evil concepts" such as *ḥulūl* and *ittiḥād*. These (actually synonymous) theological terms expressed incarnation or "infusion," the indwelling of God in a creature, a union of divinity with human—a concept that the theologians refuted and condemned.[97] The man was detained in the local citadel, interrogated by the Ḥanbalī qadi of his town, and forced to go back on his ideas and proclaim that he was a Muslim. Another local qadi, this time a Ḥanafī, who is described as an ignoramus (*jāhil*), approved of the decision. However, the man was later sent (together with the report of the investigation) to Damascus, presented to Taqī al-Dīn, the *shaykh al-Islām*, who transferred his case to the Shāfiʿī qadi. Interrogated a second time, the man reiterated his original idea and, subsequently, was returned to Taqī al-Dīn. A ritual of humiliation was then conducted, whereby his head was exposed bare, and he was put in fetters and sent to the *ḥabs al-dam*, which would imply that he was expected to be executed. What actually happened to him remains unknown.[98] Another man described as a *rāfiḍī* (? Shīʿī; it is unclear what the term denotes here) was also imprisoned in the *ḥabs al-dam* for an unspecified reason and died, possibly in the course of interrogation.[99] Earlier in this book a controversy was detailed between Taqī al-Dīn and another prominent Shāfiʿī, Burhān al-Dīn al-Biqāʿī, during his stay in Damascus, in the course of which the former ruled that al-Biqāʿī's stand amounted to apostasy (*takfīr*). Perhaps because in this case two of the most distinguished Shāfiʿīs were at odds, and the accusation leveled at one of them was severe, the viceroy got himself involved but then decided to defer the hearing till the qadis of all four schools were present in the city. The only case of execution on religious grounds we learn about was, as demanded by law, of a renegade who went back to Christianity.[100]

---

96 Ibn Ṭawq, *Taʿlīq* 603.

97 See Ḥulūl, *EI*²; Ittiḥād, *EI*²; Zindīḳ, *EI*². For similar cases in Egypt and further discussion, see Geoffroy, *Soufisme* 379–380, 383, 439–443, 472–476.

98 Ibn Ṭawq, *Taʿlīq* 163–164; Ibn al-Ḥimṣī, *Ḥawādith* i, 273 is shorter and less clear; Ibn Ṭūlūn, *Mufākahat al-khillān* 48, copied from him.

99 Ibn Ṭawq, *Taʿlīq* 102.

100 Ibn Ṭawq, *Taʿlīq* 1479.

As to wine, in one instance Taqī al-Dīn was informed that the preacher of al-Mizza had at his residence two drunkards.[101] When someone was sent to verify it, the preacher opened the door, and it turned out that he was drunk as well, and two vessels full of wine were found. The two guests managed to escape, but the preacher was detained. At Taqī al-Dīn's residence, with the Mālikī qadi and his professional witnesses present, the man confessed, was stripped of his clothes, and was flogged "according to the law" (*ḍarb al-ḥadd*) 80 lashes on his shoulders. However, when the governor's officials arrived to arrest him, Taqī al-Dīn objected. A week later, perhaps after his release, they were able to put their hands on him, and he was fined 2,000 dirhams. In another case, a man caught drinking in a woman's company was detained and brought to a hearing (a protocol was recorded), after which he was delivered to the viceroy and released after paying 100 dinars.[102] In his capacity as a deputy qadi, al-Buṣrawī provides a detailed report on a tribunal in Cairo, to which he was summoned, to review a case of wine drinking. It involved a Damascus man pretending to be a *faqīh* but known to drink wine and consume hashish, associating with sinners (*fussāq*) and even taking pride in that. For his drinking he had already been brought to trial in Damascus before al-Buṣrawī himself, but he then asked to present his case to the sultan. At the session in Cairo there was a dispute between al-Buṣrawī and the Egyptian Ḥanafī qadi, who argued that the accusation established in Damascus was on the grounds that the accused man acted of his own choice (*mukhtāran*). Al-Buṣrawī "silenced" his colleague by retorting that such a condition was required by the Ḥanafīs but not by his Shafiʿī school. A second issue of contention was whether one punishment for all the offenses was permissible. Al-Buṣrawī cited the opinion of Shāfiʿī authorities that the number of lashes for drinking wine could go anywhere between 40 and 80 and subsume all other related offenses. A third legal issue that came up in this framework was whether to publicize the case. Once again, al-Buṣrawī cited opinions of his school about the deterrent effect that publicity might have on potential offenders.[103]

It is known that the Mālikīs were the most conservative in denying repentance for blasphemy, and in the course of the fourteenth century most cases of execution resulted from decisions made by qadis of the Mālikī school. In oppo-

101 For the treatment of wine in the Mamluk state earlier, see Stilt, *Islamic law* 92–95. For Syria in the period here considered, see Martel-Thoumian, *Déliquance* 289–298.

102 Ibn Ṭawq, *Taʿlīq* 366–367, 656, 659 (Martel-Thoumian, *Délinquance* 187), 1114. For other cases briefly mentioned, see e.g. 58, 124, 213, 233, 239, 426, 460, 1206, 1860.

103 al-Buṣrawī, *Tārīkh* 64–66.

sition stood Taqī al-Dīn al-Subkī (d. 756/1355), the Shāfiʿī qadi of Damascus and one of the leading scholars of his time, who opined that a qadi of any school could authorize repentance.[104] Ibn Ṭawq's material demonstrates that the difference between schools was practiced in his own day. Thus a youth adhering to the Shāfiʿī school was accused of blasphemy (*fī ḥaqq Allāh*) in making some unspecified statement and was sent by the Mālikī deputy qadi to prison to be put to death. Against that verdict, the Shāfiʿī deputy qadi declared that the youth remained a believer nevertheless. Then, the Mālikī retaliated by putting more pressure on the accused. Only Taqī al-Dīn's intervention put an end to the confrontation, and the youth was released.[105] In another case a Mālikī made some unacceptable declaration and even propagated it in mosques, for which the qadi of his *madhhab* decided to put him in the *ḥabs al-dam*. Unsurprisingly, the man and his supporters were given protection by the (Shāfiʿī) *shaykh al-Islām*, who acted against his arrest.[106]

Let us conclude with a relatively detailed report on the descendants of a Jewish woman, a daughter of Shamla (?) the perfume dealer, whose conversion to Islam had been certified some decades earlier by the Shafiʿī qadi. She then wished to go back to her origins but, after being threatened with death, stayed in Islam and was married to a Muslim. Now her children and grandchildren, most likely because of suspicion about their religious standing, were detained following Taqī al-Dīn's order. It turned out that, according to a decision made by the Māliki qadi of Safed 15 years earlier—perhaps, the family originated in that town—they were considered renegades. The case reached the viceroy, and, in a session in the presence of the qadis and other leading scholars, the Shāfiʿī qadi declared that the woman was Muslim nevertheless and so were her offspring. Here, the difference between the lenient Shafiʿīs and the strict Mālikīs becomes clear. However, under pressure from his Mālikī colleague, the Shāfiʿī backed down. The session ended without decision, and, in another session following the intervention of another Mālikī scholar, it was declared that the earlier Mālikī decision was to be annulled and that the family should be regarded Muslim after all. Taqī al-Dīn issued a fatwa about it, and other lead-

---

104 Rapoport, Legal diversity 223, 225. On a detailed report of Mālikī procedure in a blasphemy case in Toledo in 464/1072 and the saga of the accused, see Muller, *Gerichtspraxis* 204–211. For a few cases of execution in tenth- and eleventh-century Spain, see Fierro, Heresy. For a case in Tlemcen in 843/1439 see the detailed analysis in Powers, *Law, society, and culture* 167–200. On al-Subkī, see al-Subkī, *EI*².

105 Ibn Ṭawq, *Taʿlīq* 37–38; Petry, *Criminal underworld* 170, relies on Ibn Ṭūlūn's version, which misses some elements.

106 Ibn Ṭawq, *Taʿlīq* 650.

ing Shāfiʿīs approved of the decision. The case was far from resolved, however, and came up again less than a year later. After several more months, a family member went to Cairo, and apparently he returned with a decree from the sultan, the caliph, and a fatwa written by the Egyptian Mālikī qadi, all confirming the family's status as Muslims. Three years later, a letter was sent to Cairo concerning this affair, now referred to as the "issue of the Jews" (*qaḍiyat awlād al-yahūd*), but further details are missing.[107]

It has recently been argued that the notion of the rulers and the jurists occupying separate spheres in the Mamluk period must be substantially revised and that institutional collaboration existed between the regime and the qadi-court; and further that, beyond interaction and symbiosis, the two groups actively competed for jurisdiction.[108] The lack of a clear demarcation line between the juridical authority of the different agencies, and the encroachment by the Mamluks on the legal arena, as well as personal conflicts among qadis, all were potential for complication.[109] The viceroy or other officeholders in the Mamluk high echelon also intervened in cases that were not normally under their jurisdiction. Ibn Ṭawq's information in this regard supports the argument about the expansion of the realm of jurisdiction of Mamluk courts by the fifteenth century at the latest.[110] An example is a hearing that took place at the Dār al-ʿAdl following an appeal by a husband whose divorcée conditioned their reunion on his payment of 10 dinars, apparently as a *ṣadāq*. The husband found it difficult to pay the sum, and the viceroy instructed his men to raise a larger sum to enable the man also to provide for his children. The ruler promised to support him whenever he was in need.[111]

Mamluks who were appealed to on legal issues inflicted punishment, sometimes quite severe, often without juridical procedure, or following the Mamluk system (*siyāsa*), which allowed certain actions that the sharīʿa did not.[112] Summons and tribulation (*miḥna*) resulted in death. This was the case for an

107 Ibn Ṭawq, *Taʿlīq* 87, 88, 89, 90, 169, 266, 651, 744. See also El-Leithy, Living documents 395.

108 Muller, Mamluk law 266, 278; Stilt, *Islamic law* 33; Petry, *Criminal underworld* 321.

109 See the general statement in Hallaq, *Sharīʿa* 202–203.

110 Rapoport, Royal justice; Irwin, Privatization; Hallaq, *Sharīʿa* 200–201, 209. However, the statement about the Mamluk viceroy's exceptional jurisdiction as regards civilians should be qualified. See most recently Muller, Crimes 145–146.

111 Ibn Ṭūlūn, *Mufākahat al-khillān* 245; Ibn Ṭūlūn, *Iʿlām* 199–200.

112 In one case it was explained that, unlike the *ḥukm Allāh*, which did not allow taking a document in someone's possession by force, the Mamluk system did. See Ibn Ṭawq, *Taʿlīq* 977; Siyāsa, *EI*[2]; e.g. Hallaq, *Sharīʿa* 211–212.

"eastern" (*mashriqī*) merchant who complained about Shihāb al-Dīn Aḥmad al-Raqqāwī. The latter was interrogated by the sultan's *barddār* and thrown in bad condition at the door of his house, where he died. On top of that, money he left was confiscated by the *dīwān al-mawārīth al-ḥashriyya*.[113] In another instance, a relative of Ibn Ṭawq disputed with a broker (*dallāl*) about 40 dirhams. The former claimed to have paid it and complained to the interim governor (*mutasallim*), who sent his men and they flogged the broker. However, the Mamluk was dissatisfied with this punishment and ordered also amputation. Luckily only part ("a nerve or two") was injured, and the man was sent to prison, where he bribed his guards and his condition there was improved. The issue was resolved after he paid no less than 50 ashrafīs, namely, a sum many times higher than the initial cause of the dispute.[114]

The jurists did not give up easily and on occasion could receive support from unexpected sources. Around mid century, the Māliki qadi was dismissed after disputing with the second *ḥājib* about a murder suspect who enjoyed the latter's custody. The emirs addressed the sultan about the juridical autonomy of each of the group of Mamluks (*ḥukkām al-siyāsa*) and the qadis. Significantly, the sultan decided that a suspect at a sharʿī court could not be taken to the Mamluk system.[115] A dispute between a perfume dealer and a peasant from the Ḥawrān came before a Mamluk official, who summoned the dealer, but he declined to show up, after which his and his son's residences were sealed. The two appealed to the Ḥanafī qadi, who decided to seal only the son's residence for a couple of days. Then, Mamluk officials were sent and inflicted corporal punishment on the dealer and dragged him violently into the inner city, where he was brought before the *dawādār*, flogged, and thrown into a jail known as "the oven." The Ḥanafī qadi went to see the viceroy, but the latter claimed to have no influence on the *dawādār* and that Taqī al-Dīn, the *shaykh al-Islām*, should become involved. At first, the *dawādār* declined to cooperate. Then, a session was convened by the shaykh, in which three of the qadis and other prominent scholars were present. After witnesses testified to the *dawādār*'s misconduct and the various atrocities ascribed to him, he was dismissed from his office. It is easy to see in this case too many involved with conflicting interests. Also here the Mamluks had to concede.[116] This was also true when in Muḥarram 895/November 1489 Arkimās the *dawādār* released from the Māliki qadi's residence one "of the peasants of one of the high-officers (*ulūf*)," who

113 Ibn Ṭawq, *Taʿlīq* 1877.

114 Ibn Ṭawq, *Taʿlīq* 1744. The author expresses his uneasiness with the decision.

115 Ibn Ṭūlūn, *Quḍāt Dimashq* 259.

116 Ibn Ṭawq, *Taʿlīq* 1054–1055, 1056.

had been convicted of murder. The four qadis reacted by closing the court to routine litigation for three days, and the Mamluk was compelled to rearrest the peasant and apologize. However, as Petry suggests, this show of power could be an exception in a larger context of the loss of ground by the qadis at the end of the Mamluk regime.[117]

117 Ibn Ṭawq, *Taʿlīq* 916, 917; Ibn al-Ḥimṣī, *Ḥawādith* i, 321; Ibn Ṭūlūn, *Mufākahat al-khillān* 97; Petry, *Criminal underworld* 288.

CHAPTER 6

The Family: Marriage, Divorce, and the Household

As with other subjects discussed in this book, Ibn Ṭawq is one of our best sources also as regards the medieval Muslim family, especially as we know little about the marital life of common people. The information he provides on Damascus at the end of the fifteenth century refers to three main topics: marriage, divorce, and the household, especially female slaves owned by men and, to much lesser extent, by women. This chapter presents the findings based primarily on the notary's diary, with some additional material derived from other sources.

1 Marriage[1]

Our notary's information supports what is generally known, namely, that a marriage contract (*ʿaqd*) was to be signed following oral negotiation (*takhāṭabā shafāhan*) and a "proposal and its acceptance" (*ījāb wa qabūl*) between representatives of the future couple in the presence of qualified witnesses.[2] An agent (*wakīl*) or a guardian (*walī*), usually a relative, represented the bride, but in the absence of such, someone else would do.[3] In accordance with the Ḥanafī and Shāfiʿī ruling, a mature bride had to give her consent to the marriage. The groom himself, or someone he appointed, accepted the offer.[4] The Ḥanafī school allowed the bride's mother to represent her daughter in the absence of a male relative to do it.[5] In one instance the marriage of cousins was annulled because the bride's father did not give his consent.[6]

Prior to the signing, the orally pronounced agreement could be abrogated by one of the parties. Thus our notary reports that a groom who was summoned by the qadi to be told the bad news complained: "How is it possible? We

1 For the legal norms in general, see ʿUrs, *EI*², and Nikāḥ, *EI*²; Hallaq, *Sharīʿa* 271–277; Ali, Marriage. For some references to the Mamluk period, see Frenkel, Mamluk ʿulamāʾ.

2 E.g. Ibn Ṭawq, *Taʿlīq* 613, 626, 681.

3 E.g. Ibn Ṭawq, *Taʿlīq* 536, 539, 821. For annulling a contract after it was revealed that the bride had not reached puberty, see 752.

4 Ibn Ṭawq, *Taʿlīq* 263, 292, 379, 536, 613, 626, 658, 821, 916, 1032, 1301, 1736, 1796, 1822.

5 Ibn Ṭawq, *Taʿlīq* 1787–1788.

6 Ibn Ṭūlūn, *Mufākahat al-khillān* 298–299. For this ruling, see Ali, Marriage 18–19.

 | DOI:10.1163/9789004413269_008

have decided earlier! I disagree!" Yet, to no avail.[7] Unless she had been married before, the bride was declared a virgin and had to be proven as such.[8] Contracts could be signed at different locales, such as at the bride's home (especially if she was a divorcée or a widow), at the groom's or his relative's home, at the qadi's residence, at a Sufi lodge with which the groom was associated, or at a mosque or madrasa.[9] There were cases in which a few days, weeks, and even a couple of years, depending on the specific circumstances, elapsed between the act of signing the contract and its implementation by the actual wedding (*ʿurs*); this usually happened when puberty was not yet attained.[10] Separate celebrations (*walīmat ʿurs*) on a gender basis, sometime a day apart, were held. Playing music could be controversial.[11] Consummation of the marriage (*dukhūl*) was expected during the night following the wedding party.[12] An especially piquant report is on a freshly wed young couple who went to bed, with a lady, a cousin of the bride's mother, present. Following the consummation (*naqsh*) the three went to sleep, leaving a candle burning; a fire started and caused slight burns to the lady "supervisor" but, fortunately, nothing more than that.[13]

Let us examine the details of a couple of cases of the signing a marriage contract in which Ibn Ṭawq served as a witness. Fāṭima, the daughter of Bahāʾ al-Dīn (the full name is effaced; he was also known as Ibn al-Sharīfa), a virgin, unmarried before, was married to ʿAbd al-Raḥīm, a son of the deceased qadi Burhān al-Dīn b. al-Muʿtamid. The contract was signed on the afternoon of 5 Shaʿbān 903/29 March 1498 at the bride's home in Lower Qābūn village. The bride's father authorized Taqī al-Dīn b. al-Baṭāʾinī to represent his daughter, and the groom was represented by al-Baṭāʾinī's father. The groom was to pay a marriage gift (*ṣadāq*) of 200 ("not forged") dinars. The betrothal (*khiṭāb*) was officiated by the Ḥanafī qadi. Since the groom was a qadi's son, some prominent men were present, among them the Ḥanbalī qadi, merchants, and residents of the Ṣāliḥiyya Quarter (which, as we know, was heavily populated by Ḥanbalīs).

---

7 Ibn Ṭawq, *Taʿlīq* 379.

8 E.g. Ibn Ṭawq, *Taʿlīq* 263, 292, 536, 659, 680, 821. On the custom of carrying the gown of the newly wed bride stained with blood through the neighborhood to demonstrate her virginity, see 638. In this particular case the bride appears to have remained a virgin on the morrow of the wedding, so the people's joy turned out to be premature.

9 Ibn Ṭawq, *Taʿlīq* 61, 109–110, 154, 186, 263, 292, 503, 536, 821, 1142, 1301, 1623, 1661, 1702, 1906. For the Ḥanafī ruling that marriage could be arranged only at a madrasa, see 1136–1137.

10 E.g. Ibn Ṭawq, *Taʿlīq* 292, 329, 536, 657, 1888, 1906.

11 Ibn Ṭawq, *Taʿlīq* 154, 658, 1345, 1704, 1792, 1854, 1855. Music was banned from the marriage of the notary's son.

12 Ibn Ṭawq, *Taʿlīq* 154, 581, 645, 1842.

13 Ibn Ṭawq, *Taʿlīq* 1812.

Refreshment was served, and the party then went to entertain themselves in the garden. Ibn Ṭawq could not stay for it but heard that the celebration continued till sunset.[14]

Another marriage ceremony, the details of which are relatively rich, is of Najm al-Dīn, the son of *shaykh al-Islām* Taqī al-Dīn b. Qāḍī ʿAjlūn. At 17, he married his cousin Fāṭima, the "Egyptian's" (i.e., his stepmother's) daughter from her earlier marriage to Najm al-Dīn's uncle, who had attained puberty a short time before the marriage, which would imply that she was a few years younger than the groom. The latter was represented by his relative, Kamāl al-Dīn, and the bride's representative was Abū l-Yumn, her step ("half") brother. Ibn Ṭawq signed his name on the marriage contract, and the Shāfiʿī qadi added his name. The marriage was concluded at the grandmother's (i.e., Taqī al-Dīn's mother). The shaykh (i.e., the groom's father) delivered a sermon. The part of the marriage gift to be paid immediately was 100 dinars. The wedding party took place about a couple of months later, the bride's mother (i.e., the "Egyptian" wife) being absent. Our source, who repeatedly demonstrates his dislike of her, explains that "the devil had control over her" and that she was "bewitched." The celebration went on till after midnight, and our notary knew to tell that the marriage was consummated thereafter. Incidentally, less than four years later Ibn Ṭawq reports on problems in the marriage, that a daughter was born and died aged 18 months. Three months later Fāṭima miscarried twin daughters. After another year another daughter was born, but also she died less than two years old. About nine months afterward, a son was born, and after three more years another deceased daughter is mentioned.[15] This young family, like Ibn Ṭawq's, lost almost all their children. There is no further information on them.

What were the stipulations inserted into a marriage contract? If the future husband had married and divorced before his new engagement, he could be required to declare that he did not intend to remarry his divorcée. In fact, in one case the husband declared that if he married another wife or remarried his divorcée, he would have to pay a penalty of 100 dinars to members of a *madhhab*; however, this was not put to the test, because the wife passed away only three months after concluding the marriage.[16] Other stipulations could be, for example, not letting a female slave reside close by, or that the husband should not be absent for more than a year with no legally recognized reason. A breach of that condition would give the wife the right to ask for divorce, which perhaps would be effected by the husband pronouncing the divorce formula only once

14 Ibn Ṭawq, *Taʿlīq* 1597–1598.
15 Ibn Ṭawq, *Taʿlīq* 536, 539, 581, 877, 1213, 1312, 1325, 1490, 1580, 1873.
16 Ibn Ṭawq, *Taʿlīq* 1488, 1511.

(*ṭalqa wāḥida*) instead of the three times normally required.[17] Possibly following the Ḥanafī school, if hit by her husband, or forced to move out of her home, acts for which she were able to bring two witnesses, and after giving up the rest of the *ṣadāq*, a wife would be free to divorce after only one *ṭalāq* statement.[18] One husband declared that his wife, who had previously been a slave, was entitled to his share in a house that had belonged to her former husband, a share he received through her daughter. At the same time, he made sure that both his wife and her daughter had no further claims except for the deferred *ṣadāq*.[19] These stipulations that our notary provides come close to those found in later times in Ottoman records.[20]

At this point it may be instructive to digress and discuss a brief treatise on Syrian weddings, *Aʿrās al-Shām*, by ʿAlī b. ʿAṭiyya, better known as ʿAlwān al-Ḥamāwī (d. 936/1530), a contemporary scholar of the Syrian town Ḥamā.[21] It is a devastating critique of marriage customs as then conducted, and perhaps unsurprisingly so, since the author was a Sufi shaykh known for his "commanding the right and forbidding the wrong" and for being a sort of puritan. ʿAlwān condemns the materialistic approach of his time, whereby a groom does not enquire about his bride's piety, or about her origins, but only about her beauty and the trousseau (*jihāz*) she can bring to the marriage ("Does she have enough cloth"?). A bride's ability to provide a fortune overrules any consideration of character and piety. ʿAlwān criticizes the tendency to demonstrate high status and arouse envy by, for example, writing contracts on a large piece of silk, presumably instead of paper. As the time for consummating the marriage (*dukhūl*) approaches, the groom's neighbors accompany him to the bride's quarter, and the emphasis in the meeting is on feasting. During the wedding party, people celebrate when they actually should mourn the mingling of men and women, the joyful exclamations (*zaghālīṭ*), and the expressions of excess and pride, the only aim of which is to impress and report to their friends: "This and that

17 Ibn Ṭawq, *Taʿlīq* 121, 1051, 1187–1188, 1276–1277, 1488, 1653. For al-Sakhāwī's reference to the stipulation about the husband's absence, see Musallam, Ordering 193. For a wife's demand of divorce because of her husband's prolonged absence, see also Muller, *Gerichtspraxis* 272–288.

18 Ibn Ṭawq, *Taʿlīq* 911–912. The difference between one and thrice a statement is not entirely clear. For an interesting example, see Powers, Four cases.

19 Ibn Ṭawq, *Taʿlīq* 1023.

20 Sonbol, History, esp. 87–90, 94–96, 101, 104. For contracts in general and sixteenth-century Cairo records, see Hallaq, *Sharīʿa* 188–189, 277–278.

21 See on him al-Ḥamāwī, ʿAlwān, *EI*[3]; e.g. Geoffroy, *Soufisme* 494–497. The treatise was published in al-Ḥamāwī, *Shām* 65–77. The introduction provides biographical details and a list of his works.

attended the party." Social pressure causes even the poor to spend beyond their means. The participants, who bring to mind the Iranian magians worshipping fire, go to the public bath carrying candles in front of the bride. The groom sits on an elevated chair, and women stick pieces of paper (in another version, dirhams) to his eyebrow. The odor of perfume they spread and the looks they give him are to be condemned. The writer mentions a curious custom of the bride changing her wedding dress after the party is over and putting on her head, as if in a gesture of transdressing, a learned man's turban, holding a sword, and approaching the husband, who takes it and gently hits her head three times with it as a token of dominance. A similarly curious custom is the groom's mother-in-law standing at the door and forcing the newly wed couple to crawl between her legs. In an observation also confirmed by Ibn Ṭawq in his aforementioned report, ʿAlwān states that, during the night following the marriage, the privacy of the couple is hindered by neighboring women, who peep into the bedroom to learn whether intercourse has taken place.[22]

To return to our notary, among the hundreds of notarial documents included in the *Taʿlīq* about 65 are marriage contracts with relatively rich information. This is undoubtedly the best set of data on this subject one can hope to find for a pre-Ottoman Islamic society anywhere. What does it teach us? First, and this should not come as a surprise, in most cases where the background of the parties to the marriage can be established, one observes social equality.[23] Of marriages between families of the learned elite our notary reports quite a lot. Thus Muḥammad Raḍī al-Dīn al-Ghazzī (d. 935/1528), the son of the *shaykh al-Islām* and himself a prolific Shāfiʿī scholar and a deputy qadi, married the daughter of the deceased *shaykh al Islām*, who had been his guardian after his father's death when he was barely two years old. Interestingly, despite the groom's Shāfiʿī adherence, the marriage contract was according to the Ḥanafī

---

22 For a modern commentator's note that he witnessed it in his youth, see al-Ḥamāwī, *Shām* 51–52. One may note ʿAlwān's "postmodernist" attitude that criticizes male chauvinism, for which he brings examples and compares it unfavorably with the Prophet's treatment of women.

23 The son of ʿAlāʾ al-Dīn al-Buṣrawī, the Shāfiʿī deputy qadi and historian, married the sister of the merchant Ibn al-Maʿārīkī. Ḥasan b. al-Naḥḥās, apparently a wealthy man, married the daughter of Badr al-Dīn Ḍafdaʿ, of the Qāḍī Adhriʿāt family. ʿAbd al-Ghanī, a wealthy merchant, of the Ibn al-Muzalliq family, married Saʿadāt bt. Badr al-Dīn of the Ibn Qāḍī Shuhba family of scholars. ʿAbd al-Ghanī's relative, the daughter of the deceased wealthy merchant Shams al-Dīn b. al-Muzalliq (see on him Chapter 4) was married to the *kātib al-sirr* Muḥibb al-Dīn. ʿAlī, of the wealthy al-Qārī family of merchants, married his cousin, the daughter of Shams al-Dīn Muḥammad b. al-Daqīq, apparently a sugar merchant (*sukkarī*). See Ibn Ṭawq, *Taʿlīq* 109–110, 154, 1128, 1611, 1817.

procedure (we know that the bride's mother was of a Ḥanafī family).[24] Burhān al-Dīn, a son of the notary Tāj al-Dīn al-Ṣaltī and himself a deputy qadi, married Zaynab, the daughter of qadi Muḥyī al-Dīn al-Ikhnāʾī.[25] The daughter of Shams al-Dīn Muḥammad al-Khaṭīb, whose father somehow occasionally substituted for Taqī al-Dīn in issuing fatwas, and who was also a descendant of the prominent al-Bāʿūnī family of qadis, married the nephew of the Shāfiʿī qadi Ibn Farfūr.[26] There were, as already noted, marriages between families of different legal schools[27] and between Mamluk families and families of civilian officials and bureaucrats.[28] Yet, occasionally, for unclear reasons, there were marriages reflecting social inequality. Such appears to have been the case in the marriage of Muḥibb al-Dīn b. Shahlā, possibly a real-estate broker, to a "peasant" (*falāḥa*). Abū l-Faḍl, the son of qadi Muḥyī al-Dīn al-Ikhnāʾī, married the daughter of an oil presser (*shakhṣ miʿṣarānī*) less than a year after the death of his wife due to pregnancy complications. Ibn Ṭawq's distant relative married a woman whose deceased father was a foreigner and some kind of a thief (? *aʿjamī min al-shalāḥa*).[29]

Of the close to 150 marriages recorded by Ibn Ṭawq for the period between circa 1480 and 1500, about 30 cases of marriage between first-degree cousins or more distant relatives are recorded.[30] About a dozen cases are the marriages of widows, including by the deceased husband's brother. Thus about eight months

24 Ibn Ṭawq, *Taʿlīq* 27. For a child born, see 782. See also, Ibn Ṭūlūn, *Mufākahat al-khillān* 22. For Raḍī al-Dīn, see al-Ḥaṣkafī, *Mutʿat al-adhhān* ii, 771–772. For an obituary of his father, see al-Buṣrawī, *Tārīkh* 60–61.

25 For children born, see Ibn Ṭawq, *Taʿlīq* 70, 296, 857, 1647. On Tāj al-Dīn, see 29, 140, 687.

26 Ibn Ṭawq, *Taʿlīq* 379, 657. For her father, see 90. See also al-Buṣrawī, *Tārīkh* 140.

27 For the marriage of Taqī al-Dīn and the granddaughter of the Ḥanbalī qadi, see Ibn Ṭawq, *Taʿlīq* 1734.

28 For example, Ḥaṭbā, Taqī al-Dīn's cousin, was married to a member of the Qāḍī Zarʿ family. See Ibn Ṭawq, *Taʿlīq* 579. For the son of Shihāb al-Dīn b. ʿAbd al-Ḥaqq, a scholar and notary, marrying the granddaughter of the Qāḍī Adhriʿāt family, see 967. For Shihāb al-Dīn, see 194, 293, 1063. For the marriage of the son of Muḥibb al-Dīn Muḥammad, probably *kātib al-sirr* (for whom see al-Buṣrawī, *Tārīkh* 173) and Aṣīl, a granddaughter of Badr al-Dīn, the qadi of Adhriʿāt, see 287. For the marriage of the son of the Shāfiʿī Kamāl al-Dīn al-Biqāʿī and Fāṭima, a daughter of Abū l-Faḍl al-Qudsī, a Shāfiʿī scholar and possibly a notary, see 1032–1033, 1038. For the marriage of Emir Kāsbāy's daughter to the notary Ibn ʿAlāʾ al-Dīn, see 854. A relative of the governor married the daughter of qadi Muḥibb al-Din, apparently of the Ibn Qāḍī ʿAjlūn family. See 1279. The perfume merchant (*ʿaṭṭār*) Ibn Baʿyūn, who had earlier divorced his wife, married the daughter of Iskandar, the grand emir's *ustādār*. See 1906.

29 Ibn Ṭawq, *Taʿlīq* 371 (on Ibn Shahla, see 1586 and above), 1598, 1672, 1702. For a couple defined as "equally simple-minded," see 1661.

30 Ibn Ṭawq, *Taʿlīq* 258, 430, 456, 536 (and 539), 545, 612, 666, 730, 851, 925, 929, 1034, 1057 (two

after the death of the young Badr al-Dīn al-Buṣrawī, the son of the deputy qadi and historian, who had been married for less than a year and a half to a daughter (or granddaughter) of Shams al-Dīn, the *khaṭīb* of the Saqīfa Mosque, his brother Jalāl al-Dīn, himself to become a qadi, married the young widow. As noted above, he had already a wife.[31] Ibn Ṭawq reports about an especially successful marriage between qadi Ibn al-Muzalliq and the widow of the Ḥanafī qadi Burhān al-Dīn b. al-Quṭb (d. 888/1483); she is quoted stating: "I have never seen a husband like him."[32] The status of a widow was crucial to her chances of finding a new match.

As to divorcées, only a few cases of marriage are recorded. Surely, also here a well-off divorcée had a better chance of attracting a second marriage.[33] An exceptional case must be Fāṭima's, who was divorced after a single pronouncement (*ṭalqa wāḥida*)—the husband admitted that the marriage had not been consummated and thus had to consent—who married someone else on the very same day. Another Fāṭima, the daughter of Shihāb al-Dīn b. al-Ṣāʾigh, was divorced (*firāq*, for which term see below) and less than four months later was married to a lad (*al-shābb al-ṭifl*) who liked to dress in Anatolian (? *ahl al-rūm*) clothing.[34] As to the terms, if the divorcée had young children from her previous marriage, an allowance (*nafaqa*) could be demanded from her new husband.[35]

The majority of marital relationships reported by Ibn Ṭawq appear to have been monogamous.[36] This conclusion conforms to that based on archival material for Ottoman Damascus around 1700, where polygamy was only about 10

cases), 1136, 1325, 1376, 1436, 1436–1437, 1452, 1475, 1488, 1580, 1605, 1611, 1713, 1780, 1793 (two cases), 1812, 1858, 1864, 1883.

31 Ibn Ṭawq, *Taʿlīq* 1030, 1131, 1185, 1622. Somewhat later he married also the daughter of the leading Shāfiʿī, Kamāl al-Dīn, but was forced to be separated from her because of some obscenity ascribed to him. See Ibn Ṭūlūn, *Mufākahat al-khillān* 289–290, 292. For other cases, see Ibn Ṭawq, *Taʿlīq* 186, 503, 640, 767, 1230, 1272–1273, 1301, 1350, 1546, 1842, 1864.

32 Ibn Ṭawq, *Taʿlīq* 243, 1230.

33 Ibn Ṭawq, *Taʿlīq* 70, 626, 964, 1452, 1611, 1662. See the conclusion in Musallam, Ordering 193–194, 197, based on about 500 biographies in al-Sakhāwī, that a third of the women married more than once, sometimes in close succession, and that in earlier times the rate was even higher. However, this may derive from the fact that these women were of high-bourgeois circles. For an assessment of this source see further below.

34 Ibn Ṭawq, *Taʿlīq* 1605, 1629, 1653. For an instance of the divorcée taking an oath, see 1452. In quite a number of cases it is unclear whether the bride had been a widow or a divorcée. See, e.g. 114, 363, 666, 738, 851, 964, 1114, 1192, 1361, 1477, 1545, 1589, 1592, 1611, 1646, 1672, 1678, 1728, 1785, 1815, 1866.

35 For *nafaqa* see the examples below.

36 For a somewhat impressionistic view, see Rapoport, Women and gender 30–31. For an attempt to be extremely precise ("2% polygamy"), see Musallam, Ordering 193.

percent of the recorded marriages.[37] Was it disapproved of by society?[38] Were there economic reasons, as might be suggested from some examples to follow? It is hard to tell. Still, it is of interest to mention the details provided on some polygamous cases. The Shāfiʿī qadi Bahāʾ al-Dīn al-Bāʿūnī (d. 910/1504) married his brother's widow. A couple of years after she passed away, he married two women in Egypt. Some years later, aged about 40, he married the daughter of *kabīr al-ḥarāfīsh*, the leader of the aforementioned social group.[39] The prominent Shāfiʿī Kamāl al-Dīn, of the Ibn Qaḍī ʿAjlūn family, had three wives, one of whom was the daughter of qadi Muḥibb al-Dīn, a family member, and another a daughter of qadi Ṣalāḥ al-Dīn al-ʿAdawī. Two of his wives gave birth to five daughters and a son respectively, while from the third he did not have—at least as reported—any children.[40] ʿAbd al-Qādir, who occupied at some point the post of *shaykh al-ṣāgha* (head of the goldsmiths), married Zayn al-ʿĀbidīn, a divorcée, and he vouched for a *kiswa* in addition to the *ṣadāq* and, as already noted about divorcées in general, her right to keep her residence. About a year later they had a daughter. After a few months ʿAbd al-Qādir is reported as having another wife, a qadi's granddaughter. Now he took an oath, with Zayn al-ʿĀbidīn being present, that he had legally married the second wife, perhaps because some doubt had been cast on it. Less than two years later, he divorced Zayn al-ʿĀbidīn by *khulʿ* (for which see below), but only a few weeks passed before they were remarried, then divorced yet again. However, a year and a half later she complained to the Mālikī qadi—perhaps she had her reasons to turn to this qadi in particular—and demanded to be remarried to ʿAbd al-Qādir. The qadi put pressure on him and it proved successful. After their second marriage, a son was born. Later, there was another divorce and remarriage, after which they had another son. Half a year later, Zayn al-ʿĀbidīn died. ʿAbd al-Qādir had at that time a third wife, Bt. Karurwa (?), or perhaps he had married her after one of his divorces from Zayn al-ʿĀbidīn. At one point, while she was pregnant, he divorced her as well.[41] Our source

---

37 Establet and Pascuel, *Familles* 55–57.

38 Musallam, Ordering 197.

39 Ibn Ṭawq, *Taʿlīq* 640, 869, 1197.

40 Ibn Ṭawq, *Taʿlīq* 41, 223, 423, 523, 617, 1015, 1969; Ibn Ṭūlūn, *Mufākahat al-khillān* 189.

41 Ibn Ṭawq, *Taʿlīq* 267, 852, 1156, 1242, 1317, 1335, 1338, 1363, 1403, 1504, 1673, 1684, 1725, 1864, 1894–1895. For a son born from his second wife, see 1867. His title suggests the existence of some sort of craft organization. Ibn Ṭawq refers to shaykhs of the tanners (*dabbāgha*), weavers (*ḥayyāk*), and goldsmiths (*ṣāgha*). It should be recalled that the term "shaykh" for the head of a guild features in documents from the early Ottoman period. See Cohen, *Guilds* 5, 6. Other relevant terms mentioned by our notary are *naqīb* ("head"), *ṭāʾifa* ("professional organization"), and *arbāb al-ḥiraf* ("heads of professional organizations"), such

lists further polygamous marriages. They suggest that polygamy was contingent on the man's economically elevated status.[42]

Muḥammad b. Muḥammad, known as Abū l-Yumn (d. 935/1529), the son of Zayn al-Dīn ʿAbd al-Raḥmān Ibn Qāḍī ʿAjlūn and, hence, a nephew of Taqī al-Dīn, the *shaykh al-Islām*, merits special attention.[43] We first meet him marrying Suryāy, Taqī al-Dīn's white former slave, who bore the shaykh a daughter a few weeks after her manumission. Abū l-Yumn's marriage gift to her was 25 ashrafīs, quite a generous one when compared to the sums normally paid to manumitted female slaves. Less than two years after this marriage we learn of the death of Umm Sitiyatiya, also Abū l-Yumn's wife. The widower did not wait too long before marrying Khadīja, known as Sitt al-ʿUlamāʾ, the daughter of the deceased Zayn al-Dīn ʿAbd al-Laṭīf al-Lūʾlūʾī, the wealthy "Head (? *shaykh*) of the Book Market (*sūq al-kuttāb*)."[44] Also she died less than three years later, following birth complications that resulted also in the death of her prematurely born son.[45] Barely four days passed after Sitt al-ʿUlamāʾ's death before he married the granddaughter of the former *nāʾib al-qalʿa*. Their marriage contract is the most detailed of its kind and is worthy of being quoted in full, especially as it points to a high degree of conformity to the legal norms.

> On the blessed Saturday, the 14 Ṣafar 894 [18 January 1489] was signed an engagement contract (*ʿaqd*) between Abū l-Yumn and the virgin, of sexual puberty, who had not been engaged in the past, who is free of any legal constraints (*khāliyya ʿan al-mawāniʿ al-sharʿiyya*), and who has no family relative to represent her ([*khāliyya*] *ʿan walī wa-ʿaṣaba*), the daughter of Faṭima, a daughter of [the deceased] Bardabek al-Sayfī Sūdūn al-Muḥammadī [Ibn al-Khayāṭa], who had been the *nāʾib al-qalʿa* in Damascus, may God protect her. Witnesses for the bride are Taqī al-Dīn Abū Bakr b. al-Khayāṭa and [her great uncle] Badr al-Dīn [Ibn al-Khayāṭa] and his son. Witnesses for the groom are Shihāb al-Dīn the Shāfiʿī … [other names

---

as carpenters and constructors. See Ibn Ṭawq, *Taʿlīq* 59, 71, 114, 391, 459, 1103, 1351, 1539, 1673. Lapidus, *Muslim cities* 96, 98, 101, refers to an organization of silk workers. For a guild of weavers in Egypt, see Labib, *Handelsgeschichte* 228–229. For a recent survey of scholarship that reflects the uncertainty yet suggests that guilds "clearly flourished as of the fifteenth or sixteenth centuries," see Hanna, Guilds 897, 898.

42 Ibn Ṭawq, *Taʿlīq* 213, 379, 851, 1131, 1444.

43 Ibn Ṭawq, *Taʿlīq* 536. For Zayn al-Dīn, see Chapter 3 and n. 52. I thank Dr. Torsten Wollina for saving me from errors in this regard.

44 Ibn Ṭawq, *Taʿlīq* 549, 550, 638, 659. For his death less than a year earlier, see 593. See on him also al-Ḥaṣkafī, *Mutʿat al-adhhān* i, 463–464.

45 Ibn Ṭawq, *Taʿlīq* 816.

> are effaced]. The agreement took place in the presence of the bride's mother at her residence at the "little market" (*suwayqa*) Ṣārūjā, outside [the inner wall] of Damascus, near al-Sharaf al-Aʿlā al-Shāmī. Representative (*mutawallī*) for the bride is the Shāfiʿī qadi Muḥyī al-Dīn al-Ikhnāʾī, may God help him. Representation (*tawkīl*) for the groom is by his uncle, the *shaykh al-Islām* Taqī al-Dīn Ibn Qāḍī ʿAjlūn, may God provide benefit through him. The marriage gift (*ṣadāq*) is 60 ashrafīs, paid upon request (*al-ḥāll*), of which 40 are to be paid in advance (*muqaddam*). Badr al-Dīn, the witness for the bride, testified receiving the sum, and the bride herself, as well as the groom's mother, testified that the bride received that sum through Badr al-Dīn. In addition, 500 dirhams of the Damascus currency were vouched annually for the bride's various expenses (*kiswa*), to which the bride was entitled by law. She agreed to that.[46]

The wedding feast took place some weeks later, and on the morrow the couple were allowed solitude for the consummation of the marriage. Fāṭima died three years later in the severe plague of 897/1492, leaving behind two daughters.[47] Not even four months elapsed before Abū l-Yumn contracted one more marriage, this time with Sāra, a daughter of Sharaf al-Dīn Maḥmūd, of the al-Shaybānī family. The *ṣadāq* was 55 ashrafīs. About four years later Abū l-Yumn had one more marriage, this time to his relative Āmina Zayn (also Sitt) al-ʿUlamāʾ, Taqī al-Dīn's daughter. The *ṣadāq* was the high sum of 200 ashrafīs, and the contract was concluded at Taqī al-Dīn's residence. A marriage party followed about a year later. Less than two years afterward, Abū l-Yumn asked for divorce without compensation (*majānan bi ghayr ʿiwaḍ*); it is reported that tension within the wider family was the reason.[48] All in all, Abū l-Yumn appears to have been extremely active in marital affairs; we know of six wives he had in a relatively short time span, and at least part of the time he was polygamous.

As to the financial terms, although dowry (trousseau) provided by her family could be a major factor in a wife's economic independence, and an upper-class groom in late thirteenth-century Damascus, for example, could expect his bride to bring a dowry worth as much as 2,500 dinars,[49] only four dowries are men-

---

46 Ibn Ṭawq, *Taʿlīq* 821.

47 Ibn Ṭawq, *Taʿlīq* 830, 831, 1122.

48 Ibn Ṭawq, *Taʿlīq* 1142–1143, 1436–1437 (Ibn Ṭawq appears to confuse Abū l-Yumn with his cousin Abū l-Qamarayn), 1532, 1709, 1757, 1895, 1909.

49 Rapoport, *Marriage* 84–85, 112 (possibly a highly inflated figure). See the fantastic case he cites from al-Ṭarsūsī, *Tuḥfat al-turk*. For trousseaux in the Mamluk period, see al-Wakīl, *Shiwār*.

tioned by Ibn Ṭawq, one of which was his daughter-in-law's, valued at about 300 dinars. Three more dowries lack details.[50] One wonders why. Perhaps, as suggested by scholars, because dowries were not part of the marriage contract, they were not legally required but were only a custom.[51] If this is the reason, it strikes one as substantially different from the custom in contemporary Italian cities, for example.[52] As for the groom's marriage gift (dower, *ṣadāq*; the term *mahr* is not used in our sources), the information is relatively rich. About 50 different quotations, ranging from 12 to 300 ashrafīs, with the majority being less than 100, are listed. Unsurprisingly, relatively low sums were promised in marriages to divorcées, as, for example, in the case of one Fāṭima, whose dower was 21 dinars, only 6 of which were paid immediately and the rest promised to be paid in installments of one dinar every year.[53] Widows were promised even lower sums, as also were brides of the lower classes and manumitted female slaves.[54] In one case of a marriage of a concubine, the quotation is not in ashrafīs but in silver currency, and in another case, contrary to what was stated in the contract, part of the dower was paid in silver.[55] It is possible that, by and large, sums of *ṣadāq*, even though designated in dinars, were in practice paid in silver coins.[56] Occasionally, one finds further financial stipulations. Thus Sitt Saʿādāt, Taqī al-Dīn's so-called "Egyptian wife," received 20 silver coins a day, flour (*ṭaḥūn*) in the weight of 8 *raṭls*, wood (*ḥaṭab*), house rent (*ujrat al-sukn*), and *kiswa* for her two children.[57] Brides who had children from an earlier marriage were entitled to a special allowance as long as they were in their custody.[58]

As one might expect, the highest sums were vouched by grooms coming from families of merchants, qadis, scholars, and officeholders. For his marriage with Sāra, the daughter of the deceased *khuwājā* Ibn al-Muzalliq, Taqī al-Dīn, the *shaykh al-Islām*, paid the high sum of 200 ashrafīs, which possibly reflected not only his but also the bride's high status; 150 were paid immediately—a

50 Ibn Ṭawq, *Taʿlīq* 177, 439–440, 1474. For his daughter-in-law's 15,000 dirhams, see 1854. One may note that also as regards Mamluk Egypt, there exists only scattered information on dowries among the military elite and no information on the middle class. See al-Wakīl, *Shiwār* 444–454.

51 Rapoport, Matrimonial gifts 23–24; Zomeno, Stories 26.

52 Kirshner, *Marriage*, esp. chap. 4.

53 Ibn Ṭawq, *Taʿlīq* 626.

54 E.g. Ibn Ṭawq, *Taʿlīq* 27, 110, 114, 186, 263, 287, 292, 379, 382, 407, 430, 503, 536, 545, 613, 680, 704, 708, 753, 1057, 1156, 1164, 1166, 1192, 1214, 1301, 1336, 1341–1342, 1408–1409, 1435, 1437, 1477, 1488, 1653, 1858.

55 Ibn Ṭawq, *Taʿlīq* 192, 417, 1452.

56 Rapoport, *Marriage* 54–55.

57 Ibn Ṭawq, *Taʿlīq* 744, 801.

58 E.g. Ibn Ṭawq, *Taʿlīq* 1477.

notary and the bride were entitled to count the coins, that is, unlike in many other transactions, payment in this case was not by the total weight of coins but by counting them individually.[59] In his first betrothal Ibn Ṭawq's son vouched for 69 ashrafīs, of which he paid 50 immediately. It so happened that his wife died exactly two years later in the plague,[60] and about 16 months afterward he married again and this time promised 60 ashrafīs, "paid upon demand," of which he paid 40 at the time of concluding the contract; in addition he vouched for another 8 as *kiswa*.[61] This would indicate, as might be inferred from other cases, that she had been previously married and had children in her custody.[62] The *ṣadāq* figures cited confirm an earlier conclusion, that middle-class grooms paid far less than top government officials and other members of the elite, and their sums rarely exceeded several hundred dinars.[63] However, the Damascus data differ from the average sums for marriage gifts that are quoted in the so-called Jerusalem Ḥaram documents, which range between 5 and 20 dinars.[64] This difference, if not accidental, could indicate, by and large, a better economic situation in late fifteenth-century Damascus than in fourteenth-century Jerusalem. Was the *ṣadāq* an economic asset for women? In fifteenth-century Granada the immediate *ṣadāq* could be converted into household items,[65] and a study of the Geniza documents suggests that the equivalent Jewish marriage gift (*mohar*) did contribute to the economic position of brides. Ibn Ṭawq reports only in one case that the dower was used by the bride to purchase a female slave.[66]

From what has been said thus far it is evident that dowers were divided into two installments, the so-called "immediate" and "deferred." The immediate could be demanded even prior to consummation, and the deferred was "payable upon demand."[67] Despite objection by Muslim scholars, this had been

59 Ibn Ṭawq, *Taʿlīq* 1589.

60 Ibn Ṭawq, *Taʿlīq* 1415.

61 Ibn Ṭawq, *Taʿlīq* 1736.

62 E.g. Ibn Ṭawq, *Taʿlīq* 1477.

63 Rapoport, *Marriage* 14, and eight cases for the latter in n. 15. In a Geniza marriage contract from the second half of the thirteenth century, the groom's marriage gift is 50 dinars, and in a contract dated to 1301 it is 30. See Rapoport, *Marriage* 17. For Rapoport's argument about the tendency to inflate sums for maintaining social prestige, see Rapoport, *Marriage* 54 and nn. 14–15.

64 Rapoport, *Marriage* 20.

65 Shatzmiller, *Her day* 23, 24–27, 34.

66 Friedman, *Jewish marriage* 257–262, 271–288; Ibn Ṭawq, *Taʿlīq* 1806, and see further below and n. 141.

67 E.g. Ibn Ṭawq, *Taʿlīq* 681. See also Rapoport, *Marriage* 53 (and reference to legal manuals), 56 and n. 33. For al-Ṭarsūsī's discussion in the first half of the fourteenth century, see 57.

the norm for centuries before the period here discussed.[68] It is noteworthy that in eleventh- and twelfth-century marriage contracts (*ketubbot*) of Palestinian and Egyptian Jews, various phrases are used to express the postponement of part of the dower, which possibly was a result of the influence of the Muslim custom.[69] As to the deferred part, in early days the date for its payment was specified.[70] The assumption is that later the deferred portion was due upon divorce or the husband's death, although there are indications that even then it was a complicated issue to resolve.[71] In one case the parties were ready to sign a contract, but at the last minute an agreement about the deferred sum could not be reached.[72] In another case it was stipulated that the divorcée who remarried her husband was not entitled to her (deferred) dower unless there was another divorce.[73] Exceptionally detailed is the case of two representatives, ʿImād al-Dīn, the *khaṭīb* of the Saqīfa Mosque, and ʿAbd al-Bāsiṭ al-Barzawī. As a result of negotiation and a compromise (*muṣālaḥa*) they reached, ʿImād al-Dīn agreed that his daughter-in-law, who was ʿAbd al-Bāsiṭ's sister, be paid a *ṣadāq* of 800 dirhams; she was expected to receive 600, while the rest was deferred to four months later in four installments, in between paying a monthly payment of 30 (which would practically mean a deferment of seven months) plus a *kiswa*. ʿAbd al-Bāsiṭ objected to the latter and demanded 45 per month, forfeiting the *kiswa* in return, which would fall on the wife's own family. In the event, the agreement was concluded on such terms.[74] In yet another instance, a groom divorced even before consummation, and the bride's father insisted on keeping the *ṣadāq* and denied any claim the groom might have had against it.[75] According to one example, if the husband died, it was possible to have his mother rectify a document about the details of the deferred *ṣadāq*.[76] Obviously, the death of the wife would absolve the husband from paying the deferred sum.[77]

---

68 Shatzmiller, *Her day* 23–24.

69 See n. 66 above. The Jewish custom as reflected in the Geniza suggests that the deferred payment was normally never collected. See Friedman, *Jewish marriage* 272.

70 Rapoport, Matrimonial gifts 9.

71 Shatzmiller, *Her day* 27–30; Zomeno, Islamic marriage 142. For a contract wherein it was noted, see Ibn Ṭawq, *Taʿlīq* 1259. For the example of Hājar receiving the deferred part upon divorce, see the section on divorce below.

72 Ibn Ṭawq, *Taʿlīq* 1303.

73 Ibn Ṭawq, *Taʿlīq* 1051.

74 Ibn Ṭawq, *Taʿlīq* 1239. For other examples, see 338, 531, 1272–1273.

75 Ibn Ṭawq, *Taʿlīq* 652.

76 Ibn Ṭawq, *Taʿlīq* 682.

77 Ibn Ṭawq, *Taʿlīq* 535.

The socioeconomic implication of the "payable upon demand" clause is open to more than one interpretation. It should come as little surprise that the leading Ḥanbalī scholar in Damascus, Ibn Qayyim al-Jawziyya, who was surely dissatisfied with it, was pleased to claim that the clause was not put into practice except when there was discord. Apparently, he had a clear interest in preserving the image of a harmonious marriage institution at all costs, especially as the cost usually fell on women's shoulders. Perhaps to his chagrin, however, some wives did bring their husbands to court and even brought about their imprisonment.[78] Contrary to the Damascus scholar's possible agenda, and as part of his thesis about the weakening of patriarchy (for which, see below), Rapoport thinks that "payable upon demand" undermined the notion of marriage as a harmonious, non-monetized relationship devoid of material and earthly aspects. Although I tend to side with Rapoport, I would qualify his suggestion in one respect: one could make a case for the clause of "payable upon demand" not as a symbol of the disintegration of the image but as an indication of an improvement in some women's initial situation when entering marriage. As in the aforementioned case, there probably were further instances where the bride and her family could either back down or at least improve on the proposed *ʿaqd*, for example, when it came to specifying the deferred *ṣadāq*.[79]

Finally in this section, I wish to refer to information on marital problems that our notary provides. Shihāb al-Dīn al-Raqqāwī, at one point a waqf supervisor (*mutakallim*), had a dispute with his wife ʿĀʾisha bt. [Ibn?] al-Ḥawrānī when she was in an advanced stage of pregnancy. She even left their home for two nights. Shihāb al-Dīn vowed (*ḥalafa bi-l-ṭalāq*)—more precisely, he took an "oath of divorce," to be discussed in the next section—in the presence of Ibn Ṭawq that he had not taken a concubine (*yatasarra ʿalayhā bi-jāriya*), "neither white nor black," during his earlier journey to Cairo; furthermore, that he had never taken any in the past, nor had he had sexual relations with any except for the one residing at his home. Only then did Bt. al-Ḥawrānī return home. About five weeks later she gave birth to a son, but tension persisted. Two years later Ibn Ṭawq was called by Shihāb al-Dīn to certify that he owed only the 130 ashrafīs he had taken from her as a loan, plus the deferred marriage gift. On this occasion the husband vowed once again that any other wife he took would provide sufficient ground for *ṭalāq* and his wife could free herself of the marriage after one pronouncement of divorce (*ṭalqa*); she would forfeit as little as 1 ashrafī

78 Rapoport, *Marriage* 58.

79 E.g. Ibn Ṭawq, *Taʿlīq* 1303. For examples, see also Rapoport, *Marriage* 58.

of the *ṣadāq* in her credit.[80] In another instance, less than a couple of months after the marriage of ʿAbd al-Raḥīm, the *shaykh al-Islām*'s son, and his wife, who was the granddaughter of the Ḥanbalī qadi Ibn Mufliḥ (d. 884/1479), the groom had a fight with his mother-in-law, and a few months later the couple, in the midst of a ball game (*ṭāba*), cursed and hit each other.[81] In another case, ʿAbd al-Qādir, Alf's son, was accused of beating his wife. The tension between the two persisted and led to divorce.[82] The wife of Muḥammad b. al-Muzalliq, who was the qadi's son, complained to the governor about her husband, which led to his arrest. In another case, a man known as the "Egyptian preacher" was fined in the considerable sum of 40 dinars after his wife filed a complaint against him.[83]

There were parents who intervened in the marital life of their son or daughter. Shaykh Azbak al-Nābulusī had a fight with his in-laws and he even hit them. He received a warning that any further violence would result in a "triple divorce." In another case, after the wife of Ibn al-Zarʿī gave birth, her father convinced his son-in-law that the two should move to his residence. Not only that, he further requested them not to have intercourse for a whole year. In another case, Yūsuf of Jaramānā, Ibn Ṭawq's business associate, pressed for a *khulʿ* (see below) to be given to his daughter even before the consummation of the marriage, in return for giving up the dower, to which the groom agreed. In yet another case a husband broke into the house of his in-laws and injured them severely in retaliation for their decision to enforce separation on the couple. A conflict also developed between Abū l-Yumn and his cousin, qadi Najm al-Dīn, the reason being the former's purchase of a female slave to reside with his wife. The angry Najm al-Dīn took his sister to her mother's home. Subsequently, Abū l-Yumn stated that if it weren't for his respect for Taqī al-Dīn (i.e., Najm al-Dīn's father), he would have gone to the viceroy to complain. Seemingly, the issue was resolved somehow, as on the next day Abū l-Yumn's wife returned.[84] In Ibn Ṭawq's family, at one point Khadīja, his son's second wife, said harsh words about her husband and in-laws. Understandably, our notary criticized her behavior. Then, further belligerent behavior on her part is described:

---

80 Ibn Ṭawq, *Taʿlīq* 198, 209, 402 (note the phrasing *waqaʿat baʿd* [*sic*; apparently Ibn Ṭawq's spelling error] *umūr*). Rapoport, Women and gender 31, n. 148, cites this example (apparently erroneously) in the context of polygamy.

81 Ibn Ṭawq, *Taʿlīq* 1792, 1812, 1861. For the Ḥanbalī qadi, see al-Buṣrawī, *Tārīkh* 213; ʿAbd al-Bāsiṭ, *Nayl* i, 232–233.

82 Ibn Ṭawq, *Taʿlīq* 1363, 1403.

83 Ibn Ṭawq, *Taʿlīq* 882, 1875.

84 Ibn Ṭawq, *Taʿlīq* 681 (see also Wollina, *Zwanzig* 86), 704, 976–977, 1671, 1709.

she locked herself in her private space, refusing even to eat, then spent the night at the neighbors till her uncle had to come and work for reconciliation with her husband.[85]

2 Divorce

Like with marriage, Ibn Ṭawq's data on divorce are the best one can hope for on this subject, albeit for a relatively short time span, anywhere prior to the Ottoman era. What do they reveal? First, in at least one-third of the 60 cases of divorce (*ṭalāq*) recorded, it is stated that they were initiated by the husband. However, in the light of the small number of the wife's initiative explicitly stated, the number must have been higher.[86] Divorce could take place even when the wife was in advanced pregnancy or a few hours from giving birth.[87] Normally, the grounds for divorce are unspecified. Thus ʿUthmān al-Ḥamawī, a Shāfiʿī deputy qadi, divorced his wife for the vague reason that she was a "grave sinner" (*fāsiqa*). The husband also claimed she was unfit for her job of supervising charity distributed to orphans. The Shāfiʿī qadi, who was asked to decide on the matter, ordered that the woman's house be sealed. However, sometime later the divorcée persuaded her husband to take her back "to his custody" (*ilā ʿiṣmatihi*). He unsealed the house without consulting his superior, the qadi, which cost him his job.[88]

There are only a few cases about which our source states that it was the wife who initiated a *ṭalāq*. Fāṭima was divorced by a single pronouncement (*ṭalqa wāḥida*) after her husband admitted that the marriage was not consummated. She married another man on the same day. That is, given the specific circumstances, she was not obliged to wait three cycles of menstruation to determine if she was pregnant.[89] Similarly, the daughter of *khawājā* Shams al-Dīn b. ʿAlwān al-Shuwaykī complained to the governor—her status probably enabled that, or the fact that she was married to (her cousin) Badr al-Dīn Ḥasan b. Aydakī al-Shuwaykī, possibly the son of *naqīb al-qalʿa*. In any case, she claimed he was impotent (*ʿanīn*) and that she remained a virgin. The governor agreed to a *ṭalāq*,

85 Ibn Ṭawq, *Taʿlīq* 1907–1908.

86 Ibn Ṭawq, *Taʿlīq* 96, 98, 234, 236, 595, 601, 604, 612, 634, 696, 712, 820, 852 (possibly because the wife was unable to give birth), 964, 1051, 1096, 1127, 1215, 1296, 1403, 1477, 1504, 1605, 1673, 1700, 1850, 1909.

87 Ibn Ṭawq, *Taʿlīq* 1726.

88 Ibn Ṭawq, *Taʿlīq* 414–415. For ʿUthmān al-Ḥamawī, see 83, 478–479.

89 Ibn Ṭawq, *Taʿlīq* 1605. For *ʿidda*, see Ṭalāḳ, *EI*^{2}.

but for that she had to pay the high price of 120 ashrafis, either the advanced or deferred *ṣadāq*.[90] In another instance, Kamāl al-Dīn, of the Ibn Qāḍī ʿAjlūn family, initiated the separation (*fāraqa*) of his daughter from her husband, the son of the historian Jalāl al-Dīn al-Buṣrawī. The reason alleged was the little piety (*ʿadam al-taqwa*) he was notorious for and his little care for his household. The husband had to accept it in return for the *ṣadāq* repaid to him. A couple of months later he found a new bride.[91]

About 30 cases of divorce (i.e., half of the cases detailed by our notary) were based on a *khulʿ* procedure.[92] Unlike the unilateral *ṭalāq*, this was a bilateral agreement.[93] If able to prove, for example, that her husband's character was bad or he intended to harm her, a wife could initiate a *khulʿ* in return for forfeiting the deferred marriage gift or even returning the dower already received.[94] Ibn Ṭawq notes a few exceptional *khulʿ* cases even prior to consummation.[95] There was at least one clear advantage in a divorce based on this procedure: although a new marriage contract was required in case the couple reunited, unlike in a *ṭalāq*, the husband could remarry his divorcée without her marrying another man in between. Remarriage could take place after a three-month waiting period (*ʿidda*).[96]

The large number of *khulʿ* cases compared to *ṭalāq* notwithstanding, there is a need to qualify Rapoport's argument that *khulʿ* came to be the preferred form of divorce when brought for registration to notaries, *ṭalāq* becoming a sort of dead letter and a self-defeating threat.[97] Rather, the two procedures were in

90 Ibn Ṭūlūn, *Mufākahat al-khillān* 112. For Aydakī, see Ibn Ṭawq, *Taʿlīq* 39, 126, 375.

91 Ibn Ṭūlūn, *Mufākahat al-khillān* 289–290, 292. According to Ali, Marriage 23, *fāraqa* denotes divorce decided by the qadi. However, for *firāq* as dissolution of marriage prior to divorce, see Layish, *Marriage* 123, 226. For *tafrīq* as separation, see Hallaq, *Sharīʿa* 280. For another example of a wife initiating a *ṭalāq* without further details, see Ibn Ṭawq, *Taʿlīq* 604.

92 It is variously termed as *firāq bi-khulʿ bāʾin, khulʿ sharʿī, khulʿ sharʿī ʿāriyan ʿan lafẓ al-ṭalāq wa-niyyatihi*. See Ibn Ṭawq, *Taʿlīq* 56, 114 (two cases), 157, 278, 429, 449, 626, 695, 704, 706, 747, 768, 809, 810, 872, 1037, 1062, 1096, 1109, 1195, 1231, 1257, 1317, 1318, 1323, 1335, 1435, 1452, 1517, 1593, 1629, 1729, 1798.

93 For Rapoport's "consensual separation," see e.g. *Marriage* 4. See also Hallaq, *Sharīʿa* 283–286.

94 al-Asyūṭī, *Jawāhir al-ʿuqūd* ii, 89, 94. This is a fifteenth-century book of legal stipulations (*shurūṭ*) by an Egyptian of the Shāfiʿī school. See also Rapoport, *Marriage* 69–70; Ali, Marriage 42, n. 236; Tucker, *Women* 97–98.

95 Ibn Ṭawq, *Taʿlīq* 704, 1435.

96 Ibn Ṭawq, *Taʿlīq* 1096–1097. For another case, see 1477. See further Ali, *Marriage* 146; Powers, Four cases 385; Rapoport, *Marriage* 95, 98 and n. 42; Hallaq, *Sharīʿa* 284.

97 As he concedes, the historical material at his disposal is insufficient to support this conclusion, and he admits that al-Sakhāwī "makes no consistent distinction between repudiation

use. This much can be said, however: the increase in consensual divorce in the late Mamluk era anticipates a phenomenon that is documented for the early Ottoman period.[98] This procedure, as already noted, implied financial loss for women. Thus Bulbul bt. ʿAbdallāh, formerly a manumitted slave, had to give up the deferred marriage gift (*ṣadāq*) of 10 ashrafīs as well as any claim to unpaid maintenance (*nafaqa*) and clothing expenses (*kiswa*). She had to cede also any claim for support in the house rent she had to pay during the three-month waiting period, as well as "any other legal claim concerning marital relationship in the past." In addition, a loan in the amount of 10 ashrafīs the husband had taken from her was to be repaid in installments because—so it was claimed—she knew he could not return it otherwise. Ibn Ṭawq, who wrote the draft and the final document (*waraqa qāʾima*) handed it to Bulbul.[99] In another case, Sitt Saʿādāt, the so-called "Egyptian wife" of Taqī al-Dīn Ibn Qāḍī ʿAjlūn, when she was separated by *khulʿ*, expected to receive only the token sum of one silver coin. However, other financial terms fixed before that, such as her right to *kiswa* and *nafaqa*, were retained till the actual dissolution of the marriage. Incidentally, the couple reunited exactly a year later but after ten years divorced again by *khulʿ*.[100] Further cases of financial loss to divorcées resulting from *khulʿ* are noted.[101] Especially grave was the situation of manumitted slaves and concubines who initiated dissolution.[102]

Rapoport's suggestion that the legal phrasing of *khulʿ* cases makes it apparent that it was always wives who initiated consensual divorce[103] is not supported by Ibn Ṭawq, who lists only 6 such cases out of a total of 30, while 2 more are equivocal.[104] Since, unlike in a *ṭalāq*, husbands could receive a financial gain from this procedure, by regaining or at least keeping part of their marriage gift, it stands to reason that such initiative was also beneficial to them.[105]

---

and consensual separation" and that the precise legal form of the divorce was perhaps unknown to al-Sakhāwī, and probably irrelevant. See Rapoport, *Marriage* 69, 70, 72, 84–85, 112.

98 Zilfi, "We don't get along" 272, 275.

99 Ibn Ṭawq, *Taʿlīq* 429. For Ḥanafī discussion in Ottoman time of the issue of *nafaqa* in a *khulʿ* case, see Tucker, *Women* 97–98.

100 Ibn Ṭawq, *Taʿlīq* 747, 801–802, 833, 1729.

101 E.g. Ibn Ṭawq, *Taʿlīq* 157, 429, 704, 768, 1037.

102 For Mubāraka, Taqī al-Din's former *jāriya*, divorced by *khulʿ* and receiving only 30 dirhams and forfeiting another 40, see Ibn Ṭawq, *Taʿlīq* 278.

103 Rapoport, *Marriage* 69, 72 and n. 22, for tenuous evidence. Note that on pp. 84–85, on the basis of only four examples, he advances his argument that it was a wife who commonly initiated divorce proceedings.

104 Ibn Ṭawq, *Taʿlīq* 429, 449, 704 (the bride's father asks for it), 1037, 1195, 1318, 1517, 1662.

105 For the wife of qadi Ibn al-Muzalliq forfeiting her deferred *ṣadāq* of 16 dinars, see Ibn

Why and when *khulʿ* became a serious alternative to *ṭalāq* are intriguing questions. In accordance with his suggestion about wives as normally initiators of this procedure, Rapoport's explanation is that Muslim women were more economically independent than is commonly thought.[106] Two objections may be raised, however. First, as we have seen, it is far from certain that wives were always the initiators. Second, like later in the Ottoman period, we may consider *khulʿ* as an "early course adjustment" for those not long married, with or without children.[107] Furthermore, if records for eighteenth-century Istanbul are indicative, then, contrary to Rapoport's hypothesis, it was not affluence but just the opposite, economic hardship, that exposed couples to the risk of break-up. In any case, what is significant about Ibn Ṭawq's material is that, unlike al-Sakhāwī's biographical dictionary, which is Rapoport's main source, and which is of an elite and bourgeois provenance, our source reports about ordinary women who had significantly less resources than the women al-Sakhāwī reported about. One can hardly associate the women discussed by Ibn Ṭawq with economic independence and the daring initiative of walking out of marriage regardless of the economic risks involved—incidentally, a model not even overwhelmingly tenable in currently affluent societies. That the case is just to the contrary can be supported by examples that our source relates and which will be considered shortly. My point is that, if indeed *khulʿ* became a common divorce procedure in the Mamluk period—and this, given the information provided by our sources, is far from certain—it was rather despite economic uncertainty for the divorced women but in return for a promise for immediate relief.

Now, the fact is that on occasion divorcées were desperate to remarry their former husbands and even turned to the court for support.[108] A case that receives some detail is of the aforementioned Zayn al-ʿĀbidīn, who had been divorced by Zayn al-Dīn ʿAbd al-Qādir al-Akārī, our notary's neighbor, and later remarried him. More than five years later, she was divorced again, after which

Ṭawq, *Taʿlīq* 1317. Exceptional appears a session at the Dār al-ʿAdl, already referred to earlier in another context, as regards a husband claiming that his divorcée conditioned their remarriage on 10 dinars, apparently the marriage gift. See Ibn Ṭūlūn, *Mufākahat al-khillān* 245.

106 Rapoport, *Marriage* 74–78.

107 Ivanova, Divorce 118.

108 Ibn Ṭawq, *Taʿlīq* 29, 69 (the woman returned, but half a year later there was another *ṭalāq*), 114, 157, 267, 601, 1051. For a couple remarrying, then remarrying once again two years later, obviously after one more divorce, see 393, 647. See also 1338 (two cases). For Suʿūd returning to her husband only one month after their *khulʿ* agreement for 1 ashrafī, which appears to have been a token sum in several cases, see 1318. For Alf (or Ilf), see 44.

she bore a son. Four more years elapsed and we find her married, now to ʿAbd al-Qādir, the head of the goldsmiths. Perhaps she had a weak spot for that name, for it was not only the *kunya* of her two husbands but also her father's name. About a year later the couple had a daughter, then two more years went by and they divorced by *khulʿ*, but only a few weeks passed before they were remarried. Tension continued and six months later they divorced by *ṭalāq*. However, a year and a half after that Zayn al-ʿĀbidīn complained to the Mālikī qadi and demanded to be remarried to ʿAbd al-Qādir. The qadi put pressure on him and ʿAbd al-Qādir complied, promising just 1 ashrafī, while his wife forfeited 500 dirhams (i.e., close to the 10 dinars given to her for an unclear purpose). After their second marriage, a son was born. Later, there was another divorce and remarriage, after which they had another son. Here is an exceptional case of a couple marrying and divorcing multiple times. Half a year later Zayn al-ʿĀbidīn died.[109]

Another case serves as clear evidence for the power husbands enjoyed in marital affairs. Badr al-Dīn b. al-Yāsūfī, a man in his 30s, who would become a deputy Shāfiʿī qadi, divorced (*firāq bi-khulʿ bāʾin*) Āsya, the daughter of Ibrāhīm b. Jaʿbarī al-Bayṭār. Apparently, very soon thereafter he married the daughter of Badr al-Dīn Ḥasan b. Nabhān, who previously had been divorced by the merchant Ibn al-Takrītī, also known as the "youngster" (*shābb*). Shortly thereafter (*fī thānī yawm*), "for an unknown reason," Badr al-Dīn took back (*radda*) his divorcée, that is, al-Bayṭār's daughter, and separated himself (*abāna*) from his second wife. But this was not the end of the story. Only 20 days elapsed before Badr al-Dīn took back also his second wife, Ibn Nabhān's daughter. This took place at her father's residence. Badr al-Dīn now vowed not to marry a third wife, not to send Ibn Nabhān's daughter to her parents, and to ensure that his two spouses would be kept at a safe distance from one another and not live in the same neighborhood (*maḥalla*). We are told that, to be on the safe side, the engagement was rectified twice (*juddida al-ʿaqd thānī marra iḥtiyāṭan*); as in the first version, there was a clause about the couple residing at the wife's residence, and about the husband's divorcing his first wife or not taking her back. Less than two years later we learn that al-Yāsūfī had from Āsya a son who died aged seven months.[110] It should be noted that the tendency to remarry as

109 Ibn Ṭawq, *Taʿlīq* 267, 413, 414, 852, 1156, 1242, 1317, 1335, 1338, 1363, 1403, 1504, 1673, 1684, 1725, 1864, 1894–1895. For al-Akārī, see 514, 661.

110 Ibn Ṭawq, *Taʿlīq* 114, 121, 253, 302. See also Rapoport, Women and gender 31, where this example is placed in the context of "limited polygamy." On this case, see also El-Leithy, Living documents 414. On Yāsūfī reading before Taqī al-Dīn in a teaching session, see Ibn Ṭawq, *Taʿlīq* 207. For his involvement in a legal case, see 1787. For serving as a deputy to

revealed in the *Taʿlīq* is supported by about 200 documents from seventeenth-century Cairo, whereby 30 percent of divorce cases ended in remarriage.[111]

Of all the divorce cases reported by Ibn Ṭawq, that of Hājar, the daughter of the notary Muḥammad al-Ḥimṣī, is exceptionally detailed and merits attention. Her story exemplifies the hardship a woman might experience in her marital life. After being divorced by Shihāb al-Dīn Aḥmad al-Bakkār, accompanied by her brother, Hājar came before Ibn Ṭawq in his capacity as a notary to settle financial matters with her former husband. She acknowledged receiving a monthly allowance (*nafaqa*) of five silver coins for their two daughters, aged four and six, in addition to support for their clothing (*kiswa*) and house rent. Incidentally, Fāṭima, the older daughter, was found at age eight spending the night on the roof with the neighbor's son; a wet nurse claimed they had sexual intercourse and that blood was found on her, but this was later proven false. The younger of the two, named Saʿādāt, would die about 11 years later, aged 15, at the time of her death already married.[112] Half a year after her divorce, Hājar's financial matters with her former husband were not yet settled, and the two appeared again before Ibn Ṭawq. A financial arrangement resulted in Ibn al-Bakkār having to pay 38 ashrafīs, and further payments followed.[113]

In the meantime, about five months after the divorce, Hājar concluded a marriage contract with Khalīl al-Bayṭār, a dark-skinned man (*asmar al-lawn*) from the Palestinian town of Ramla. The marriage gift was 19 ashrafīs and 300 silver coins. The husband also agreed to pay 200 dirhams (*fiḍḍa*) annually for clothing (*kiswa*) and a *nafaqa* for Fāṭima, by then about seven years old, and a daily sum of 1 dirham for her younger sister. Beyond that, he had no formal obligation.[114] This marriage did not last long. Approximately half a year later Hājar received, through her brother as intermediary, a sum of 500 silver coins owed her by Khalīl as a deferred *ṣadāq*. Here one may see a rarely mentioned example of the deferred part of the marriage gift paid upon divorce. Also, one may add that the payment was made in silver, not in gold coins. Further sums followed.

Less than two years later we read about Hājar being married for a third time, now to Muḥammad b. Ibrāhīm al-Qudsī, known as Ibn al-Kutubī, who earned

---

Ibn Farfūr, see al-Nuʿaymī, *al-Dāris* ii, 355. For his death in 916/1510 after being summoned for questioning about the Umayyad Mosque, see Ibn Ṭūlūn, *Mufākahat al-khillān* 280; Ibn al-ʿImād, *Shadharāt* ix, 109–110.

111 Hanna, Marriage 356.

112 Ibn Ṭawq, *Taʿlīq* 131, 137, 1128. For her father's death, see 136–137. For her sister Fāṭima, see 265, 266.

113 Ibn Ṭawq, *Taʿlīq* 177, 233, 238, 239, 246, 247, 250, 252, 257, 269.

114 Ibn Ṭawq, *Taʿlīq* 169. The marriage was consummated a couple of weeks later. See 172.

his living in the cloth industry (*daqqāq fī l-qumāsh*). Once again, she was represented by her brother Aḥmad, who held the office of *naqīb al-fuqarāʾ*, probably at a certain Sufi association. As a marriage gift Hājar received 15 ashrafis and 400 dirhams. Ibn al-Kutubī also promised to pay her 30 silver coins each month for *kiswa* for her two daughters. Again, anything beyond that would be at his discretion. Also the third marriage did not last long. Less than a year and a half later, accompanied by her son Muḥibb al-Dīn Muḥammad, about whose existence we now learn for the first time—clearly, he was born into her first marriage—her brother Aḥmad, and her nephew ʿAbd al-Qādir al-Shallāḥ, Hājar returned (*raddat*) to Ibn al-Kutubī, obviously following a divorce. No details are given, but, as no interim husband is mentioned, it could have been of the *khulʿ* type. The marriage gift was 200 silver coins and the deferred part 10 ashrafis; it is noteworthy that while the immediate sum was in silver, the deferred sum was cited in gold terms, probably to ensure its value. There was also a promise for an allowance (*nafaqa*) of 4 dirhams, plus 1 dirham daily for clothing. Hājar was also granted the right to a divorce after only one declaration (*ṭalqa*) in case her husband attacked (*hajjaja*) her children, prevented them from being with their mother, married another woman, or returned to the wife he had divorced, "even be it by proxy (*nikāḥ al-fuḍūl*)." However, also this remarriage was not destined to survive for long, and a year later a *ṭalāq* took place.[115]

Hājar was divorced at least four times. It is a sad record by any standard. Was she unbearable? Did blame lie with the husbands? Was it a mixture of both? Were there details that Ibn Ṭawq chose not to tell? These are intriguing questions that cannot be answered. It is not superfluous to note that in each of her financial agreements with the divorcing husbands, Hājar settled for very low sums. Whatever the precise details of her life, the little information we have in her case and other cases discussed above is sufficient to point to one tentative conclusion: married women in fifteenth-century Damascus were, perhaps more frequently than not, on the losing side when their marriage was dissolved. Hence, not even a triple *ṭalāq* was necessarily the last word for them, and there were reunions even after divorce, by either of the two divorce procedures. Undoubtedly, life for such women involved social, economic, and emotional challenges. Despite all the costs involved, remarriage for them was a viable and practical option.

115 Ibn Ṭawq, *Taʿlīq* 235, 417–418, 608 (*nikāḥ al-fuḍūl*), 696. Note that the name of the daughter Fāṭima is here given differently and may be the editor's error. For Muḥibb al-Dīn's own marriage, see 626. The term *nikāh al-fuḍūl* denotes betrothal through someone who is neither a *wakīl* nor a *walī*. See Ibn Nujaym, *Rasāʾil iqtiṣādiyya*, 303–308. For *ʿaqd al-fuḍūlī* as a contract made on behalf of someone, see Hallaq, *Sharīʿa* 246.

Further issues concerning divorce need now be taken up. First is Rapoport's thesis that, compared to medieval Latin Europe, the most distinctive feature of the marital regime in urban Islam was the ubiquity of divorce. Furthermore, over long periods of time, premodern Middle Eastern societies consistently had higher rates of divorce than they have today. Rapoport concedes that the evidence is qualitative rather than quantitative, and it pertains to Muslims in North Africa and al-Andalus, and to Copts and Jews in Cairo. In addition, it is based on entries for nearly 500 fifteenth-century Cairo women found in al-Sakhāwī's biographical compendium, where somewhat over 150 (i.e., one-third of the women listed there) were married more than once, and many married three times or more.[116]

What were the reasons for the allegedly high divorce rate? Muslim women, Rapoport argues, were not as dependent on their husbands as Islamic marital law might suggest. Although divorce was a uniquely patriarchal privilege, it also reflected the high degree of economic independence enjoyed by women. High divorce rates were generated by the expansion of the textile industry beginning in the thirteenth century and the opportunities it offered to female spinners, seamstresses, and embroiderers. The changing economic situation increased the monetary value of marriage contracts, and more cash was allocated to support the needs of women, enabling them to enjoy financial independence. By the fifteenth century, Rapoport suggests, the *ṣadāq* and other means of support meant that a marriage relationship increasingly resembled a business partnership.[117]

Now, certainly as regards Damascus, it would be difficult to support Rapoport's conclusion that divorce was pervasive.[118] As already noted, Ibn Ṭawq has about 60 divorce cases for a period of about 20 years. Too small a sample to draw a meaningful picture for a city inhabited at the time of his writing by an estimated 40,000 to 60,000 people, this figure can by no means support an argument about a high rate of divorce.[119] The second related issue is of women's

116 Rapoport, *Marriage* 2, 3–4, 5, 111. Although Rapoport's data pertain to Cairo, Damascus, and Jerusalem, he speaks occasionally of medieval Islamic society in general. See also Musallam, Ordering 193.

117 Rapoport, *Marriage* 6, 32, 46, 50, 52–53, 58–59, 111, 113. One of Rapoport's few supporting references is in *Marriage* 49 n. 111, where he refers to a work by Khazrajī. However, this is a treatise (in verse) lacking any concrete context.

118 Rapoport, *Marriage* 5. See also 1.

119 It may be noted that also as regards Cairo, Rapoport's conclusions may be questioned on several grounds. First, al-Sakhāwī's biographical entries about a few hundred divorcées, randomly coming to his notice, do not tell us anything meaningful about the tens of thousands of married women who lived in Cairo in the course of the fifteenth century CE,

economic independence resulting from their increased participation in the textile industry. Rapoport's hypothesis, which is crucial to his major argument, is nowhere evidenced.[120] Here it would be indicative to point out that in industrial societies such a development as Rapoport suggests took place only toward the end of the nineteenth century.[121]

The hypothesis about high divorce rates allows Rapoport to question the strength of patriarchy in traditional Islamic society. He urges historians to rethink the nature of gender relations in that society and the economic and legal dimensions that these relations involved in particular. As he puts it, "By their very nature, the high rates of divorce severely and institutionally undermined the ideal patriarchal order, in which society was imagined as composed of households led by men who exercised control over their wives, children and slaves."[122]

Ibn Ṭawq's information about Damascus calls into question Rapoport's attempt, tempting as it may be, to read modernity into traditional Islamic society more than 500 years in the past. It should be added that our notary, the best available source on this topic, reports about 20 cases of *ṭalāq* and consensual divorce that were followed by remarriage. Furthermore, the majority of remarriage cases, as already noted, appear to have been the result of divorcées wanting to return to their husbands, occasionally for only a slight increase in the immediate and deferred marriage gift or even worse terms.[123] While we are not informed about the reasons that lay behind reunion, it is possible that economic hardship and the need to recover the right to a deferred *ṣadāq* might have forced it. Be that as it may, the information given by Ibn Ṭawq on divorce can hardly suggest that there was any real challenge to the entrenched structure of patriarchy. If anything, despite some changes in

---

let alone about women in other urban communities in the Muslim world. Second, al-Sakhāwī's materials are skewed in favor of the scholarly milieu, the Mamluk elite, and the high bourgeoisie. For Rapoport's own reservations, see Rapoport, *Marriage* 82–83, 84–85. A more recent study by Mouton, Sourdel, and Sourdel-Thoumine, *Mariage*, esp. 35–63, which is based on 32 marriage contracts and 30 divorce documents from Damascus for the 350-odd years between 948 and 1299 CE, suffers from similar problems. As interesting as the documents surviving from this period may be in themselves, one should resist the temptation to generalize on the basis of such sparse data.

120 Rapoport, *Marriage* 32–38, 47–48.

121 See, e.g. Canning, Gender.

122 Rapoport, *Marriage* 111. See also 6.

123 Ibn Ṭawq, *Taʿlīq* 29, 44, 114, 157, 414–415, 449, 601, 608, 634, 911, 1037, 1051, 1062, 1096, 1215, 1317, 1322–1323, 1548, 1726, 1855. On financial terms in remarriage as they appear in early Ottoman records from Egypt, see Abdal-Rehim, Family 106–108.

the marriage/divorce procedures for the benefit of women, patriarchy retained its stability under the Mamluks.

Finally, let us turn to another aspect of divorce, which Rapoport has termed "oath on pain of divorce," and which implies the husband taking an oath that created the conditions for a future divorce, or briefly put, divorce on condition. For example, an oath stating "May my wife be repudiated if I enter this house" required repudiation if the husband in fact entered the house.[124] It was granted special status by Sunnī law and was prevalent in Mamluk society but at the same time was subject to legal circumvention. The oath, when said only once, was considered revocable (*ṭalqa rajʿiyya*),[125] but when pronounced three times, as in a straightforward *ṭalāq* case, made repudiation of one's wife contingent on the fulfillment of the sworn undertaking. According to Rapoport, in Mamluk Damascus the "oath on pain" became a controversial issue due to Ibn Taymiyya's treatise on the subject, which went against the then current concept; its aim was to restrain the adverse marital effects. Ibn Taymiyya, one of the leading authorities of the Ḥanbalī school, reasoned that the oath did not require the actual dissolution of marriage and could be avoided by an act of atonement. A number of his followers were arrested and humiliated for endorsing his views, especially the one that renders ineffective a single pronouncement of the "triple repudiation" (*ṭalāq thalāthan*) or three made on one and the same occasion.[126]

It would be instructive to examine discussions of the issue among Shāfiʿī scholars in late fifteenth-century Damascus. One could gingerly suggest that Ibn Taymiyya's sensible attitude toward divorce was adopted by the Shāfiʿīs a long time after the Ḥanbalī scholar's death. At one point a question came up about a man taking the oath when banning his manumitted female slave (*ʿatīq*) from entering his home. What would have happened if she actually entered? It was decided that a divorce was not to follow because of the lack of intention (*lā shuʿūr lahu bi-wujūd al-yamīn*). This recalls Ibn Taymiyya's argument about intention as crucial for effecting divorce. Thus one can see Shāfiʿī scholars in fifteenth-century Damascus dissenting from their predecessors, such as Taqī al-Dīn al-Subkī (d. 756/1355) and his attack on Ibn Taymiyya's interpretation,[127]

124 Rapoport, *Marriage* 89–90. For examples pertaining to the different social strata, see 91–96.

125 E.g. Ibn Ṭawq, *Taʿlīq* 1477.

126 For Ibn Taymiyya's original interpretation, see Rapoport, *Marriage* 96–101. For the debate and his arrest, see 101–105. For a more elaborate discussion of Ibn Taymiyya's position as regards the "triple divorce," see al-Matroudi, *Ḥanbalī school* 172–185.

127 Rapoport, *Marriage* 96–97, 101–102. See al-Subkī, *EI*².

now moving closer to the Ḥanbalī ruling. The Shāfiʿī al-Buṣrawī cites the opinion of Badr al-Dīn b. Qāḍī Shuhba, his contemporary, who was asked about a man who took the oath on condition that his wife left the house without his permission. What would have happened if, on her asking permission, the husband burst out laughing, and she understood his reaction as consent? It had a precedent (*hadhihi lahā mushābahāt qablihi*) in a question brought before al-Bulqīnī, an Egyptian scholar and another Shāfiʿī authority, about a man taking the oath against his wife's entering a hammam. What would have happened if another man had told her that the husband had changed his mind but it turned out that he had lied? Was divorce to follow? Al-Bulqīnī's answer was negative because the woman did not go to the bath in order to challenge the husband (*murāgham lahu*). However, Ibn Qāḍī Shuhba's opinion implied that in the case under consideration separation was required (apparently, leading to divorce, *firāq*) because the consent had to be pronounced by the husband himself and not someone else. Al-Buṣrawī's own view was that this was an unclear case, in which the wife came to think (*ẓann*) that the man had told her the truth, and one should see it as a "suspected permission." In yet another case al-Buṣrawī reproduced a discussion he had heard about a man taking the oath, the condition being not repaying a debt. In this case, Taqī al-Dīn, the Shāfiʿī mufti, opined that if at the time of taking the oath the man knew that he could not repay, a *ṭalāq* ought to come into effect.[128]

Apart from such theoretical discussions, did the oath result in actual cases of divorce? At least in the case of Sitt Faraḥ, who initiated a *khulʿ* from Zayn al-Dīn, the merchant, because of an oath he made that he would not speak to his son, the couple reconciled after the *ʿidda* period.[129] Ibn Ṭawq relates about his own son's "oath of divorce" in case he did not return the sum he borrowed from his mother within three months. Apparently, Ibn Ṭawq was worried that his son would not be able to make it (which would force him to divorce), and therefore borrowed from his wife 1 ashrafī in order to give it to his son. However, the *shaykh al-Islām* relieved the father of his anxiety, stating that the period of three months was too short and did not legally necessitate a divorce. Alī b. Qabās made an oath of the triple *ṭalāq* in case his mother-in-law continued to reside in his wife's residence till the month of Ramadan of that year. As the deadline approached, the mother-in-law left for a couple of days, most likely in order to avoid the oath coming into effect. Taqī al-Dīn ruled leniently that, had the woman not known of the oath, no *ṭalāq* was mandatory. However, it

128 al-Buṣrawī, *Tārīkh* 53–54, 211. On Ibn Qāḍī Shuhba, see Ibn Ḳāḍī Shuhba, *EI*².

129 Ibn Ṭawq, *Taʿlīq* 1195.

appears that the husband decided on a *khulʿ* procedure anyway, but, as in many other cases already mentioned, the couple reunited.[130] Taqī al-Dīn's decisions in both cases conform to his general principal as regards divorce as put in his legal writing—unnecessary divorce should be avoided, and if one is obliged, one divorce is enough.[131]

3 The Household: Slaves, Female Slaves, and Concubines

We know of domestic slaves, both black (*ʿabd*, occasionally *ʿabd aswad*) and white (*ghulām, mamlūk, ṣabī*) in late Mamluk Damascus.[132] Our notary reports of at least one slave market located in Ḥarāt al-Baghīl, possibly below the citadel—it was also a center of prostitutes—and the names of a few slave dealers (*dallāl al-jawārī, tājir fī l-raqīq*). As he relates, slaves arrived on a regular basis from Egypt and the Sudan.[133]

We are much better informed on female slaves. Here, one has to begin by clarifying terminology and by drawing attention to two different categories established by the sharīʿa, the female slave (*jāriya*) and the concubine (*surriya*). Legally, a *jāriya* was purchased primarily for housework and a *surriya* for sexual relations and in many cases would bear children to her master.[134] In reality the distinction was not always retained, and—if Ibn Ṭawq used the terms with precision, which is far from certain—female slaves often bore children as well and thus became like concubines.[135]

Female slaves and concubines were owned by middle- and lower-middle-class men. Rapoport brings half a dozen or so examples of fifteenth-century men, with one exception all Egyptian, some of whom of modest background, who kept concubines as a substitute for a wife, most likely an indication of their

130 For his son, see Ibn Ṭawq, *Taʿlīq* 1915. For Ibn Qabās, see 810. See also 1857. The text is not entirely clear to me.

131 Ibn Ṭūlūn, *Iʿlām* 150.

132 E.g. Ibn Ṭawq, *Taʿlīq* 67, 201, 234, 256, 259, 258, 269, 299, 335, 420, 423, 439, 441, 443, 479, 480, 494, 530, 616, 629, 636, 762, 777, 872, 901, 902, 910, 930, 1057, 1060, 1087, 1089, 1113, 1124, 1143, 1154, 1307, 1333, 1363, 1406, 1461, 1478, 1504, 1507, 1510, 1513 (two cases), 1516, 1530, 1596, 1602, 1650, 1676, 1681, 1722, 1740, 1758, 1783, 1871, 1882.

133 Ibn Ṭawq, *Taʿlīq* 627, 1198. See also al-Shihābī, *Muʿjam Dimashq* i, 151. For prostitution elsewhere in the city, see Ibn Ṭūlūn, *Mufākahat al-khillān* 21. For dealers, see Ibn Ṭawq, *Taʿlīq* 116, 292, 309, 491, 1295, 1500.

134 For this distinction, see ʿAbd, *EI*[2], 24b and 28a respectively.

135 On occasion our notary uses the term *jāriya* and adds to it *surriya*, or he notes that the *jāriya* was meant to be a concubine (*li-l-tasarrī*). See Ibn Ṭawq, *Taʿlīq* 198, 1504, 1672.

poor economic situation.[136] However, the available information on Damascus shows that this was not necessarily the case. Thus Jamāl al-Dīn Yūsuf b. ʿAbd al-Hādī, also known as Ibn al-Mibrad, a leading Ḥanbalī scholar and a contemporary of Ibn Ṭawq, had a slave named Bulbul, with whom he cohabited for ten years till her death in the plague of 883/1479 and from whom he had a son and a daughter. In a booklet in her memory he indulged in her praise, especially her piety ("She never left our house, she did not even attend my brother's wedding, although he expressed his wish to see her there"). However, according to the cliché, life must go on, and after her death the scholar purchased at least two more female slaves, who bore him children.[137] Also qadi Muḥibb al-Dīn (it is unclear whether the Shāfiʿī, or his namesake the Ḥanafī) was attached to his concubine, mourned her death, and buried her beside the grave of his parents. About a year later he lost his suckling toddler (*raḍī*), most likely born from the deceased concubine.[138] It appears that later he took another concubine, ʿAyn al-Ḥayā ("Source of Life"), who bore him a son. Eventually, he manumitted her and she was married to the prominent Shāfiʿī Kamāl al-Dīn and gave birth to a daughter. This daughter died aged two months, and her mother also died a few years later as a result of the plague. Ibn Ṭawq alludes to strained relations between her and Kamāl-al-Dīn's mother and other female members of the family. At one point she even complained to the authorities about her master.[139]

Although most of the female slaves that are mentioned by our notary were the property of male masters, some are identified by their lady owners.[140] Thus, about a month after her marriage to ʿAbd al-Raḥīm, Taqī al-Dīn's son, his wife, who had received from him 20 ashrafīs as a marriage gift, borrowed from him another 20 and spent it on buying a female slave.[141]

Ibn Ṭawq reports about 50 female slaves and concubines, both white and dark-skinned, in the Damascus of his day.[142] In his capacity as an official witness to transactions, he provides interesting information on some cases. The often-

136 Rapoport, Women and gender.

137 Frenkel, Slave girls. I am indebted to Prof. Frenkel for allowing me to see a copy of the article prior to its publication; Rapoport, Women and gender 13–16.

138 Ibn Ṭawq, *Taʿlīq* 82, 175.

139 Ibn Ṭawq, *Taʿlīq* 804, 873, 889, 1501.

140 Ibn Ṭawq, *Taʿlīq* 55, 61, 246, 408, 413, 512, 528, 619, 765, 814, 845, 866, 872, 965, 971, 1010, 1035, 1122, 1464, 1504, 1533, 1593.

141 Ibn Ṭawq, *Taʿlīq* 1792, 1806.

142 Ibn Ṭawq, *Taʿlīq* 106, 258, 353, 450, 619, 635, 648, 662, 698, 730, 783, 799, 842, 922, 965 (two cases), 1006, 1035, 1051, 1119 (two cases), 1121, 1123, 1124, 1125, 1127 (three cases), 1128, 1134, 1237, 1363, 1454, 1478, 1500, 1501, 1503, 1504, 1505, 1512, 1516, 1530, 1538, 1557, 1582, 1595, 1607, 1608, 1621, 1672.

mentioned Shāfiʿī scholar Kamāl al-Dīn, of the Ibn Qāḍī ʿAjlūn family, purchased a breastfeeding *jāriya*, together with her suckling daughter, as required by the sharīʿa.[143] Buying her through ʿAṣfūr, the same slave dealer with whom Ibn Ṭawq contracted one of his own transactions, the agent for Kamāl al-Dīn was able to reduce the price by 10 dirhams, a trifling 1 percent of the deal. About half of the sum was paid by an order of payment (*ḥawāla*).[144] Abū l-Yumn, another member of the same family, owned a female slave and got into trouble with his wife Sitt al-ʿUlamāʾ, Taqī al-Dīn's daughter, for accommodating the slave at her residence.[145] Ibn Ṭawq also served as a witness to a purchase made by his relative, the lady Bt. al-Khātūn, of Fāʾida, the Egyptian, who had been previously owned by shaykh Abū l-Faḍl, most likely our notary's colleague and close friend. She was purchased together with her (young) daughter. Incidentally, at one point Fāʾida ran away; this, as we shall see, was not the only case of an escaping female slave.[146] Ibn Ṭawq also drafted and witnessed a sale contract for three partners who purchased another of Abū l-Faḍl's slaves, dark-skinned and "of obscure origin" (*al-majhūla al-jins*).[147]

More than 20 female slaves, half of them black, are reported to have given birth to children of their masters.[148] The term used is *umm walad* for a son, *umm sitt* for a daughter, and *umm awlād* for a son and daughter[149] Some concubines were very young and therefore of questionable puberty.[150] However, when considered in the light of the age of brides, it was not exceptional.[151] A dark-skinned child indicates that the mother must have been a black concubine.[152] When Abū l-Yumn sold his black female slave to one of the prison guards, she claimed

---

143 For the ruling that a child below seven years cannot be separated from his/her mother when sold as a slave, see ʿAbd, *EI*².

144 Ibn Ṭawq, *Taʿlīq* 308–309.

145 Ibn Ṭawq, *Taʿlīq* 1709.

146 Ibn Ṭawq, *Taʿlīq* 411, 627, 628. For two of Abū l-Faḍl's female slaves who ran away, one of them with a child, see 209, 654. For further cases of escape, see 662, 1136; Martel-Thoumian, *Délinquance* 306 n. 8.

147 Ibn Ṭawq, *Taʿlīq* 655.

148 Ibn Ṭawq, *Taʿlīq* 45, 106, 150, 238, 379, 448, 498, 542, 633, 814, 816, 838, 868, 873, 1030, 1119, 1121, 1122, 1125, 1127 (two cases), 1150, 1240, 1272, 1318, 1465, 1499, 1601.

149 See, however, Ibn Ṭawq's reference to his wife as noted in Chapter 1. For concubines and slaves who bore children, see e.g. Ibn Ṭawq, *Taʿlīq* 45, 81, 245, 492, 735, 768, 779, 845, 846, 868, 891, 964, 1006, 1030, 1504, 1557.

150 For the *khaṭīb* Ibrāhīm al-Nājī purchasing an eleven-year-old white concubine, see Ibn Ṭawq, *Taʿlīq* 175.

151 Information on two prominent scholars illustrates it: al-Sakhāwī married an eleven-year-old girl, and al-Maqrīzī's mother married when she was twelve. See Rapoport, *Marriage* 39.

152 E.g. Ibn Ṭawq, *Taʿlīq* 1628, 1724.

to be already pregnant by him. Though Abū l-Yumn denied it, he intimated to our notary that he had twice had sexual intercourse with her.[153] Similar was the case of Ibrāhīm al-Kurdī, the husband of Ibn Ṭawq's relative Bt. al-Khātūn. However, he took the aforementioned "oath of pain" (*ḥalafa bi-l-ṭalāq*) that he was not the child's father, as at the relevant time he had been away in Cairo.[154]

As to prices, Shahdiya, Ibn Ṭawq's white slave, was priced at 2,000 dirhams, about 38 ashrafīs.[155] However, price quotations for female slaves are mostly 1,100 and 1,200 dirhams. Given a rate of exchange of 1:52 for the ashrafī that obtained in these transactions, the average price was 21 to 23 dinars, including a dealer's commission and a notary's fee.[156] These prices are possibly for dark-skinned slaves and are similar to what we find in the Jerusalem Ḥaram documents as the highest prices for black slaves at the end of the fourteenth century.[157] In other words, on the basis of this sparse material we may gingerly conclude that the price of female slaves had not undergone a dramatic change in the course of the fifteenth century. This should question Rapoport's assumption about the decline in the "supply" of female slaves in the fifteenth century. It compares with the highest range of prices for similar slaves in contemporary Egypt.[158] Payment was sometimes made in a mixture of gold and silver currency.[159] Oftentimes only down payment was made, the rest being paid later, some time within a fixed period.[160]

There were sales in which prices were even lower. The notary Muḥibb al-Dīn b. ʿAbd al-Bāsiṭ, who was known for dealing in slaves (*bayyāʿ al-raqīq*), bought from Taqī al-Dīn's son a black *jāriya* named Nawfara who was weak and suffered from stomach aches (*mabṭūna*). The relatively low price in this case, 450 dirhams, less than half the normal price, and deferred to a month later, had probably to do with her medical condition. It was stipulated that in case she failed to do her job, the transaction would be annulled and the money returned.[161] A seller would be expected to guarantee that the slave was not pregnant, that she was in good physical condition, and that she did not suffer

153 Ibn Ṭawq, *Taʿlīq* 1209.
154 Ibn Ṭawq, *Taʿlīq* 408.
155 Ibn Ṭawq, *Taʿlīq* 96, 97.
156 Ibn Ṭawq, *Taʿlīq* 118, 120, 288, 290, 308–309, 334, 411, 594, 604, 655, 730, 1148.
157 Rapoport, Women and gender 14 and n. 57. For a price quotation of 24 ashrafīs that our notary gives for a black female slave in Egypt, see Ibn Ṭawq, *Taʿlīq* 1758.
158 Rapoport, Women and gender 15. For the ducat and the ashrafī having a comparable value, see Bacharach, Dinar, esp. 89–90.
159 Ibn Ṭawq, *Taʿlīq* 96, 604, 655, 1148.
160 Ibn Ṭawq, *Taʿlīq* 411, 594, 730.
161 Ibn Ṭawq, *Taʿlīq* 926.

from mental problems. We saw earlier that Ibn Ṭawq, when selling his *jāriya*, revealed, among other things, her physical problems.[162]

An owner's death required immediate manumission. The "honorable lady" (*al-sayyida al-sharīfa*), the sister of Kamāl al-Dīn and niece of Taqī al-Dīn, stated shortly before her death, in the presence of her brother, that she manumitted her black *jāriya* and after her lady's death she would be free to do whatever she decided. Other slave owners manumitted their slaves during their lifetime and provided them with a certificate (*waraqat iʿtāq*).[163] Manumission enabled marriage even to a man of an elevated status, as well as the acquisition of residence.[164] This was the case of Taqī al-Dīn's Mubāraka, either of Christian or Anatolian origin (*rūmiyya*), the mother of the shaykh's son Muḥammad. After her manumission she was married to Abū Bakr al-Fāmī (or al-Hāmī), the muezzin. The marriage gift she received was 300 dirhams (6 dinars), 100 of which was paid immediately, thus significantly lower than the *ṣadāq* paid to freeborn women.[165] Suryāy, another of the shaykh's manumitted concubines, was married to Abū l-Yumn, the shaykh's nephew, from whom she received a generous marriage gift of 25 ashrafīs, close to sums received by freeborn wives.[166] Possibly, it was the result of the bride being Taqī al-Dīn's concubine and the groom a member of the family. Others of the shaykh's manumitted concubines married as well.[167]

There are a few reports about the sexual harassment of and various scandals related to female slaves and the reaction of the authorities. In one case, Ismāʿīl, known as "the Ḥanafī," raped a white female slave and she became pregnant. For some reason the case came before the sultan, who decided to castrate Ismāʿīl. Had this harsh decision to do with the fact that the rape had taken place during Ramadan?[168] In another case, Taqī al-Dīn's suckling (*murḍiʿā*) slave, in her fourth month, blamed one Ibrāhīm al-Ḥawrānī for her pregnancy. He

162 Ibn Ṭawq, *Taʿlīq* 96, 97, 655, 730.

163 Ibn Ṭawq, *Taʿlīq* 363, 523, 528, 1030.

164 E.g. Ibn Ṭawq, *Taʿlīq* 59, 512, 804, 858, 1039, 1412.

165 Ibn Ṭawq, *Taʿlīq* 192. For another case, see 417.

166 Ibn Ṭawq, *Taʿlīq* 549, 550.

167 Suryāy married for the considerably lesser sum of 5 ashrafīs. See Ibn Ṭawq, *Taʿlīq* 1464. The Ethiopian Jawhara, who bore him a daughter named Āsya, at the time still suckling, was married to Muḥammad al-Buṣrawī for a marriage gift of 700 dirhams, only 135 of which she received at the time of the marriage. See Ibn Ṭawq, *Taʿlīq* 1030, 1036–1037, 1038. For other cases, see 59 (and 406), 428, 804, 858, 863, 943, 964, 1023, 1039, 1049, 1195, 1206, 1240, 1254, 1315, 1360, 1412, 1422, 1683.

168 Ibn Ṭawq, *Taʿlīq* 667.

agreed to marry her, but it remains unclear whether this in fact happened.[169] Another *jāriya* accused her master and his male slave for her pregnancy, yet the master denied it and put the blame on his neighbor. The issue came before the *ḥājib al-ḥujjāb*, who arrested the slave. No sanction against his master is reported, but animosity was generated between the master and the accused neighbor.[170] A man twice caused the abortive pregnancy of his daughter's black female slave and, in the complication caused in the second pregnancy, she died. The man was fined 50 ashrafīs.[171] There are reports of similar cases.[172]

Some female slaves tried to escape. A noteworthy case is that of Surūr, the shaykh's slave, whose praise Ibn Ṭawq relates. He puts the blame for her wish to run away on the "Egyptian wife." Now Surūr was able to drill a hole in the wall and escape through it to the house of one of the shaykh's former female slaves, who was now married, but her husband betrayed her and reported about her whereabouts for the negligible reward of 10 dirhams. Her failure to escape did not deter Surūr from another attempt. Apparently also this one did not bring an end to her employment problems, for we read about a third attempt, after which Surūr was sold. Perhaps, more than having problems at one specific household, Surūr was a sort of rebellious slave who had difficulties accepting her unfortunate status.[173]

Despite its obvious deficiencies, the information our notary provides for a 20-year period about several dozen female slaves and concubines suggests that these were part of the Damascus scene and its social fabric. In bourgeois, middle-, and lower-class families or the homes of single men, one could find female slaves and concubines, sometime more than one at the same time, in addition

169 Ibn Ṭawq, *Taʿlīq* 454, 466, 467.

170 Ibn Ṭawq, *Taʿlīq* 462. The involvement of the *ḥājib* in these affairs confirms the argument about the growing involvement of *ḥājibs* in judicial affairs in the latter Mamluk period. See Irwin, Privatization, and Chapter 5 in this book.

171 Ibn Ṭawq, *Taʿlīq* 1789, 1794.

172 When a young man and the female slave of a shaykh's spouse were found in an intimate situation somewhere in the preacher's quarters within a mosque complex, the slave was injured as a result of the harsh reaction of the man who spotted them; her partner threw himself into the river. See Ibn Ṭawq, *Taʿlīq* 61. Raḍī al-Dīn al-Ghazzī, the Shāfiʿī deputy qadi, beat the white slave of his mother-in-law because he suspected her of letting a foreign man, most likely a European (*ajnabī*), enter the house. She found shelter at the viceroy's palace and in revenge reported about money that al-Ghazzī kept at his residence. See Ibn Ṭawq, *Taʿlīq* 650. The son of the Mālikī qadi and another young man (*al-ḥadath*) had sex (*dakhala ʿalā*) with a female slave. They were caught and brought before the governor, yet we are not told what the verdict was. Ibn Ṭawq, *Taʿlīq* 942.

173 Ibn Ṭawq, *Taʿlīq* 419, 662.

to legal wives. Whether this was in numbers that remained stable compared to earlier times or, as Rapoport suggests, albeit with much fewer data, in declining figures, is surely impossible to say. One can only regret that no one else left similar records and surely marvel, once again, at Ibn Ṭawq's importance as a unique source.

Epilogue

The published text of Ibn Ṭawq's diary terminates at the end of 906/summer 1501. From that point onward, until the dramatic capture of Damascus by the Ottomans, our information, based as it is on other sources, dwindles substantially. We are now dependent mostly on Ibn Ṭūlūn's *Mufākahat al-khillān* and *Iʿlām al-warā*, both conventional history books that lack all that is so special about the *Taʿlīq*. Ibn al-Ḥimṣī, another source who is by now familiar to the reader, spent the years 900–914/1494–1509 in Cairo and reported very little on Damascus during these years. One could say that, with our notary's reports no longer available, the microhistory of the city is shrouded again to a large extent in mist. However, by and large, Ibn Ṭūlūn's reports tell us that problems in Damascus on the eve of the Ottoman conquest only intensified.

First and foremost, the plague continued to strike without mercy. After the last plague outbreak that Ibn Ṭawq mentioned for 905/1499–1500, another occurred in Jumādā 909/November 1503, in which one of the viceroy's sons was among the victims. Then, there was respite for a dozen of years till Ramaḍān 917/November–December 1511. Then, for Jumādā I 919/July 1513, the figure of 75,000 deaths is senseless, of course, and is most likely above the size of the entire population. More plausible is the figure of 3,000 for the Ṣāliḥiyya Quarter, which is high in itself and is about 5 percent of the estimated population. On that basis, adding the deaths in other quarters, one could suggest that a quarter to a third of the residents perished in that outbreak, which conforms to usual estimates of plague mortality. At the end of that year, that is, the beginning of 1514, a collective prayer, led by the governor of the province, was said in the hope of bringing the disaster to an end, and a fast for three days was decreed. A few months later the plague hit the viceroy's own family and his daughter died.[1]

The chaotic situation within the governing circles intensified, reflecting a great deal of mistrust among the Mamluks, and measures were taken against various functionaries. At the same time, Cairo was losing its control in Syria. Seen in this light, the betrothal between the sultan's son and the viceroy's nine-year-old daughter in Jumādā I 920/July 1514 appears to have been a political step. The sum of 20,000 dinars reportedly spent on this occasion demonstrates total ignorance of the context and that the ruler in Damascus had lost touch

1 Ibn Ṭūlūn, *Mufākahat al-khillān* 219; Ibn Ṭūlūn, *Iʿlām* 176–177, 221; Ibn al-Ḥimṣī, *Ḥawādith* ii, 225, 250, 251, 253, 259. The figure of 75,000 is accepted uncritically by Miura, *Dynamism* 62, n. 52.

 | DOI:10.1163/9789004413269_009

with the bitter reality. Similarly, the precious gifts exchanged between Sultan al-Ghawrī and the viceroy when the former stopped in Damascus on his way to battle the Ottomans in Rabīʿ II 922/May 1516, a battle in which he would meet his death, looks ironic in hindsight.

Under these dire circumstances, all sorts of criminals found an opportunity to murder and plunder.[2] Food prices rose substantially and, at the same time, heavy taxation continued to weigh heavily on the people. The "infantry tax" (*mushāt*), imposed on all the city's quarters, and other ad hoc taxes are mentioned frequently. For example, in Rabīʿ II 907/October 1501 the Maydān al-Ḥaṣā and the Ṣāliḥiyya quarters were taxed with 1,000 and 500 dinars respectively to enable the newly appointed *ustādār* to pay for his office; other quarters similarly suffered. Even the Mālikī qadi and other notables (*aʿyān*) failed to avert confrontation between the Shāghūr Quarter inhabitants and the mamluks. Ibn Ṭūlūn's report reveals the weakness of the authorities, who in the end had to accept several of the people's demands to ease the burden and take further measures. However, later in the year, 100,000 dinars, most likely an imagined figure, were imposed on the entire city and then reduced to 30,000 dinars. As a result, people were forced to vacate their homes and shops. The tax was then further reduced to 20,000 dinars. Even if these figures are inflated, they indicate an unbearable burden. The governor was blamed for imposing taxes for his own needs (*li nafsihi*), in addition to what was imposed by the sultan. Also villages suffered from pillage. The hated Ibn al-Fuqhāʿī, the tax collector (*ballāṣī*), who had not been removed from his office despite public demand, was murdered on his way to the public bath. Some days later another tax collector suffered the same fate. Waqf money was taken.[3] In Jumādā I 912/September 1506, as troops were sent to the Jordan Valley to raid the bedouins, each of the city's quarters had to send men to the infantry units or raise money for upkeep. Eight years later, around the time of Ramadan, an order was issued that the city must recruit a total of 4,000 and in addition a tax of 25 dinars to each infantryman, which would make a total sum of 100,000.[4]

Also villages in the vicinity, including Jarūd, Ibn Ṭawq's ancestral village, suffered from pillage by the troops. In al-Mizza a dispute about a dog that the sultan's representative requested and the owner refused to give away resulted

2 Ibn Ṭūlūn, *Iʿlām* 143–231, *passim*. For the murder of a Sufi shaykh who was favored by the viceroy, see 181. For theft and execution, see e.g. 188–189, 195, 196.

3 E.g. Ibn Ṭūlūn, *Mufākahat al-khillān* 199, 200, 202, 203, 204, 205, 206, 209, 212, 222, 224, 249, 250, 254, 255, 257; Ibn Ṭūlūn, *Iʿlām* 160, 161–162, 166, 179, 205, 221–222, 228–229; Ibn al-Ḥimṣī, *Ḥawādith* ii, 4, 146–147; Elbendary, *Crowds* 127–128. For *ballāṣī* see Miura, Urban society 167.

4 Ibn Ṭūlūn, *Iʿlām* 200, 201, 203, 222–224.

in the latter being murdered. If this was not enough, the entire village was punished. In Muḥarram 911/June 1505 each property owner in Damascus had to pay a two-month rent, and in Jumādā 916/August 1510 the property of Europeans was confiscated. The end of 909/1504 witnessed one more assassination of an official at al-Mizza, and a couple of months later there was another political murder, in Maydān al-Ḥaṣā, of "the greatest supporter of evil" (*akbar aʿwān al-zukma*), whose corpse was dragged from one site to another. At his funeral the people pelted stones. Less than a week elapsed before a youngster of a noble family of the ʿAbbāsiyūn Quarter was executed for no blame. This provoked another riot, aimed at the interim viceroy, in the course of which the residences of mamluks were pillaged and some were killed. Ibn Ṭūlūn mostly reports for these years about confrontation between the people and the authorities in which it is unclear who fared better. When a couple of months later a new governor arrived, there was anxiety in the city, which the *mutasallim* (the interim viceroy? synonym for *nāʾib al-ghayba*?) tried to calm. The governorship appears to have been in a chaotic state.[5]

It is about the activity of the *zuʿr* and the governor's retaliation against them that we learn quite a lot. Some of their leaders, such as Ibn al-Ustādh of Maydān al-Ḥaṣā, were detained and executed. Their activity at the Shāghūr Quarter resulted in a confrontation with the viceroy's troops and widespread destruction. In Muḥarram 909/July 1503 there was one out of several attempts at curbing the activity of these local gangsters, and an announcement was made that *zaʿāra* was abolished and the carrying of weapon was forbidden, as well as a special hair style (*qarʿaniyan*) and a special mode of dress (*lā yuqlab thiyābuhu ʿalā katfihi*). Two merchants who propagated for the *zuʿr* were punished. All this worked only to a limited extent, and criminal activity of attacking officials and murdering continued. It reached the point that in Jumādā II 910/November 1504, an interim period between two viceroys, qadis made the *zuʿr* swear that they would join the sultan's forces on condition that they place a representative ("emir") in each of the quarters. Later Abū Ṭāqiya from the Shaghūr Quarter assembled *zuʿr* of many quarters and villages; they confiscated money from the people and received help from an emir, frustrated that he was not being appointed governor. The Mamluk troops were helpless against the gangsters, whose leader received a robe of honor. It appears as the heyday in the history of the local *zuʿr*, and Abū Ṭāqiya enjoyed power for a while. In Shaʿbān 911/ January 1506, *zuʿr* of some quarters accompanied the governor of Aleppo on his

5 Ibn Ṭūlūn, *Mufākahat al-khillān* 200, 203, 204, 205–206, 221, 225–226, 229, 230, 231; Ibn Ṭūlūn, *Iʿlām* 164–165, 221; Ibn al-Ḥimṣī, *Ḥawādith* ii, 200, 204, 233, 234, 236, 240.

way from Damascus, and he was reprimanded for cooperating with the aforementioned Abū Ṭāqiya. When a new governor was appointed some months later, there was a ban on carrying arms, and gangsters of the Ṣāliḥiyya Quarter were detained. The public was satisfied, because they feared the many who carried daggers, but it turns out that some continued to do so nevertheless.[6]

As in earlier years, Mamluk policy was inconsistent, and, in contrast to severe measures applied against the *zuʿr* on the one hand, the viceroy occasionally bestowed robes of honor on their leaders. One who received it was Ibn Ṭabbākh, the *kabīr al-zuʿr* of the Shāghūr Quarter. Some Mamluk officers are reported to have had units of *zuʿr* at their service. The gangsters of a number of quarters held parties for the *dawādār al-sulṭān*. Shortly afterward, the governor called upon them to go before him in a procession, carrying their armor, and they participated in a reception of a delegate coming from the Ottomans. One, referred to as "the rightly guided" (*al-muhtadī*), became the shaykh of the Maydān al-Ḥaṣā Quarter and participated in the governor's processions. In Ṣafar 914/June 1508 the *zuʿr* of all the quarters were even called upon to be mobilized for an expedition to the Ḥawrān. They are still referred to on the eve of the Ottoman conquest, and in 922/1516, after the defeat of Mamluk forces became known, they roamed in the city and murdered people, including seven residents of the Ṣāliḥiyya Quarter, together with the head of the quarter (*ʿarīf*). They plundered residences, even those of high-ranking officers who had left for Egypt, and they intended to murder the Ḥanafi qadi. Undoubtedly, they terrorized the city's inhabitants.[7]

The internal chaos that is reported almost continuously for the last years of the Mamluk era was coupled by bedouin attacks on the outskirts of Damascus, pillaging grain and devastating land. Here and there, punitive expeditions were sent against them. In Rajab 907/March 1502 a subtribe (*ʿashīr*) even arrived at al-Maydān al-Akhḍar (the "Green Hippodrome"), slightly west of the old city. In the following years there were raids, such as against the Ibn Muqallad clan. In Rabīʿ II 920/June 1514 the bedouins living on the outskirts of the city were expelled after the mamluks received the land as *iqṭāʿ*s in what appears to have been an attempt to defend the city by using old systems. For no less than seven years, till the beginning of 922/1516, the hajj convoy could not set out because of the danger posed by the tribes, and only a settlement, by which they were

---

6 Ibn Ṭūlūn, *Mufākahat al-khillān* 209–210, 211, 212, 218, 226, 227, 228–229, 231, 232, 238, 241, 242, 254, 255, 267; Ibn Ṭūlūn, *Iʿlām* 167–168, 169–170, 183–184, 187, 191, 195 (especially critical account), 196–197, 205.

7 E.g. Ibn Ṭūlūn, *Iʿlām* 175; Ibn Ṭūlūn, *Mufākahat al-khillān* 204, 212–213, 216, 267, 268, 334, 336–337.

promised 4,000 dinars annually, changed the dismal situation.[8] As with the *zuʿr*, the authorities had a problem, and their policy toward the bedouins kept changing. At one point Ibn Saʿīd, a chief of a tribe, came to Damascus and received a robe of honor from the governor after earlier concluding a treaty with the sultan.[9]

All this was reflected in the grave situation of the most basic needs of the people, namely in food prices. As the figures provided in the Appendix clearly show, compared to the figures of the early 1480s, the price of bread rose enormously 15 and 20 years later; in fact, it more than doubled. The year 919/1513 witnessed another severe plague, and grain prices more than doubled when compared to the beginning of that year. Two years later, the price of wheat and meat hit a new record.[10] A severe plague, which took a high toll and brought about high prices, thus started the year 922/1516 for the people of Damascus. In Jumādā I/June of that year, the sultan Qanṣūh al-Ghawrī arrived in the city, accompanied by his leading emirs and many officials. He stayed there a week, and then moved on northward to Aleppo, followed by Sibāy, the viceroy, and his troops. An envoy sent to Aleppo by the Ottoman sultan Selim failed to reach reconciliation, and the Mamluk ruler entered Ottoman territories. The understanding among the Damascus population was that the Ottomans deceived and that they were interested in a war. In Rajab/August, the battle at Marj Dābiq outside Aleppo ensued, in the course of which the Mamluk sultan died under unclear circumstances. His forces were defeated and suffered heavy losses. On 20 Shaʿbān/19 August, Ottoman troops arrived in Damascus to find its population starving and miserable. They probably did not know what readers of this book have learnt—that Damascus had been in a situation of crisis for years. The people surrendered, and ten days later Selim himself entered the city.[11] A new era had begun.

8 Ibn Ṭūlūn, *Mufākahat al-khillān* 198–199, 211, 234, 246, 253, 274, 290, 291; Ibn Ṭūlūn, *Iʿlām* 192, 217; Ibn al-Ḥimṣī, *Ḥawādith* ii, 190, 197, 258, 276. For their causing problems also in the early Ottoman period, see Berger, *Gesellschaft* 131.

9 Ibn Ṭūlūn, *Iʿlām* 208, 210, 211–212, 213, 215, 216, 217, 218; Ibn al-Ḥimṣī, *Ḥawādith* ii, 221–222, 227.

10 For figures see Appendix.

11 Ibn Ṭūlūn, *Mufākahat al-khillān* 333–335; Ibn al-Ḥimṣī, *Ḥawādith* ii, 283–291.

APPENDIX

Food Prices 873–921/1468–1516

Sources: al-Buṣrawī, *Tārīkh* 34, 35, 36, 37, 38, 43, 45, 110, 125, 169, 197; Ibn al-Ḥimṣī, *Ḥawādith* i, 188, 289; ii, 243, 277; Ibn Ṭawq *Taʿlīq*, 27, 39, 45, 71, 72, 89, 125, 180, 181, 188, 252, 262, 274, 282, 286, 287, 289, 290, 291, 292, 294, 297, 319, 332, 350, 366, 368, 425, 455–456, 547, 548, 553, 598, 620, 639, 667, 675, 726, 727, 730, 735, 763, 767, 1007, 1098, 1147, 1164, 1201, 1212, 1238, 1242, 1243, 1248, 1274, 1282, 1297, 1353, 1387, 1390, 1459, 1462, 1467, 1489, 1590, 1607, 1633, 1694, 1902, 1773, 1779, 1802, 1831, 1900; Ibn Ṭūlūn, *Mufākahat al-khillān* 71, 77, 82–83, 129, 216, 235, 298, 304; Ibn Ṭūlūn, *Iʿlām* 174, 188, 189, 209.

Wheat[1]

Ṣafar 873	420
Rabīʿ I 873	900
Jumādā II 873	900
Rajab 873	1,018
Shaʿbān 873	2,000; 40 dinars
Ramaḍān 873	1,000, then 1,500
Dhū l-Qaʿda 873	1,000
Rajab 874	500
Ramaḍān 874	300
Jumādā I 888	180
Rajab 888	8 ashrafīs (= 416 dirhams)
Shawwāl 888	400, then 420, then 450
Dhū l-Qaʿda 888	350, then 500
Dhū l-Ḥijja 888	460, then 450
Muḥarram 889	480, then 460
Rabīʿ I 889	500 plus, then 520
Jumādā II 889	300
Rabīʿ I 890	400
Rabīʿ I 891	260, then 360
Dhū l-Ḥijja 891	320
Muḥarram 892	250–350
Dhū l-Ḥijja 892	380, then 420
Muḥarram 893	380, then 160
Ṣafar 893	less than 400
Jumādā I 893	420, then 400
Dhū l-Qaʿda 898	240
Rabīʿ I 899	322, 7 ashrafīs [= ca. 385 dirhams]
Rajab 899	ca. 500, then 350
Shaʿbān 899	380
Shawwāl 899	less than 400
Rabīʿ I 901	300
Rabīʿ I 902	300
Shawwāl 906	360–400
Muḥarram 909	200
Dhū l-Ḥijja 918	400, then 500
Muḥarram 919	24 ashrafīs [= 1,248 dirhams]
Dhū l-Ḥijja 921	26 ashrafīs [= 1,352 dirhams]

1 Prices in dirhams for 1 *gharāra*.

Barley

Ṣafar 873	210
Rabīʿ I 873	300
Jumādā II 873	500
Rajab 873	650
Shaʿbān 873	900, then 500
Ramaḍān 873	500, then 800
Dhū l-Ḥijja 873	300
Rajab 874	200
Ramaḍān 874	100
Muḥarram 886	60
Shaʿbān 887	92
Jumādā I 888	110
Shawwāl 888	220 [more likely 120]
Dhū l-Qaʿda 888	120, then 250
Muḥarram 889	130, then 140
Rabīʿ I 889	150
Jumādā II 889	130
Rabīʿ I 890	ca. 200
Dhū l-Ḥijja 891	110
Muḥarram 892	120
Dhū l-Ḥijja 892	160, then 180
Muḥarram 893	180
Ṣafar 893	200
Jumādā I 893	200
Shaʿbān 893	220
Dhū l-Qaʿda 898	100 plus
Rabīʿ I 899	4 ashrafīs [= ca. 220 dirhams]
Shaʿbān 899	180
Rabīʿ I 901	100
Rabīʿ II 902	150

Bread[2]

Shaʿbān 873	8
Muḥarram 886	ca. 7 (119 for quarter *qinṭār* = ca. 12 kg)
Jumādā II 886	1.25, then 1, fixed (*khubz mafrūk*)
Shaʿbān 893	1.5
Muḥarram 909	1–1.75
Ramaḍān 910	3, 1.5–2 (fixed)
Rabīʿ I 911	2–3
Dhū l-Ḥijja 918	4 (fixed)

Meat (mutton)[3]

Shaʿbān 873	7
Shawwāl 885	4
Shaʿbān 886	4
Muḥarram 887	3.5
Shaʿbān 887	ca. 1.7 (44 per *qinṭār* = 47.5 kg)
Jumādā II 888	4.5
Shawwāl 888	4
Dhū l-Qaʿda 888	4
Rabīʿ I 889	3
Muḥarram 890	4
Dhū l-Ḥijja 890	5 to 9 (holiday), then fixed at 4
Jumādā I 891	3, then 3.5–4 (shortage)
Muḥarram 892	4
Rabīʿ I 896	4.5
Rabīʿ I 897	4.5 (people eat fish)
Rabīʿ I 898	4.5
Ramaḍān 898	4
Rabīʿ II 899	0.5

2 Prices in dirhams for 1 *raṭl* (= 1.85 kg).

3 Prices in dirhams for 1 *raṭl*.

Shawwāl 899	3.5, then 4	Shaʿbān 904	4, then 3.5
Shawwāl 900	4	Jumādā I 905	5
Rabīʿ I 901	5 (fixed)	Jumādā II 905	6
Rabīʿ II 901	4.5 (fixed)	Rajab 905	4 (fixed)
Rabīʿ II 902	3.5, then 4.5	Shawwāl 905	5, then 3 (fixed)
Jumādā I 902	4, then 6	Rajab 906	4 (fixed)
Ramaḍān 902	4	Ramaḍān 910	6, then fixed at 4
Rajab 903	4 (fixed)	Dhū l-Ḥijja 914	6
Ramaḍān 903	3.5	Dhū l-Ḥijja 918	8 (beef 6)
Dhū l-Qaʿda 903	5 (fixed)	Dhū l-Ḥijja 919	4 (fixed)
Rajab 904	5–6 (beef 4)	Jumādā I 921	2

Bibliography

Sources

ʿAbd al-Bāsiṭ, Zayn al-Dīn b. Khalīl b. Shāhīn, *al-Majmaʿ al-mufannan bi-l-muʿjam al-muʿanwan*, ed. ʿUmar al-Tadmurī, 2 vols., Beirut 2011.

ʿAbd al-Bāsiṭ, Zayn al-Dīn b. Khalīl b. Shāhīn, *Nayl al-amal fī dhayl al-duwal*, 8 vols., Beirut 2002.

ʿAlwān al-Ḥamāwī, *al-Shām aʿrāsuhā wa-faḍāʾil suknāhā*, ed. Nashwah al-ʿAlwānī, Damascus 1997.

Anṣārī, Sharaf al-Dīn Mūsā, *Nuzhat al-khāṭir wa bahjat al-nāẓir*, 2 vols., Damascus 1991.

al-Asadī, Muḥammad b. Muḥammad, *al-Taysīr wa-l-iʿtibār wa-l-taḥrīr wa-l-ikhtibār fīmā yajib min ḥusn al-tadbīr wa-l-taṣarruf wa-l-ikhtiyār*, ed. ʿAbd al-Qādr Aḥmad Ṭulaymāt, Cairo 1968.

al-Asyūṭī, Shams al-Dīn Muḥammad al-Minhajī, *Jawāhir al-ʿuqūd wa muʿīn al-quḍāt wa-l-muwaqqiʿīn wa-l-shuhūd*, 2 vols., Beirut 1996.

al-Balāṭunusī, Muḥammad Taqī al-Dīn, *Taḥrīr al-maqāl fīmā yaḥill wa-yuḥram min bayt al-māl*, ed. Fatḥallāh Muḥammad Ghāzī al-Ṣabāgh, al-Manṣūra 1989.

al-Buṣrawī, ʿAlāʾ al-Dīn ʿAlī, *Tārīkh al-Buṣrawī*, Damascus 1988.

al-Ghazzī, Najm al-Dīn Muḥammad, *al-Kawākib al-sāʾira bi aʿyān al-miʾa al-ʿāshira*, 3 vols., Beirut 1979.

al-Ḥaṣkafī, Aḥmad b. Muḥammad, *Mutʿat al-adhhān min al-tamatuʿ bi-l-aqrān bayna tarājim al-shuyūkh wa-l-aqrān*, 2 vols., Beirut 1999.

Ibn al-Ḥimṣī, *Ḥawādith al-zamān wa-wafāyāt al-shuyūkh wa-l-aqrān*, 3 vols., Beirut 1999.

Ibn al-ʿImād, *Shadharāt al-dhahab*, 10 vols., Beirut 1986–1993.

Ibn Iyās, *Badāʾiʿ al-zuhūr fī waqāʾiʿ al-duhūr*, 5 vols., Cairo, 1960–1975.

Ibn Kannān, Muhammad b. ʿĪsā, *al-Mawākib al-Islāmiyya fī l-mamālik al-shāmiyya*, ed. ʿAbd al-Jābir al-Buḥayrī, Cairo 2001.

Ibn Mibrad, Yūsuf b. ʿAbd al-Hādī, *Sayr al-ḥathth ilāʿ ilm al-ṭalāq al-thalāth*, Beirut 1997.

Ibn Nujaym, *Rasāʾil Ibn Nujaym al-iqtiṣādiyya*, Cairo 1998–1999.

Ibn Sibāṭ, *Tārīkh* (= *Ṣidq al-akhbār*), 2 vols., Tripoli 1993.

Ibn Ṭawq, *al-Taʿlīq*, 4 vols., Damascus 2000–2007.

Ibn Ṭūlūn, *Dhakhāʾir al-qaṣr fī tarājim nubalāʾ al-ʿaṣr*, 2 vols., Amman 2015.

Ibn Ṭūlūn, *al-Fulk al-mashḥūn fī aḥwāl Muḥammad Ibn Ṭūlūn*, Beirut 1996.

Ibn Ṭūlūn, *Ḥawādith Dimashq al-yawmiyya*, ed. Ahmed Ibesch, Damascus 2002.

Ibn Ṭūlūn, *Iʿlām al-warā bi-man waliya nāʾiban min al-atrāk bi-Dimashq al-Shām al-Kubrā*, Damascus 1984.

Ibn Ṭūlūn, *Mufākahat al-khillān fī ḥawādith al-zamān*, Beirut 1998.
Ibn Ṭūlūn, *al-Muʿizza fīmā qīla fī l-Mizza*, Damascus 1983.
Ibn Ṭūlūn, *Naqd al-ṭālib li zaghl al-manāṣib*, Beirut 1992.
Ibn Ṭūlūn, *al-Qalāʾid al-jawhariyya fī tārīkh al-Ṣāliḥiyya*, 2 vols., Damascus 1981.
Ibn Ṭūlūn, *Quḍāt Dimashq*, Damascus 1956.
Ibn Ṭūlūn, *Qurrat al-ʿuyūn fī akhbār Bāb Jīrūn*, Damascus 1964.
al-Nuʿaymī, *al-Dāris fī tārīkh al-madāris*, 2 vols., Beirut 1990.
al-Sakhāwī, *al-Ḍawʾ al-lāmiʿ fī aʿyān al-qarn al-tāsiʿ*, 6 vols., Cairo 1966.
al-Ṣayrafī, *Inbāʾ al-haṣr bi-abnāʾ al-ʿaṣr*, Cairo 1970.
Yāqūt, *Muʿjam al-buldān*, 5 vols., Beirut 1977.

Studies

ʿAbd al-Hādī, Ṣafwat, *al-Imām Yūsuf ʿAbd al-Hādī*, Damascus 2007.
Abdal-Rehim, Abdal-Rahman, The family and gender laws in Egypt during the Ottoman period, in Amira El Azhary Sonbol (ed.), *Women, the family, and divorce laws in Islamic history*, Syracuse 1996, 96–111.
Ali, Kecia, Marriage in classical Islamic jurisprudence: A survey of doctrines, in Asifa Quraishi and Frank E. Vogel (eds.), *The Islamic marriage contract: Case studies in Islamic family law*, Cambridge, MA 2008, 11–45.
Ali, Kecia, *Marriage and slavery in early Islam*, Cambridge, MA 2010.
Allin, Michael, *Zarafa: A giraffe's true story from deep in Africa to the heart of Paris*, New York 1998.
Ashtor, Eliyahu, *Histoire des prix et des salaries dans l'orient medieval*, Paris 1969.
Ashtor, Eliyahu, *Les métaux précieux et la balance des payements du proche-orient a la basse époque*, Paris 1971.
Ashtor, Eliyahu, Levantine sugar industry in the late Middle Ages: A case of technological decline, in A.L. Udovitch (ed.), *The Middle East, 700–1800: Studies in economic and social history*, Princeton 1981, 91–132.
L'autorité de l'écrit au moyen age (Orient Occident), Paris 2009.
Bacharach, Jere L., The dinar versus the ducat, in *IJMES* 4 (1973), 77–96.
Badrān, ʿAbd al-Qādir, *Munādamat al-aṭlāl wa musāmarat al-khayāl*, Damascus 1960.
al-Badrī, Abū l-Baqāʾ ʿAbdallāh, *Nuzhat al-anām fī maḥāsin al-Shām*, Beirut 1980.
Bayley, Sally, *The private life of the diary: From Pepys to tweets*, London 2016.
Behrens-Abuseif, Doris, The fire of 884/1479 at the Umayyad Mosque in Damascus and an account of its restoration, in *MSR* 8 (2004), 279–297.
Berger, Lutz, *Gesellschaft und Individuum in Damaskus 1550–1791*, Wurzburg 2007.
Bouden, Frederic, Mamluk-era documentary studies: The state of the art, in *MSR* 9 (2005), 15–60.

Braudel, Fernand, *The Mediterranean and the Mediterranean world in the age of Philip II*, London 1972.

Brinner, William M., Dār al-Saʿāda and Dār al-ʿAdl in Mamluk Damascus, in Myriam Rosen-Ayalon (ed.), *Studies in memory of Gaston Wiet*, Jerusalem 1977, 235–247.

Brinner, William M., The significance of the *ḥarāfish* and their "sultan," in *JESHO* 6 (1963), 190–215.

Canning, Kathleen, Gender and the politics of class formation: Rethinking German labor history, in *The American Historical Review* 97 (1992), 736–768.

Cohen, Amnon, *The guilds of Ottoman Jerusalem*, Leiden 2001.

Cohen, Esther, Law, folklore and animal lore, in *Past and Present* 110 (1986), 6–37.

Conermann, Stephan, Ibn Ṭūlūn (d. 955/1548): Life and works, in *MSR* 8 (2004), 115–140, repr. in Stephan Conermann, *Mamlukica: Studies on the history and society of the Mamluk period*, Goettingen 2013, 213–236.

Conermann, Stephan, and Tilman Seidensticker, Some remarks on Ibn Tawq's (d. 915/1509) journal *al-Taliq*, Vol. I (885/1480 to 890/1485), in *MSR* 9/2 (2007), 121–135, repr. in Stephan Conermann, *Mamlukica: Studies on the history and society of the Mamluk period*, Goettingen 2013, 237–250.

Cuno, Kenneth M., Was the land of Ottoman Syria *miri* or *milk*? An examination of juridical differences within the Hanafi school, in *SI* 81 (1995), 121–152.

Davis, Natalie Zemon, *The return of Martin Guerre*, Cambridge, MA 1983.

Davis, Natalie Zemon, The shapes of social history, in *Storia della Storiografia* 17 (1990), 28–34.

Deguilhem, Randi, The waqf in the city, in Salma K. Jayyuysi (ed.), *The city in the Islamic world*, ii, Leiden 2008, 923–950.

Dols, Michael W., *The Black Death in the Middle East*, Princeton 1977.

Drori, J., The role of Banū Faḍl in fourteenth century north Syria, in U. Vermeulen, D. De Smet, and K. D'Hulster (eds.), *Egypt and Syria in the Fatimid, Ayyubid and Mamluk eras*, v, Leuven 2007, 471–485.

Duhmān, Muḥammad, Aḥmad, *Dimashq fī ʿahd al-mamālīk*, Damascus 1964.

Elbendary, Amina, *Crowds and sultans: Urban protest in late medieval Egypt and Syria*, Cairo 2015.

El-Leithy, Tamer, Living documents, dying archives, in *Qanṭara* 32 (2011), 389–434.

El-Zawahreh, Taisir Khalil Muhammad, *Religious endowments and social life in the Ottoman province of Damascus in the sixteenth and seventeenth centuries*, Karak 1992.

Ephrat, Daphna, Sufism and sanctity: The genesis of the Wali Allah in Mamluk Jerusalem and Hebron, in David J. Wasserstein and Ami Ayalon (eds.), *Mamluks and Ottomans: Studies in honour of Michael Winter*, London 2006, 4–18.

Ephrat, Daphna, and Hatim Mahamid, The creation of Sufi spheres in medieval Damascus (mid-6th/12th to mid-8th/14th centuries), in *JRAS* 25/2 (2015), 189–207.

Establet, Colette, and Jean-Paul Pascuel, *Familles et fortunes à Damas: 450 foyers damascains en 1700*, Damascus 1994.

Eychenne, Mathieu, La production agricole de Damas et de la Ghūṭa au XIV siècle: Diversite, taxation et prix des cultures maraicheres d'apres al-Jazarī (m. 739/1338), in *JESHO* 56 (2013), 569–630.

Fernandes, Leonor, Between qadis and muftis: To whom does the Mamluk sultan listen? in *MSR* 6 (2002), 95–108.

Fierro, Maria Isabel, Heresy in al-Andalus, in Salma Khadra Jayyusi (ed.), *The legacy of Muslim Spain*, Leiden 1994, 895–908.

A Florentine Diary from 1450 to 1516 by Luca Landucci continued by an Anonymous Writer till 1542 with notes by Iodoco del Badia, trans. Alice de Rosen Jervis, Freeport 1927, repr. 1971.

Frenkel, Yehoshua, *Awqāf* in Mamluk Bilād al-Shām, in *MSR* 13 (2009), 149–166.

Frenkel, Yehoshua, *Ḍaw' al-sārī li-maʿrifat habar Tamīm al-Dārī: On Tamīm al-Dārī and his waqf in Hebron*, Leiden 2014.

Frenkel, Yehoshua, *Fikāk al-asīr*: The ransoming of Muslim captives in the Mamlūk sultanate, in Hike Grieser and Nicole Priesching (eds.), *Gefangenenloskauf im Mittelmeerraum, ein interreligioser Vergleich*, Hildesheim 2015, 143–155.

Frenkel, Yehoshua, Mamluk ʿulamāʾ on festivals and rites de passage: Wedding customs in 15th-century Damascus, in U. Vermuelen and K. D'Hulster (eds.), *Egypt and Syria in the Fatimid, Ayyubid and Mamluk eras VI: Proceedings of the 14th and 15th International Colloquium organized at the Katholieke Universiteit*, Leuven 2010, 279–289.

Frenkel, Yehoshua, Slave girls and learned teachers: Women in Mamluk sources, in Yuval Ben-Bassat (ed.), *Developing perspectives in Mamluk history: Essays in honor of Amalia Levanoni*, Leiden 2017, 158–176.

Frenkel, Yehoshua, *Volksroman* under the Mamluks: The case of the Tamim ad-Dārī popular sīra, in Stephan Conermann (ed.), *History and society during the Mamluk period (1250–1517)*, Goettingen 2014, 21–36.

Friedman, Mordechai Akiva, *Jewish marriage in Palestine: A Cairo Geniza study*, i, *The ketubba traditions*, Tel Aviv 1980.

Geoffroy, Eric, *Le soufisme en Egypte et en Syrie sous les derniers Mamelouks et les premiers Ottomans*, Damascus 1995.

Ghazaleh, Pascale, Introduction: Pious foundations: From here to eternity? in Pascale Ghazaleh (ed.), *Held in trust: Waqf in the Islamic world*, Cairo 2011, 1–22.

Giladi, Avner, *Children of Islam: Concepts of childhood in medieval Muslim society*, Houndmills 1992.

Ginzburg, Carlo, *The cheese and the worms: The cosmos of a sixteenth-century miller*, Baltimore 1980.

Grehan, James, *Everyday life & consumer culture in 18th-century Damascus*, Seattle 2007.

Guellil, Gabriela Linda, *Damszener Akten des 8./14. Jahrhunderts nach aṭ-Tarsūsī Kitāb al-Iʿlām*, Bamberg 1985.

Guo, Li, al-Biqāi's chronicle: A fifteenth-century learned man's reflection on his time and world, in Hugh Kennedy (ed.), *The historiography of Islamic Egypt (c. 950–1800)*, Leiden 2001, 121–148.

Guo, Li, *Commerce culture and community in a Red Sea port in the fifteenth century: The Arabic documents from Quseir*, Leiden 2004.

Guo, Li, *The performing arts in medieval Islam: Shadow play and popular poetry in Ibn Danyal's Mamluk Cairo*, Leiden 2011.

Guo, Li, al-Taʿlīq: Yawmiyāt Shihāb al-Dīn Aḥmad Ibn Ṭawq, in *MSR* 12/1 (2008), 210–218.

Hallaq, Wael B., The *qāḍī's dīwān (sijjil)* before the Ottomans, in *BSOAS* 61/3 (1998), 415–436.

Hallaq, Wael B., *Sharīʿa: Theory, practice, transformations*, Cambridge 2009.

Hanna, Nelly, Guilds in recent historical scholarship, in Salma K. Jayyusi (ed.), *The city in the Islamic world*, Leiden 2008, 895–921.

Hanna, Nelly, Guild waqf: Between religious law and common law, in Pascale Ghazaleh (ed.), *Held in trust: Waqf in the Islamic world*, Cairo 2011, 135–153.

Hanna, Nelly, Marriage and the family in 17th-century Cairo, in Daniel Panzac (ed.), *Histoire economique et sociale de l'Empire ottoman et de la Turquie (1326–1960)*, Paris 1995, 349–358.

Hirschler, Konrad, From archive to archival practices: Rethinking the preservation of Mamluk administrative documents, in *JAOS* 136/1 (2016), 1–28.

Hitz, Benjamin, *Kampfen um Sold: Eine Alltags- und Sozialgeschichte schweizerischer Soldner in der Fruhen Neuzeit*, Koln 2015.

Igarashi, Daisuke, *Land tenure, fiscal policy, and imperial power in medieval Syro-Egypt*, Chicago 2015.

al-ʿIlabī, Akram Ḥasan, *Khiṭat Dimashq: dirāsa tārikhiyya shāmila*, Damascus 1989.

Irwin, Robert, The privatization of "justice" under the Circassian Mamluks, in *MSR* 6 (2002), 63–70.

Ivanova, Svetlana, The divorce between Zubaida Hatun and Esseid Osman Aga, in Amira El Azhary Sonbol (ed.), *Women, the family, and divorce laws in Islamic history*, Syracuse 1996.

Johnson, Alexandra, *A brief history of diaries: From Pepys to blogs*, London 2011.

Jones, P.J., Florentine families and Florentine diaries in the fourteenth century, in *Papers of the British School at Rome* 24 (1956), 183–205.

Khayr, Ṣafūḥ, *Madinat Dimashq: dirāsa fī jughrāfiyat al-mudun*, Damascus 1969.

Kirshner, Julius, *Marriage, dowry, and citizenship in late medieval and Renaissance Italy*, Toronto 2015.

Labib, Subhi, *Handelsgeschichte Aegyptens in Spatmittlealter 1171–1517*, Wiesbaden 1965.

Lapidus, Ira Marvin, *Muslim cities in the later Middle Ages*, Cambridge, MA 1967.

Layish, A., *Marriage, divorce and succession in the Druze family*, Leiden 1982.

Lejeune, Phillippe, *On diary*, Honolulu 2009.

Lev, Yaacov, *Charity, endowment, and charitable institutions in medieval Islam*, Gainesville 2005.

Levanoni, Amalia, *Takfīr* in Egypt and Syria during the Mamlūk period, in Camilla Adang, Hassan Ansari, Maribel Fierro, and Sabine Schmidtke (eds.), *Accusations of unbelief in Islam: A diachronic perspective on takfīr*, Leiden 2016, 155–188.

Little, Donald P., *History and historiography of the Mamluks*, London 1986.

Lutfi, Huda, *al-Quds al-Mamlukiyya: A history of Mamluk Jerusalem based on the Ḥaram documents*, Berlin 1985.

Luz, Nimrod, *The Mamluk city in the Middle East: History, culture, snd the urban landscape*, Cambridge 2014.

Mahamid, Hatim, Mosques as higher educational institutions in Mamluk Syria, in *JIS* 20/2 (2009), 188–212.

Mahamid, Hatim, *Waqf, education and politics in late medieval Syria*, Saarbrucken 2013.

Makdisi, George, The diary in Islamic historiography: Some notes, in *History and Theory* 25 (1986), 173–185.

Malti-Douglas, Fedwa, *Mentalités* and marginality: Blindness and Mamluk civilization, in C.E. Bosworth (ed.), *The Islamic world from classical to modern times*, Princeton 1989, 211–237.

Martel-Thoumian, Bernadette, Le converti à travers quelques écrits historiques du IX/XV siècle, in U. Vermeulen and J.M.F. van Reeth (eds.), *Law, Christianity and modernism in Islamic society*, Leuven 1998, 171–184.

Martel-Thoumian, Bernadette, *Délinquance et ordre social: L'État mamlouk syro-égyptien face au crime à la fin du IX–XV siècle*, Paris 2012.

Martel-Thoumian, Bernadette, Muḥibb ad-Dīn Salāma b. Yūsuf al-Aslamī, un secretaire à Damas sous les derniers sultans mamlouks, in U. Vermeulen and J. van Steenbergen (eds.), *Egypt and Syria in the Fatimid, Ayyubid and Mamluk eras*, iii, Leuven 2001, 219–269.

Martel-Thoumian, Bernadette, The sale of office and its economic consequences during the rule of the last Circassians (872–922/1468–1516), in *MSR* 9/2 (2005), 49–83.

Martin, Sergio Carro, and Amalia Zomeno, Identifying the ʿudūl in fifteenth-century Granada, in Maaike van Berkel, Léon Buskens, and Petra M. Sijpesteijn (eds.), *Legal documents as sources for the history of Muslim societies: Studies in honour of Rudolph Peters*, Leiden 2017, 109–128.

Masud, Muhammad Khalid, Brinkley Messick, and David S. Powers (eds.), *Islamic legal interpretation: Muftis and their fatwas*, Cambridge, MA 1996.

al-Matroudi, Abdul Hakim I., *The Ḥanbalī school of law and Ibn Taymiyya: Conflict or conciliation*, Abingdon, UK 2006.

Mattern, Marlies, *Leben in Abseits: Fraun und Manner in Tauferturm (1525–1550), eine Studie zur Alltagsgeschichte*, Frankfurt am Main 1998.

Melcak, Miroslav, Reconstruction of the lost Ayyubid waqf. Madrasa al-Shāmīya al-Juwwānīya in Damascus as depicted in the *fatāwā* of Taqī al-Dīn al-Subkī (d. 756/1355), in *Archiv Orientali* 80 (2012), 1–39.

Mikhail, Alan, *Nature and empire in Ottoman Egypt: An environmental history*, Cambridge 2011.

Miura Toru, *Dynamism in the urban society of Damascus: The Ṣāliḥiyya Quarter from the twelfth to the twentieth centuries*, Leiden 2016.

Miura, Toru, The Ṣāliḥiyya Quarter of Damascus at the beginning of Ottoman rule: The ambiguous relations between religious institutions and waqf properties, in Peter Sluglett and Stefan Weber (eds.), *Syria and Bilād al-Shām under Ottoman rule: Essays in honour of Abdul Karim Rafeq*, Leiden 2010, 269–291.

Miura, Toru, The structure of the quarter and the role of the outlaws: The Ṣāliḥiya Quarter and the zuʿr in the Mamlūk period, in Takeshi Yukawa (ed.), *Proceedings of the International Conference on Urbanism in Islam*, iii, Tokyo 1989, 401–437.

Miura, Toru, Urban society in Damascus as the Mamluk era was ending, in *MSR* 10 (2006), 157–189.

Mouton, Jean-Michel, Dominique Sourdel, and Janine Sourdel-Thoumine, *Mariage et séparation à Damas au moyen age*, Paris 2013.

Muller, Christian, Crimes without criminals? Legal documents on fourteenth-century injury and homicide cases from the Haram collection in Jerusalem, in Maaike van Berkel, Léon Buskens, and Petra M. Sijpesteijn (eds.), *Legal documents as sources for the history of Muslim societies: Studies in honour of Rudolph Peters*, Leiden 2017, 129–179.

Muller, Christian, *Gerichtspraxis im Stadtsstaat Cordoba: zum Recht der Gesellschaft in einer mālikitisch-islamischen Rechtstradition des 5./11. Jahrhunderts*, Leiden 1999.

Muller, Christian, The Ḥaram al-Sharīf collection of Arabic legal documents in Jerusalem: A Mamlūk court archive? in *Qanṭara* 32 (2011), 435–459.

Muller, Christian, *Der Kadi und seine Zeugen: Studie der mamlukischen Ḥaram-Dokumente aus Jerusalem*, Goettingen 2013.

Muller, Christian, A legal instrument in the service of people and institutions: Endowments in Mamluk Jerusalem as mirrored in the Ḥaram documents, in *MSR* 12 (2008), 173–191.

Muller, Christian, Mamluk law: A reassessment, in Stephan Conermann (ed.), *Ubi sumus? Quo vademus? Mamluk Studies—State of the art*, Goettingen 2013, 263–283.

Musallam, Basim, The ordering of Muslim societies, in Francis Robinson (ed.), *The Cambridge illustrated history of the Islamic world*, Cambridge 1996, 164–207.

Pascual, Jean-Paul, *Damas à la fin du XVIe siècle*, i, Damascus 1983.

Petry, Carl F., Class solidarity vs. gender gain: Women as custodians of property in later medieval Egypt, in Nikki Keddie and Beth Baron (eds.), *Women in Middle Eastern history: Shifting boundaries in sex and gender*, New Haven 1991, 122–142.

Petry, Carl F., *The criminal underworld in a medieval Islamic society: Narratives from Cairo and Damascus under the Mamluks*, Chicago 2012.

Petry, Carl F., *Protectors or praetorians? The last Mamlūk sultans and Egypt's waning as a great power*, Albany 1994.

Pouzet, Louis, *Damas au VII/XIII siècle, vie et structures religigieuses d'une métropole islamique*, Beirut 1988.

Pouzet, Louis, Maghrebins à Damas au VII/XIII siècle, in *BEO* 28 (1975), 167–199.

Powers, David S., *The development of Islamic law and society in the Maghrib: Qāḍīs, muftīs and family law*, Farnham, UK 2011.

Powers, David S., Four cases relating to women and divorce in al-Andalus and the Maghrib, 1100–1500, in Muhammad Khalid Masud, Rudolph Peters, and David S. Powers (eds.), *Dispensing justice in Islam: Qadis and their judgments*, Leiden 2006, 383–409.

Rabbat, Nasser O., The ideological significance of the Dār al-Adl in the medieval Islamic Orient, in *IJMES* 27 (1995), 3–28.

Rabie, Hassanein, The size and value of the iqṭāʿ in Egypt, 564–741 A.H. 1169–1341 A.D., in M.A. Cook (ed.), *Studies in the economic history of the Middle East from the rise of Islam to the present day*, London 1970, 129–138.

Rapoport, Yossef, Legal diversity in the age of *taqlīd*: The four chief qadis under the Mamluks, in *Islamic Law and Society* 10 (2003), 210–228.

Rapoport, Yossef, *Marriage, money and divorce in medieval Islamic society*, Cambridge 2005.

Rapoport, Yossef, Matrimonial gifts in early Islamic Egypt, in *Islamic Law and Society* 7/1 (2000), 1–36.

Rapoport, Yossef, Royal justice and religious law: *Siyāsah* and sharīʿah under the Mamluks, in *MSR* 16 (2012), 71–102.

Rapoport, Yossef, Women and gender in Mamluk society: An overview, in *MSR* 11 (2007), 1–47.

Reilly, James A., Rural waqfs of Ottoman Damascus: Rights of ownership, possession and tenancy, in *AO* 51 (1990), 27–46.

Reinfandt, Lucian, Die Beurkundung einer mamlukenzeitlichen Familienstiftung vom 12. Gumādā II 864 (4. April 1460), in Astrid Meier, Johannes Pahlitzsch, and Lucian Reinfandt (eds.), *Islamische Stiftungen zwischen juristicher Norm und sozialer Praxis*, Berlin 2009, 117–152.

Richards, Donald, Glimpses of provincial Mamluk society from the documents of the Ḥaram al-Sharīf in Jerusalem, in Michael Winter and Amalia Levanoni (eds.), *The Mamluks in Egyptian and Syrian politics and society*, Leiden 2004, 45–57.

Robinson, Chase F., *Islamic historiography*, Cambridge 2003.

Roujon, Yves, and Luc Vilan, *Le Midān: Actualité d'un faubourg ancien de Damas*, Damascus 1997.

Roujon, Yves, and Luc Vilan, *Les faubourgs de Damas: Atlas contemporain des faubourgs anciens*, Damascus 2010.

Sajdi, Dana, *The Barber of Damascus: Nouveau literacy in the eighteenth-century Ottoman Levant*, Stanford 2013.

al-Salāma, Nāṣir b. Suʿūd, *Muʿjam muʾallafāt Yūsuf b. Ḥasan b. ʿAbd al-Hādī al-Ḥanbalī*, Riyadh 1999.

Shatzmiller, Maya, *Her day in court: Women's property rights in fifteenth-century Granada*, Cambridge, MA 2007.

al-Shihābī, Qutayba, *Muʿjam Dimashq al-Tārīkhī*, 3 vols., Damascus 1999.

Shoshan, Boaz, From silver to copper: Monetary changes in fifteenth-century Egypt, in *SI* 56 (1982), 97–116.

Shoshan, Boaz, Grain riots and the "moral economy": Cairo, 1350–1517, in *Journal of Interdisciplinary History* 3 (1980), 459–478.

Shoshan, Boaz, Jokes, animal lore, and *mentalité* in medieval Egypt, in *Arabica* 45 (1998), 129–135.

Shoshan, Boaz, Mini-dramas by the water: On irrigation rights and disputes in fifteenth-century Damascus, in Roxani Eleni Margariti, Adam Sabra, and Petra M. Sijpesteijn (eds.), *Histories of the Middle East: Studies in Middle Eastern society, economy and law in honor of A.L. Udovitch*, Leiden 2011, 233–244.

Shoshan, Boaz, Notes sur les epidemies de peste en Égypte, in *Annales de démographie historique*, 1981, 387–404.

Shoshan, Boaz, On divorce in Damascus, 1480–1500 CE, in U. Vermeulen, K. D'Hulster, and J. Van Steenbergen (eds.), *Egypt and Syria in the Fatimid, Ayyubid and Mamluk eras*, viii, Leuven 2016, 533–542.

Shoshan, Boaz, On the marital regime in Damascus, 1480–1500 CE, in Stephan Conermann (ed.), *History and society during the Mamluk period (1250–1517): Studies of the Annemarie Schimmel Institute for Advanced Study*, ii, Goettingen 2016, 7–27.

Shoshan, Boaz, Popular Sufi sermons in late Mamluk Egypt, in David J. Wasserstein and Ami Ayalon (eds.), *Mamluks and Ottomans: Studies in honour of Michael Winter*, London 2006, 106–113.

Sonbol, Amira El-Azhari, A history of marriage contracts in Egypt, in Asifa Quraishi and Frank E. Vogel (eds.), *The Islamic marriage contract: Case studies in Islamic family law*, Cambridge, MA 2008, 87–122.

Stilt, Kristen, *Islamic law in action: Authority, discretion, and everyday experiences in Mamluk Egypt*, Oxford 2011.

Tarawneh, Taha Thelji, *The province of Damascus during the second Mamluk period (784/1382–922/1516)*, Muta 1994.

Taylor, Christopher S., *In the vicinity of the righteous: Ziyāra & the veneration of Muslim saints in late medieval Egypt*, Leiden 1999.

Tucker, Judith E., *Women, family, and gender in Islamic law*, Cambridge 2008.

Tyan, Émile, *Le notariat et le regime de la prevue par ecrit dans la pratique du droit musulman*, Beirut 1945, Harissa ²1959.

Varlik, Nukhet, *Plague and empire in the early modern Mediterranean world: The Ottoman experience, 1347–1600*, New York 2015.

al-Wakīl, Fā'iza, *al-Shiwār: Jihāz al-ʿarūs fī Miṣr fī ʿasr salāṭīn al-mamālīk*, Cairo 2001.

Walker, Bethany J., *Jordan in the late Middle Ages: Transformation of the Mamluk frontier*, Chicago 2011.

Walker, Bethany J., Popular responses to Mamluk fiscal reforms in Syria, in *BEO* 58 (2009), 51–68.

Wiederhold, Lutz, Blasphemy against the prophet Muḥammad and his Companions (*sabb al-rasūl, sabb al-ṣaḥābah*): The introduction of the topic into Shāfiʿī legal literature and its relevance for legal practice under Mamluk rule, in *JSS* 42/1 (1997), 39–70.

Winter, Michael, Inter-madhab competition in Mamluk Damascus: al-Ṭarsūsī's counsel for the Turkish sultan, in *JSAI* 25 (2001), 195–211.

Winter, Michael, Mamluks and their households in late Mamluk Damascus: A waqf study, in Michael Winter and Amalia Levanoni (eds.), *The Mamluks in Egyptian and Syrian politics and society*, Leiden 2004, 297–316.

Wollina, Torsten, Ibn Ṭawq's *Taʿlīq*: An ego-document for Mamluk studies, in Stephan Conermann (ed.), *Ubi sumus? Quo vademus? Mamluk studies—State of the art*, Goettingen 2013, 337–362.

Wollina, Torsten, A view from within: Ibn Ṭawq's personal topography of 15th-century Damascus, in *BEO* 61 (2012), 271–295.

Wollina, Torsten, *Zwanzig Jahre Alltag: Lebens-, Welt- und Selbstbild im Journal des Aḥmad Ibn Ṭawq*, Goettingen 2014.

Woods, John E., *The Aqquyunlu: Clan, confederation, empire*, Salt Lake City 1999.

Zilfi, Madeline C., "We don't get along": Women and *hul* divorce in the eighteenth century, in Madeline C. Zilfi (ed.), *Women in the Ottoman Empire: Middle Eastern women in the early modern era*, Leiden 1997.

Zomeno, Amalia, The Islamic marriage contract in al-Andalus (10th–16th centuries), in Asifa Quraishi and Frank E. Vogel (eds.), *The Islamic marriage contract: Case studies in Islamic family law*, Cambridge, MA 2008, 136–155.

Zomeno, Amalia, The stories in the fatwas and the fatwas in history, in Boudouin Dupret, Barbara Drieskens, and Annelies Moors (eds.), *Narratives of truth in Islamic law*, London 2008, 25–49.

Index